John Milner, Fielding Lucas

The end of religious controversy

in a friendly correspondence between a religious society of Protestants and a

Roman Catholic divine

John Milner, Fielding Lucas

The end of religious controversy
in a friendly correspondence between a religious society of Protestants and a Roman Catholic divine

ISBN/EAN: 9783741112294

Manufactured in Europe, USA, Canada, Australia, Japa

Cover: Foto ©Lupo / pixelio.de

Manufactured and distributed by brebook publishing software (www.brebook.com)

John Milner, Fielding Lucas

The end of religious controversy

THE

END OF RELIGIOUS CONTROVERSY,

In a Friendly Correspondence

BETWEEN A

RELIGIOUS SOCIETY OF PROTESTANTS,

AND A CATHOLIC DIVINE.

———

BY THE RIGHT REV. JOHN MILNER, D. D.

———

TO WHICH IS ADDED,

The Author's Postscript.

———•———

BALTIMORE:

PRINTED AND PUBLISHED BY JOHN MURPHY & CO.

METROPOLITAN PRESS, 182 BALTIMORE STREET.

PITTSBURG: GEORGE QUIGLEY.

Sold by Catholic Booksellers generally throughout the United States.

1866.

' Let those treat you harshly, who are not acquainted with the difficulty of attaining to truth and avoiding error. Let those treat you harshly, who know not how hard it is to get rid of old prejudices. Let those treat you harshly, who have not learned how very hard it is to purify the interior eye and render it capable of contemplating the sun of the soul, truth. But as to us: we are far from this disposition towards persons who are separated from us, not by errors of their own invention, but by being entangled in those of others. We are so far from this disposition that we pray to God, that, in refuting the false opinions of those, whom you follow, not from malice, but imprudence, he would bestow upon us that spirit of peace, which feels no other sentiment than charity, no other interest than that of Jesus Christ, no other wish but for your salvation." *St. Austin, Doctor of the Church, A. D. 400, contra Ep. Fund. c. i. c. ii.*

" There are many other things which keep me in the bosom of the Catholic Church. The agreement of different people and nations keeps me there. The authority established by Miracles, nourished by hope, increased by charity, and confirmed by antiquity, keeps me there. The succession of bishops in the See of St. Peter, the apostle, (to whom our Lord, after his resurrection, committed his sheep, to be fed) down to the present bishop, keeps me there. Finally, the very name of CATHOLIC, which, among so many heresies, this church alone possesses, keeps me there." *St. Augustin, Doctor of the Church, A. D. 400, contra Epist. Fundam. c. 4.*

" It is a shame to charge men with what they are not guilty of, in order to make the breach wider, already too wide." *Dr. Montague, bishop of Norwich. Invoc. of Saints, p. 60.*

" Let them not lead people by the nose to believe they can prove their supposition, that the Pope is Antichrist, and the Papists idolaters, when they cannot." *Dr. Herbert Thorndike, prebendary of Westminster. Just Weights and Measures, p. 11.*

" The object of their (the Catholics) adoration of the B. Sacrament is the only true and eternal God, hypostatically joined with his holy humanity, which humanity they believe actually present under the veil of the sacramental signs: and if they thought him not present, they are so far from worshipping the bread in this case that themselves profess it to be idolatry to do so." *Dr Jeremy Taylor. bishop of Down. Liberty of prophesying, chap xx*

THE EDITOR TO THE READER.

In this work, entitled " The End of Religious Controversy," the author and his correspondents having established the certainty of divine revelation and the truth of the Christian religion, he proposes the means by which, among the various discordant creeds of those who profess Christianity, the *true faith* which Jesus Christ brought down from heaven, and the *true church* which he established on earth, may be discovered. He undertakes to prove that we are provided with the certain *means* of making this discovery, and that Christ himself has left us a *rule of faith*, adapted to the *capacities of all*, by which we may come to the knowledge of *true religion*.

Before he attempts to show what this rule is, he notices certain methods, which have been adopted as rules of faith, and proves them to be insufficient and fallacious. *Private inspiration*, he maintains, cannot be a *rule of faith*, because private inspiration is in itself a *questionable* pretension; may be claimed by one as well as by another, and all alike; and has, in fact, been claimed and acted upon by *different* sectaries, in support of *different* and *contradictory* tenets; at the same time that it has, in many instances, led the pretenders to it into the greatest *absurdities* and most shocking *impieties*. Another rule of faith, the rule adopted by the reformed churches in general, is the *scripture* or the *written* word of God, left to the *interpretation of each individual*: for as no *supreme, unerring* authority is acknowledged by Protestants to determine the *sense* and *meaning* of Scripture, or to decide and announce what articles of faith are necessary for salvation, individual judgment is made the guide to individuals, the necessity of preachers is done away, and the commission of Jesus Christ to his apostles, "Go, *teach* all nations," is annulled. Where there is no *obligation* to *hear* and *obey*, there can be no *authority* to *teach* and *instruct*. The church, as an infallible teacher, is discarded, but its powers are transferred to each individual person; each person possesses *infallibility* in himself, each person is himself a church, accordingly as he may please to form his creed; and every possible contradictory opinion is *equally* defensible, as resting upon the interpretation of Scripture, adopted by the person who maintains it. This rule, like private inspiration, is shown to be fallacious; since, like the former, it has led, as it is calculated to lead, to *opposite conclusions* on numberless points of faith: and since there is no acknowledged *judge* on earth to *decide*, it necessarily follows that either contradictory doctrines are *favored* by the sacred volume, and revealed, as *equally true*, by the God from whom that sacred volume came, or else that it was intended by the God of *peace*, as an *apple of discord*, and *meant* by the God of *truth* for the propagation of *falsehood*. But as such intentions can never be imputed to the Deity, nor can it be imagined that our Redeemer established a church to succeed to the Jewish dispensation, and to last *till the end of the world*, so vague and indeterminate in its creed, so uncertain as to its form or even existence, in one place professing, on the authority of God's infallible word, articles and doctrines which, in another place, it anathematizes and disclaims on the same unerring authority, —the author maintains that the Scripture *alone* does not furnish this *certain* and *attainable* rule adapted to the capacities and situations of mankind at large.

Still he maintains that a *rule* does exist, and ever has existed since the time of Christ, by which the *faith of his disciples is secured from error*, and *his true religion*, with all its *doctrines* and *articles of belief* proclaimed to them with equal certainty, by means of his *protecting Spirit*, his promised *Paraclete*, as if He were visibly *seen* by them, and were *heard* by them speaking in his own person, as when he conversed with his disciples upon earth. This rule, he contends, is *the word of God, written* and *unwritten*, as it is interpreted and explained by his appointed oracle, HIS CHURCH, which he has *authorized and commissioned to teach all nations*, while he has *commanded* all mankind to *hear his church*. This *rule of faith*, subject to the interpretation of an *infallible expositor*, inspired by *himself*, and guided by *his Holy Spirit, the Spirit of Truth*, must *necessarily* communicate *his* revelations, must *infallibly* teach *his truth*, the *whole* truth, and the truth *alone*. This rule, thus unerringly explained by the *Light of Light*, inevitably implies teachers *instituted by* JESUS CHRIST *himself*, and a *succession* of teachers *kept up by Him* and *inspired by Him*. It secures their followers from the danger of error, in adopting their own conjectures, and the teachers it preserves from the spirit of innovation and imposture, from all the attempts of ambitious or interested dogmatizers. He then proceeds to show, that the church dispersed throughout the world and in communion with the See of Rome (commonly called the CATHOLIC CHURCH) alone adopts and follows this infallible rule; and he produces numberless arguments to prove that, whereas Christians have, in every age since that of the apostles, professed their belief of *One, Holy, Catholic*, and *Apostolic* Church,—the Church in *communion with the See of Rome*, and presided over by *the successor of St. Peter in that see*, exclusively exhibits these four *essential marks* of the church of Christ, viz., UNITY, in *doctrine, liturgy, government*, and *constitution*; SANCTITY, in *doctrine*, in the *means* of holiness, and the *fruits* of holiness; CATH-

ELICITY, or *universality*, in its *extent*, as to *time* and place, no less than its *name*, which it has borne from time immemorial; and, finally, APOSTOLICITY, in its *descent* and regular *succession* of *ministers*, from the time of the apostles, as well as in its *sacraments* and *sacred institutions*. He then proceeds to show, that these marks are deficient to *every* Christian society, except that *which is in communion with the See of Rome*, and which exclusively enjoys, as it ever has enjoyed, the distinctive appellation of the *Catholic Church*.

Here, strictly speaking, his work is at an end and *controversy* concluded. For the infallible superintendence and inspiration of Jesus Christ promised and preserved, and the marks, by which *his* church may be distinguished from every other society or congregation, being ascertained and applied, it follows of consequence, (without *particular* proof with regard to each *particular* article,) that *every* doctrine of a *church so guarded and protected*, must be the doctrine of *Jesus Christ himself*, and the church *secure from error*. However, for the sake of *candid* and *sincere* inquirers, the author condescends to *particular* examination; brings forward the principal *charges* that are usually made against the Roman Catholic Church, and proves them to be either the involuntary errors of mistaken *ignorance*, or the unfair means resorted to by *misrepresentation*, with the view to blacken and disfigure the *spouse of Christ*. He draws aside the mask which malice had held up as her genuine countenance, and displays her form and features in all their native beauty and loveliness. For further satisfaction, he explains and justifies those particular doctrinal points, which are excepted against by the separatists from the Church of Rome.

Such are the nature and character of the work now presented to the public; such is the object of the pre-eminent writer, which if he have attained, he has without question put an *End to Religious Controversy*, and fully justified the title given to his matchless performance. Let the reader juage.

CONTENTS.

PART I.

Page

LETTER VIII.
To James Brown, Esq.

LETTER IX.
To James Brown, Esq.

LETTER X.
To James Brown, Esq.

LETTER XI.
To James Brown, Esq.

LETTER XII.
To James Brown, Esq.

Contents.

PART II.

Contents

Contents.

Page

LETTER XXVIII.
To James Brown, Esq.

LETTER XXIX.
To James Brown, Esq.

LETTER XXX.
To James Brown, Esq.

POSTSCRIPT.

PART III.

Contents.

Contents.

Contents.

ADDRESS.

TO

THE RIGHT REVEREND

LORD BISHOP OF ST. DAVID'S.

MY LORD,

THE following Letters, with some others belonging to the
same series, were written in the latter part of the year 1801, and
the first months of 1802, though they have since that time been
revised, and, in some respects, altered. They grew out of the
controversy, which the principal writer of them was obliged to
sustain against an eminent author, a prebendary of the cathedral,
and the chancellor of the diocese of Winchester, who had personally challenged him to the field of argument, in a book, called
Reflections on Popery. That controversy having made some noise
in the public, and even in the houses of parliament, particularly
in the upper house, where the lord chancellor,* and a predecessor
of your lordship, then the light and glory of the established
church,† expressed opposite opinions on the issue of it, certain
powerful personages expressed an earnest wish for its termination. For this purpose, the usual method of silencing authors
was at first resolved upon with respect to the writer, and a Catholic gentleman of name, still living, was commissioned to sound
him on the business : but, in conclusion, it was thought most ad
visable to employ the influence which the prelate alluded to had
so justly acquired over him. This method succeeded ; and, accordingly, these Letters, which, otherwise, would have been published fifteen years ago, have slept in silence ever since.

I trust your lordship will not be the person to ask me, why the
Letters, after having been so long suppressed, now appear ?—You
are witness, my lord, of the increased and increasing virulence of

---

* The Right Hon. the Earl of Loughborough.

† The Right Rev. Dr. Horsely, successively bishop of St. David's, Rochester, and St. Asaph's.

the press against Catholics; and this, in many instances, directed by no ignoble or profane hands. . Abundant proofs of this will be seen in the following work. For the present, it is sufficient to mention, that one of your most venerable colleagues publishes and re-publishes, that we stand convicted of *idolatry, blasphemy,* and *sacrilege.* Another proclaims to the clergy, assembled in Synod, that we are *enemies of all law, human and divine.* More than one of them has charged us with the guilt of that Anti-Christian conspiracy on the continent, of which we were exclusively the victims. This dignitary accuses us of *Antinomianism;* that maintains our religion to be *fit only for persons weak in body and in mind.* In short, we seldom find ourselves, or our religion, mentioned in modern sermons, or other theological works, unaccompanied with the epithets of *superstitious, idolatrous, impious, disloyal, perfidious,* and *sanguinary.* One of the theologues alluded to, who, like many others, has gained promotion by the fervour of his NO POPERY zeal, has exalted his tone to the pitch of proclaiming that our religion *is calculated for the meridian of hell!!*— Thus solemnly, and almost continually, charged before the tribunal of the public, with crimes against society and our country, no less than against religion, and yet conscious, all the while, of our entire innocence, it is not only lawful, but also a duty, which we owe to our fellow-subjects and ourselves, to repel these charges, by proving that there was *reason,* and *religion,* and *loyalty,* and *good faith* among Christians, before 'Luther quarreled with Leo X., and Henry VIII. fell in love with Ann Bullen; and that, if we ourselves have not yet been persuaded by the arguments, either of the monk or the monarch, to relinquish the faith originally preached in this island, above 1300 years before their time, we are, at least, possessed of *common sense, virtuous principles,* and *untainted loyalty.*

The writer might assign another reason for making the present publication; namely, the number and acrimony of his own public opponents on subjects of religion. To say nothing of the groundless charges, by word of mouth, of certain privileged personages, the following writers are some of those who have published books, pamphlets, essays, or notes against him, on subjects of a religious nature; the deans of Winchester and Peterborough; chancellor Sturges; prebendary Poulter; the doctors Hoadly, Ash, Ryan, Ledwich, Le Mesurier,* and Elrington; Sir Richard Musgrave,

---

* To one only objection of his adversaries, the writer wishes here to give an answer, that of having *quoted falsely;* which, however, has been advanced by very few of them, and is confined, as far as he knows, to two instances. The first of these, is, that the writer, in his *History of Winchester,* vol. i. p. 61, " quotes Gildas, for the exploits of king Arthur, who never once mentions his name." This objection was first started by Dr. O'Conor, in his *Columbanus,* was borrowed from him, by the Rev. Mr. Le Mesurier, in his *Bampton Lectures,* and was adopted from the latter by the Rev. Mr. Grier, in his *Answer to Ward's Errata.*—After all, this pretended *forgery of the writer*

John Reeves, Esq. the Reverend Messrs Williamson, Bazeley, Churton, Grier, and Roberts; besides numerous anonymous rifle-men in the Gentleman's Magazine, the Monthly Magazine, the Anti-Jacobin Review, the Protestant Advocate, the Antibiblion, and other periodical works, including newspapers. By some of these he has been challenged into the field of controversy, and when he did not appear there, he has been posted as a *coward.*

A still more cogent reason, my lord, for the appearance of this work, which was heretofore suppressed, at the desire of a former bishop of St. David's, has been furnished by his present successor, in the work the latter has lately published, called THE PRO-TESTANT'S CATECHISM. This is no ordinary effusion of NO POPERY zeal. It was not called for by the increase of the ancient religion in his lordship's diocese, which teems with Me-thodist jumpers, to the danger of his cathedral and parish church-es being left quite empty; while not one Catholic family, is, per-haps, to be found in it. It was not provoked by any late attempt on the established church, or on Protestantism in general; as the bishop does not pretend that such thing has taken place. Never-theless he comes forward in his Episcopal mitre, bearing in his hands a new *Protestant Catechism*, to be learnt by Protestants of every description, which teaches them to *hate* and *persecute* their elder brethren, the authors of their Christianity and civilization! In fact, this Christian bishop, begins and ends his *Protestant Cate-chism*, with a quotation from a Puritan regicide, declaring, that *" Popery is not to be tolerated,* either in public or *in private,* and that *it must be thought how to remove it,* and hinder the growth thereof:" adding, " if they say, that, by removing their idols we violate their consciences, we have *no warrant to regard conscience,* which is not grounded on Scripture."* This, your lordship must

will be found, on consulting the passage referred to above, to be nothing else but *a blunder of his critics;* since it will appear that he quotes William, of Malmsbury, for *the exploits* of Arthur and Gildas, barely for *the year* in which *one* of them, the battle of Mons Badonicus, took place! The second accusation of this nature, was inserted by one of the above named writers, in the *Gentleman's Magazine,* namely, that the writer had advanced, *without any historical authority,* that James 1. used to call November 5, " *Cecil's holi-day."* In answer to this charge, he gave notice in the next number of the Magazine, that he had sent up to the editor's office, as he had done, there to remain, during a month, for public inspection, lord Castlemain's *Catholique Apology,* which contains the fact, and the authorities on which it is advanced The writer is far from claiming inerrancy; but he should despise himself, if he, knowingly, published any falsehood, or hesitated to retract any one that he was proved to have fallen into.

* Milton's prose works, vol. 4. The prose writings of this secretary of the Long parliament are execrable, for their regicide and anti-prelatic principles, as his poetry is super-excellent for its sublimity and sweetness. Four other English authors are brought forward, by the bishop of St. David's, to justify that persecution of Catholics, which he recommends. The first of these is the Socinian Locke, who will not allow of Catholics being *tolerated,* on the demonstrated false pretext, that they cannot tolerate other Christians. The

know, is the genuine cant of a Mar-Preate Independent; the same
cant which brought Laud, and Charles I. to the block; the same
cant which overthrew the church and state in the grand rebellion.
But what chiefly concerns my present purpose, in this, the bishop's twice repeated quotation from Milton, is to observe that it
breathes the whole persecuting spirit of the sixteenth century, and
calls for the fines and forfeitures, dungeons and halters, and
knives, of Elizabeth's reign, against the devoted Catholics; since,
it is evident, that the *idolatry of Popery*, as it is termed, exercised
in private, cannot *be removed* without such persecuting and sanguinary measures. The same thing is plain from the nature of
the different legal offences which the Right Rev. prelate lays to
their charge. In one place, he accuses the Catholics of England
and Ireland, that is to say, more than a quarter of his majesty's
European subjects, of "acknowledging the jurisdiction of the Pope,
in *defiance of the laws*, and of the *allegiance due to their rightful
sovereigns*" though he well knows, that they have abjured the
Pope's jurisdiction in *all civil and temporal cases*, which is all that
the king, lords and commons required of them, in their Acts of
1791 and 1793. Again, the prelate describes their opposition to
the *veto* (though equally opposed in the appointment of their respective pastors by all Protestant dissenters, who constitute more
than another fourth part of his majesty's subjects,) as "*treasonable by statute*," p. 35. Now, every one knows that the legal punishment of a subject, acting in *defiance of his allegiance*, and con-
tracting the guilt of *treason*, is nothing less than *death*. Nay, so
much bent on the persecution of Catholics is this modern bishop,
as to arraign parliament itself as guilty of *a breach of the Constitution*, by the latter of the above mentioned tolerating Acts;

true cause was, that his hands being stained by the blood of twenty innocent
Catholics, who were immolated by the sanguinary policy of his master Shaftsbury, in Oates' infamous plot, he was obliged to find a pretext for excluding
them from the legal toleration, which he stood in need of himself.—Bishop
Hoadly, who had no religion at all of his own, would not allow the Catholics to
enjoy theirs, because, he says; " no oaths and solemn assurances, no regard to
truth, justice, or honour, can restrain them." This is the hypocritical plea
for intolerance, of a man who was in the constant habit of violating all his
oaths and engagements to a church which had raised him to rank and fortune, and who systematically pursued its degradation, into his own anti-
Christian Socinianism, by professed *deceit* and *treachery*, as will be seen in the
Letters.—Blackstone, being a crown lawyer, and writing when the penal
laws were in force, could not but defend them : but, judge as he was, and
writing at the above mentioned time, he, in the passage following that quoted
by Dr. Burgess, expressed a hope, that the time " was not distant, when the
fears of a Pretender having vanished, and the influence of the Pope becoming feeble, the rigorous edicts against the Catholics would be revised," b. iv.
c. 4.; which event, accordingly, soon took place. As to Burke, the last author whom the bishop quotes against Catholic emancipation, it is evident,
from his speech at Bristol, his letter to lord Kenmare, and the whole tenor of
his conduct, that he was not only a warm friend, but, in some degree, a martyr to it.

where he says : " If the elective franchise be really *inconsistent with the Constitutional Statutes* of the revolution, *it ought to be repealed,* like all other concessions, that are *injurious to loyalty and religion.*"—He adds, " But it does not follow that because parliament had been *guilty of one act of prodigality,* that it should, therefore, like a thoughtless and *unprincipled spendthrift,* plunge itself into inextricable ruin," pp. 53, 54. Thus, my lord, though the prelate alluded to, after advertising, in his table of contents, A CONCLUSION, showing " the means of co-operating with the laws for preventing the danger and increase of Popery," when he comes to the proper place for inserting it, apologizes for *deferring its publication,* as " being connected with the *credit of the ecclesiastical establishment,*" yet, we see as clearly, from the substance and drift of *the Protestant's Catechism,* what his Conclusion is, as if he had actually published it ; namely, he would have the whole code of penal laws, with all their incapacities, fines, imprisonment, hanging, drawing, and quartering, re-enacted, to prevent even the *private practice of idolatry ;* and he would have the bishops, clergy, churchwardens, and constables, employed in enforcing them, according to the forms of Inquisition, prescribed by the Canons of 1597, 1603, and 1640.

Before the writer passes from the present subject of loyalty and the laws, to others more congenial with his studies, and those of the prelate, he wishes to submit to your lordship's reflection two or three questions connected with it. First: Is it strictly legal, even for a lord of parliament, and is it edifying for a bishop, to instruct the public, especially in these days of insubordination and commotion, that the reigning king, and the two houses of parliament, have acted against the Constitutional Statutes, by affording religious relief to a large and loyal portion of British subjects ; as king William, George I. and George II. had afforded it to other portions of them ? We all know what outcries are continually raised about violating the Constitution, and we know what effect these are intended to produce : now, if a turbulent populace are made to believe that the present legislature has acted *illegally* and *unconstitutionally* in some of its acts, is there no danger that they may form the same notion concerning some of its other acts, which are peculiarly obnoxious to them, and that they may rank these among the *Fictitious Statutes,* as this prelate terms the *Acts of Parliament* of three former reigns ?—Secondly · The writer wishes to ask your lordship, whether or no you think it is for the peace and safety of the sister isle, to alarm the bulk of its inhabitants with the threat of their being dispossessed of the elective franchise, which they have now enjoyed for a quarter of a century ? In like manner, is it conducive to this important end, for a person of his lordship's character and consequence to assure this people, that the Pope's jurisdiction, and England's dominion over them, " were introduced into Ireland by the mercenary compact of the Pope and Henry II." p. 24, "founded on a fiction of the grossest kind, the pretended donation of Constantine," p. v. though, by the bye, this was never once mentioned or hinted at by either of the parties?—Lastly: The writer would be glad to be informed by your lordship, whether it is for the advantage of the established church so highly to extol John Wickliffe, who maintained that clergymen ought to have no sort of temporal possessions? And is it for the security of the state to hold up lord Cobham as " a great and good man, and the martyr of Protestantism," p. vii.*, who was convicted in the King's Bench, and in open parliament, of raising an insurrection of twenty thousand men, for the purpose of killing the king and his brother, and the lords spiritual and temporal, and who was executed for the same, merely because he was a *Wickliffite?* How innocent was colonel Despard, compared with sir John Oldcastle, called lord Cobham!

The writer has spoken of the object of the publication which has lately appeared, under the name of a Rt. Rev. bishop of the established church: he now proceeds to say something of its contents.

It professes to be THE PROTESTANT'S CATECHISM. From this title, most people will suppose it to be *an elementary book, for the instruction of Protestants of every description, in the doctrine and morality taught by Jesus Christ:* but not a word can the writer find in it about Christ, or God, or any *doctrinal* matter whatever; except that, " They, who do not hold the worship of the church of Rome to be idolatrous, are not Protestants, whatever they may profess to be," p. 46.; which is a sentence of excommunication against many of the brightest lights and chief ornaments of the bishop's own church. Nor does this novel Catechism contain any moral or practical lesson; except that, " Every member of parliament's conscience is pledged against the Catholic claims;" and, what has been mentioned before, that as " Popery is idolatrous, it is *not to be tolerated* either in public or in *private*," and that " it must be now thought how to remove it," p. 3. Had the Catechism appeared without a name, it might be supposed to be a posthumous work of lord George Gordon; but, had its origin been traced to the mountains of Wales, it would certainly be attributed to some itinerant Jumper, rather than to a successor of St. Dubritius and St. David. What, however, chiefly distinguishes *The Protestant Catechism* from other *No Popery* publications, is, not so much the strength of its acrimony, as the boldness of its paradoxes. These, for the most part, stand in contradiction to all ancient records and modern authors, Protestant as well as Catholic, being supported by the bare word of the bishop of St. David's: and what is still more extraordinary, they sometimes stand in contradiction to the word of the bishop of St.

* See Walsingham's Historia Major. Knighton Leicest. Collier's Eccles Hist. Stow, &c

David's himself; resting in this case, on the word of Dr. Thomas Burgess, I purpose exhibiting a few of the paradoxes I refer to.

The great and fundamental paradox of the Right Rev. *Catechist* is, that Protestantism subsisted many hundred years *before Popery*, at the same time that he marks its essence consist in *a renunciation of, and opposition to, Popery!* for his lordship lectures his Protestant pupils in the following manner: "Question. What is Protestantism? Answer. The abjuration of Popery and the exclusion of Papists from all power, ecclesiastical and civil." p. 12. "Question. What is Popery? Answer. The religion of the church of Rome, so called because the church of Rome is subject to the jurisdiction of the Pope." p. 11. "Question. When was this jurisdiction assumed over the whole church? Answer. At the beginning of the seventh century." p. 15. The writer does not here refute the various errors of the Right Rev. bishop on these heads; this refutation will be found in the following letters; he barely exhibits one of the bishop's leading paradoxes. It may be here stated as another very favourite paradox of the prelate, since he has maintained it in a former work, that, because Venantius Fortunatus, a poet of the sixth century, sings that "the *stylus*, or writings of St. Paul, had run east, west, north and South, and passed into Britain and the remote Thule," and because Theodoret, an author of the fifth century, says, "St. Paul, brought salvation to the islands in the sea," (namely, Malta and Sicily, *Acts* xxvii.) it follows that the British church was *founded* by St. Paul! p. 19.* This paradox might be stated and even granted, for any thing it makes in favour of the bishop's object, which is to invalidate the supremacy of St. Peter. For it matters not which apostle founded this church or that church, while it is evident from the words of Christ, in St. Matthew, c. xvi. v. 18, and in other texts, and from the concurring testimony of the fathers, and all antiquity, that Christ built the whole church on the foundation of the apostles and prophets, he himself being the chief corner stone, so as still to ground it, next after himself, on the *Rock*, Peter.† This will be found demonstrated in the following work, Letter xlvi. A third paradox of the prelatic *Catechist* is this: Having undertaken to prove that "The church of Rome

---

* The falsity of this inference and the weakness and unfairness of the bishop's arguments on the whole subject, have been well exposed by an able and learned writer, the Rev. John Lingard, in his *Examination of Certain Opinions advanced by the Rev. Dr. Burgess*, &c. 1813. Syers, Manchester; Keating and Brown, London.

† The Right Rev. prelate seems to have been forced out of his former cavil concerning the difference of gender between Πετρος and Πετρα in the text, Matt. xvi. by a learned colleague of his [Landaff from remote ages was a thorn in the side of Menevia] who has shown him that Christ did not speak Greek but Syriac, and on this occasion, made use of the word *Cephas*, *Rock*, which admits of no variation of genders.

was founded by St. Paul," p. 13, no less than the church of Britain, he attempts to draw an argument *from their different discipline* in the observance of Easter; that the latter was "independent" of the former, p. 23. Hence it would follow that St. Paul established *one* discipline, that which the prelate himself now follows, at Rome; and *another,* "that of the church of Ephesus, and the eastern churches, in Britain," p. 17. The truth is, his lordship has quite bewildered himself in the ancient controversy about the right time of keeping Easter. He will learn, however, from the following letters, that the British church originally agreed with that of Rome, in this, no less than in the other points, as the emperor Constantine expressly declares in his letter on that subject,[*] and as farther appears by the Acts of the Council of Arles, which the British bishops, there present, joined with the rest in subscribing. And when, after the Saxon invasion, the British churches got into a wrong computation, they did not follow that of the Asiatic Quarto-decimans, but always kept Easter-day on a Sunday, differing from the practice of the continent once only in seven years. A fourth paradox of the Catechism maker, is, that, admitting, as he does, the existence of our Christian king, Lucius, in the second century, he, nevertheless, rejects his conversion by the missionaries of Pope Eleutherius, Fagatius and Duvianus, as "a mere Romish fiction, and a monkish fable," p. 23; notwithstanding both facts rest on exactly the same authority, namely, that of all the original writers, British, Saxon, English, Roman, and Gallic.[†] A fifth paradox of the bishop's, is, that "The British churches were Protestant before they were Popish," p. 23: "six centuries elapsed before Popery had any footing in this island," p. 28; and that "the British bishop's showed their independence of the Pope's authority by rejecting the overtures of Austin, and by refusing to acknowledge any authority but that of their own metropolitan," p. 24. And yet it is demonstrated that the British bishops were present not only at the Councils of Arles and Nice, which acknowledged the Pope's authority, but also that of Sardica in Illyrium, held in 347,[‡] where the right of appeal to the Pope in all ecclesiastical causes, from every part of the world, was confirmed.[§] It is equally certain, that in the former part of the following century, Pope Celestine sent St. Palladius to convert the Scots, St. Patrick to convert the Irish, and St. Germanus to reclaim such Britons as had

---

[*] Euseb. Vit. Constant. L. iii. c. 19.

[†] Nennius' Hist. Briton, c. xviii. Girald. Cambr. De Jur. Menev. P. ii. Angel. Sac. p. 541. Silvest. Girald. Camb. Descript. c. xviii. The Ancient Register of Landaff, quod Teilo vocatur. Angel. Sacra, vol. ii. Gildas Historicus, quoted by Rudborn. Galfrid Monument. Ven. Bede, L. i. c. 4. The Saxon Chronicle. Gul. Malm. Antiq. Glaston. Martyr Rom. Raderus, &c. &c.

[‡] St. Athan. Apolog. 2. See also Usher.

[§] Can. iii.

fallen into the Pelagian heresy.* Each of these facts is expressly affirmed by a contemporary author of the highest character, St. Prosper; and the last mentioned fact is conformable to the British records, which represent this foreign bishop, as exercising high acts of jurisdiction in Britain, which he never could have exercised but in virtue of the Papal supremacy, of which he and his companion, St. Lupus, bishop of Treves, were the delegates; such as consecrating bishops in different parts of the island, and constituting St. Dubritius archbishop of the *Right Side of it*, or of Wales.† But how many other proofs of the dependency of the ancient British church on the See of Rome, has not our episcopal antiquary met with, in his own favourite author and predecessor, Giraldus Cambrensis,‡ especially where the latter gives an account of his pleading before the Pope for the Archiepiscopal dignity of St. David's, which the latter asserted was formerly decorated even with the *Pallium*, the mark of Papal legatine jurisdiction; till one of his predecessors, Sampson, as he asserted, flying into Britany, transferred it to Dol? He maintained, however, that, excepting the use of the Pallium, the church of St. David possessed the whole metropolitical dignity, and was " subject to no other church *except that of Rome*, and to that *immediately*."§ The modern prelate does but add to the wonder of his learned readers by appealing to the conference between St. Austin, Pope Gregory's missionary and legate in England, and the Welsh bishops, A. D. 502, and to the latters " rejecting the overtures" of the former, in proof of their " rejecting the Pope's authority," p. 24. For, what were these overtures? They were these three: that they, the Welsh bishops, would keep Easter at the right time; that they would adopt the Roman ritual in the

---

* St. Prosper. "Papa Celestinus Germanum Antisidorensem Episcopum *VICE SUA* mittit, et deturbatis hæreticis Britannos ad Catholicam fidem dirigit." Chron. ad An. 429. See also Archbish. Usher De Brit. Eccl. Prim.

† " Post quam prædicti Seniores (Germanus et Lupes) Pelagianam hæresim extirpaverant; Episcopos, in pluribus locis Britanniæ Insulæ consecraverunt. Super omnes autem Britannos dextralis partis Britanniæ B. Dubritium, summum Doctorem, a Rege et ab omni parochiâ electum, Archiepiscopum consecraverunt." Ex Antiq. Eccl. Landav. Registro. Angl. Sacr. P. ii. p. 667.

‡ The New Biographical Dictionary divides Silvester Giraldus Cambrensis into two different persons, whereas, it is plain, from this author's Description of Wales, p. 882, Edit. Cambden, that these three names belong to one and the same author.

§ " Usque ad Anglorum Regem Henricum I. totam Metropoliticam dignitatim, præter usum Pallii, Ecclesia Menevensis obtinuit; nulli Ecclesiæ prorsus, *nisi Romanæ tantum*, et illi *immediate*, sicut nec Ecclesia Scotica, subjectionem debens." De Jur. Menev. Ecc. Angl. Sac. P. ii. p. 541.— The rival See of Landlaff bears equal testimony to the supremacy of Rome. "Sicut Romana Ecclesia excedit dignitatem omnium Ecclesiarum Catholicæ fidei, ita Ecclesia illa Landavia excedit omnes Ecclesias totius dextralis Britanniæ." Ex Antiq. Regist. Landav. Angl. Sac. P. ii. p. 669.

3

administration of baptism; and that they would join with the Roman missionaries in preaching the word of God to the Pagan English.* This last overture demonstrates, that neither on the two former points, nor on any other point, and least of all on that of the Pope's supremacy, was there, in the opinion of St. Austin, any difference, of essential consequence, between his doctrine and that of the Welsh bishops. For, if there had been such a difference, and especially if they had denied the supremacy of his master, the Pope, would he have invited, and even pressed them, to join with him in preaching the gospel to his new and increasing flock in England? As well may we believe that a faithful shepherd would collect together, and turn into his fold a number of hungry wolves! It is true they then said they would not receive St. Augustin for their *archbishop*:† but neither did he nor the Pope require them to do so; nor is the vindication of the rights of an ancient church, at any time, a denial of the Pope's general supremacy. So far from this, within two years from the holding of that conference, we find Oudoceus, bishop of Landaff, going to Canterbury to receive consecration from the same St. Austin, and we find him received, on his return into Wales, by the king, princes, clergy and people, with the highest honour.‡ We have moreover, the testimony of the above quoted British register, that the bishops of Landaff, from this period, were always subject and obedient to the archbishop of Canterbury, who was at all times the Pope's legate. The right Rev. bishop's argument to prove that the Irish church was not, anciently, in communion with the church of Rome, namely, because it was in communion with the British bishops, p. 24, is as great a paradox as any of the above-mentioned: since it has been proved that the British bishops themselves were always in communion with the church of Rome. Of the same description are the assertions, that no legate was appointed by the Pope in Ireland "before Gillebert, in the twelfth century," and that "the Pope's jurisdiction was first introduced into Ireland by the mercenary compact of the Pope and Henry II." p. 25. To expose the inconsistency of these assertions, nothing more is necessary than to consult the *Antiquities* of Usher himself, on whose authority they are said to be grounded. This Protestant archbishop then testifies from ancient records, which he cites, that, first St. Palladius, and after him St. Patrick, was sent into Ireland by Pope Celestine, to convert its inhabitans from Pagan idolatry; the former in 431, the latter in 432; that St. Patrick, "having established the church of Ireland, and ordained bishops and priests throughout the whole island, went to Rome, in 462, where he procured from Pope

* "Ut genti Anglorum una nobiscum prædicetis verbum Domini." Bed. Eccl. Hist. L. ii. c. 2.

† Bed. Eccl. Hist. L. ii. c. 2.

‡ Vita Oudocei, quoted by Godwin De Præsul, and Usher.

Hilary, the confirmation of whatever he had done in Ireland, together with the Pallium, and the title of *Pope's legate;*"[*] that in 540 the celebrated St. Finan, of Clonard, having spent seven years at Rome, and being consecrated bishop, returned into Ireland, where he instituted schools and convents, one of which contained three thousand monks.[†] It appears from the same annalist, that in 580, the renowned St. Columban passed from Ireland to the continent, where he was protected by different bishops and princes, for his orthodoxy and piety, and even by the Popes themselves, with whom he corresponded; that in 630, a deputation was sent from Ireland, of learned and holy men, " to the fountain of their baptism, like children to their mother,"[‡] namely, to the apostolic See of Rome, to consult with it on matters of religion; that among these was St. Lasrean, who was consecrated bishop by Pope Honorius, and appointed his *legate in Ireland;*[§] that in 640, Tomianus, and four other bishops, being still anxious about the right observance of Easter, and about the Pelagian heresy, wrote to consult Pope Severinus, and that they received an answer to their letter from his successor, Pope John.—Numerous other testimonies, not only of the *communion* of the church of Ireland, with that of Rome, but also of its *acknowledging the Pope's supremacy,* may be collected from Usher, Ware, and other Protestants, no less than from the original Catholic writers, down to the very time of Gillebert, bishop of Limerick, whom the Catechist admits to have been the Pope's legate in Ireland. This happened, according to Usher, in 1130, twenty-five years before the date of what the Catechist calls " the mercenary compact of the Pope and Henry II. by which," he says, " the Pope's jurisdiction was *first* introduced into Ireland," and forty years before the latter invaded Ireland; which island, after all, as every child knows, he invaded, not as the executor of Pope Adrian's legacy, but as the ally of the dethroned king, Dermot.

In speaking of the beginning and progress of the religion of our own ancestors, the English, it might be expected the Right Rev. Catechist would have paid more attention to truth and consistency than he has done with respect to the foregoing more obscure histories This, however, is not the case. But, previously to the writer's entering on this particular subject he wishes to observe, what is more fully demonstrated in the following work, that the Catechist totally misrepresents our apostle, Pope Gregory the Great, as having " reprobated the spiritual supremacy,"

* Usher's Antiq. Index Chronol.   † Usher Primord.
‡ Usher.
§ Gilbert was succeeded in the legatine office by St. Malachy, who, by a special authority, erected the See of Tuam into an archbishopric. After his death Cardinal Papario was sent by Pope Eugenius III. into Ireland, namely, in 1151, with four Palliums for the four archbishoprics. So false is the prelate's account of the origin of the Pope's jurisdiction in Ireland !

and also "his successor Boniface as being the first Pope to assume it," p. 16.   In short, the question, at issue, is not concerning the *title*, but the *power* of a head bishop; which power, as it
will appear below, no Pope exercised more frequently or extensively " than the learned and virtuous St. Gregory," to use
the prelate's own epithets.   His lordship does not deny that
our ancestors, the Anglo-Saxons, were converted to Christianity by " the Pope's missionaries," p. 26, namely, by St.
Austin and his companions, sent hither by the above-mentioned Pope Gregory, in 597; nor does he contradict the account of our venerable historian, Bede, who describes the whole
jurisdiction and discipline of our church, as being regulated by
that Pope and his successors.   Still the prelate most paradoxi-
cally denies that " the Pope ever exercised jurisdiction in England or Ireland, except during the four centuries before the Reformation!" p. 11; and he maintains, in particular, that "the
Anglo-Saxon churches differed from the church of Rome in their
objection to image worshipping, the invocation of Saints, transubstantiation, and other errors," p. 28.   Here are two paradoxes to
be refuted; one concerning the *spiritual power*, the other concerning the *doctrine* of the See of Rome.   With respect to the
former: is it not a fact, my lord, known to every ecclesiastical
antiquary, that each one of our primates, from St. Austin down
to Stigand, exclusively, who was deposed soon after the conquest,
either went to Rome to fetch, or had transmitted to him from
Rome, the emblem and jurisdiction of legatine authority, by which
he held and exercised the power of a metropolitan over his suffre
gan bishops?   An original author, Radulph Diceto, exhibits a succinct but clear demonstration of this, in a series of all the archbishops, and a list of the different Popes, from whom the former
respectively received the Pallium.   Did not St. Wilfrid, archbishop of York, appeal to the Pope from the uncanonical seques-
tration of his diocess by the primate Theodore?   Did not Offa,
the powerful Mercian king, engage Pope Adrian to transfer six
suffregan bishoprics from the See of Canterbury to that of Litchfield, constituting it, at the same time, an archbishopric?   A hundred other instances of the exercise of the Pope's ecclesiastical
jurisdiction in England, previously to the conquest, could be
produced, if they were wanted.—As to the pretended difference
between the *doctrine* of the Anglo-Saxons and the church of
Rome, the Catechist was bound to inform his readers when it
took place; and who were the authors of it; that is, who first
persuaded the whole English nation to reject the religion they
had been taught by their apostles, Pope Gregory and his missionaries; and whether this change was effected by slow degrees, or all
of a sudden.*   If so absurd a paradox, as the above-mentioned..

* To make some brief confutation of each of the Catechist's alleged dif
ferences between the Anglo-Saxon church and that of Rome : Bede testifies

required a serious refutation, it might be stated that, in 610, bishop Melitus, who afterwards became primate, went to Rome to
obtain the Pope's confirmation of certain regulations which had
been made in England, that he subscribed to the Acts of an
Episcopal Synod, then held in that city, which Acts he brought
back with him to England,* and that, in 680, St. Wilfrid, going
to Rome, to prosecute his appeal, was present at a council of one
hundred and twenty-five Bishops, where, " In the name of all the
churches in the north part of Britain, Ireland, and the nations of
the Scots and Picts, he made open profession of the true Catholic
faith, confirming it also by his subscription." †

Other paradoxes of the Right Rev. prelate, relating to matters
of a later date, are these, that Pope Adrian IV. grounded his
right to give away Ireland on " the forged donation of Constantine," though he never once alluded to it, but assigned quite
other grounds for what he did ; and that "the Pope now owes the
whole of his temporal and spiritual power on the continent, to
this gross fiction, and the Decretal Epistles," p. v. Alas ! what
must the learned Catholics of the continent, who were the first to
detect these literary frauds of the eighth century, and to trace
them to the place of their birth in Lower Germany, think of the
literature of this country, when they hear a bishop, and a member
of our learned societies, telling them that they would not acknowledge the Pope to be prince of Rome or head of the church,
were it not for those spurious pieces! A similar paradox is, that
" The Popish bishops and Popish clergy were the real authors of
the fictitious statutes (Acts of Parliament) of Richard II. Henry IV.
and Henry V." against the Lollards ; though they neither did,
nor were permitted to interfere in those Acts ; and though it is
notorious from all contemporary history, that these severe edicts
were occasioned by what that anarchial faction had done, and
threatened to do. They had, under the command of Wat Tyler,
and John Ball, a Wickliffite priest, *actually* put to death, by public execution, the lord chancellor, the lord treasurer, and the lord
chief justice of England : and they had *threatened* to kill the king,

that when St. Austin and his fellow missionaries preached the gospel to
king Ethelbert, they carried a cross for their ensign, with a painted picture
of Christ, L. i. c. 25. Will. Malmsb. mentions that, among other pious
images, preserved at Glastonbury, were those of Christ and his apostles,
made of silver and given by king Ina. De Antiq. Glaston. We learn from
archbishop Cuthred's letter to Lullus, successor of St. Boniface, bishop and
martyr of Mentz, that a Synod of Anglo-Saxon bishops had chosen this saint,
and St. Gregory, and St. Austin, to be their " patrons and intercessors."
Inter Epist. Bonif. That our ancestors, believed in transubstantiation, is
clear, from Osborn's relation of archbishop Odo's rendering this visible.
Angl. Sac. P. ii. 82. One of his successors, Lanfrank, was the principal
defender of this doctrine against Berengarius. It may be added, that the
original faith concerning purgatory, the mass, and perhaps every other
controverted point, can be proved from Bede's History alone.

 * Bede, L. ii. c. 4.   † Ibid. L. v. c. 20.

3*

the lords spiritual and temporal, and all the *pen and ink-horn men*, as
they called the lawyers; as also to put down all the clergy, except
the begging friars, and to divide among themselves all their lands
and property.* Such were the levellers of the fifteenth century,
whom a modern bishop eulogizes.—The following are theological
paradoxes, being such as will infallibly non-plus every *regular*
student in divinity. 1st. " The apostles were not bishops," p.
15. By the same rule bishops are not priests.—2dly. " To retain the *obsolete language* of ancient Rome, in prayer, is *an error,*
p. 39.—3dly. The Irish were guilty of " *a heresy of discipline !*
p. 60.

But the political paradoxes, my lord, of this new Catechis
are still more inexplicable than the theological ones. The first
of them, which I shall mention, is contained in the following question and answer. " Q. What is it excludes Pagans, Jews, and
Mahometans from our churches and from parliament? A. Religion," p. 44.—Your lordship will permit the writer to observe,
in the first place, that it is impossible either for the simple catechumens of Wales, or even for the learned reviewers of England,
to gather from this passage, whether the Rt. Rev. prelate means
to say, that it is the religion of *Pagans, Jews,* and *Turks,* or that
of *Protestants,* which excludes the former from Parliament, for
example : nevertheless, the passage, taken either way, is perfectly
paradoxical. For can that prelate, or any one else, cite a precept of the Vedam, or the Talmud, or the Koran, which prohibits
its respective votaries from sitting and voting in the British
parliament if they can get entrance into it? Or can he show
any thing in *Protestantism* (which he defines to be " The abjuration of Popery, and the exclusion of Papists from all power, ecclesiastical or civil") that prevents a man, who publicly proclaims Mahomet, or who publicly denies Jesus Christ, or who
publicly worships the obscene and blood-stained idol Juggernaut,
from being a member of either house of the legislature? No, my
lord, there is no one article in any one of these religions, if they
may be called so, which excludes them from our parliament; the
only condition for rendering them fit and worthy to enter into it,
and becoming legislators, being their *calling God to witness,* that
" there is no transubstantiation in the mass," and that " the *worship of the Virgin Mary* and the saints, as practised in the church
of Rome, (upon both which points the worshippers of Juggernaut
and English Protestants are, for the most part, equally well instructed,) are *Idolatrous !*———A second political paradox in
this Catechism is, that " the inviolable covenants of the two
unions show the injustice and unconstitutional nature of the Ro
man Catholic claims," p. viii. This, my lord, is equally incomprehensible; since the act of union with Scotland neither men-

* Hist. Major T. Walsingham, Knighton De vent. Angl. Collier's Eccl.
Hist.

tions these claims, nor alludes to them : and since that of the union with Ireland expressly admits the principle of their being conceded, and prepares the minds of men for their actual concession ; as it is therein enacted, that " Members of the united parliament shall take and subscribe the usual oaths and declarations UNTIL THE SAID PARLIAMENT SHALL OTHERWISE PROVIDE." Art. IV.——The last of these paradoxes, which the writer will extract from the incomprehensible Catechism, is the following. It teaches, at page 35, that " Not to consent to the *veto,* is not to acknowledge the *king's supremacy,* which it is *treasonable,* by statute, to oppose." And immediately after, at p. 36, it teaches that " *the veto,* or the king's nomination is *unprotestant* and *illegal :*" to which the bishop adds, in the words of his friend Mr. Sharp ; "it is highly improper and even *illegal* for the crown of England to *accept* the power of the proposed *veto;* or to have *any concern in the appointment of unreformed bishops,*" p. 56. Can any one, my lord, reconcile these opposite doctrines ? To the plain sense of the writer it appears, that if it be *illegal* for his majesty to *accept of the veto,* it would be *criminal* in the Catholics *to offer it* to him ; so far from its being *treasonable* to refuse giving it !

MY LORD BISHOP,

The wise man has said, in the Sacred Text, *of making many books there is no end,* Eccles. xii. 12. ; and we are certain, from reason and experience, that, least of all, will there be an end of making books, and disputing on subjects of religion, with respect to those who have no fixed rule, or none but a false one, for deciding on religious controversies, or who suffer wordly interest, pride, or the prejudices of education, to take place of the sincerity, humility and piety, which ought to guide them in a matter of such infinite moment. The writer trusts that, in the *first part* of the following Letters, he has shewn the *rule* appointed by Christ, for clearly discerning the truths he has revealed, and which conducts to the same end; that he has, in his *second part,* clearly pointed out Christ's *true church,* which cannot but teach his *true doctrine.* With men of *good will,* who follow either of these ways in the uprightness and fervour of their souls, a satisfactory end to their religious discussions and doubts, will quickly be found. But who can subdue or soften the above-mentioned passions and prejudices ? No one, certainly, but God alone ; and, as the greater part of mankind is notoriously under their influence, the writer is so far from expecting to make these persons proselytes to his demonstrations, that he has prepared his mind for the opposition and obloquy which he is sure to experience from them. He is aware, that most statesmen, and other great personages, regard religion merely as a political engine for managing the population, and therefore wish to keep one as well as the other as quiet as possible. On this principle, had they been counsellors to king Ethelbert, they would have persuaded him to banish St. Austin, and to continue the worship of Thor and Woden. The multitude, in this age of infidelity and dissipation, nauseate religious inquiries and instructions; and, when they must hear them, like the Jews of old; *they say to the seer, see not; and to the prophet, prophesy not to us right things: speak unto us smooth things; prophesy deceits,* Isai. xxx. 10. The critics and reviewers are, for the most part, as *smooth* in this respect, as the prophets: if they lead the public opinion in matters of less consequence, they follow it in those of greater.—But whatever *excuse* there may be for the inconsistency of other men, in religious matters, there would, evidently, be none for persons of your lordship's and the writer's profession and situation, should they for their temporal advantage, or their prejudices, mislead others in a matter of eternal consequence. Such conduct would be hypocritical, and doubly perfidious and ruinous. It would be *perfidious* to the individuals so misguided, and to the church or sect which they profess to serve; since nothing can injure that so much, as the appearance of insincerity and human passions in its official defenders. Accordingly it will be seen, in the following work, that the most fruitful source of conversions to the Catholic church, are the detected calumnies and misrepresentations of her bitterest enemies. Such conduct would also be utterly *ruinous;* first, to its immediate victims; and secondly, to the persons of your lordship's and the writer's profession and character. In fact, my lord, if, as Christ assures us, at the great day of universal trial, some of the arraigned will *rise up in judgment against others and condemn them* for their peculiar guilt, *Matt.* xii. 41.; how heavy a condemnation will poor bewildered souls call down upon those faithless guides who have led them astray! Or rather, how severe a vengeance will the *Good Shepherd* himself (then also the Judge of the living and the dead) *who hath laid down his life for his sheep,* take of those hirelings, who have not only *left his sheep to be caught and scattered by the wolf,* but have themselves *killed and destroyed them!* John x.

For all these important motives, let us, my lord, dismiss every selfish interest, human respect, and prejudice from our minds, in the discussion of religious subjects, and follow *truth,* whithersoever she leads us, with the utmost sincerity and ardour of our souls. The writer of this, for his part, disgusted, as he is, at seeing the most serious and sacred of all subjects become a mere field of exercise for the talents, the learning, and the passions of different writers, and averse, as he is, from taking a part in such contests, nevertheless holds himself bound, not only *to render an account of the hope that is in him, to every one who asketh it of him*, in the sincerity of an upright heart, but also to yield the palm to your lordship thankfully and publicly, should you be able to prove (not, however, by extravagant and unsupported assertions, but by sound and convincing theological arguments) that the rule of faith, which he maintains, is not the one appointed by Christ and his apostles, for guiding Christians into all truth; or that the church to which he adheres, has not exclusively those marks of the true church, which your lordship ascribes to it, in the creeds you repeat, equally with the writer. Until one or other of these points is proved, he will hold himself bound to stick close both to the rule and the church, in spite of calumny, misrepresentation, ridicule, clamour, persecution, and to maintain, in opposition to your lordship, that there is no just cause for either making or continuing any penal laws against the professors of the original faith.

The writer has the honour to remain, my lord,

Your lordship's obedient servant,

J. M. D. D.

W———, *May 3, 1818.*

THE END

OF

RELIGIOUS CONTROVERSY.

LETTER I.

From JAMES BROWN, Esq. to the Rev. J. M.
D. D. F. S. A

INTRODUCTION.

New Cottage, near Cressage, Salop, Oct. 13, 1801.

Reverend Sir,

I SHOULD need an ample apology for the liberty I take, in thus addressing you without having the honour of your acquaintance, and still more for the heavy task I am endeavouring to impose upon you, if I did not consider your public character, as a pastor of your religion, and as a writer in defence of it, and likewise your personal character for benevolence, which has been described to me by a gentleman of your communion, Mr. J. C—ne, who is well acquainted with us both.   Having mentioned this, I need only add, that I write to you in the name of a society of serious and worthy Christians, of different persuasions, to which I myself belong, who are as desirous as I am, to receive satisfaction from you, on certain doubts, which your late work, in answer to Dr. Sturges, has suggested to us.*

However, in making this request of our society to you, it seems proper, Reverend sir, that I should bring you acquainted with the nature of it, by way of convincing you, that it is not unworthy of the attention, which I am desirous you should pay to it. We consist then of above twenty persons, including the ladies, who, living at some distance from any considerable town, meet together once a week, generally at my habita-

---

* *Letters to a Prebendary*, in answer to *Reflections on Popery*, by the Rev. Dr. Sturges, *Prebendary and Chancellor of Winchester*.

A

tion of New Cottage; not so much for our amusement and re-
fection, as for the improvement of our minds, by reading the
best publications of the day, which I can procure from my
London bookseller, and sometimes an original essay written by
one of the company.

I have signified that many of us are of different religious per
suasions : this will be seen more distinctly from the following
account of our members. Among these I must mention, in
the first place, our above named learned and worthy rector, Dr
Carey. He is, of course, of the church of England ; but like
most other of his learned and dignified brethren, in these times,
he is of that free, and as it is called, liberal turn of mind, as to
explain away the mysteries and a great many of its other articles, which, in my younger days, were considered essential to
it. Mr. and Mrs. Topham, are Methodists of the Predesti-
narian and Antinomian class, while Mr. and Mrs. Askew are
mitigated Arminian Methodists, of Wesley's connection. Mr.
and Mrs. Rankin are honest Quakers. Mr. Barker and his
children term themselves *Rational Dissenters*, being of the
old Presbyterian lineage, which is now almost universally
gone into Socinianism. I, for my part, glory in being a
stanch member of our happy establishment, which has kept
the golden mean among the contending sects, and which I am
fully persuaded, approaches nearer to the purity of the apostol
ic church, than any other which has existed since the age of
it. Mrs. Brown professes an equal attachment to the church ;
yet, being of an inquisitive and ardent mind, she cannot refrain from frequenting the meetings, and even supporting the
missions of those self-created apostles, who are undermining
this church on every side, and who are no where more active
than in our sequestered valley.

With these differences among us, on the most interesting or
all subjects, we cannot help having frequent religious controversies : but reason and charity, enables us to manage these
without any breach of either good manners or good will to each
other. Indeed, I believe that we are, one and all, possessed of
an unfeigned respect and cordial love for christians of every
description, one only excepted. Must I name it on the present occasion?—Yes, I must ; in order to fulfil my commission in a proper manner. It is then the church that you,
Rev. sir, belong to ; which, if any credit is due to the eminent
divines, whose works we are in the habit of reading, and more
particularly to the illustrious bishop Porteus, in his celebrated
and standing work, called A BRIEF CONFUTATION OF
THE ERRORS OF THE CHURCH OF ROME, *extracted from archbishop Secker's* V. SERMONS AGAINST

POPERY,* is such a mass of absurdity, bigotry, superstition, idolatry, and immorality, that, to say we respect and love those who obstinately adhere to it, as we do other Christians, would seem a compromise of reason, Scripture, and virtuous feeling. -

And yet even of this church, we have formed a less revolting idea, in some particulars, than we did formerly. Thi has happened, from our having just read over your controver sial work against Dr. Sturges, called LETTERS TO A PREBENDARY, to which our attention was directed by the notice taken of it in the house of parliament, and particularly by the very unexpected compliment paid to it, by that ornament of our church, bishop Horsley.. We admit then (at least I, for my part, admit) that you have refuted, the most odious of the charges brought against your religion, namely, that it is, necessarily, and, upon principal, intolerant and sanguinary, requiring its members to persecute, with fire and sword, all persons of a different creed from their own, when this is in their power. You have also proved that Papists may be good sub-, jects to a Protestant sovereign ; and you have shown, by an interesting historical detail, that the Roman Catholics of this kingdom have been conspicuous for their loyalty, from the time of Elizabeth, down to the present time. Still most of the absurd and anti scriptural doctrines and practices, alluded to above, relating to the worship of saints and images, to transubstantiation and the half communion, to purgatory, and shutting up the Bible, with others of the same nature, you have not, to my recollection, so much as attempted to defend. In a word, I write to you, Rev. sir, on the present occasion, in the name of our respectable society, to ask you whether you fairly give up these doctrines and practices of Popery, as untenable, or otherwise, whether you will condescend to interchange a few letters with me on the subject of them, for the satisfaction of me and my friends, and with the sole view of mutually discovering and communicating religious truths. We remark that you say, in your first letter to Dr. Sturges : " Should I have occasion to make another reply to you, I will try if it be not possible to put the whole question at issue between us, into such a shape as shall remove the danger of irritation on both sides, and still enable us if we are mutually so disposed, to agree together in the acknowledgment of the same religious truths."—If you still think that this is possible, for God's sake and your neighbours' sake, delay not to undertake

* The Norrisian professor of divinity, in the university of Cambridge speaking of this work, says, " The refutation of the Popish errors is now reduced into a small compass by archbishop Secker and bishop Porteus."—*Lectures in Divinity, Vol. IV. p.* 71.

4

it. The plan embraces every advantage we wish for, and excludes every evil we deprecate.   You shall manage the discussion in your own way, and we will give you as little interuption
as possible.—Two of the essays above alluded to, with which
our worthy rector lately furnished us, I, with your permission,
enclose, to convince you, that genius and sacred literature are
cultivated round the Wrekin, and on the banks of the Severn.

I remain, Rev. Sir, with great respect,

Your faithful and obedient servant,

JAMES BROWN.

ESSAY I.

ON THE EXISTENCE OF GOD, AND OF NATURAL RELIGION.

BY THE REV. SAMUEL CAREY, LL. D.

FORESEEING that my health will not permit me, for a
considerable time, to meet my respected friends at New Cottage, I comply with the request, which several of them have
made me, in sending them in writing, my ideas on the two
noblest subjects which can occupy the mind of man ; *the existence of God, and the truth of Christianity.* In doing this,
I profess not to make new discoveries, but barely to state certain arguments, which I collected in my youth, from the learned
Hugo Grotius, our judicious Clark, and other advocates of
natural and revealed religion. I offer no apology for adopting
the words of Scripture, in arguing with persons who are supposed not to admit its authority, when these express my meaning as fully as any others can do.

The first argument for the existence of God, is thus expressed by the royal prophet ; *Know ye that the Lord he is God: it
is he that hath made us, not we ourselves.* Ps. c. 3. In fact,
when I ask myself that question, which every reflecting man
must sometimes ask himself: *How came I into this state of existence ? Who has bestowed upon me the being which I enjoy ?* I
am forced to answer: *It is not I that made myself;* and each of
my forefathers, if asked the same question, must have returned
the same answer. In like manner, if I interrogate the several

beings with which I am surrounded, the earth, the air, the water, the stars, the moon, the sun, each of them, as an ancient father says, will answer me, in its turn: *It was not I that made you ; I, like you, am a creature of yesterday, as incapable of giving existence to you, as I am of giving it to myself.* In short, however often each of us repeats the question: *How came I hither ? Who has made me what I am ?* we shall never find a rational answer to them, till we come to acknowledge that there is an *eternal, necessary self-existent Being,* the author of all contingent beings, which is no other than GOD. It is this *necessity of being*, this *self-existence*, which constitutes the nature of God, and from which all his other perfections flow. Hence when he deigned to reveal himself, on the flaming mountain of Horeb, to the holy legislator of his chosen people, being asked by this prophet, what was his *proper name ?* he answered : I AM THAT I AM. *Exod.* iii. 14. This is as much as to say: *I alone exist of myself: all others are created beings, which exist by my will.*

From this attribute of *self-existence*, all the other perfections of the Deity, eternity, immensity, omnipotence, omniscience, holiness, justice, mercy, and bounty, each in an infinite degree, necessarily flow, because there is nothing to limit his existence and attributes, and because whatever perfection is found in any created being, must, like its existence, have been derived from this universal source.

This proof of the existence of God, though demonstrative and self-evident to reflecting beings, is, nevertheless, we have reason to fear, lost on a great proportion of our fellow creatures ; because they hardly reflect at all ; or at least, never consider, *who made them,* or *what they were made for ;* but that other proof, which results from the magnificence, the beauty, and the harmony of the creation, as it falls under the senses, so it cannot be thought to escape the attention of the most stupid or savage of rational beings. The starry heavens, the fulminating clouds, the boundless ocean, the variegated earth, the organized human body, all these, and many other phenomena of nature, must strike the mind of the untutored savage, no less than that of the studious philosopher, with a conviction that there is an infinitely powerful, wise and bountiful Being, who is the author of these things : though, doubtless, the latter, in proportion as he sees more clearly and extensively than the former, the properties and economy of different parts of the creation, possesses a stronger physical evidence, as it is called, of the existence of the great Creator. In fact, if the Pagan physician, Galen,*

* De Usu Partium.

from the imperfect knowledge which he possessed of the structure of the human body, found himself compelled to acknowledge the existence of an infinitely wise and benificent Being, to make it such as it is, what would he not have said, had he been acquainted with the circulation of the blood, and the uses and harmony of the arteries, veins, and lacteals! If the philosophical orator, Tully, discovered and enlarged on the same truth, from the little knowledge of astronomy which he possessed,[*] what strains of eloquence would he not have poured forth upon it, had he been acquainted with the discoveries of Galileo and Newton, relative to the magnitude and distances of the stars, the motions of the planets and comets! Yes, all nature proclaims that there is a Being, who is *wise in heart and mighty in strength: who doth great things and past finding out; yea, wonders without number:—who stretcheth out the north over the empty places, and hangeth the earth upon nothing.—The pillars of heaven tremble and are astonished at his reproof.—Lo! these are a part of his ways; but how little a portion is heard of him! The thunder of his power who can understand!* Job. ix.—xxvi.

The proofs, however, of God's existence, which can least be evaded, are those which come immediately home to a man's own heart; convincing him, with the same evidence he has of his own existence, that there is an all-seeing, infinitely just, and infinitely bountiful Master above, who is witness of all his actions and words, and of his very thoughts. For whence arises the heart-felt pleasure which the good man feels on resisting a secret temptation to sin, or in performing an act of benificence, though in the utmost secrecy? Why does he raise his countenance to heaven, with devotion, and why is he then prepared to meet death with cheerful hope, unless it be that his conscience tells him of a munificent rewarder of virtue, the spectator of what he does? And why does the most hardened sinner, tremble and falter in his limbs, and at his heart, when he commits his most secret sins of theft, vengeance, or impurity? Why, especially, does he sink into agonies of horror and despair at the approach of death, unless it be that he is deeply convinced of the constant presence of an all-seeing witness, and of an infinitely holy, powerful, and just Judge, *into whose hands it is a terrible thing to fall.* —*In vain does he say: Darkness encompasseth me and the walls cover me: no one seeth: of whom am I afraid?*—for his conscience tells him that, *The eyes of the Lord are far brighter than the sun, beholding round about all the ways of men.* Eccles. xxiii. 26, 28

This last argument, in particular, is so obvious and convincing, that I cannot bring myself to believe there ever was a hu-

---

[*] De Natura Deorum. l. ii.

man being, of sound sense, who was really an Atheist. Those persons who have tried to work themselves into a persuasion that there is no God, will generally be found, both in ancient and modern times, to be of the most profligate manners, who, dreading to meet him as their Judge, try to persuade themselves that he does not exist. This has been observed by St. Austin, who says: "No man denies the existence of God, but such a one whose interest it is that there should be no God." Yet even they who pretend to disbelieve the existence of a Supreme Being, in the broad day-light, and among their profligate companions, in the darkness and solitude of the night, and, still more, under the apprehension of death, fail not to confess it; as Seneca, I think, has somewhere observed.*

A son heareth his father, and a servant his master, says the prophet Malachi. *If then I be a father, where is mine honour? and if I be a master, where is my fear? saith the Lord of Hosts*, i. 6. In a word: it is impossible to believe in the existence of a Supreme Being, our Creator, our Lord, and our Judge, without being conscious, at the same time, of our obligation to worship him exteriorly and interiorly, to fear him, to love him, and to obey him. This constitutes *natural religion*: by the observance of which the ancient patriarchs, together with Melchisedec, Job, and, we trust, very many other virtuous and religious persons of different ages and countries, have been acceptable to God, in this life, and have attained to everlasting bliss, in the other; still we must confess, with deep sorrow, that the number of such persons has been small, compared with those of every age and nation, who, as St. Paul says, *When they knew God, glorified him not as God; neither were they thankful, but became vain in their imaginations; and their foolish hearts were darkened;—who changed the truth of God into a lie, and worshipped and served the creature more than the Creator, who is blessed for ever more.* Rom. i. 21, 25.

SAMUEL CAREY.

* It is proper here to observe, that a large proportion of the boasting Atheists who signalized their impiety during the late French revolution, when they came to die, acknowledged that their irreligion had been affected, and that they never doubted, in their hearts, of the existence of God and the truths of Christianity. Among these were Boulanger, La Metrie Collot d'Herbois. Egalité duke of Orleans, &c.

4*

ESSAY II.

ON THE TRUTH OF THE CHRISTIAN RELIGION.

BY THE REV. SAMUEL CAREY, LL. D.

THOUGH the light of nature is abundantly sufficient, as I trust I have shown in my former essay, to prove the existence of God, and the duty of worshipping and serving him, yet this was not the only light that was communicated to mankind in the first ages of the world concerning these matters, since many things relating to them were revealed by God to the patriarchs, and, through them, to their contemporaries and descendants. At length this knowledge was almost universally obliterated from the minds of men, and the light of reason itself was so clouded by the boundless indulgence of their passions, that they seemed, every where, sunk almost to a level with the brute creation. Even the most polished nations, the Greeks and the Romans, blushed not at unnatural lusts, and boasted of the most horrid cruelties. Plutarch describes the celebrated Grecian sages, Socrates, Plato, Xenophon, Cebes, &c. as indulging freely in the former* and every one knows that the chief amusement of the Roman people, was to behold their fellow creatures murdering one another in the amphitheatres, sometimes by hundreds and thousands at a time. But the depravity and impiety of the ancient Pagans, and I may say the same of those of modern times, appears chiefly in their religious doctrines and worship. What an absurd and disgusting rabble of pretended deities, marked with every crime that disgraces the worst of mortals, lust, envy, hatred and cruelty, did not the above named refined nations worship, and that, in several instances, by the imitation of their crimes! Plato allows of drunkenness in honour of the gods: Aristotle admits of indecent representations of them. How many temples were every where erected, and prostitutes consecrated to the worship of Venus?† And how generally were human sacrifices offered up in honour of Moloch, Saturn, Thor, Diana, Woden, and other pretended gods, or rather real demons, by almost every Pagan nation, Greek and barbarian,

---

* De Isid et Osirid. Even the refined Cicero and Virgil did not blush at these infamies.

† Strabo tells us, that there were a thousand prostitutes attached to the temple of Venus, at Corinth. The Athenians attributed the preservation of their city to the prayers of its prostitutes.

and among the rest by the ancient Britons, inhabitants of this
island! It is true, some few sages of antiquity, by listening to
the dictates of nature and reason, saw into the absurdity of the
popular religion, and discovered the existence and attributes of
the true God; but then how unsteady and imperfect was their
belief, even in this point! and when *they knew God, they dia
not glorify him as God, nor give him thanks, but became vain in
their thoughts.* Rom. i. 21. In short, they were so bewildered on the whole subject of religion, that Socrates, the wisest of
them all, declared it " impossible for men to discover this, unless the Deity himself deigned to reveal it to them."† Indeed
it was an effort of mercy, worthy the great and good God, to
make such a revelation of himself, and of his acceptable worship, to poor, benighted, and degraded man. This he did, first,
in favour of a poor, afflicted captive tribe on the banks of the
Nile, the Israelites, whom he led from thence into the country
of their ancestors, and raised up to be a powerful nation, by a
series of astonishing miracles, instructing and confirming them
in the knowledge and worship of himself by his different prophets. He afterwards did the same thing in favour of all the
people of the earth, and to a far greater extent, by the promised
Messiah, and his apostles. It is to this latter divine legation
I shall here confine my arguments : though indeed, the one confirms the other ; since Christ and the apostles continually bear
testimony to the mission of Moses.

All history, then, and tradition prove that in the reign of
Tiberius, the second Roman emperor after Julius Cæsar, an
extraordinary personage, Jesus Christ, appeared in Palestine,
teaching a new system of religion and morality, far more sublime and perfect than any which the Pagan philosophers, or even
than the Hebrew prophets, had inculcated. He confirmed the
truths of natural religion and of the Mosaic revelation; but
then he vastly extended their sphere, by the communication of
many heavenly mysteries, concerning the nature of the one true
God, his economy in redeeming man by his own vicarious suf
ferings, the restoration and future immortality of our bodies
and the final decisive trial we are to undergo before him, our
lestined Judge. He enforced the obligation of loving our
heavenly Father, above all things, of praying to him continually
and of referring all our thoughts, words, and actions to his di
vine honour. He insisted on the necessity of denying, not one
or other of our passions, as the philosophers had done, who, as
Tertullian says, *drove out one nail with another ;* but the whole
collection of them, disorderly and vitiated as they are, since the

---

† Plato Dialog. Alcibiad.

fall of our first parent. In opposition to our innate avarice, pride, and love of pleasure; he opened his mission by teaching that, *blessed are the poor in spirit; blessed are the meek; blessed are they that mourn, &c.* With respect to our fellow creatures; teaching, as he did, every virtue, he singled our fraternal charity for his peculiar and characteristic precept; requiring that his disciples should love one another as they love themselves, and even as he himself has loved them; he who laid down his life for them! and he extended the obligation of this precept to our enemies, equally with our friends.

Nor was the morality of Jesus a mere speculative system of precepts, like the systems of the philosophers: it was of a practical nature, and he himself confirmed, by his example, every virtue which he inculcated, and more particularly the hardest of all others to reduce to practice, the love of our enemies. Christ had *gone about*, as the Sacred Text expresses it, *doing good to all*, Acts x. 38. and evil to no one. He had cured the sick of Judea and the neighbouring countries, had given sight to the blind, hearing to the deaf, and even life to the dead; but above all things, he had enlightened the minds of his hearers with the knowledge of pure and sublime truths, capable of leading them to present and future happiness: yet was he every where calumniated and persecuted, till at length, his inveterate enemies fulfilled their malice against him by nailing him to a cross, thereon to expire, by lengthened torments. Not content with this, they came before his gibbet, deriding him in his agony with insulting words and gestures. What, now, is the return which the author of Christianity makes for such unexampled barbarity? He excuses the authors of it! He prays for them! *Father, forgive them: for they know not what they do!* Luke xxiii. 34. No wonder this proof of supernatural charity should have staggered the most hardened infidels; one of whom confesses that, " if Socrates has died like a philosopher, Jesus alone has died like a God!"* The precepts and the example of the master have not been lost upon his disciples.—These have ever been distinguished by their practice of virtue, and, particularly by their charity and forgiveness of injuries. The first of their who laid down his life for Christ, St. Stephen, while the Jew were stoning him to death, prayed thus, with his last voice, *Lord, lay not this sin to their charge!* Acts vii. 59.

Having considered the several systems of paganism, which have prevailed, and that still prevail, in different parts of the world, both as to belief and practice, together with the speculations of the wisest infidel philosophers concerning them; and ha-

---

* Rousseau Emile.

ving contemplated, on the other hand, the doctrine of the New Testament on both of them, namely, theory and practice, I would ask any candid believer, where he thought Jesus Christ could have acquired the idea of so sublime, so pure, so efficacious a religion as Christianity is, especially when compared with the others above alluded to? Could he have acquired it in the workshop of a poor artisan of Nazareth, or among the fishermen of the lake of Genezareth? Then, how could he and his poor unlettered apostles succeed in propagating this religion, as they did throughout the world, in opposition to all the talents and power of philosophers and princes, and all the passions of all mankind? No other answers can be given to these questions, than that the religion itself has been *divinely revealed*, and that it has been *divinely assisted*, in its progress throughout the world.

In addition to this *internal evidence* of Christianity, as it is called, there are *external proofs*, which must not be passed over. Christ, on various occasions, appealed to the miracles which he wrought, in confirmation of his doctrine and mission; miracles public and indisputable, which, from the testimony of Pilate himself, were placed on the records of the Roman empire,[*] and which were not denied by the most determined enemies of Christianity, such as Celsus, Porphyrius, and Julian, the apostate. Among these miracles, there is one of so extraordinary a nature, as to render it quite unnecessary to mention any others, and which, therefore, is always appealed to by the apostles, as the grand proof of the gospel they preached: I mean the *resurrection of Christ from the dead;* to which must be added its circumstances, namely, that he raised himself to life *by his own power*, without the intervention of any living person; and that he did this *in conformity with his prediction, at the time, which he had appointed* for this event, and in *defiance of the efforts of his enemies*, to detain his body in the sepulchre. To elude the evidence resulting from this unexampled prodigy, one or other of the following assertions must be maintained, either that the *disciples were deceived* in believing him to be risen from the dead, or that *they combined to deceive the world* into a belief of that imposition.—Now it cannot be credited, that they themselves were deceived in this matter, being many in number, and having the testimony of their eyes, in seeing their master repeatedly, during forty days; of their ears, in hearing his voice; and one, the most incredulous among them of *his feeling in touching* his person and *probing* his wounds; nor can it be believed that they *conspired to propa-*

---

gate an unavailing falsehood of this nature throughout the nations of the earth, namely, that a person, put to death in Judea, had risen again to life, without any prospect to themselves *for this world,* but that of persecution, torments, and a cruel death, which they successively endured, as did their numerous disciples after them, in testimony of this fact; or, *for the other world,* but the vengeance of the God of truth.

Next to the miracles, wrought by Christ, is the fulfilment of the ancient prophecies concerning him, in proof of the religion taught by him.   To mention a few of these: he was born just *after the sceptre had departed from the tribe of Juda,*Gen. xlix. 10.; at the *end of seventy-two weeks* of years from the restoration of Jerusalem, *Dan.* ix. 24; while the *second temple* of Jerusalem was *in being,* Hagg. ii. 7.   He was born in *Bethlehem,* Mic. v. 2.; worked the identical *miracles foretold of him, Isai.* xxxv. 5.   He was *sold* by his perfidious disciple for *thirty pieces of silver,* which were laid out in the *purchase of a potter's field,* Zach. xi. 13. He was *scourged, spit upon,* Isai. l. 6.; placed *among malefactors,* Isai. xxxiii. 12.   His *hands and feet were transfixed* with nails, *Ps.* xxii. 16.; and his *side was opened* with a spear, *Zach.* xii. 10.   Finally, he *died,* was *buried with honour,* Isai. liii. 9.; and *rose again* to life *without experiencing corruption.* Ps. xvi. 10.   The sworn enemies of Christ, the Jews, were, during many hundred years before his coming, and still are in possession of the Scriptures, containing these and many other predictions concerning him, which were strictly fulfilled.

The very existence, and, other circumstances respecting this extraordinary people, the Jews, are so many arguments in proof of Christianity. They have now subsisted, as a distinct people, for more than four thousand years, during which they have again and again been subdued, harassed, and almost extirpated.   Their mighty conquerors, the Philistines, the Assyrians, the Persians, the Macedonians, the Syrians, and the Romans, have, in their turns, ceased to exist and can no where be found as distinct nations: while the Jews exist in great numbers, and are known in every part of the world.   How can this be accounted for? Why has God preserved them alone, amongst the ancient nations of the earth? The truth is, they are still the subject of prophecy, with respect to both the Old and New Testament.   They exist as monuments of God's wrath against them; as witnesses to the truth of the Scriptures which condemn them; and as the destined subjects of his final mercy before the end of the world.   They are to be found in every quarter of the globe; but in the condition which their great legislator Moses threatened them with, if they forsook

the Lord, namely, that he would *remove them into all the kingdoms of the earth.* Deut. xxviii. 25. That they should become
an astonishment, and a by-word, among all nations, ibid. 37.
That they should *find no ease, neither should the sole of their
foot have rest,* ibid. 65. Finally, they are every where seen, but
carrying, written on their foreheads, the curse which they pronounced on themselves in rejecting their Messiah: *his blood be
upon us and upon our children.* Mat. xxvii. 25. Still is this
raordinary people preserved, to be, in the end, converted,
nd to find mercy. *Rom.* xi. 26, &c.

SAMUEL CAREY.

LETTER II.

TO JAMES BROWN, Esq. &c.

PRELIMINARIES.

Winton, October 20, 1801.

Dear Sir,

YOU certainly want no apology for writing to me on the
subject of your letter. For if, as St. Peter inculcates, each
Christian ought to be *ready always to give an answer to every
man that asketh him a reason of the hope that is in him,* 1 Pet.
iii. 15. how inexcusable would a person of my ministry and
commission be, who am *a debtor both to the Greeks and to the
Barbarians, both to the wise and the unwise,* Rom. i. 14. were
I unwilling to give the utmost satisfaction in my power, respecting the Catholic religion, to any human being whose inquiries appear to proceed from a serious and candid mind,
desirous of discovering and embracing religious truth, such as
I must believe yours to be. And yet this disposition is exceedingly rare among Christians. Infinitely the greater part
of them, in choosing a system of religion, or in adhering to one,
are guided by motives of interest, worldly honour, or convenience. These inducements not only rouse their worst passions,
but also blind their judgement; so as to create hideous phantoms to their intellectual eyes, and to hinder them from seeing
the most conspicuous objects which stand before them. To
such inconsistent Christians, nothing proves so irritating as the

attempt to disabuse them of their errors, except the success of it, by putting it out of their power to defend them any longer. These are they; and O! how infinite is their number! of whom Christ says, *they love darkness rather than light*, John iii. 16.; and who say to the prophets, *Prophesy not unto us right things. speak unto us smooth things.* Isai. xxx. 10. They form to themselves *a false conscience*, as the Jews did, when they mur dered their Messiah, *Acts* iii. 17.; and as he himself foretold many others would do, in murdering his disciples. *John* xvi. 2. I cannot help saying that I myself have experienced something of this spirit, in my religious discussions with persons who have been loudest in professing their candour and charity. Hence, I make no doubt that, if the elucidation which you call for at my hands, for your numerous society, should happen, by any means to become public, that I shall have to *eat the bread of affliction, and drink the water of tribulation*, 1 Kings xxii. 27. for this discharge of my duty, perhaps for the remain- der of my life. But, as the apostle writes, *none of these things move me; neither count I my life dear to me, so that I may finish my course with joy, and the ministry which I have re- ceived from the Lord Jesus.* Acts xx. 24.

It remains, sir, to settle the conditions of our correspondence. What I propose is, that, in the first place, we should mutually, and indeed all of us who are concerned in this friendly contro- versy, be at perfect liberty to speak, without offence to any one, of doctrines, practices, and persons, as we judge best for the discovery of truth: secondly, that we should be disposed, in common, as far as poor human nature will permit, to investi- gate truth with impartiality; to acknowledge it, when disco- vered, with candour; and, of course, to renounce every error and unfounded prejudice that may be detected, on any side, whatever it may cost us in so doing. I, for my part, dear sir, here solemnly promise, that I will publicly renounce the reli- gion, of which I am a minister, and will induce as many of my flock, as I may have influence over, to do the same, should it prove to be that "mass of absurdity, bigotry, superstition, ido- latry, and immorality," which you, sir, and most Protestants conceive it to be; nay, even if I should not succeed in clearing it of these respective charges. To religious controversy, when originating in its proper motives, a desire of serving God and securing our salvation, I cannot declare myself an enemy, with- out virtually condemning the conduct of Christ himself, who, on every occasion, arraigned and refuted the errors of the Pha- risees: but I cannot conceive any hypocrisy so detestable as that of ascending the pulpit or employing the pen on sacred subjects to serve our temporal interest, our resentment, or our pride,

under pretext of promoting or defending religious truth.—To
inquirers, in the former predicament, I hold myself a debtor,
as I have already said; but the circumstances must be extraordinary to induce me to hold a communication with persons in
the latter. Lastly, as you appear, sir, to approve of the plan I
spoke of in my first letter to Dr. Sturges, I mean to pursue it
on the present occasion. This, however, will necessarily throw
back the examination of your charges to a considerable distance; as several other important inquiries must precede.

I am, &c.

J. M.

LETTER III.

From *JAMES BROWN*, Esq. to the Rev. J. M. D. D.

PRELIMINARIES.

New Cottage, Oct. 30, 1801.

REVEREND SIR,

I HAVE been favoured, in due course, with yours of the
20th instant, which I have communicated to those persons of
our society, whom I have had an opportunity of seeing. No
circumstance could strike us with greater sorrow, than that you
should suffer any inconvenience from your edifying promptness
to comply with our well meant request, and we confidently trust
that nothing of the kind will take place through our fault. We
agree with you, as to the necessity of perfect freedom of speech,
where the discovery of important truths is the real object of
inquiry.   Hence, while we are at liberty to censure many of
your popes, and other clergy, Mr. Topham will not be offended
with any thing that you can prove against Calvin; nor will Mr.
Rankin quarrel with you for exposing the faults of George Fox
and James Naylor; nor shall I complain of you for any thing
that you can make out against our venerable Latimer or Cranmer; I say the same of doctrines and practices, as of persons.
If you are guilty of Idolatry, or we of heresy, we are respectively unfortunate, and the greatest charity we can do, is to
point out to each other the danger of our respective situations,
to their full extent. Not to renounce error and embrace truth

of every kind, when we clearly see it, would be folly; and to
neglect doing this, when the question is about religious truth,
would be folly and wickedness combined together.   Finally,
we cheerfully leave you to follow what course you please, and
o whatever extent you please, provided you only give us such
satisfaction as you can give, on the subjects I mentioned in my
former letter.

I am, Rev. Sir, &c.

JAMES BROWN.

LETTER IV.

To JAMES BROWN, Esq. &c.

DISPOSITIONS FOR RELIGIOUS INQUIRY.

DEAR SIR,

THE dispositions which you profess, on the part of your
friends, as well as yourself, I own, please me, and animate me
to undertake the task you impose upon me.   Nevertheless,
availing myself of the liberty of speech which you and your
friends allow me, I am forced to observe that there is nothing
in which men are more apt to deceive themselves, than in thinking themselves to be free from religious prejudices, and sincere
in seeking after, and resolved to embrace and follow the truth
of religion, in opposition to their preconceived opinions and
wordly interests.   How many imitate Pilate, who, when he
had asked our Saviour the question, *What is truth?* presently
went out of his company, before he could receive an answer to
it! *John* xviii. 38.   How many others resemble the rich young
man, who, having interrogated Christ, *What good thing shall
I do that I may have eternal life?* when this divine master answered him, *If thou wilt be perfect, go and sell what thou hast
and give to the poor;—went away sorrowful!* Mat. xix. 22. Finally, how many more act like certain presumptuous disciples
of our Lord, who, when he had propounded to them a mystery
beyond their conception, that of the real presence, in these
words, *My flesh is meat indeed, and my blood is drink indeed;—*

said, this is a hard saying; who can hear it?—and went back and walked no more with him! John vi. 56. O! if all Christians, of the different sects and opinions, were but possessed of the sincerity, disinterestedness, and earnestness, to serve their God, and save their souls, which a Francis Walsingham, kinsman to the great statesman of that name, a Hugh Paulin Cressy, dea of Laughlin, and prebendary of Windsor, and an Anthon Ulric, duke of Brunswick and Lunenburgh, prove themselves to have been possessed of; the first, in his *Search into Matters of Religion;* the second, in his *Exomologesis, or Motives of Conversion, &c.;* and the last, in his *Fifty Reasons;* how soon would all and every one of our controversies cease, and we be all united in one faith, hope, and charity! I will here transcribe, from the preface to the *Fifty Reasons,* what the illustrious relative of his majesty says, concerning the dispositions, with which he set about inquiring into the grounds and differences of the several systems of Christianity, when he began to entertain doubts concerning the truth of that in which he had been educated; namely, Lutheranism.   He says, "First, I earnestly implored the aid and grace of the Holy Ghost, and with all my power, begged the light of true faith, from God, the father of lights," &c. "Secondly, I made a strong resolution, by the grace of God, to avoid sin, well knowing that *Wisdom will not enter into a corrupt mind, nor dwell in a body subject to sin,*" Wisd. i. 4. "and I am convinced, and was so then, that the reason why so many are ignorant of the true faith, and do not embrace it, is because they are plunged into several vices, and particularly into carnal sins." Then, "Thirdly, I renounced all sorts of prejudices, whatever they were, which incline men to one religion more than another, which unhappily I might have formerly espoused, and I brought myself to a perfect indifference, so as to be ready to embrace whichsoever the grace of the Holy Ghost, and the light of reason, should point out to me, without any regard to the advantages and inconveniences, that might attend it in this world." "Lastly, I entered upon this deliberation and this choice, in the manner I should wish to have done it, at the hour of my death, and in a full conviction that, at the day of judgment, I must give an account to God, why I followed this religion in preference to all the rest." The princely inquirer finishes this account of himself with the following awful reflections: Man has but one soul, which will be eternally either damned or saved. *What doth it avail a man to gain the whole world and lose his own soul?* Matt. xvi. 26. Eternity knows no end.   The course of it is perpetual.   It is a series of unlimited duration.   There is no comparison between things infinite and those which are not so.   O! the happiness of the

C

eternity of the saints! O! the wretchedness of the eternity of the damned.   One of these two eternities awaits us!"

I remain, Sir, yours, &c.

J. M.

LETTER V.

To JAMES BROWN, Esq.

METHOD OF FINDING OUT THE TRUE RELIGION.

Dear Sir,

IT is obvious to common sense, that, in order to find out any hidden thing, or to do any difficult thing, we must first discover, and then follow, the proper method for such purpose. If we do not take the right road to any distant place, it cannot be expected that we should arrive at it.   If we get hold of a wrong clue, we shall never extricate ourselves from a labyrinth. Some persons choose their religion as they do their clothes, by fancy.   They are pleased, for example, with the talents of a preacher, when presently they adopt his creed.   Many adhere to their religious system, merely because they were educated in it, and because it was that of their parents and family; which, if it were a reasonable motive for their resolution, would equally excuse Jews, Turks, and Pagans, for persisting in their respective impiety, and would impeach the preaching of Christ and his apostles! Others glory in their religion, because it is the one established in this their country, so renowned for science, literature, and arms: not reflecting that the polished and conquering nations of antiquity, the Egyptians, Assyrians, Persians, Greeks, and Romans, were left, by the inscrutable judgments of God, *in darkness and the shadow of death*, while a poor oppressed and despised people on the banks of the Jordan, were the only depositary of divine truth, and the sole truly enlightened nation.   But, far the greater part even of Christians, of every denomination, make the business of eternity subservient to that of time, and profess the religion which suits best their interest, their reputation, and their convenience   I trust that none of your respectable society fall under any of these descriptions. They. all have, or fancy they have, a rational method of discovering religious truth, in other words an adequate *rule of faith.* Before I enter into any disquisition on this all-important controversy, concerning the *right rule of faith,* on which the determination of every other depends, I will lay down three fundamental maxims the truth of which, I believe, no rational Christian will dispute.

First, *our divine master, Christ, in establishing a religion here on earth, to which all the nations of it were invited,* Matt. xviii. 19, *left some* RULE *or* method, *by which those persons, which sincerely seek for it, may certainly find it.*

Secondly, *this rule or method, must be* SECURE *and never-failing; so as not to be ever liable to lead a rational, sincere inquirer, into error, impiety, or immorality, of any kind.*

Thirdly, *This rule or method must be* UNIVERSAL, *that is to say, adapted to the abilities and other circumstances, of all those persons, for whom the religion itself was intended; namely the great bulk of mankind.*

By adhering to these undeniable maxims, we shall quickly, dear sir, and clearly, discover the method appointed by Christ for arriving at the knowledge of the truths which he has taught, in other words, at *the right rule of faith.* Being possessed of this rule, we shall have nothing else, of course, to do than to make use of it, for securely, and, I trust, amicably, settling all our controversies. This is the short and satisfactory method of composing religious differences, which I alluded to in my above mentioned letter to Dr. Sturges. To discuss them all, separately, is an endless task, whereas this method reduces them to a single question.

5*   I am, &c.

J. M.

LETTER VI.

TO JAMES BROWN, Esq.

THE FIRST FALLACIOUS RULE OF FAITH.

DEAR SIR,

AMONG serious Christians, who profess to make the discovery and practice of religion their first and earnest care, three different methods or rules have been adopted for this purpose. The first consists in a supposed *private inspiration*, or an immediate light and motion of God's spirit, communicated to the individual. This was the rule of faith and conduct formerly professed by the Montanists, the Anabaptists, the Family of Love, and is now professed by the Quakers, the Moravians, and different classes of the Methodists. The second of these rules is the *written Word of God*, or THE BIBLE, *according as it is understood by each particular reader or hearer of it.* This is the professed rule of the more regular sects of Protestants, such as the Lutherans the Calvinists, the Socinians, the Church of England men. The third rule is THE WORD OF GOD, *at large, whether written in the Bible, or handed down from the apostles in continued succession by the Catholic church, and as it is understood and explained by this church.* To speak more accurately, besides their *rule* of faith, namely, *Scripture* and *tradition*, Catholics acknowledge *an unerring judge of controversy*, or sure guide in all matters relating to salvation, namely, THE CHURCH. I shall now proceed to show that the first mentioned rule, namely, a supposed *private inspiration*, is quite fallacious, in as much as *it is liable to conduct, and has conducted many, into acknowledged errors and impiety.*

About the middle of the second age of Christianity, Montanus, Maximilla and Priscilla, with their followers, by adopting this enthusiastical rule, rushed into the excess of folly and blasphemy. They taught that the Holy Spirit, having failed to save mankind, by Moses, and afterwards by Christ, had enlightened and sanctified them to accomplish this great work. The strictness of their precepts, and apparent sanctity of their lives, deceived many, till at length the two former proved what spirit they were guided by, in hanging themselves.[*] Several

---

[*] Euseb. Eccles. Hist. l. v. c. 15.

other heretics became dupes of the same principles in the primitive and the middle ages; but it was reserved for the time of religious licentiousness, improperly called the Reformation, to display the full extent of its absurdity and impiety.   In less than five years after Luther had sounded the trumpet of evangelical liberty, the sect of Anabaptists arose in Germany and the Low Countries.   They professed to hold immediate communication with God, and to be ordered by him to despoil and kill all the wicked, and to establish a kingdom of the just,* who, to become such, were all to be rebaptized.   Carlostad, Luther's first disciple of note, embraced this *Ultra-Reformation ;* but its acknowledged head, during his reign, was John Bockhold, a taylor of Leyden, who proclaimed himself king of Sion, and who, during a certain time, was really sovereign of Münster, in Lower Germany, where he committed the greatest imaginable excesses, marrying eleven wives at a time, and putting them, and numberless other of his subjects to death, at the motion of his supposed interior spirit.† He declared that God had made him a present of Amsterdam and other cities, which he sent parties of his disciples to take possession of.   These ran naked through the streets, howling out, " Wo to Babylon ; wo to the wicked ;" and, when they were apprehended, and on the point of being executed for their seditions and murders, they sung and danced on the scaffold, exulting in the imaginary light of their spirit.‡ Herman, another Anabaptist, was moved by his spirit to declare himself the Messiah, and thus to evangelize the people, his hearers : " Kill the priests, kill all the magistrates in the world : repent: your redemption is at hand."§   One of their chief and most accredited preachers, David George, persuaded a numerous sect of them, that " the doctrine both of the Old and New Testament was imperfect, but that his own was perfect, and that he was the *true Son of God.*"‖   I do not notice these impieties and other crimes for their singularity or their atrociousness, but because they were committed *upon the principle and under a full conviction of an individual and uncon trolable inspiration,* on the part of their dupes and perpetrators.

Nor has our own country been more free from this enthusiastic principle than Germany and Holland.   Nicholas, a disci-

---

* " Cum Deo colloquium esse et mandatum habere se dicebant, ut, impiis omnibus interfectis, novum constituerent mundum, in quo pii solum et innocentes viverent et rerum, potirentur."—Sleidan. De Stat. Rel. et Reip. Comment. l. iii. p. 45.

† Hist. Abreg. de la Reform. par Gerard Brandt, tom. i. p. 46. Mosheim, Eccles Hist. by Maclaine, vol. iv. p. 452.

‡ Brandt, p, 49, &c.   § Brandt, p. 51.   ‖ Mosheim, vol. iv. p. 484

ple of the above mentioned David George, came over to England with a supposed commission from God to teach men that the essence of religion consists in the feelings of divine love, and that all other things relating either to faith or worship, are of no moment.*   He extended this maxim even to the fundamental precepts of morality, professing to continue in sin that grace might abound.   His followers, under the name of the *Familists*, or *The Family of Love*, were very numerous at the end of the sixteenth century, about which time, Hacket, a Calvinist, giving way to the same spirit of delusion, became deeply persuaded that the spirit of the Messiah had descended upon him ; and, having made several proselytes, he sent two of them, Arthington and Coppinger, to proclaim through the streets of London, that Christ was come thither with his fan in his hand. This spirit, instead of being repressed, became still more ungovernable at the sight of the scaffold and the gibbet, prepared in Cheapside for his execution.   Accordingly he continued till the last, exclaiming, " Jehova, Jehova ; don't you see the heavens open, and Jesus coming to deliver me, &c."† Who has not heard of Venner, and his Fifth Monarchy-men, who, guided by the same private spirit of inspiration, rushed from their meeting house in Coleman street, proclaiming that they would " acknowledge no sovereign but king Jesus, and that they would not sheathe their swords, till they had made Babylon (that is monarchy) a hissing and a curse, not only in England, but also throughout foreign countries ; having an assurance that one of them would put a thousand enemies to flight, and two of them ten thousand ?" Venner being " taken and led to execution, with several of his followers, protested it was not he, but Jesus, who had acted as their leader."‡   I pass over the unexampled follies and the horrors of the grand rebellion, having detailed many of them elsewhere.§   It is enough to remark that, while many of these were committed from the licentiousness of private interpretation of Scripture, many others originated in the enthusiastic opinion which I am now combating, that of an immediate individual inspiration, equal, if not superior, to that of the Scriptures themselves.‖

It was in the midst of these religious and civil commotions that the most extraordinary people of all those who have adopted the fallacious rule of private inspiration, started up at the call of George Fox, a shoe-maker of Leicestershire.   His funda

* Ibid. Brandt.
† Fuller's Church Hist. b. ix. p. 113.   Stow's Annals, A. D. 1591.
‡ Echard's Hist. of Eng. &c.
§ Letters to a Prebendary.   Reign of Charles I.
‖ See the remarkable history of the military preachers at Kingston.   Ibid

mental propositions, as laid down by the most able of his fol-lowers,[*] are, that, " *The Scriptures are not the adequate prima-ry rule of faith and manners,—but a secondary rule, subordi-nate to the spirit,* from which they have their excellency and certainty :"[†] that the testimony of the spirit is that alone by which the true knowledge of God hath been, is, and can be re-vealed :"[‡] that " all true and acceptable worship of God is of-fered in the inward and immediate moving and drawing of his own spirit, which is neither limited to places, times, nor per-sons."[§] Such are the avowed principles of the people called Quakers : let us now see some of the fruits of those principles, as recorded by themselves, in their founder and first apostles.

George Fox tells of himself, that at the beginning of his mis-sion he was "moved to go to several courts and steeple-houses, (churches) at Mansfield, and other places, to warn them to leave off oppression and oaths, and to turn from deceit, and to turn to the Lord."[‖] On these occasions the language and behaviour of his spirit was very far from the meekness and respect for constituted authorities of the Gospel spirit, as appears from dif-ferent passages in his Journal.[¶] He tells us of one of his disci-ples, William Simpson, who was "moved of the Lord to go, at several times, for three years, naked and barefoot before them, as a sign unto them, in markets, courts, towns, cities, to priests' houses, and to great men's houses, telling them, *so should they be all stripped naked.* Another Friend, one Robert Hunting-don was moved of the Lord to go into Carlisle steeple-house with a white sheet about him."[**] We are told of a female Friend who went "stark naked in the midst of public worship, into Whitehall chapel, when Cromwell was there;" and ano-

---

[*] Robert Barclay's Apology for the Quakers.

[†] Propos. III. In defending this proposition, Barclay cites some of the Friends, who, being unable to read the Scriptures, even in the vulgar lan-guage, and being pressed by adversaries with passages from it, *boldly denied, from the manifestation of truth in their own hearts, that such passages were con-tained in the Scriptures, p,* 82.

[‡] Propos. II.   [§] Propos. XI.

[‖] See the Journal of George Fox, written by himself, and published by his disciple Penn, son of admiral Penn, folio, p. 17.

[¶] I shall satisfy myself with citing part of his letter, written in 1660, to Charles II.——" King Charles, thou camest not into this nation by sword nor by victory of war, but by the power of the Lord. And if thou dost bear the sword in vain, and let drunkenness, oaths, plays. May-games, with fiddlers, drums, and trumpets to play at them, with such like abominations and vanities, be encouraged, or go unpunished, as setting up of May-poles, with the image of the crown a-top of them, the nation will quickly turn, like Sodom and Go-morrah, and be as bad as the old world, who grieved the Lord, till he over-threw them : and so he will you, if these things be not suddenly prevented." &c. G. F.'s Journal, p. 225

[**] Journal. p. 230

ther woman, who came into the parliament house with a trencher in her hand, which she broke in pieces, saying, *thus shall he be broke in pieces.*"—One came to the door of the parliament house with a drawn sword, and wounded several, saying, *he was* inspired by the Holy Spirit to kill every man that sat in that house."* But on no one occasion have the Friends, with George Fox himself, been so embarrassed to save their *rule of faith*, as they have been to reconcile with it the conduct of James Naylor.† When certain low and disorderly people in Hampshire, disgraced their society and became obnoxious to the laws, G. Fox disowned them,‡ but, when a Friend of James Naylor's character and services§ became the laughing-stock of the nation for his presumption and blasphemy, there was no other way for the society to separate his cause from their own, but by abandoning their fundamental principles, which leaves every man *to follow the spirit within him, as he himself feels it.* The fact is, James Naylor, like so many other dupes of a supposed private spirit, fancied himself to be the Messiah, and in this character rode into Bristol, his disciples spreading their garments before him, and crying, *Holy, holy, holy, hosannah in the highest:* and when he had been scourged by order of parliament, for his impiety, he permitted the fascinated women, who followed him, to kiss his feet and his wounds, and to hail him "the prince of peace, the rose of Sharon, the fairest of ten thousand,"‖ &c.

I pass over many sects of less note, as the Muggletonians, the Labbadists, &c. who, by pursuing the meteor of a supposed inward light, were led into the most impious and immoral practices. Allied to these are the Moravian brethren, or Hernhutters, so called from Hernhuth in Moravia, where their apostle, count Zinzendorf, made an establishment for them. They are now spread over England, with ministers and bishops appointed by others resident at Hernhuth. Their rule of faith, as laid down by Zinzendorf, is an imaginary inward light, against

---

* Maclaine's note on Mosheim, vol. v. p. 470.

† See History of the Quakers, by William Sewel, folio, p. 138. Journal of G. Fox, p. 220.

‡ Journal of G. Fox, p. 320.

§ Ibid. p. 220. Sewel's Hist. of Quakers, p. 140.

‖ Echard's Hist. Maclaine's Mosheim. Neal's Hist. of Puritans. In closing this account of the Quakers, we may remark that there is no appearance yet of the fulfilment of the confident prophecy with which Barclay concludes his Apology : " That little spark (Quakerism) that hath appeared, shall grow to the consuming of whatsoever shall stand up to oppose it. The mouth of the Lord hath spoken it ! Yea; he that hath risen in a small remnant, shall arise and go on by the same arm of power in his spiritual manifestation until he hath conquered all his enemies : until all the kingdoms of the earth become the kingdom of Jesus Christ."

which the true believer cannot sin. This they are taught to wait for in quiet, omitting prayer, reading the Scriptures, and other *works*.* They deny that even the moral law contained in the Scriptures is a rule of life for believers. Having considered this system in all its bearings, we are the less surprised at the disgusting obscenity, mingled with blasphemy, which is to be met with in the theological tracts of the German count.†

The next system of delusion which I shall mention, as proceeding from the fatal principle of an *interior rule of faith!* though framed in England, was also the work of a foreign nobleman, baron Swedenborg. His first supposed revelation was at an eating-house in London, about the year 1745. "After I had dined," says he, "a man appeared to me sitting in the corner of the room, who cried out to me, with a terrible voice, *Don't eat so much.* The following night the same man appeared to me, shining with light, and said to me, *I am the Lord, your Creator and Redeemer, I have chosen you to explain to men the interior and spiritual sense of the Scriptures: I will dictate to you what you are to write.*"‡ His imaginary communications with God and the angels were as frequent and familiar as those of Mahomed, and his conceptions of heavenly things were as gross and incoherent as those of the Arabian impostor. Suffice it to say that his *God* is a mere *man*, his *angels* are *male* and *female*, who marry together and follow various *trades and professions.* Finally, his *New Jerusalem*, which is to be spread, over the whole earth, is so little different from this sublunary world that the entrance into it is *imperceptible.*§ So far is true, that the New Jerusalemites are spread throughout England, and have chapels in most of its principal towns.‖

* Wesley, in a letter which he inscribes "To the church of God at Hernhuth,' says, " There are many whom your brethren have advised, though not in their public preaching, not to use the Ordinances—reading the Scripture, praying, communicating ; as the doing these things is *seeking salvation by works.* Some of our English brethren (Moravians) say, *You will never have faith till you leave off the church and the sacraments: as many go to hell by praying as by thieving.*" Journal, 1740. John Nelson, in his own Journal, tells us, that the Moravians call their religion *the Liberty*, and the *Poor Sinnership*, adding, that " they sell their prayer books, and leave off reading and praying to follow the Lamb.

† See Maclaine's Hist. vol. vi. p. 23, and bishop Warburton's Doctrine of Grace, quoted by him.

‡ Baruel's Hist. du Jacobinisme, tom. iv. p. 118.

§ Baruel's Hist. du Jacobinisme, tom. iv. p. 118.

‖ Since the above letter was written, another sect, the Joannites, or disciples of Joanna Southcote, have risen to notice by their number and the singularity of their tenets. This female apostle has been led by her spirit to believe herself to be the woman of Genesis, destined to crush the head of the infernal serpent, with whom she supposes herself to have had daily battles, to the effusion of his blood. She believes herself to be, likewise, the woman of

I am sorry to be obliged to enter upon the same list with these enthusiasts, a numerous class, many of them very respectable, of modern religionists, called Methodists: yet, since their avowed system of faith is, that this consists in an *instantaneous illapse of God's spirit into the souls of certain persons*, by which they are *convinced of their justification and salvation*, without reference to Scripture or any thing else, they cannot be placed, as to their rule of faith, under any other denomination. This, according to the founder's doctrine, is the *only article of faith;* all other articles he terms *opinions*, of which he says, "the Methodists do not lay any stress on them, whether right or wrong."* He continues: "I am sick of opinions; I am weary to bear them; my soul loaths this frothy food."† Conformably to this latitudinarian system, Wesley opens heaven indiscriminately to churchmen, Presbyterians, Independents, Quakers, and even to Catholics.‖ Addressing the last named, he exclaims, "O that God would write in your hearts the rules of self-denial and love laid down by Thomas á Kempis; or that you would follow in this and in good works, the burning and shining light of your own church, the marquis of Renty.‡ Then would all who know and love the truth, rejoice to acknowledge you as the church of the living God."§

At the first rise of Methodism in Oxford, A. D. 1729, John Wesley and his companions were plain, serious church of England men, assiduous and *methodical* in praying, reading, fasting, and the like. What they practised themselves, they preached to others both in England and America, till becoming intimate with the Moravian brethren and particularly with Peter Boh-

---

the Revelations crowned with twelve stars, which are so many ministers of the established church. In fact, one of these, a richly beneficed rector, and of a noble family, acts as her secretary, in writing and sealing passports to heaven, which she supposes herself authorized to issue, to the number of 144,000, at a very moderate price. One of these passports, in due form, is in the writer's possession. It is sealed with three seals. The first exhibits two stars, namely, the morning star, to represent Christ, the evening star, to represent herself. The second seal exhibits the lion of Juda, supposed to allude to the insane prophet, Richard Brothers. The third shows the face of Joanna herself. Of late, her inspiration has taken a new turn: she believes herself to be pregnant of the Messiah, and her followers have prepared silver vessels of various sorts for his use, when he is born.

* Wesley's Appeal, P. III. p. 134.   † Ibid. p. 135.
‖ Wesley's Appeal.
‡ His life written in French, by Père St. Jure, a Jesuit, and abridged in English by J. Wesley.
§ In his "*Popery Calmly Considered*," p. 20, Wesley writes: "I firmly believe that many members of the church of Rome have been holy men, and that many of them are so now." He elsewhere says, "Several of them (Papists) have attained to as high a pitch of sanctity as human nature is capable f arriving at "

ler, one of their elders, John Wesley, "became convinced of unbelief, namely, a *want of that faith whereby alone we are saved.*"* Speaking of his past life and ministry, he says, " I was fundamentally a Papist, and knew it not."† Soon after this persuasion, namely, on May 24, 1739, " Going into a society in Aldersgate street," he says, " whilst a person was reading Luther's Preface to the Romans, about a quarter before nine, I felt my heart strangely warmed : I felt I did trust in Christ, in Christ alone for salvation, and *an assurance was given me that he had taken away my sins, even mine, and saved me from the law of sin and death.*"‡

What were now the unavoidable consequences of a diffusion of this doctrine among the people at large ? Let us hear them from Wesley's most able disciple and destined successor Fletcher, of Madeley. " Antinomian principles and practices," he says, " have spread like wild-fire among our societies. Many persons, speaking in the most glorious manner of Christ and their interest in his complete salvation, have been found living in the greatest immoralities.—How few of our societies, where cheating, extorting, or some other evil hath not broke out, and given such shakes to the ark of the Gospel, that, had not the Lord interposed, it must have been overset !"§—" I have seen them who pass for believers, follow the strain of corrupt nature; and when they should have exclaimed against Antinomianism, I have heard them cry out *against the legality of their wicked hearts,* which they said, *still suggested that they were to do something for their salvation.*"‖—" How few of our celebrated pulpits, where more has not been said *for sin* than *against it !*"¶—The same candid writer, laying open the foulness of his former system, charges Sir Richard Hill, who persisted in it, with maintaining that, " Even adultery and murder do not hurt the pleasant children, but rather work for their good."**—" God sees no sin in believers, whatever sin they

---

* Whitehead's life of John and Charles Wesley, vol. ii. p. 68.

† Journal, A. D. 1739. Elsewhere, Wesley says, " O what a work has God begun, since Peter Bohler came to England ; such a one as shall never come to an end, till heaven and earth pass away."

‡ Vide Whitehead. vol. ii. page 79. In a letter to his brother Samuel, John Wesley says, " By a Christian, I mean one who so believes in Christ that death hath no dominion over him, and in this obvious sense of the word I was not a Christian till 24th of May, last year." Ibid. 105.

§ Checks to Antinom. vol. ii. p. 22.   ‖ Ibid. page 200.

¶ Ibid. page 215.

** Fletcher's Works, vol. iii. page 50. Agricola, one of Luther's first disciples, is called the founder of the Antinomians. These hold that the faithful are bound by no law, either of God or man, and that good works of every kind are useless to salvation; while Amsdorf, Luther's pot-companion, taught that they are an impediment to salvation. Mosheim's Eccles. Hist.

commit. My sins might displease God; my person is always acceptable to him. Though I should outsin Manasses, I shoulc not be less a pleasant child, because God always views me in Christ. Hence, in the midst of adulteries, murders and incests, he can address me with, *Thou art all fair my love, my undefiled, there is no spot in thee.*"*—"It is a most pernicious error of the schoolmen to distinguish sins according to the *fact*, and not according to the *person*."—"Though I blame those who say, *Let us sin that grace may abound*, yet adultery, incest, and murder, shall, upon the whole, make me *holier on earth*, and *merrier in heaven.*"†

These doctrines and practices, casting great disgrace on Methodism, alarmed its founder. He therefore held a synod of his chief preachers, under the title of *a Conference*, in which he and they unanimously abandoned their past *fundamental principles*, in the following confession which they made.—"*Quest*. 17. Have we not unawares, leaned too much to Calvinism? *Ans.* We are afraid we have. *Quest.* 18. Have we not also leaned too much to Antinomianism? *Ans.* We are afraid we have. *Quest.* 20. What are the main pillars of it? *Ans.* 1. That Christ abolished the moral law: 2. That Christians therefore are not obliged to observe it: 3. That one branch of Christian liberty, is liberty from observing the commandments of God," &c.‡ The publication of this retraction, in 1770, raised the indignation of the more rigid Methodists, namely, the Whitefieldites, Jumpers, &c. all of whom were under the particular patronage of lady Huntingdon: accordingly her chaplain, the Hon. and Rev. Walter Shirley, issued a circular letter by her direction, calling a general meeting of her connexion, as it is called, at Bristol, to censure this "*dreadful heresy*," which, as Shirley affirmed, "injured the very fundamentals of Christianity."§

Having exhibited this imperfect sketch of the errors, contradictions, absurdities, impieties, and immoralities, into which numberless Christians, most of them, no doubt, sincere in their belief, have fallen, by pursuing phantoms of their imagination or divine illuminations, and adopting a supposed immediate and personal revelation as the *rule of their faith and conduct*, I would request any one of your respectable society, who may,

by Maclaine, vol iv. p. 35. p. 328. Eaton, a Puritan, in his *Honeycomb of Justification*, says: "Believers ought not to mourn for sin, because it was pardoned before it was committed."
* Fletcher, vol. iv. p. 97.
† Quoted by Fletcher. See also Daubeny's Guide to the Church, p. 82.
‡ Apud Whitehead, p. 213. Benson's Apology, p. 208.
§ Fletcher's Works, vol. ii. p. 5. Whitehead. Nightingale's Portrait of Methodism, p. 463.

still adhere to it, to reconsider the self-evident maxim laid down in the beginning of this letter; namely, *that cannot be the rule of faith and conduct which is liable to lead us, and has lea very many well meaning persons into error and impiety*; I would remind him of his frequent mistakes and illusions respecting things of a temporary nature; then, painting to his mind the all-importance of ETERNITY, that is of happiness or misery inconceivable and everlasting, I would address him in the words of St. Augustine, " What is it you are trusting to, poor, weak soul, and blinded with the mists of the flesh: what is it you are trusting to?

J. M.

LETTER VII.

TO JAMES BROWN, Esq. &c.

OBJECTIONS ANSWERED.

DEAR SIR,

I HAVE just received a letter from Friend Rankin, of Wenlock, written much in the style of George Fox, and another from Mr. Ebenezer Topham, of Brozeley. They both consist of objections to my last letter to you, which they had perused at New Cottage; and the writers of them both request that I would address whatever answer I might give them, to your villa.

Friend Rankin is sententious, yet civil. He asks, first, Whether " Friends at this day and in past times, and even the faithful servant of Christ, George Fox, have not condemned the vain imaginations of James Naylor, Thomas Bushel, John Perot, and the sinful doings of many others, through whom the word of life was blasphemed in their day among the ungodly ?" He asks, secondly, " Whether numberless follies, blasphemies, and crimes, have not risen up in the Roman Catholic as well as in other churches ?" He asks, thirdly, Whether the " learned Robert Barclay in his glorious Apology, hath not shown forth, that *the testimony of the spirit is that alone by which the true knowledge of God, hath been, is, and can be revealed* and confirmed ; and this not only by the outward testimony of Scripture, but also by that of Tertullian, Hierom, Augustin, Gregory the Great, Bernard, yea also by Thomas a Kempis, F. Pacificus Baker,* and many others of the Popish communion, who, says Robert Barclay, have known and tasted the love of God, and felt the power and virtue of God's spirit working within them for their salvation ?"†

I will first consider the arguments of Friend Rankin. I grant him, then, that his founder, George Fox, does blame certain extravagancies of Naylor, Perot, and others, his followers, at the same time that he boasts of several committed by himself by Simpson, and others.‡ But how does he confute them, and guard others against them? Why, he calls their authors *ranters* and charges them with *running out!*§ Now what kind of argument is this in the mouth of G. Fox against any fanatic, however furious, when he himself has taught him, that he is to *listen to the spirit of God within himself, in preference to the authority of any man and of all men, and even of the Gospel?* G. Fox was not more strongly moved to believe that he was the *messenger of Christ*, than J. Naylor was to believe that *he himself was Christ*: nor had he a firmer conviction that the Lord forbade *hat-worship*, as it is called, *out of prayer*, than J. Perot‖ and his company had that they were forbidden to use it *in prayer.*¶ Secondly, with respect to the excesses and crimes committed by many Catholics, of different ranks, as well as by other men, in all ages, I answer, that these have been committed, *not in virtue of their rule of faith and conduct*, but *in direct opposition to it*, as will be more fully seen, when we come to treat of that rule; whereas the extravagancies of the Quakers were the *immediate dictates of the imaginary spirit* which they followed as their *guide.* Lastly, when the doctors of the Catholic church teach us, after the inspired writers, *not to extinguish*, but to *walk in the spirit* of God, they tell us, at the same time,

* An English Benedictine Monk, author of *Sancta Sophia*, which is quoted at length by Barclay.

† Apology, p. 351.

‡ See Journal of G. Fox, passim.

§ Speaking of James Naylor, he says, "I spake with him, for I saw *he was out* and *wrong*; he slighted what I said, and was *dark* and *much out.*" Journ. p. 220,

‖ Journ. 310. This and another friend, John Love, went on a mission to Rome, to convert the Pope to Quakerism; but his Holiness not understanding English, when they addressed him with some course English epithets in St. Peters church, they had no better success than a female friend, Mary Fisher, had, who went into Greece to convert the Great Turk. See Sewel's Hist.

¶ "Now he (Fox) found also that the Lord forbade him to put off his hat to any men either high or low; and he required to *Thou* and *Thee* every man and woman, without distinction, and not to bid people *Good morrow*, or *Good evening*; neither might he bow, or scrape with his leg." Sewell's Hist. v. 18. See there a Dissertation on *Hat-worship*.

that this holy spirit invariably and necessarily leads us to hear the church, and to practise that humility, obedience, and those other virtues, which she constantly inculcates: so that, if it were possible for *an angel from heaven to preach another Gospel than what we have recieved*, he ought to be rejected, as a spirit of *darkness*. Even Luther, when the Anabaptists first broached many of the leading tenets of the Quakers, required them to demonstrate their pretended commission from God, by incontestable miracles.* or submit to be guided by his appointed ministers.

I have now to notice the letter of Mr. Topham.† Some of his objections have already been answered, in my remarks on Mr. Rankin's letter. What I find particular, in the former, is the following passage: "Is it possible to go against conviction and facts? namely, the experience that very many serious Christians feel, in *this day of God's power*, that they are made partakers of Christ and of the Holy Ghost? Of very many that hear him saying to the melting heart, with his still, small, yet penetrating and renovating voice, *Thy sins are forgiven thee: be thou clean: thy faith hath made thee whole?* If an exterior proof were wanting, to show the certainty of this interior conviction, I might refer to the conversion and holy life of those who have experienced it."—To this I answer, that the facts and the conviction which your friend talks of, amount to nothing more than a certain strength of imagination and warmth of sentiment, which may be natural, or may be produced by that *lying spirit*, whom God permits sometimes to *go forth*, and to *persuade* the presumptuous to their destruction. 1 *Kings* xxii. 22. I presume Mr. Topham will allow, that no experience he has felt or witnessed exceeds that of Bockhold, or Hacket, or Naylor, mentioned above, who, nevertheless, were confessedly betrayed by it into most horrible blasphemies and attrocious crimes. The virtue most necessary for enthusiasts, because the most remote from them, is an humble diffidence in themselves. When Oliver Cromwell was on his death-bed, Dr Godwin being present, among other ministers, prophesied that the Protector would recover: death, however, almost immediately ensuing, the Puritan, instead of acknowledging his error, cast the blame upon Almighty God, exclaiming, "Lord, thou hast deved us and we have been deceived!"‡ With respect to the

Sleidan.

† It was originally intended to insert these and the other letters of the same description: but as this would have rendered the work too bulky, and as the whole of the objections may be gathered from the answers to them, that intention has been abandoned.

‡ See Birch's Life of Archbishop Tillotson, p 17.

6*

alleged purity of Antinomian saints, I would refer to the history of the lives and deaths of many of our English regicides, and to the gross immoralities of numberless *Justified Methodists*, described by Fletcher, in his *Checks to Antinomianism.**

I am, &c.

J. M.

LETTER VIII.

To *JAMES BROWN*, *Esq.*

SECOND FALLACIOUS RULE.

Dear Sir,

I TAKE it for granted, that my answers to Messrs. Rankin and Topham have been communicated to you, and I hope that they, in conjunction with my preceding letters, have convinced those gentlemen, of what you, dear sir, have all along, been convinced, namely, of the inconsistency and fanaticism of every pretension on the part of individuals, now-a-days, to a new and particular inspiration, as a *rule of faith.* The question which remains for our inquiry is, whether the rule or method prescribed by the church of England and other more rational classes of Protestants, or that prescribed by the Catholic church, is the one designed by our Saviour Christ for finding out his true religion. You say that the whole of this is comprised in the *written word of God*, or *the Bible*, and that *every individual is a judge* for himself of the *sense of the Bible.* Hence, in every religious controversy, more especially since the last change of the inconstant Chillingworth,† Catholics have

---

* This candid and able writer says, " The Puritans and first Quakers soon got over the edge of internal activity into the smooth and easy path of Laodicean formality. Most of us, called Methodists, have already followed them. We fall asleep under the bewitching power; we dream strange dreams; our salvation is finished; we have got above legality; we have attained Christian liberty; we have nothing to do; our covenant is sure." Vol. ii. p. 233. He refers to several instances of the most flagitious conduct which human nature is capable of, in persons who had attained to what they call *finished salvation.*

† Chillingworth was first a Protestant, of the establishment: he next became Catholic, and studied in one of our seminaries. He then returned, into his former creed: and last of all, he gave into Socinianism, which his writings greatly promoted.

Deen stunned with the cries of jarring Protestant sects and individuals, proclaiming that, *the Bible, the Bible alone is their religion:* and hence, more particularly at the present day, Bibles
are distributed by hundreds of thousands, throughout the empire and the four quarters of the globe, as the adequate means
appointed by Christ, of uniting and reforming Christians and of
converting Infidels. On the other hand, we Catholics hold that
the Word of God in general both written and unwritten, in other
words, *the Bible and tradition, taken together, constitute the rule
of faith or method for finding out the true religion:* and *that, besides the rule itself, he has provided in his holy church, a living,
speaking judge to watch over it and explain it in all matters of
controversy.* That the latter, and not the former, is the *true rule,*
I trust I shall be able to prove as clearly as I have proved that
private inspiration does not constitute it : and this I shall prove
by means of the two maxims I have, on that occasion, made
use of; namely, *the rule of faith, appointed by Christ must be*
CERTAIN *and* UNERRING, that is to say, *it must be one
which is not liable to lead any rational and sincere inquirer into
inconsistency or error*: secondly, this rule must be UNIVER-
SAL.; that is to say, *it must be proportioned to the abilities and
circumstances of the great bulk of mankind.*

I. If Christ had intended that all mankind should learn his
religion from a *book,* namely, *The New Testament,* he himself
would have written that book, and would have laid it down, as
the first and fundamental precept of his religion, the obligation
of learning to read it; whereas, he never wrote any thing at all,
unless perhaps the sins of the Pharisees with his finger upon
. the dust, *John* viii. 6.*   It does not even appear that he gave
his apostles any command to write the Gospels; though he repeatedly and emphatically commanded them to preach it, (*Matt.*
x.) and that to all the nations of the earth, *Matt.* xxviii. 19.—
In this ministry they all of them spent their lives, preaching the
religion of Christ in every country, from Judea to Spain, in one
direction, and to India in another; every where establishing
churches, and *commending their doctrine to faithful men who
should be fit to teach others also.* 2. Tim. ii. 2. Only a part of
them wrote any thing, and what these did write was, for the
most part, addressed to particular persons or congregations,
and on particular occasions. The ancient fathers tell us that
St. Matthew wrote his Gospel at the particular request of the
'Christians of Palestine,† and that St. Mark composed his at the

---

* It is agreed upon among the learned, that the supposed letter of Christ to
Abgarus, king of Edessa, quoted by Eusebius, Hist. Eccl. 1. 1. is spurious.
† Euseb. 1. 3. Hist. Eccl. Chrysos. in Mat. Hom. 1. Iren. 1. 3. c. 1. Hieron.
de Vir Illust.

E

desire of those at Rome.* St. Luke addressed his Gospel to
an individual, Theophilus, having written it, says the holy evangelist, because *it seemed good to him to do so.* Luke i. 3. St. John
wrote the last of the Gospels in compliance with the petition of
the clergy and people of Lesser Asia,† to prove, in particular, the
divinity of Jesus Christ, which Cerinthus, Ebion, and other
heretics began then to deny. No doubt the evangelists were
moved by the Holy Ghost to listen to the requests of the faithful in writing their respective Gospels; nevertheless, there is
nothing in these occasions, nor in the Gospels themselves, which
indicates that any one of them, or all of them together, contain
an entire, detailed, and clear exposition of the whole religion of
Jesus Christ. The canonical Epistles in the New Testament,
show the particular occasions on which they were written, and
prove, as the bishop of Lincoln observes, that "they are not to
be considered as regular treatises on the Christian Religion."‡

II. In supposing our Saviour to have appointed his bare written word for the rule of our faith, without any authorized judge
to decide on the unavoidable controversies growing out of it,
you would suppose that he has acted differently from what common sense has dictated to all other legislators. For where do
we read of a legislator, who, after dictating a code of laws, neglected to appoint judges and magistrates to decide their meaning, and to enforce obedience to such decisions? You, dear
sir, have the means of knowing what would be the consequence
of leaving any act of parliament, concerning taxes, or inclosures,
or any other temporal concerns, to the interpretation of the individuals whom it regards. Alluding to the Protestant rule,
the illustrious Fenelon has said, "It is better to live without
any law, than to have laws which all men are left to interpret
according to their several opinions and interests."§ The bishop of London appears sensible of this truth, as far as regards
temporal affairs, where he writes, "In matters of property indeed, some decision, right or wrong, must be made: society
could not subsist without it:"‖ just as if peace and unity were
less necessary in the *one sheepfold of the one shepherd,* the
church of Christ, than they are in civil society!

III. The fact is, this method of determining religious ques
tions by Scripture only, according to each individual's interpretation, whenever and wherever it has been adopted, has always
produced endless and incurable dissentions, and of course errors; because truth is one, while errors are numberless. The

---

* Euseb. l. 2. c. 15. Hist. Eccl. Epiph. Hieron. de Vir. Illust.
† Euseb. l. 6. Hist. Eccl. Hieron.　.
‡ Elem. of Christ. Rel. vol. i. p. 277.
§ Life of Archbp. Fenelon, by Ramsey　　　　‖ Brief Confut. p. 18

ancient fathers of the church reproached the sects of heretics and schismatics with their endless internal divisions; "See," says St. Augustine, "into how many morsels those are divided, who have divided themselves from the unity of the church!"* Another father writes, "It is natural for error to be ever changing.† The disciples have the same right in this matter that their masters had."

To speak now of the Protestant reformers. No sooner had their progenitor, Martin Luther, set up the tribunal of his private judgment on the sense of Scripture, in opposition to the authority of the church, ancient and modern,‡ than his disciples, proceeding on his principle, undertook to prove, from plain texts of the Bible, that his own doctrine was erroneous, and that the Reformation itself wanted reforming. Carlostad,§ Zuinglius,‖ Œcolompadius, Muncer,¶ and a hundred more of his followers wrote and preached against him and against each other, with the utmost virulence, still each of them professing to ground his doctrine and conduct on the written word of God alone. In vain did Luther claim a superiority over them; in vain did he denounce hell-fire against them;** in vain did he threaten to return back to the Catholic religion:†† he had put the Bible into each man's hand to explain it for himself: this his followers continued to do in open defiance of him;‡‡ till their mutual contradictions and discords became so numerous and

---

* St. Aug.   † Tertul. de Præscrip.

‡ This happened in June, 1520, on his doctrine being censured by the Pope. Till this time, he had submitted it to the judgment of the Holy See.

§ He was Luther's first disciple of distinction, being archdeacon of Wittemberg. He declared against Luther in 1521.

‖ Zuinglius began the reformation in Switzerland, sometime after Luther began it in Germany; but taught such doctrine, that the latter termed him a pagan, and said, he despaired of his salvation.

¶ He was the disciple of Luther, and founder of the Anabaptists, who, in quality of *the just*, maintained that the property of *the wicked* belonged to them, quoting the second beatitude: *blessed are the meek for they shall possess the land.* Muncer wrote to the several princes of Germany, to give up their possessions to him; and, at the head of forty thousand of his followers, marched to enforce this requisition.

** He says to them, "I can defend you against the Pope—but when the devil shall urge against you (the heads of these changes) at your death, these passages of Scripture. *they ran and I did not send them,* how shall you withstand him! He will plunge you headlong into hell."—Oper. tom. vii. fol. 274.

†† "If you continue in these measures of your common deliberations, I will recant whatever I have written or said, and leave you. Mind what I say."—Oper. tom. vii fol. 276. edit. Wittemb.

‡‡ See the curious challenge of Luther to Carlostad to write a book against the *real presence*, when one wishes the other to *break his neck*, and the other retorts, *may I see thee broken on the wheel.*—Variat b. ii. n. 12.

scandalous, as to overwhelm the thinking part of them with grief and confusion.*

To point out some few of the particular variations alluded to ; for to enumerate them all, would require a work vastly more voluminous than that of Bossuet on this subject: it is well known that Luther's fundamental principle was that of *imputed justice*, to the exclusion of all acts of virtue and good works whatsoever. His favourite disciple and bottle-companion, Amsdorf, carried this principle so far as to maintain that *good works are a hinderance to salvation.*† In vindication of his fundamental tenet, Luther vaunts as follows: This article shall remain, in spite of all the world: it is I, Martin Luther, evangelist, who say it: let no one therefore attempt to infringe it, neither the emperor of the Romans, nor of the Turks, nor of the Tartars ; neither the Pope, nor the monks, nor the nuns, nor the kings, nor the princes, nor all the devils in hell. If they attempt it, may the infernal flames be their recompense. What I say here is to be taken for an inspiration of the Holy Ghost."‡— Notwithstanding, however, these terrible threats and imprecations of their master, Melancthon, with the rest of the Lutherans, immediately after his death, abandoned this article, and went over to the opposite extreme of Semipelagianism ; namely, they not only admitted the necessity of good works, but they also taught that these are prior to God's grace. Still on this single subject, Osiander, a Lutheran, says, " there are twenty several opinions, *all drawn from the Scripture*, and held by different members of the Augsburg, or Lutheran Confession."§

Nor has the unbounded license of explaining Scripture, each one in his own way, which Protestants claim, been confined to mere errors and dissensions ; it has also caused mutual persecution and bloodshed ;‖ it has produced tumults, re-

---

* Capito, minister of Strasburg, writing to Farel, pastor of Geneva, thus complains to him: " God has given me to understand the mischief we have done, by our precipitancy in breaking with the pope, &c. The people say to us, I know enough of the Gospel: I can read it for myself. I have no need of you." Inter Epist. Calvini. In the same tone, Dudith writes to his friend Beza, " Our people are carried away with every wind of doctrine. If you know what their religion is to-day, you cannot tell what it will be to-morrow. In what single point are those churches which have declared war against the pope agreed among themselves ? There is not one point which is not held by some of them as an article of faith, and by others as an impiety." In the same sentiment, Calvin, writing to Melancthon, says, " It is of great importance that the divisions, which subsist among us, should not be known to future ages; for nothing can be more ridiculous than that we, who have broken off from the whole world, should have agreed so ill among ourselves, from the very beginning of the Reformation."

† Mosheim Hist. by Maclaine, vol. iv. p. 328. ed. 1790. ‡ Visit. Saxon.
§ Archdeacon Blackburn's Confessional, p. 16.

‖ See Letters to a Prebendary, chapter, Persecution. Numberless other proofs of Protestants persecuting, not only Catholics, but also their fellow Protestants, to death, on account of their religious opinions, can be adduced.

bellions, and anarchy, beyond recounting. Dr. Hey asserts, that " The misinterpretation of Scripture brought on the miseries of the civil war ;"* and lord Clarendon, Madox, and other writers, show that there was not a crime committed by the Puritan rebels, in the course of it, which they did not profess to justify by texts and instances drawn from the sacred volumes.† Leland, Bergier, Baruel, Robison, and Kett, abundantly prove that the poisonous plant of Infidelity, which has produced such dreadful effects of late years on the continent, was transplanted thither from this Protestant island ; and that it was produced, nourished, and increased to its enormous growth by that principle of private judgment in matters of religion, which is the very foundation of the Reformation. Let us hear the two last mentioned authors, both of them Protestant clergymen, on this important subject. " The spirit of free inquiry," says Kett, quoting Robinson, " was the great boast of the Protestants, and their only support against the Catholics ; securing them, both in their civil and religious rights. It was, therefore, encouraged by their governments, and sometimes indulged to excess. In the progress of this contest, their own Confessions did not escape censure ; and it was asserted, that the Reformation, which these confessions express, was not complete. Further reformation was proposed. The Scriptures, the foundation of their faith, were examined by Clergymen of very different capacities, dispositions, and views, till, by explaining, correcting, allegorizing, and otherwise twisting the Bible, men's minds had hardly any thing to rest on, as a doctrine of revealed religion. This encouraged others to go further, and to say that revelation was a solecism, as plainly appears by the irreconcilable differ es among the enlighteners of the public, as they were called ; and that man had nothing to trust to, but the dictates of natural reason. Another set of writers, proceeding from this, as from a point settled, proscribed all religion whatever, and openly taught the doctrines of Materialism and Atheism. *Most of these innovations were the work of Protestant divines, from t causes that I have mentioned.* But the progress of Infideli was much accelerated by the establishment of a *Philanthropi* or academy of general education in the principality of Anh Dessau. The professed object of this institution was to unit the three Christian communions of Germany, and to make it possible for the members of them all not only to live amicably. and to worship God in the same church, but even to communi cate together. This attempt gave rise to much speculation and

* Dr. Hey's Theological Lectures. vol. i. p. 77.
† Hist. of Civ. War. Examin. of Neal's Hist. of Puritans.

refinement ; and the proposal for the amendment of the formulas, and the instructions from the pulpit, were prosecuted with so much keenness, that the ground-work of Christianity was refined and refined, till it vanished altogether, leaving Deism, or natural, or, as it was called, *philosophical religion*, in its place. *The Lutherans and Calvinists, prepared by the causes before mentioned,* to become dupes to this masterpiece of art, were enticed by the specious liberality of the scheme, and the particular attention which it promised to the morals of youth: but *not one Roman Catholic could Basedow allure to his seminary of practical ethics.*"*

IV. You have seen, dear sir, to what endless errors and impieties, the principle of private interpretation of Scripture, no less than that of private inspiration of faith, has conducted men, and, of course, is ever liable to conduct them ; which circumstance, therefore, proves, that it cannot be the rule for bringing us to religious truths, according to the self-evident maxim stated above. Nor is it to be imagined, that, previously to the formation of the different national churches, and other religious associations, which took place in several parts of Europe, at what is called " The Reformation," the Scriptures were diligently consulted by the founders of them, and that the ancient system of religion was exploded, and the new systems adopted, conformably with their apparent sense, as Protestant controvertists would have you believe. No, sir, princes and statesmen had a great deal more to do with these changes, than theologians ; and most of the parties concerned in them were evidently pushed on by very different motives from those of religion. As to Martin Luther, he testifies, and calls God to witness the truth of his testimony, that it was *not willingly*, (that is, not from a previous discovery of the falsehood of his religion) but *from accident*, (namely, a quarrel with the Dominican friars, and afterwards with the Pope) that he fell into his broils about religion.† With respect to the Reformation in

---

* Robison's Proofs of a Conspiracy against all Religions, &c. Kett's History the Interpreter of prophecy, Vol. ii. p. 158.

† Casu non voluntate in has turmas incidi : Deum testor."—The Protestant historian, Mosheim, with whom Hume agrees, admits that several of the principal agents in this revolution " were actuated more by the impulse of passions and views of interests than by a zeal for true religion." Maclaine, vol. iv. p. 135. He had before acknowledged that king Gustavus introduced Lutheranism into Sweden, in opposition to the clergy and bishops, "not only as agreeable to the genius and spirit of the Gospel, but also as favourable to the temporal state and political constitution of the Swedish dominions," p. 79, 80. He adds, that Christiern, who introduced the reformation into Denmark, was animated by no other motive than those of ambition and avarice, p. 82. Grotius, another Protestant, testifies that it was " sedition and violence which gave birth to the Reformation in his country," Holland. Append. de Antichristo.

our own country, we all know that Henry VIII., who took the first step towards it, was, at the beginning of his reign, so zealous against it that he wrote a book, which he dedicated to Pope Leo X. In opposition to it, and in return, obtained for himself and his successors, from this pontiff, the title of *Defender of the Faith.* Becoming afterwards enamoured of one of his queen's maids of honour, Ann Bullen, and the reigning Pope refusing to sanction an adulterous marriage with her, he caused a statute to be passed, abrogating the Pope's supremacy, and declaring himself *supreme head of the church of England.** Thus he plunged the nation into schism, and opened a way for every kind of heresy and impiety. In short, nothing is more evident than that the king's inordinate passion, and not the word of God, was the rule followed in this first important change of our national religion. The unprincipled duke of Somerset, who next succeeded to supreme power in the church and state, under the shadow of his youthful nephew, Edward VI. for his own ambitious and avaricious purposes, pushed on the Reformation, so called, much further than it had yet been carried. He suppressed the remaining colleges and hospitals, which the profligacy of Henry had spared, converting their revenues to his own and his associates' uses. He forced Cranmer and the other bishops, to take out fresh commissions for governing their dioceses during his nephew's, that is, his own *good pleasure.*† He made a great number of important changes in the public worship by his own authority, or that of his visitors ;‡ and when he employed certain bishops and divines in forming fresh articles and a new liturgy, he punished them with imprisonment if they

The same was the case in France, Geneva, and Scotland. It is to be observed, that in all these countries the reformers, as soon as they got the upper hand, became violent persecutors of the Catholics. Berger defies Protestants to name so much as a town or village in which, when they became masters of it, they tolerated a single Catholic.

* Archbishop Parker records, that the bishops assembled in Synod in 1531, offered to sign this new title, with the following salvo, "*In quantum per Christi leges licet :*" but that the king would admit of no such modification Antiq. Brit. p. 325. In the end, they surrendered the whole of their spiritual jurisdiction to him (all except the religious bishop of Rochester, Fisher, who was put to death for his refusal) and were content to publish *Articles of Religion devised by the King's Highness.* Heylin Hist. of Reform. Collier, &c.

† "Licentiam concedimus ad nostrum beneplacitum dumtaxat duraturam." Burnet Hist. Ref. Rec. P. II. B. i. N. 2.

‡ See the Injunctions of the Council to Preachers, published before the parliament met, concerning the mass in the Latin language, prayers for the dead, &c. See also the order sent to the primate against palms, ashes, &c. in Heylin, Burnet, and Collier. The boy Edward VI. just thirteen years old, was taught by his uncle to proclaim as follows: "We would not have our subjects so much to mistake our judgment, &c. as though we could not discern what is to be done, &c. God be praised, we know what, by his word, is fit to be redressed," Collier, vol. ii. p. 246.

7

were not obsequious to his orders*.　He even took on himself
to alter their work, when sanctioned by parliament, in compliment to the church's greatest enemy, Calvin.†　Afterwards,
when Elizabeth came to the throne, a new reformation, different in its articles and liturgy, from that of Edward VI., was
set on foot, and moulded, not according to Scripture, but to
her orders.　She deposed all the bishops except one, " *the ca-
lamity of his see*," as he was called ;‡ and she required the new
ones, whom she appointed, to renounce certain exercises, which.
they declared to be *agreeable to the Word of God*,§ but which
she found not to agree with her system of politics.　She even
in full parliament, threatened to depose them all, if they did
not act conformably to her views.‖

V. The more strictly the subject is examined, the more
clearly it will appear, that it was not in consequence of any
investigation of the Scriptures, either public or private, that
the ancient Catholic religion, was abolished, and one or other of
the new Protestant religions set up, in the different northern
kingdoms and states of Europe, but in consequenc of the politics of princes and statesmen, the avarice of the nobility and
gentry, and the irreligion and licentiousness of the people.　I
will even advance a step further, and affirm that there is no appearance of any individual Protestant, to whatever sect he belongs, having formed his creed by the rule of *Scripture alone.*
For do you, sir, really believe that those persons of your communion, whom you see the most diligent and devout in turning
over their Bibles, have really found out in them the Thirty-
nine Articles, or any other creed which they happen to profess?
To judge more certainly of this matter, I wish those gentlemen
who are the most zealous and active in distributing Bibles
among the Indians, and Africans, in their different countries,
would procure, from some half dozen of the most intelligent
and serious of their proselytes, who have heard nothing of the
Christian faith by any other means than their Bibles, a summa-
ry of what they respectively understand to be the doctrine and
the morality taught in that sacred volume. What inconsistent and

* The bishops Heath and Gardiner were both imprisoned for non-compli-
ance.

† Heylin complains bitterly of Calvin's pragmatical spirit, in quarrelling with
the English liturgy, and soliciting the protector to alter it.　Preface to Hist.
of Reform.　His letters to Somerset on the subject may be seen in *Fox's Acts
and Monum.*

‡ Anthony Kitch n, so called by Godwin, De Præsul, and Camden.

§ This took place with respect to what was termed *prophesying*, then practised by many Protestants, and defended by archbishop Grindal and the other
bishops, as *agreeable to God's word :* nevertheless, the queen obliged them
to suppress it.　Col Eccl. Hist. P. II. p. 554, &c.

‖ See her curious speech in parliament, March 25, 1585, in Stow's Annals.

nonsensical symbols should we not witness! The truth is, Protestants are tutored from their infancy, by the help of catechisms and creeds, in the systems of their respective sects;they are guided by their parents and masters, and are influenced by the opinions and example of those with whom they live and converse, some particular texts of scripture are strongly impressed upon their minds, and others of an *apparent* different meaning, are kept out of their view, or glossed over; and above all, it is constantly inculcated to them, that their religion is built upon Scripture alone; hence, when they actually read the Scriptures, they fancy they see there what they have been otherwise taught to believe; the Lutheran for example, that Christ is really present in the sacrament; the Calvinist, that he is as far distant from "it as heaven is from earth;" the churchman, that baptism is necessary for infants; the Baptist, that it is impiety to confer it upon them; and so of all the other forty sects of Protestants, enumerated by Evans, in his *Sketch of the different Denominations of Christians*, and of twice forty other sects, whom he omits to mention.

When I remarked that our blessed Master Jesus Christ wrote no part of the New Testament himself, and gave no orders to his apostles to write it, I ought to have added that, if he had intended it, together with the Old Testament, to be the sole rule of religion, he would have provided means for their being able to follow it; knowing, as he certainly did, that ninety-nine in every hundred, or rather nine hundred and ninety-nine in every thousand, in *different ages and countries*, would not be able to read at all, and much less to comprehend a page of the sacred writings: yet no such means were provided by him: nor has he so much as enjoined it to his followers in general to study letters.

Another observation on this subject, and a very obvious one is, that among those Christians, who profess that the Bible alone is the rule of their religion, there ought to be no articles, no catechisms, no sermons, nor other instructions. True it is, that the abolition of these, however incompatible they are with the rule itself, would quickly undermine the established church, as its clergy now begin to understand, and, if universally carried into effect, would in the end, efface the whole doctrine and morality of the Gospel:* but this consequence only shows more clearly the falsehood of that exclusive rule. In fact, the

* The Protestant writers, Kett and Robinson, have shown, in the passage above quoted, how the principle of private judgment tends to undermine Christianity at large; and archdeacon Hook, in his late Charge, shows, by an

most enlightened Protestants find themselves here in a dilemma,
and are obliged to say and unsay, to the amusement of some
persons, and the pity of others.*　They cannot abandon the
rule of *the Bible alone*, as explained by each one for himself,
without proclaiming their guilt in refusing to hear the Catholic
church; and they cannot adhere to it, without opening the flood-
gates to all the impiety and immorality of the age upon their
own communion.—I shall have occasion hereafter to notice the
claims of the established church to authority, in determining
the sense of Scripture, as well as in other religious controversies: in the mean time, I cannot but observe that her most able
defenders are frequently obliged to abandon their own, and
adopt the Catholic rule of faith. The judicious Hooker, in his
defence of the church of England, writes thus, "Of this we are
right sure, that nature, Scripture, and experience itself, have
taught the world to seek for the ending of contentions, by sub-
mitting to some judicial and definite sentence, whereunto nei
ther party that contendeth may, under any pretence or colour,
refuse to stand. This must needs be effectual and strong. As
for other means, without this, they seldom prevail."†　Another most clear-headed writer, and renowned defender of the
establishment, whom I had the happiness of being acquainted
with, Dr. Balguy,‡ thus expresses himself, in a *Charge to the
clergy* of his archdeaconry: "The opinions of the people are
and must be founded more on authority than reason. Their
parents, their teachers, their governors, in a great measure, determine for them, what they are to believe and what to practise. The same doctrines uniformly taught, the same rites constantly performed, make such an impression on their minds,
that they hesitate as little in admitting the articles of their

exact statement of capital convictions in different years, that the increase of
immorality has kept pace with that of the Bible societies.

* One of the latest instances of the distress in question was exhibited by
the Rt. Rev. Dr. Marsh. In his publication, *The Inquiry*, p. 4, he said, very
truly, that "the poor (who constitute the bulk of mankind) cannot without
assistance understand the Scriptures." Being congratulated on this important, yet unavoidable concession, by the Rev. Mr. Gandolphy, he tacks about,
in a public letter to that gentleman, and says, that what he wrote, in his *In
quiry*, concerning the necessity of a further rule than mere Scripture only,
regards the *establishment* of religion, not the *truth* of it: just as if that rule
were sufficient to conduct the people to the *truth of religion*, while he expressly says they *cannot understand it*.

† Hooker's Eccles. Politic. Pref. art. 6.

‡ Discourses on various Subjects, by T. Balguy, D. D. archdeacon and
prebendary of Winchester. Some of these discourses were preached at the
consecration of bishops, and published by order of the archbishop; some in
Charges to the Clergy. The whole of them are dedicated to the king, whom
the writer thanks for naming him to a high dignity (the bishopric of Gloucester), and for permitting him to decline accepting of it.

faith, as in receiving the most established maxims of common life."* With such testimonies before your eyes, can you, dear sir, imagine that the bulk of Protestants have formed their religion by the standard of Scripture? He goes on to say, speaking of controverted points: "Would you have them (the people) think for themselves? Would you have them hear and decide the controversies of the learned? Would you have them enter into the depths of criticism, of logic, of scholastic divinity? You might as well expect them to compute an eclipse, or decide between the Cartesian and Newtonian philosophy. Nay, I will go farther: for I take upon myself to say, there are more men capable, in some competent degree, of understanding Newton's philosophy, than of forming any judgment at all concerning the abstruser questions in metaphysics and theology." Yet the persons, of whom the doctor particularly speaks, were all furnished with Bibles; and the abstruse questions, which he refers to, are: "Whether Christ did or did not come down from heaven?" whether "he died or did not die for the sins of the world?" whether "he sent his Holy Spirit to assist and comfort us or whether he did not send him?"† The learned doctor elsewhere expresses himself still more explicitly on the subject of Scripture, without church authority. He is combating the dissenters, but his weapons are evidently as fatal to his own church as to theirs. "It has long been held among them, that Scripture only is the rule and test of all religious ordinances; and that human authority is to be altogether excluded. Their ancestors, I believe, would have been not a little embarrassed with their own maxim, if they had not possessed a *singular talent of seeing every thing in Scripture which they had a mind to see.* Almost every sect could find there its own peculiar form of church government; and *while they enforced only their own imaginations, they believed themselves to be executing the decrees of heaven.*"‡

I conclude this long letter, with a passage to the present purpose from our admired theological poet:

> " As long as words a different sense will bear,
> And each may be his own interpreter,
> Our airy faith will no foundation find:
> The words a weathercock for every wind."§

I am, Dear Sir, &c.

J. M.

* Discourses on various Subjects, by T. Balguy, D. D. p. 257.　† Ibid.
‡ Discourse VII. p. 126.　§ Dryden's Hind and Panther, Part I.
7*

LETTER IX.

TO JAMES BROWN, Esq.

SECOND FALSE RULE.

DEAR SIR,

AFTER all that I have written concerning the rule of faith, adopted by yourself and other more rational Protestants, I have only yet treated of the extrinsic arguments against it. I now, therefore proceed to investigate its *intrinsic nature*, in order to show more fully the inadequacy, or rather the falsehood of it.

When an English Protestant gets possession of an English Bible, printed by Thomas Basket, or other "printer to the king's most excellent majesty," he takes it in hand with the same confidence, as if he had immediately received it from the Almighty himself, as Moses received the Tables of the Law on Mount Sina, amidst thunder and lightening. But how vain is this confidence, whilst he adheres to the foregoing rule of faith! How many questionable points does he assume, as proved which cannot be proved, without relinquishing his own principles and adopting ours!

I. Supposing then you, dear sir, to be the Protestant I have been speaking of; I begin with asking you, by what means have you learnt the *canon* of Scripture, that is to say, which are the books which have been written by divine inspiration; or indeed that any books at all, have been so written? You cannot discover either of these things by your rule, because the Scripture, as your great authority Hooker shows,* and Chillingworth allows cannot bear testimony to itself. You will say that the Old Testament was written by Moses and the prophets, and the New Testament by the apostles of Christ and the evangelists. But admitting all this; it does not of itself prove that they *always* wrote, or indeed that they ever wrote, under the influence of *inspiration.* They were, by nature, fallible men: how have you learnt that they were infallible writers? In the next place, you receive books, as canonical parts of the Testament which were not written by apostles at all; namely, the Gospels of St Mark and St. Luke, whilst you reject an authentic work of great excellence,† written by one who is termed in Scripture

* Eccles. Polit. b. iii. sec. 8.
† St. Barnaby.   See Grabe's Spicileg. and Cotlerus's Collect.

*an apostle,** and declared to be *full of the Holy Ghost,*† I speak of St Barnaby. Lastly, you have no sufficient authority for asserting that the sacred volumes are the genuine composition of the holy personages whose names they bear, except the tradition and living voice of the Catholic church, since numerous apochryphal prophecies and spurious gospels and epistles, under the same or equally venerable names, were circulated in the church, during its early ages, and accredited by different learned writers and holy fathers: while some of the really canonical books were rejected or doubted of by them. In short, it was not until the end of the fourth century, that the genuine canon of Holy Scripture was fixed: and then it was fixed by the *tradition and authority of the church*, declared in the Third Council of Carthage and a Decretal of P. Innocent I. Indeed, it is so clear that the canon of Scripture is built on the tradition of the church, that most learned Protestants,‡ with Luther himself, have§ been forced to acknowledge it, in terms almost as strong as those in the well known declaration of St Augustine.‖

II. Again, supposing the divine authority of the Sacred Books themselves to be established; how do you know that the copies of them translated and printed in your Bible are authentic? It is agreed upon amongst the learned, that the original text of Moses and the ancient prophets was destroyed, with the temple and city of Jerusalem by the Assyrians under Nebuchadnezzar;¶ and, though they were replaced by authentic copies, at the end of the Babylonish captivity, through the pious care of the prophet Esdras or Ezra, yet that these also perished in the subsequent persecution of Antiochus;** from which time we have no evidence of the authenticity of the Old Testament till this was supplied by Christ and his apostles, who transmitted it to the church. In like manner, granting, for example, that St. Paul wrote an inspired Epistle to the Romans, and another to the Ephesians; yet as the former was intrusted to an individual, the deaconess Phebe, to be conveyed by her to its destination,†† and the latter to his disciple Tychicus,‡‡ for the same purpose, it is impossible for you to entertain a rational conviction that these Epistles as they stand in your Testament,

---

* Acts xiv. 24. † Acts xi. 24.

‡ Hooker, Eccl. Polit. C. iii. S. 8 Dr. Lardner, in Bishop Watson's Col. vol. ii. p. 20.

§ "We are obliged to yield many things to the Papists—that with them is the word of God, which we received from them; otherwise we should have known nothing at all about it." Comment. on John c. 16.

‖ "I should not believe the Gospel itself, if the authority of the Catholic church did not oblige me to do so." Contra Epist. Fundam.

¶ Brett's Dissert. in bishop Watson's Collect. vol. iii. p. 5.

** Ibid. †† Rom. xvi. See Calmet, &c. ‡‡ Ephes. vi. 21.

are exactly in the state in which they issued from the apostle's
pen or that they are his genuine Epistles at all, without recurring to the tradition and authority of the Catholic church concerning them.   To make short of this matter, I will not lead
you into the labyrinth of Biblical criticism, nor will I show you
the endless varieties of readings with respect to words and
whole passages, which occur in different copies of the Sacred
Text, but will here content myself with referring you to your
own Bible Book, as printed by authority. Look then at psalm
xiv, as it occurs in the Book of Common Prayer, to which
your clergy swear their "consent and assent;" then look at the
same psalm in your Bible: you will find four whole verses in the
former, which are left out of the latter! What will you here
say, dear sir? You must say that your church has added to, or
else that she has *taken away from, the words of this prophecy!*

III. But your pains and perplexities concerning your rule of
faith must not stop even at this point : for though you had demonstrative evidence, that the several books in your Bible are
canonical and authentic, in the originals, it would still remain
for you to inquire whether or no they are *faithfully translated
in your English copy.* In fact, you are aware that they were
written, some of them in Hebrew and some of them in Greek,
out of which languages they were translated, for the last time,
by about fifty different men, of various capacities, learning,
judgment, opinions, and prejudices.† In this inquiry, the Catholic church herself can afford you no security to build your
faith upon ; much less can any private individuals whosoever.
The celebrated Protestant divine, Episcopius, was so convinced
of the fallibility of modern translations, that he wanted all sorts
of persons, labourers, sailors, women, &c. to learn Hebrew and
Greek.   Indeed, it is obvious that the sense of the text may
depend upon the choice of a single word in the translation: nay,
it sometimes depends upon the mere *punctuation* of a sentence,
as may be seen below.‡ Can you then, consistently, reject the

---

* The verses in question being quoted by St. Paul, Rom. iii. 13, &c. there
is no doubt but the common Bible is *defective* in this passage.—On the other
hand, the bishop of Lincoln has published his conviction that the most important passage in the New Testament, 1 John v. 7, for establishing the
divinity of Jesus Christ, "is spurious." Elem. of Theo. vol. ii. p, 90
    † See a list of them in Ant. Johnson's Hist. Account. Theo. Collect. p.
95.
    ‡ One of the strongest passages for the divinity of Christ is the following,
as it is pointed in the Vulgate : *Ex quibus est Christus, secundem carnem, qui
est super omnia Deus benedictus in sæcula.* Rom. ix. 5. But see how Grotius
and Socinus deprive the text of all its strength, by merely substituting a
point for a comma : *Ex quibus est Christus, secundem carnem. Qui est super
omnia Deus benedictus in sæcula.*

authority of the great universal church, and yet build upon that
of some obscure translator in the reign of James I.? No, sir;
you must yourself have compared your English Bible with the
originals, and have proved it to be a faithful version, before
you can build your faith upon it as upon the *Word of God.* To
say one word now of the Bibles themselves, which have been
published by authority, or generally used by Protestants, in
this country. Those of Tindal, Coverdale, and queen Elizabeth's bishops, were so notoriously corrupt, as to cause a
general outcry against them, among learned Protestants, as
well as among Catholics, in which the king (James I.) joined
himself,* who accordingly ordered a new version of it to be made,
being the same that is now in use, with some few alterations
made after the restoration.† Now, though these new translators have corrected many wilful errors of their predecessors,
most of which were levelled at Catholic doctrines and discipline,‡ yet they have left a sufficient number of these behind,
for which I do not find that their advocates offer any excuse.§

IV. I will make a further supposition, namely, that you had
the certainty even of revelation, as the Calvinists used to pretend they had, that your Bible is not only *canonical, authentic,*
and *faithful,* in its English garb; yet what would all this avail
you, towards establishing your rule of faith, unless you could
be equally certain of your *understanding the whole of it rightly?*
For, as the learned Protestant bishop Walton says,‖ "The
Word of God does not consist in mere letters, whether written
or printed, but in the true sense of it;¶ which no one can better interpret than the true church, to which Christ committed
this sacred pledge." This is exactly what St. Jerom and St.
Augustin had said many ages before him. "Let us be persuaded," says the former, "that the Gospel consists not in the
words, but in the sense. A wrong explanation turns the Word

* Bishop Watson's Collect. vol. iii. p. 98.   † Ibid.
‡ These may be found in the learned Greg. Martin's treatise on the subject,
and in Ward's Errata to the Protestant Bible.
§ Two of these I had occasion to notice, in the *Inquiry into the Character
of the Irish Catholics,* namely, 1 *Cor.* xi. 27, where the conjunctive *and* is put
for the disjunctive *or;* and *Mat.* xix. 11, where *cannot* is put for *do not;* to
the altering of the sense, in both instances. Now, though these corruptions
stand in direct opposition to the original, as the Rev. Mr. Grier and Dr. Ryan
themselves quote it, yet these writers have the confidence to deny they are
corruptions, because they pretend to prove, from other texts, that *the cup is
necessary,* and that *continency is not necessary!!* Answer to Ward's Errata,
p. 1. page 33.
‖ In the Prolegomena to his Poliglott, cap. v.
* This obvious truth shows the extreme absurdity of our Bible societies and
modern schools, which regard nothing but the mere *reading of the Bible,*
leaving persons to embrace the most opposite interpretations of the same
texts.

of God into the word of man, and what is worse, into the word
of the devil; for the devil himself could quote the text of
Scripture."* Now that there are in Scripture *things hard to be
understood, which the unlearned and unstable wrest unto their
own destruction,* is expressly affirmed in it.† The same thing
is proved by the frequent mistakes of the apostles themselves,
with respect to the words of their divine Master. These obscurities are so numberless throughout the sacred volumes,
that the last quoted father, who was as bright and learned a
divine as ever took the Bible in hand, says of it, "There are
more things in Scripture that I am ignorant of than those I
know."‡ Should you prefer a modern Protestant authority to
an ancient Catholic one, listen to the clear-headed Dr. Balguy.
His words are these: "But what, you will reply, is all this to
Christians? to those who see, by a clear and strong light, the
dispensation of God to mankind? We are not *as those who
have no* hope. *The day-spring from on high hath visited us.
The spirit of God shall lead us into all truth.*—To this delusive
dream of human folly, founded only on mistaken interpretations of Scripture; I answer, in one word: Open your Bibles:
take the first-page that occurs in either Testament, and tell me
without disguise; is there nothing in it too hard for your understanding? If you find all before you *clear* and *easy*, you may
thank God for giving you a privilege which he has denied to
many thousands of sincere believers."§

Manifold is the cause of the obscurity of Holy Writ; 1st,
the sublimity of a considerable part of it, which speaks either
literally or figuratively of the Deity and his attributes; of the
Word incarnate; of angels, and other spiritual beings:—2dly,
the mysterious nature of prophecy in general:—3dly, the peculiar idioms of the Hebrew and Greek languages:—lastly,
the numerous and bold figures of speech, such as allegory,
irony, hyperbole, catachresis, and antiphrasis, which are so
frequent with the sacred penmen, particularly the ancient
prophets.‖ I should like to hear any one of those, who pretend to find the Scripture so easy, attempting to give a clear
explanation of the 67th, alias the 68th, psalm; or the last chapter of Ecclesiastes. Is it any easy matter to reconcile certain
well-known speeches of each of the holy patriarchs, Abraham,
Isaac, and Jacob, with the incommutable precept of truth? I
may here notice, among a thousand other such difficulties, that

---

when our Saviour sent his twelve apostles to preach the Gospel to the lost sheep of the house of Israel, he told them, according to *St. Matthew* x. 10, *Provide neither gold nor silver—neither shoes nor yet staves :* whereas *St. Mark* vi. says, *He commanded them that they should take nothing for their journey, save a staff only.* You may indeed answer, with Chillingworth and bishop Porteus, that whatever obscurities there may be in certain parts of Scripture, it is clear in all that is necessary to be known. But on what authority do these writers ground this maxim? They have none at all; but they *beg the question,* as logicians express it, to extricate themselves from an absurdity, and in so doing they overturn their fundamental rule. They profess to gather their articles of faith and morals from mere Scripture : nevertheless, confessing that they understand only a part of it; they presume to make a distinction in it, and to say this part is necessary to be known, the other part is not necessary. But to place this matter in a clearer light, it is obvious that if any articles are particularly necessary to be known and believed, they are those which point to the God whom we are to adore, and the moral precepts which we are to observe. Now, is it demonstratively evident, from *mere Scripture,* that Christ is God, and to be adored as such? Most modern Protestants of eminence answer NO ; and, in defence of their assertion, quote the following among other texts : *The Father is greater than I,* John xiv. 28 ; to which the orthodox divines oppose those texts of the same evangelist, *I and the Father are one,* x. 30. *The Word was God,* &c. i. 1. Again we find the following among the moral precepts of the Old Testament : *Go thy way ; eat thy bread with joy, and drink thy wine with a merry heart : for God now accepteth thy works. Let thy garments be always white, and let thy head lack no ointment. Live joyfully with the wife whom thou lovest,* &c. Eccles. ix. 7, 8, 9. In the New Testament, we meet with the following seemingly practical commands. *Swear not at all,* Mat. v. 34. *Call no man father upon earth—neither be you called masters, for one is your master, Christ,* Mat. xxiii, 9. 10. *If any man sue thee at law, to take away thy coat, let him have thy cloak also,* v. 46. *Give to every man that asketh of thee ; and of him that taketh away thy goods ask him not again,* Luke vi. 33. *When thou makest a dinner or a supper, call not thy friends nor thy brethren.* xiv. 12. These are a few among hundreds of other difficulties, regarding our moral duties, which, though confronted by other texts, seemingly of a contrary meaning, nevertheless show that the Scripture is not, of itself, demonstratively clear in points of first rate importance, and that the divine law, like human laws, without an authorized interpreter, must ever be a source of doubt and contention.

V. I have said enough concerning the *contentions* among Protestants; I will now, by way of concluding this letter, say a word or two of their *doubts*. In the first place, it is certain, as a learned Catholic controvertist argues,* that a person who follows your rule *cannot make an act of faith*, this being, according to your great authority, bishop Pearson, an assent to the revealed articles, with a *certain and full persuasion* of their revealed truth ;† or, to use the words of your primate, Wake, " When I give my assent to what God has revealed, I do it, not only with a *certain assurance* that what I believe *is true*, but with an *absolute security that it cannot be false.*"‡ Now the Protestant, who has nothing to trust to but his own talents, in interpreting of the books of Scripture, especially with all the difficulties and uncertainties which he labours under, according to what I have shown above, never can rise to this *certain assurance* and *absolute security*, as to what is revealed in Scripture: the utmost he can say is, *Such and such appears to me, at the present moment, to be the sense of the texts before me :* and, if he is candid, he will add, *but perhaps, upon further consideration, and upon comparing these with other texts, I may alter my opinion.* How far short, dear sir, is such mere opinion from the certainty of faith! I may here refer you to your own experience. Are you accustomed, in reading your Bible, to conclude, in your own mind, with respect to those points which appear to you most clear, *I believe in these, with a certain assurance of their truth, and an absolute security that they cannot be false;* especially when you reflect that other learned, intelligent, and sincere Christians have understood those passages in quite a different sense from what you do? For my part, having sometimes lived and conversed familiarly with Protestants of this description, and noticed their controversial discourses, I never found one of them absolutely fixed, for any long time together, in his mind, as to the whole of his belief. I invite you to make the experiment on the most intelligent and religious Protestant of your acquaintance. Ask him a considerable number of questions, on the most important points of his religion: note down his answers, while they are fresh in your memory. Ask him the same questions, but in a different order, a month afterwards, when I can almost venture to say, you will be surprised at the difference you will find between his former and his lat-

---

* Sheffmacher *Lettres d'un Docteur Cat. a un Gentilhomme Prot.* vol. i. p 48.

 † On the Creed, p. 15   ‡ Princip. of Christ. Rel. p. 27.

ter creed. After all, we need not use any other means to discover the state of doubt and uncertainty in which many of your
greatest divines and most profound Scriptural students have
passed their days, than to look into their publications. I shall
satisfy myself with citing the pastoral Charge of one of them,
a living bishop, to his clergy. Speaking of the Christian doctrines, he says, " I think it safer to tell you *where they are contained*, than *what they are*. They are contained in the Bible ;
and if, in reading that Book, your sentiments concerning the doctrines of Christianity should be different from those of your
neighbour, or from *those of the church*, be persuaded, on you.
part, that infallibility appertains as little to you as it does to the
church."* Can you read this, my dear sir, without shuddering ?
If a most learned and intelligent bishop and professor of divinity, as Dr. Watson certainly is, after studying all the Scriptures, and all the commentators upon them, is forced publicly
to confess to his assembled clergy, that *he cannot tell them what*
the *doctrines of Christianity are*, how unsettled must his mind
have been! and, of course, how far removed from the assurance
of faith! In the next place, how fallacious must that rule of
the mere Bible be, which, while he recommends it to them, he
plainly signifies, will not lead them to a uniformity of sentiments one with another, not even with their church!

There can be no doubt, sir, but those who entertain doubts
concerning the truth of their religion, in the course of their
lives, must experience the same, with redoubled anxiety, at the
approach of death. Accordingly there are, I believe, few of our
Catholic priests, in an extensive ministry, who have not been
frequently called in to receive dying Protestants into the Catholic church,† while not a single instance of a Catholic wishing to die in any other communion than his own can be produced.‡ O death, thou great enlightener! O truth-telling death,

---

* Bishop Watson's Charge to his Clergy, in 1795.

† A large proportion of those grandees who were the most forward in promoting the Reformation, so called, and, among the rest, Cromwell, earl of Essex,
the king's ecclesiastical vicar, when they came to die, returned to the Catholic church. This was the case also with Luther's chief protector, the elector
of Saxony, the persecuting queen of Navarre, and many other foreign Protestant princes. Some bishops of the established church; for instance, Goodman and Cheyney, of Gloucester, and Gordon, of Glasgow, probably also Halifax, of St. Asaph's, died Catholics. A long list of titled or otherwise distinguished personages, who have either returned to the Catholic faith, or for the
first time, embraced it on their death-beds, in modern times, might be named
here, if it were prudent to do so.

‡ This is remarked by sir Toby Matthews, son of the archbishop of York,
Hugh Cressy, Canon of Windsor and dean of Laughlin, F. Walsingham, and
Ant. Ulric, duke of Brunswick, all illustrious converts. Also by Beurier, in
his *Conferences*, p. 400.

how powerful art thou in confuting the blasphemies, and dissipating the prejudices, of the enemies of God's church!—Taking it for granted, that you, dear sir, have not been without your doubts and fears about the safety of the road in which you are walking to eternity, more particularly in the course of the present controversy, and being anxious, beyond expression, that you should be free from these when you arrive at the brink of that vast ocean, I cannot do better than address you in the words of the great St. Augustine, to one in your situation: "If you think you have been sufficiently tossed about, and wish to see an end to your anxieties, follow the rule of Catholic discipline, which came down to us through the apostles from Christ himself, and which shall descend from us to the latest posterity."* Yes, renounce the fatal and foolish presumption of fancying that you can interpret the Scripture better than the Catholic church, aided, as she is, by the tradition of all ages, and the *spirit of all truth.*† But I mean to treat this latter subject at due length in my next letter.

I am, Dear Sir, &c.

J. M

LETTER X.

TO JAMES BROWN, Esq.

THE TRUE RULE.

Dear Sir,

I HAVE received your letter, and also two others from gentlemen of your society, on what I have written to you concerning the insufficiency of Scripture, interpreted by individuals, to constitute a secure rule of faith. From these, it is plain that my arguments have produced a considerable sensation in

---

* Du Util. Cred. c. 8.

† Bossuet, in his celebrated *Conference with Claude,* which produced the conversion of Mlle. Duras, obliged him to confess, that, by the Protestant rule, "every artisan and husbandman may and ought to believe that he can understand the Scriptures better than all the fathers and doctors of the church, ancient and modern, put together."

the society; insomuch that I find myself obliged to remind them of the terms on which we mutually entered upon this correspondence, namely, that each one should be at perfect liberty to express his sentiments on the important subject under consideration, without complaint or offence of the other. The strength of my arguments is admitted by you all: yet you all bring invincible objections, as you consider them, from Scripture and other sources, against them. I think it will render our controversy more simple and clear, if, with your permission, I defer answering these, till after I have said all that I have to say concerning the Catholic rule of faith.

The Catholic rule of faith, as I stated before, is not merely *the written Word of God*, but *the whole Word of God, both written and unwritten ;* in other words, *Scripture and tradition*, and these *propounded and explained by the Catholic church.* This implies that we have a *two-fold rule*, or *law*, and that we have *an interpreter*, or *judge to explain it*, and to decide upon it in all doubtful points.

1. I enter upon this subject with observing that all *written laws* necessarily suppose the existence of *unwritten laws*, and indeed depend upon them for their force and authority. Not to run into the depths of ethics and metaphysics on this subject, you know, dear sir, that, in this kingdom, we have *common* or *unwritten law*, and *statute* or *written law*, both of them binding; but that the former necessarily precedes the latter. The legislature, for example, makes a written statute; but we must learn, before-hand, from the common law, *what constitutes the legislature*, and we must also have learnt from the natural and the divine laws, that *the legislature is to be obeyed in all things which these do not render unlawful.* " The municipal law of England," says judge Blackstone, " may be divided into *Lex Non Scripta*, the unwritten or common law, and the *Lex Scripta*, or statute law."* He afterwards calls the common law, " the first ground and chief corner-stone of the laws of England."† " If," continues he, " the question arises, *how these customs or maxims are to be known*, and *by whom their validity is to be determined ?* The answer is, *by the judges in the several courts of justice. They are the depositaries of the laws*, the *living oracles*, who must *decide in all cases of doubt*, and who are *bound* by oath to decide according to the law of the land."‡ So absurd is the idea of binding mankind by written laws, *without laying an adequate foundation* for the authority of those laws, and without constituting *living judges* to decide upon them!

---

* Comment. on the Laws, Introduct. sect. 3.
† Ibid. p. 73. 8th edit.   ‡ Ibid. p. 69.

Neither has the divine wisdom, in founding the spiritual kingdom of his church, acted in that inconsistent manner. The Almighty did not send a Book, the New Testament, to Christians, and, without so much as establishing the authority of that Book, leave them to interpret it, till the end of time, each one according to his own opinions or prejudices. But our blessed Master and legislator, Jesus Christ, having first demonstrated his own divine legation from his heavenly Father, by undeniable miracles, commissioned his chosen apostles, *by word of mouth*, to proclaim and explain, *by word of mouth*, his doctrines and precepts to all nations, promising to be with them, in the execution of this office of his heralds and judges, even *to the end of the world*. This implies the power he had given them, of ordaining successors in this office, as they themselves were only to live the ordinary term of human life. True it is, that during the execution of their commission, he inspired some of them and their disciples to write certain parts of these doctrines and precepts, namely, the canonical Gospels and Epistles, which they addressed, for the most part, to particular persons, and on particular occasions; but these inspired writings by no means rendered void Christ's commission to the apostles and their successors, of *preaching and explaing his word* to the nations, or his promise of *being with them* till the end of time. On the contrary, the inspiration of these very writings, is not otherwise known, than by the *viva voce* evidence of these depositaries and judges of the revealed truths. This analysis of revealed religion, so conformable to reason and the civil constitution of our country, is proved to be true, by *the written Word* itself—by the *tradition and conduct of the apostles*—and by the constant testimony and practice of the fathers and doctors of the church, in all ages.

II. Nothing then, dear sir, is further from the doctrine and practice of the Catholic church than to slight the Holy Scriptures. So far from this, she had religiously preserved and perpetuated them, from age to age, during almost fifteen hundred years, before Protestants existed. She has consulted them, and confirmed her decrees from them, in her several councils. She enjoins her pastors, whose business it is to instruct the faithful, to read and study them without intermission, knowing, that *all Scripture is given by inspiration of God, and is profitable for doctrine, for reproof, for correction, for instruction in righteousness.* 2 Tim. iii. 16. Finally, she proves her perpetual right to announce and explain the truths and precepts of her divine Founder, by several of the strongest and clearest passages contained in Holy Writ.* Such, for example, is the last commission of Christ, alluded to above: *Go ye therefore and teach all nations, baptizing them in the name of the Father, and of the Son, and of the Holy Ghost: teaching them to observe all things whatsoever I have commanded you, And lo! I am with you all days, even to the end of the world.* Matt. xxviii. 19, 20. And again, *Go ye into all the world, and preach the Gospel to every creature.* Mark xvi. 15. It is *preaching* and *teaching* then, that is to say the *unwritten Word,* which Christ has appointed to be the general method of propagating his divine truths; and, whereas he promises to be *with his apostles to the end of the world:* this proves *their authority* in expounding, and that the same was to *descend to their legitimate successors* in the sacred ministry, since they themselves were only to live the ordinary term of human life. In like manner, the following clear texts prove the authority of the apostles and their successors *forever;* that is to say, of *the ever-living and speaking tribunal of the church,* in expounding our Saviour's doctrine: *I will pray the Father, and he shall give you another Comforter, that he may abide with you for ever.— The Comforter, which is the Holy Ghost whom the Father will send in my name; he shall teach you all things, and bring all things to your remembrance, whatsoever I have said unto you.* John xiv. 16, 26. St. Paul, speaking of both the unwritten and the written Word, puts them upon a level, where he says, *Therefore, brethren, stand fast and hold the tradition ye have been taught, whether by word or our Epistle.* 2. Thess. v. 13. Finally, St. Peter pronounces, that, *No prophecy of Scripture is of any private interpretation.* 2 Pet. i. 20.

III. That the apostles, and the apostolical men, whom they formed, followed this method prescribed by their Master, is unquestionable; and we have positive proofs from Scripture, as well as from ecclesiastical history, that they did so. St. Mark, after recording the above cited admonition of *preaching the Gospel,* which Christ left to his apostles, adds, *And they went forth and preached every where; the Lord working with them, and confirming the word with signs following.* Mark xvi. 20. St. Peter preached throughout Judea, and Syria, and last of all in Italy and at Rome; St. Paul, throughout Lesser Asia, Greece, and as far as Spain; St. Andrew penetrated into Scythia; St. Thomas and St. Bartholomew into Parthia and India, and so of the others; every where converting and instructing thousands, *by word of mouth;* founding churches,

* St. Austin uses this argument against the Donatists, "In Scripturis discimus Christum in Scripturis discimus, Ecclesiam Si Christum teneatis, quare Ecclesiam non tenetis."

8*

and ordaining bishops and priests to do the same.* If any of them wrote, it was on some particular occasion, and, fo the most part, to a particular person or congregation, without either giving directions, or providing means of communicating their Epistles or their Gospels to the rest of the Christians throughout the world. Hence, it happened, as I have before remarked, that it was not till the end of the fourth century, that the canon of Holy Scriptures was absolutely settled as it now stands. True it is, that the apostles, before they separated to preach the Gospel to different nations, agreed upon a short symbol or profession of faith, called *The Apostles' Creed*; but even this they did not commit to writing :† and whereas they made this, among other articles of it, *I believe in the Holy Church*,‡ *they made no mention at all of the Holy Scriptures*. This circumstance confirms what their example proves, that the Christian doctrine and discipline might have been propagated and preserved by the *unwritten Word*, or tradition, joined with the authority of the church, though the Scriptures had not been composed; however *profitable* these most certainly are *for doctrine, for reproof, for correction, and for instruction in righteousness*. 2 Tim. iii. 16. I have already quoted one of the ornaments of your church, who says, that "the canonical Epistles" (and he might have added the Gospels) " are not regular treatises upon the Christian religion ;"§ and I shall have occasion to show, from an ancient father, that this religion did prevail and flourish soon after the age of the apostles, among nations which did not even know the use of letters.

IV. However light Protestants of this age may make of the ancient fathers, as *theological authorities*,‖ they cannot object to them as *faithful witnesses* of the doctrine and discipline of the church in their respective times. It is chiefly in the latter character that I am going to bring a certain number of them

---

* *They ordained them priests in every church.* Acts xiv. 22. *For this cause I left thee in Crete, that thou shouldst set in order the things that are wanting, and shouldst ordain priests in every city, as I had appointed thee.* Tit. i. 5. *The things that thou hast heard of me among many witnesses, the same commit thou to those faithful men, who shall be able to teach others also.* 2. Tim. ii. 2.

† Ruffin inter Opera Hieron.

‡ The title *Catholic* was afterwards added, when heresies increased.

§ Elements of Theology, vol. ii.

‖ Jewel, Andrews, Hooker, Morton, Pearson, and other Protestant divines of the sixteenth and seventeenth centuries laboured hard to press the fathers into their service ; but with such bad success, that the succeeding controversialists gave them up in despair. The learned Protestant, Causabon, confessed that the fathers were all on the Catholic side ; the equally learned Obrecht testifies that, in reading their works, " he was frequently provoked to throw them on the ground, finding them so full of Popery ;" while Middleton heaps every kind of obloquy upon them.

forward, namely, to prove that during the five first ages of the church, no less than in the subsequent ages, the unwritten Word, or tradition, was held in equal estimation by her with the Scripture itself, and that she claimed a divine right of propounding and explaining them both.

I begin with the disciple of the apostles, St. Ignatius, bishop of Antioch: it is recorded of him that, in his passage to Rome, where he was sentenced to be devoured by wild beasts, he exhorted the Christians, who got access to him, "to guard themselves against the rising heresies, and to adhere with the utmost firmness to the *tradition of the apostles.*"* The same sentiments appear in this saint's Epistles, and also in those of his fellow martyr, St. Polycarp, *the angel of the church of Smyrna.*†

One of the disciples of the last mentioned holy bishop was St. Irenæus, who passing into Gaul, became bishop of Lyons. He has left twelve books against the heresies of his time, which abound with testimonies to the present purpose; some few of which I shall here insert.—He writes, "Nothing is easier to those who seek for the truth, than to remark, in every church, *the tradition,* which the apostles have manifested to all the world. We can name the bishops appointed by the apostles in the several churches, and the successors of those bishops down to our own time, none of whom ever taught or heard of such doctrines as these heretics dream of"‡ This holy father emphatically affirms that, "In explaining the Scriptures, Christians are to attend to the *pastors of the church*, who, by the ordinance of God, have *received the inheritance of truth*, with the succession of their Sees."§ He adds, "The tongues of nations vary, but the virtue of *tradition is one and the same* every where; nor do the churches in Germany believe or teach differently from those in Spain, Gaul, the East, Egypt, or Lybia."‖—"Since it would be tedious to enumerate the succession of all the churches, we appeal to the faith and *tradition* of the greatest, most ancient, and best known church, that of Rome, founded by the apostles, SS. Peter and Paul; for with this church all others agree, in as much as in her is preserved the tradition which comes down from the apostles."¶—"SUPPOSING THE APOSTLES HAD NOT LEFT US THE SCRIPTURES, OUGHT NOT WE STILL TO HAVE FOLLOWED THE ORDINANCE OF TRADITION, which they consigned to those to whom they committed the churches? It is this ordinance of *tradition* which many nations of barbarians, believing in Christ, follow, without the use of letters or ink."**

* Euseb. Hist. l. iii. c. 30.   † Revel. ii. 8.   ‡ Advers. Hæres. l. iii. c. f.
§ L. iv. c. 43.   ‖ L. i. c. 3.   ¶ L. iii. c. 2   ** L. iv. c. 64

Tertullian, who flourished two hundred years after the Christian era, among his other works, has left us one of the same nature, and almost the same title with that last cited. In this, speaking of the contemporary heretics, he says, "They meddle with the Scriptures, and adduce arguments from them: for, in treating of faith, they pretend that they ought not to argue upon any other ground than the written documents of faith: thus they weary the firm, catch the weak, and fill the middle sort with doubt. We begin, therefore, with laying down as a maxim, that these men ought not to be allowed to argue at all from scripture. In fact, these disputes about the sense of Scripture have generally no other effect than to disorder either the stomach or the brain. It is, therefore, the wrong method to appeal to the Scriptures, since these afford either no decision, or, at most, only a doubtful one. And even if this were not the case, still, in appealing to Scripture, the natural order of things requires that we should first inquire to whom the Scriptures belong? From whom, and by whom, and on what occasion, and to whom, that tradition was delivered by which we became Christians? For where the truth of Christian discipline and faith is found, there is the truth of Scripture, and of the interpretation of it, and of all Christian traditions."* He elsewhere says, "that doctrine is evidently true which was first delivered: on the contrary, that is false which is of a later date. This maxim stands immoveable against the attempts of all late heresies. Let such then produce the origin of their churches: let them show the succession of their bishops from the apostles, or their disciples.—If you live near Italy, you see before your eyes the Roman church: happy church! to which the apostles have left the inheritance of their doctrine with their blood! Where Peter was crucified, like his Master; where Paul was beheaded, like the Baptist!—If this be so, it is plain, as we have said, that heretics are not to be allowed to appeal to Scripture, since they have no claim to it.—Hence it is proper to address them as follows:—*Who are you? Whence do you come? What business have you strangers with my property? By what right are you, Marcion, felling my trees? By what authority are you, Valentine, turning the course of my streams? Under what pretence are you, Apelles, removing my land-marks? The estate is mine: I have the ancient, the prior possession of it I have the title deeds delivered to me by the original proprietors. I am the heir of the apostles; they have made their will in my favour; while they disinherited and cast you off, as strangers and enemies.*"† In another of his works,‡ this eloquent father

---

* Praescrip. Advers. Haeres. edit. Rhenan, pp. 36, 37.
† Ibid.   ‡ De Corona Milit.

proves, at great length, the absolute necessity of admitting *tra-dition*, no less than *Scripture* as the rule of faith, inasmuch as many important points which he mentions, cannot be proved without it.

I pass by other shining lights of the third century, such as St. Clement of Alexandria, St. Cyprian, Origen, &c. all of whom place apostolical tradition on a level with Scripture, and describe the church as the expounder of them both: I must, however, give the following words, from the last named great Biblical scholar. He says, "We are not to credit those, who, by citing real canonical Scripture, seem to say, *behold the Word is in your houses*: for we are not to desert our *first ecclesiastical tradition*, nor to believe otherwise than as the churches of God have, in their perpetual succession, delivered to us."

Among the numerous and illustrious witnesses of the fourth age, I shall be content with citing St. Basil and St Epiphanius. The former says, "There are many doctrines preserved and preached in the church, derived partly from written documents, partly from apostolical *tradition*, which have equally *the same force* in religion, and which no one contradicts who has the least knowledge of the Christian laws."* The latter of these fathers, says, with equal brevity and force, "We must make use of tradition: for all things are not to be found in Scripture."†

St. John Chrysostom flourished at the beginning of the fifth century, who, though he strongly recommends the reading of the holy Scriptures, yet, expounding the text, 2 *Thess.* ii. 14. says, "Hence it is plain that the apostles did not deliver to us every thing by their Epistles, but many things without writing. These are equally worthy of belief. Hence, let us regard the tradition of the church, as the subject of our belief. Such and such a thing *is a tradition: seek no farther*."—It would fill a large volume to transcribe all the passages which occur in the works of the great St. Austin, in proof of the Catholic rule, and the authority of the church in making use of it: let therefore two or three of them speak for the rest.— "To attain to the *truth of the Scriptures*," he says, "we must follow the sense of them entertained by the universal church, to which the Scriptures themselves bear testimony. True it is the Scriptures themselves cannot deceive us; nevertheless, to prevent our being deceived in the question we examine by them, it is necessary we should advise with that church, which these certainly and evidently point out to us."‡—"This (the unlawfulness of rebaptizing heretics) is not evidently read either by you

* In Lib. de Spir. Sanc.   † De Hæres N. 61.
‡ L. i. contra Crescon.

or by me; nevertheless, if there were any wise man, to whom Christ had borne testimony, and whom he had appointed to be consulted on the question, we could not fail to do so: now Christ bears testimony to his church. Whoever, therefore, refuses to follow the practice of the church resists Christ himself, who by his testimony recommends this church."* Treating elsewhere, on the same subject, he says, "The apostles, indeed, have prescribed nothing about this; but the custom must be considered as derived from their tradition, since there are many things, observed by the universal church, which are justly held to have been appointed by the apostles, though they are not written."†—It seems doing an injury to St Vincent of Lerins, who lived at the end of the fifth century, to quote a part of his celebrated *Commonitorium*, when the whole of it is so admirably calculated to refute the false rule of heretics, condemned in the foregoing testimonies, and to prove the Catholic rule, here laid down: still I can only transcribe a very small portion of it. "It is asked," says this father, "as the Scripture is perfect, what need is there of the authority of church doctrine? The reason is because the Scripture, being so profoundly deep, is not understood by all persons in the same sense, but different persons explain it different ways, so that there are almost as many meanings as there are readers of it. Novation interprets it in one sense, Photinas in another, Arius, &c. in another. Therefore it is requisite that the true road of expounding the prophets and apostles must be marked out, according to the ecclesiastical Catholic line.

"It never was, is, or will be lawful for Catholic Christians to teach any doctrine, except that which they once received; and it ever was, is, and will be their duty to condemn those who do so.—Do the heretics then appeal to the Scriptures? Certainly they do, and this with the utmost confidence. You will see them running hastily through the different books of Holy Writ, those of Moses, Kings, the Psalms, the Gospels, &c. At home and abroad, in their discourses and in their writings, they hardly produce a sentence which is not larded with the words of Scripture, &c.; but they are so much the more to be dreaded, as they conceal themselves under the veil of the divine laws. Let us, however, remember, that Satan transformed himself into an angel of light.—If he could turn the Scriptures against the Lord of Majesty, what use may he not make of them against us poor mortals!—If then Satan and his disciples, the heretics, are capable of thus perverting holy Scripture, how are Catholics the children of the church, to make use of them,

---

* De Util. Credend.　　　　　† De Bapt. contra Donat. l. v.

so as to discern truth from falsehood? They must carefully observe the rule laid down at the beginning of this treatise by the holy and learned men I referred to: THEY ARE TO IN-TERPRET THE DIVINE TEXT, ACCORDING TO THE TRADITION OF THE CATHOLIC CHURCH."*

It would be as easy to prove this rule of faith from the fathers of the sixth as the former centuries, particularly from St. Gregory the great, that holy Pope, who at the close of this century, sent missionaries from Rome to convert our Pagan ancestors: but, I am sure, you will think that evidence enough has been brought to show that the ancient fathers of the church, from the very time of the apostles, held this *whole rule of faith*, namely, the word of God *unwritten as well as written*, together with *the living, speaking tribunal of the church* to preserve and interpret both of them.

I am, &c.

J. M.

LETTER XI.

TO JAMES BROWN, Esq. &c.

THE TRUE RULE.

DEAR SIR,

THE all-importance of determining with ourselves which is the right rule or method of discovering religious truth must be admitted by all thinking Christians; as it is evident that this rule alone can conduct them to it, and that a false rule is capable of conducting them into all sorts of errors. It is equally clear why all those who are bent upon deserting the Catholic church, reject her rule, that of the *whole word of God*; together with her *living authority* in explaining it: for, while this rule and this authority are acknowledged, there can be no heresy or schism among Christians, as whatever points of religion are not clear from Scripture are supplied and illustrated by tradition; and as the pastors of the church, who possess that

---

* Vincent Lerins Commonit. Advers. Hær. edit. Baluz. An English translation of this little work has lately been published.

authority, are always living and ready to declare what is the sense of Scripture, and what the tradition on each contested point which they have received in succession from the apostles. The only resource, therefore, of persons resolved to follow their own or their forefathers' particular opinions or practices, in matters of religion, with the exception of the enthusiast, has been in all times, both ancient and modern, to appeal to mere Scripture, which being a *dead letter*, leaves them at liberty to explain it as they will.

I. And yet, with all their repugnance to tradition and church authority, Protestants have found themselves absolutely obliged, in many instances, to admit of them both.—It has been demonstrated above, that they are obliged to admit of tradition, in order to admit of Scripture itself. Without this, they can neither know that there are any writings at all dictated by God's inspiration; nor which these writings are in particular;* nor what versions, or publication of them are genuine. But, as this matter has been sufficiently elucidated, I proceed to other points of religion, which Protestants receive, either without the authority of Scripture, or in opposition to the letter of it.

The first precept in the Bible, is that of sanctifying the seventh day: *God blessed the* SEVENTH DAY, *and sanctified it.* Gen. ii. 3. This precept was confirmed by God, in the Ten Commandments: *Remember the Sabbath day to keep it holy. The* SEVENTH DAY *is the Sabbath of the Lord thy God.* Exod. xx. On the other hand, Christ declares that he is *not come to destroy the law but to fulfil it.* Mat. v. 17. He himself observed the Sabbath: *and, as his custom was, he went into the synagogue on the Sabbath day :* Luke iv. 16. His disciples likewise observed it, after his death: *They rested on the Sabbath day according to the commandment.* Luke xxiii. 56. Yet, with all this weight of Scripture authority for keeping the *Sabbath* or *seventh day* holy, Protestants, of all denominations, make this a *profane day*, and transfer the obligation of it to the *first day of the week*, or the *Sunday*. Now what authority have they for doing this? None at all, but the *unwritten Word*, or *tradition* of the Catholic church, which declares that the apostles made the change in honour of Christ's resurrection, and the descent of the Holy Ghost, on that day of the week. Then, with respect to the manner of keeping that day holy, their universal doctrine and practice are no less at variance

---

* Amongst all the learned Protestants of this age, Dr. Porteus is the only one who pretends to discern Scripture, " partly on account of its own reasonableness, and the characters of divine wisdom in it." Brief Confut. p. 9. I could have wished to ask his lordship, whether it is by these characters that he has discovered the *Canticle or Song of Solomon* to be inspired scripture?

with the Sacred Text. The Almighty says, " From even unto
even shall you celebrate your Sabbath," Levit. xxiii. 32, which
is the practice of the Jews down to the present time ; but not
of any Protestants that ever I heard of. Again, it is declared
in Scripture to be unlawful to dress victuals on that day, Exod.
xvi. 23, or even to make a fire, *Exod.* xxxv, 3. Again, where
is there a precept in the whole Scripture more express than that
against eating blood ? God said to Noah, *Every moving thing
that liveth shall be meat to you—but flesh with the life thereof,
which is the blood thereof, shall you not eat,* Gen. ix. 4. This
prohibition we know was confirmed by Moses, *Levit.* xvii. 11
Deut. xii. 23, and by the apostles, and was imposed upon the
Gentiles, who were converted to the faith, *Acts.* xv. 20. Nevertheless, where is the religious Protestant who scruples to eat
gravy with his meat, or puddings made of blood ? At the same
time if he be asked, *Upon what authority* do you act in contradiction to the express words of both the Old and the New Testament? he can find no other answer than that he has learned
from *the tradition of the church,* that the prohibition was only
temporary.—I will confine myself to one more instance of Protestants abandoning *their own rule,* that of Scripture alone, to
follow *ours,* of Scripture explained by tradition. If any intelligent Pagan, who had carefully perused the New Testament, were
asked, which of the ordinances mentioned in it, is most explicitly
and strictly enjoined? I make no doubt but he would answer
that it is, *The washing of feet.* To convince yourself of this,
be pleased to read the first seventeen verses of St. John, c. xiii.
Observe *the motive* assigned for Christ's performing the ceremony, there recorded ; namely, his " love for his disciples :"
next *the time* of his performing it; namely, when he was about
to depart out of this world : then *the stress* he lays upon it, in
what he said to Peter, *If I wash thee not thou hast no part,
with me:* finally, *his injunction,* at the conclusion of it, *If I
your Lord and Master, have washed your feet, ye also ought
to wash one another's feet.* I now ask, on what pretence can
those who profess to make *Scripture alone* the rule of their religion, totally disregard this institution and precept? Had this
ceremony been observed in the church when Luther and the
other first Protestants began to dogmatize, there is no doubt
but they would have retained it: but, having learnt from her
that it was only figurative, they acquiesced in this decision,
contrary to what appears to be the plain sense of Scripture.

II. But I asserted that Protestants find themselves obliged
not only to adopt the rule of our church, on many the most important subjects, but also to *claim her authority.* It is true as
9

a late dignitary of the establishment observes,* that, "When Protestants first withdrew from the communion of the church of Rome, the principles they went upon were such as these: Christ, by his gospel, hath called all men to *the liberty*, the glorious liberty, *of the sons of God*, and restored them to the privilege of working out their own salvation by their own understanding and endeavours. For this work, sufficient means are afforded in the Scriptures, without having recourse to the doctrines and commandments of men. Consequently, faith and conscience, having no dependence on man's laws, are not to be compelled by man's authority."—What now was the consequence of this fundamental rule of Protestantism? Why, that endless variety of doctrines, errors, and impieties, mentioned above, followed by those tumults, wars, rebellions, and anarchy, with which the history of every country is filled, which embraced the new religion. It is readily supposed that the princes, and other rulers of those countries, ecclesiastical as well as civil, however hostile they might be to the ancient church, would wish to restrain these disorders, and make their subjects adopt the same sentiments with themselves. Hence, in every Protestant state, articles of religion, and confessions of faith, differing from one another, yet each one agreeing with the opinion, for the time being, of those princes and rulers, were enacted by law, and enforced by excommunication, deprivation, exile, imprisonment, torture, and death. These latter punishments indeed, however frequently they were exercised by Protestants against Protestants, as well as against Catholics, during the sixteenth and seventeenth centuries,† have not been resorted to during the last hundred years; but the terrible sentence of excommunication, which includes outlawry, even now hangs over the head of every Protestant bishop, as well as other clergyman, in this country,‡ who interpret those passages of the Gospel, concerning Jesus Christ, in the sense which it appears from their writings a number of them entertain; and none of them can take possession of a living, without subscribing the Thirty-nine Articles, and publicly declaring his *unfeigned assent and consent* to them, and *to every* thing contained in the Book of Common Prayer.§ Thus, by adopting a false rule of

* Archdeacon Blackburn in his celebrated Confessional, p. 1.

† See the letter on the *Reformation* and on *Persecution*, in *Letters to a Prebendary.* See also Neal's History of the Puritans, Delaune's Narrative, Sewel's History of the Quakers, &c.

‡ See many excommunicating canons, and particularly one, A. D. 1640, against "the damnable and cursed heresy of Socinianism," as it is termed, in Bishop Sparrow's Collection.

§ 1st Eliz. cap. 2.—14 Car. ii. c. 4. Item Canon 36 et 38.

religion, thinking Protestants are reduced to the cruel extremity of palpable contradiction! They cannot give up "the glorious liberty," as it is called above, of explaining the Bible, each one for himself, without, at once, giving up their cause to the Catholics; and they cannot adhere to it without many of the above mentioned fatal consequences, and without the speedy dissolution of their respective churches. Impatient of the constraint in being obliged to sign articles of faith which they do not believe, many able clergymen of the establishment have written strongly against them, and have even petitioned parliament to be relieved from the alleged *grievance* of subscribing the professed doctrine of their own church.* On the other hand, the legislature, foreseeing the consequences which would result from the removal of the obligation, have always rejected their prayer: and the judges have even refused to admit the following *salvo* in addition to the subscription: "I assent and consent to the Articles and the Book, *as far as they are agreeable to the word of God.*"† In these straits, many of the most able as well as the most respectable of the established clergy, have been reduced to such sophistry and casuistry, as to move the pity of their very opponents. One of these, the Norrisian professor of divinity at Cambridge,‡ as one way of excusing his brethren for subscribing articles which they do not believe in, cites the example of the divines of Geneva, where, he says, "a complete tacit *reformation* seems to have taken place. The Genevese have now, in fact, quitted their Calvinistic doctrines, though, *in form*, they retain them. — When the minister is admitted, he takes an oath of assent to the Scriptures, and professes to teach them *according to the Catechism of Calvin;* but this last clause about Calvin, *he makes a separate business*, speaking lower, or altering his posture, or speaking after a considerable interval."§ Such a change of posture, or tone of voice, in the swearer, our learned professor considers as sufficient to excuse him from the guilt of prevarication, in swearing contrary to the plain meaning of his oath! It is not, however, intimated that the professor himself has recourse to this expedient: his particular system is, that "the church of England, like that of Geneva, has, of late, undergone a complete *tacit reformation*,|| and hence that the sense of its

* There was such a petition, signed by a great number of clergymen, and supported by many others, in 1772.
† See Confessional, p. 183.
‡ Lectures in Divinity, delivered in the university of Cambridge, by J. Hey, D. D. as Norrisian professor, 1797, vol. ii. p. 57.
§ Ibid.
|| Ibid. p. 48, (particularly in its approach to Socinianism, from which he signifies it is divided only by a few "unmeaning words.")

articles of faith is to be determined *by circumstances.** Thus
he adds (referring, I presume, to the statutes of King's college, Cambridge) the oath, "I will say so many masses for
the soul of Henry VI., may come to mean, I will perform the
religious duties required of me!!"† The celebrated moralist,
Dr. Paley, justifies a departure from the original sense of the
articles of religion subscribed, by an *INCONVENIENCE,
which is manifest beyond all doubt!!*‡ Archdeacon Powell,
master of St. John's college, defends the English clergy from
the charge of subscribing what they do not believe, because, he
says, "The crime is impossible: as that cannot be the sense of
the declaration which no one imagines to be its sense; nor can
that interpretation be erroneous which all have received!‡ And
yet such prelates as Secker, Horseley, Cleaver, Pretyman, with
all the judges, strongly maintain that the literal meaning of the
Articles must be strictly adhered to!

I could cite many other dignitaries, or other leading clergymen, of the establishment, and nearly the whole host of dissenters, who have recourse to such quibbles and evasions, in
order to get rid of the plain sense of the articles and creeds, to
which they have solemnly engaged themselves before the Creator, as, I am convinced they would not make use of in any contract with a fellow creature: but I hasten to take in hand the
admired Discourses of my friend, Dr. Balguy. He was the
champion, the very Achilles, of those who defended the subscription of the Thirty-nine Articles, against the petitioners
for the abrogation of it, in 1772. And how think you, dear
sir, did he defend it? Not by vindicating the truth of the articles themselves, much less by any of the quibbles mentioned
or alluded to above; but upon the principle, that an exterior
show of uniformity in the ministers of religion is necessary for
the support of it; and that, therefore, they ought to subscribe
and teach the doctrine prescribed to them by the law, whatever
they may inwardly think of it. Thus it was that he and many
of his friends imagined it possible to unite religious liberty
with ecclesiastical restrictions. But I will give you the archdeacon's own words, in one of his charges to his clergy. "The
articles, we will say, are not exactly *what we might wish them
to be.* Some of them are expressed in *doubtful terms;* others
are *inaccurate,* perhaps, *unphilosophical:* others again may
chance to *mislead* an ignorant reader into some *erroneous opi-*

---

* Lectures in Divinity, &c. p. 49.   † Ibid. p. 62
‡ Moral and Polit. Philos. Not having this work, or Dr. Powell's Sermon
at hand, I here quote from Overton's *True Churchman,* p. 337.
§ Serm. on Subscrip.

*nions:** but is there any one among them that leads to *immorality?* Is there one in the number that will make us revengeful or cruel?" &c.† On this principle, you might, in the Eastern world, conscientiously swear your assent and consent to the fables of the Koran or the Vedam!! But, to proceed: he says, " Nothing is clearer than that the *uniform appearance* of religion is the cause of its general and easy reception. Destroy this uniformity, and you cannot but introduce doubt and perplexity in to the minds of the people."‡ Again, he says, "I am far from wishing to discourage the clergy of the established church from thinking for themselves, or from speaking what they think, nor even from writing. I say nothing against the right of private judgment or speech, I only contend that men ought not to attack the church from those very pulpits, in which they were placed for her defence."§ What is this doctrine of the subscription champion, dear sir, I appeal to you, but a defence of the most vile and sacrilegious hypocrisy that can possibly be imagined? He leaves the clergy at liberty to *disbelieve in*, to *talk*, and even to *write*, *against the doctrine of their church;* but requires them *in the pulpit to defend it!* I agree with him that contradictory doctrines publicly maintained by ministers of the same religion, is the way to make the adherents of it renounce it entirely: but will not that effect more certainly follow from the people's discovering, as they must in the case supposed discover, that their clergy *do not themselves believe in the doctrines which they preach!*

But this system of deceiving the people is not peculiar to Dr. Balguy: it is avowed by his friend and master, bishop Hoadley, and represented by archdeacon Blackburn, from whom I take the following passage, as being very generally adopted.‖—" In all proposals and schemes to be reduced to practice," the bishop says, " we must suppose the world to be *what it is, and what it ought to be.* We must propose, not merely what is absolutely good in itself, but what is so with respect to the prejudices, tempers, and constitutions, we know and are sure to be among us. It is represented that the world was never less disposed to be serious and reasonable than at

---

* Which articles they are that the doctor particularly objects to, we can easily gather, from his general language concerning mysteries, the sacraments, and our redemption by Christ. On this last head, he seriously cautions us against "censuring or persecuting our brethren because their *non sense* and our's wears a different dress." Charge ii. p. 192.

† Charge vi. p. 293.

‡ Charge v. p. 257.

§ Disc. vii. p. 120. Discourses by Thomas Balguy D. D. archdeacon and prebendary of Winchester, &c. dedicated to the king. Lockyer Davies, 1785.

‖ Confessional, p. 375, p. 385.

this period. Religious reflection, we are informed, is not the *humour* of the times. We are therefore advised to keep our prudence and our patience a little longer; to wait till our people are in a better temper, and in the mean time, to bear with their manners and dispositions; *gently and gradually correcting their foolish notions and habits; but still taking care not to throw in more light upon them, at once, than the weak optics of men, so long used to sit in darkness, are able to bear."* His lordship's words are guarded, but perfectly intelligible. Bishop Hoadley had undermined the church he professed to support, in her doctrine and discipline, as has been elsewhere demonstrated,* and he wished all the clergy to co-operate in diffusing his Socinian system; but he advised them to attempt this *gently and gradually*, bearing with the people's *foolish notions*, and not *throwing too much light upon them at once :* in other words, continuing to subscribe the Articles and to preach them from the pulpit, being inwardly persuaded at the same time, that they are not only false, but also *foolish !*—Thus, dear sir, you have seen the necessity to which the different Protestant societies have found themselves reduced, of occasionally appealing to tradition, and of assuming authority to dictate confessions and articles of religion in direct violation of their boasted charter of private judgment; and you have seen that this inconsistency has rendered *the remedy worse than the disease.* These weapons, not being natural to them, have been turned against them, and have mortally wounded them: and " the church of England in particular," as one of its principal defenders complains, " is like an oak, cleft to shivers with wedges made out of its own body."† You will now see with what ease and success the Catholic church wields these weapons; but, first, I think it best to add something by way of confirming and elucidating this Catholic rule.

III. What has been said above in proof of the Catholic rule, namely, that Christ established it when he sent his apostles to preach the Gospel, and that the apostles followed it, when they established churches throughout different nations, is so incontestible as not to be denied by any of our learned opponents : still less will they deny, that the ancient fathers and the doctors of the church, in every age, maintained this rule. Accordingly, one of the latest and most learned Protestant controvertists writes thus, " No one will deny that Jesus Christ laid the foundation of his church *by preaching :* nor can we deny that the unwritten Word was the first rule of

---

* Letter, to a Prebendary, Art. Hoadleyism.
† Daubeny's Guide to the Church, Append.

Christianity."* This being granted, it was incumbent on his lordship to demonstrate, and this by no less an authority than that which established the rule, at what precise period it was abrogated. Was it when this Gospel or that Gospel, when this Epistle or that Epistle, was written, though known only to particular congregations or persons, that the pastors of the church lost their authority of proclaiming, *So we have received from the apostles, or the disciples of the apostles: so all the other pastors of the Catholic church believe and teach?* Or was this abrogation of the *first rule of Christianity* deferred till the canon of Scripture was fixed, at the end of the fourth century? So far from there being divine authority, there is not even a hint in ecclesiastical history on which to ground this pretended alteration in the rule of faith. His Lordship's only foundation is his *own conjecture:* " It is extremely improbable," he says, " that an all-wise Providence, in imparting a new revelation to mankind, would suffer any doctrine or article of faith to be transmitted to posterity by so precarious a vehicle as that of oral tradition."† The bishop of London‡ had before said nearly the same thing, as well with respect to tradition being the *original rule* as to the *improbability* of its continuing to be so, " considering," as he says, " how liable the easiest story, transmitted by the word of mouth, is to be essentially altered in the course of one or two hundred years." But, to the *opinions* of these learned prelates, I oppose, in the first place, undeniable *facts.* It is, then, certain, that the whole doctrine and practice of religion, including the rites of sacrifice, and, indeed, the whole Sacred History, was preserved by the patriarchs, in succession, from Adam down to Moses, during the space of twenty-four hundred years, by means of tradition : and, when the law was written, many most important truths, regarding a future life, the emblems and prophecies concerning the Messiah, and the inspiration and authenticity of the Sacred Books themselves, were preserved in the same way.— Secondly, it is unwarrantable in these prelates to compare the essential traditions of religion, with ordinary stories : in the truth of these no one has an interest, and no means have been provided to preserve them from corruption ; whereas, *the faith once delivered to the saints,* the church has ever guarded as *the apple of her eye,* and all ecclesiastical history witnesses the extreme care and pains which were taken in ancient times by the pastors to instruct the faithful in the tenets and practices of

* Comparative View of the Churches, p. 61, by Dr. (now bishop) Marsh.

† Ibid p. 67   ‡ Dr. Porteus, Brief Confut.

their religion, previously to their being baptized :* the same are generally taken by their successors previously to the confirmation and first communion of their neophytes at the present day. Thirdly, when any fresh controversy arises in the church, the fundamental maxim of the bisops and Popes, to whom it belongs to decide upon it, is, not to consult their own private opinion or interpretation of Scripture, but to inquire *what is and ever has been the doctrine of the church*, concerning it. Hence, their cry is and ever has been, on such occasions, as well in council as out of it: So we have received : so the universal church believes: let there be no new doctrine : none but what has been delivered down to us by tradition.†— Fourthly, the tradition of which we now treat, is *not a local* but a *universal* tradition, as widely spread as the Catholic church itself is, and being found every where the same. The maxim of the sententious Tertullian must be admitted: " Error," he says, " of course, varies, but that doctrine which is one and the same among many, is not an error but a tradition."‡ However liable men, and particularly illiterate men, are to believe in fables ; yet if, on the discovery of America, the inhabitants of it, from Hudson's Bay to Cape Horn, had been found to agree in the same account of their origin and general history, we should certainly give credit to them. But, fifthly, in the present case, they are not the Catholics of different ages and nations alone who vouch for the traditions in question, I mean those rejected by Protestants, but all the subsisting heretics and schismatics of former ages without exception. The Nestorians and Eutychians, for example, deserted the Catholic church, in defence of opposite errors, near fourteen hundred years ago, and still form regular churches under bishops and patriarchs throughout the East : in like manner the Greek schismatics, properly so called, broke off from the Latin church, for the last time, in the eleventh century. Theirs is well known to be the prevailing religion of Christians throughout the Turkish and Russian empires. Nevertheless, these and all the other Christian sectaries of ancient date, agree upon every article in dispute between Catholics and Protestants (except that of the Pope's supremacy) with the former and condemn the latter.§ Let Dr. Porteus and the other controvertists, who declaim

* See Fleury's Mœurs des Chret. Hartley, in bishop Watson's Col. vol. v. p. 91.

† " Nil innovetur : nil nisi quod traditum est." Steph. Papa I.

‡ " Variasse deberet error, sed quod unum apud multos invenitur, non est erratum, sed traditum." Præscrip. advers. Hæret.

§ See the proofs of this, in the *Perpetuite de la Foi*, copied from the original documents, in the French king's library.

against the alleged ignorance and vices of the Catholic clergy and laity during the five or six ages preceding the Reformation, and pretend to show how the tenets which they object to might have been introduced into our church, explain how precisely the same could have been quietly received by the Nestorians at Bagdad, the Eutychians at Alexandria, and the Greeks at Moscow! All these, and particularly the last named, were ever ready to find fault with us upon subjects of comparatively small consequence, such as the use of unleavened bread in the sacrament, the days and manner of our fasting, and even the mode of shaving our beards; and yet, so far from objecting to the pretended novelties of prayers for the dead, addresses to the saints, the mass, the real presence, &c. they have always professed, and continue to profess, these doctrines and practices as zealously as we do.

Finally, by way of the farther answer to his lordship's shameful calumny, that the ancient "clergy and laity were so universally and monstrously ignorant and vicious, that nothing was too bad for them to do or too absurd for them to believe," thereby insinuating that the former invented and the latter were duped into the belief of the articles on which the Catholic church and the church of England are divided; as also by way of farther confirming the certainty of tradition, I maintain that it would have been much easier for the ancient clergy to corrupt the Scriptures than the religious belief of the people. For, it is well known that the Scriptures were chiefly in the hands of the clergy, and that, before the use of printing, in the fifteenth century, the copies of it were renewed and multiplied in the monasteries by the labour of the monks, who, if they had been so wicked, might with some prospect of success, have attempted to alter the New Testament, in particular, as they pleased; whereas, the doctrines and practices of the church were in the hands of the people of all civilized nations, and, therefore, could not be altered without their knowledge and consent. Hence, wherever religious novelties were introduced, a violent opposition to them, and, of course, tumults and schisms, would have ensued. If they had been generally received in one country, as for example, in France, this would have been the occasion of their being rejected with redoubled antipathy in a neighbouring hostile nation, as, for instance, England. Yet none of these disturbances or schisms do we read of, respecting any of the doctrines or practices of our religion, objected to by Protestants, either in the same kingdom, or among the different states of Christianity. I said that the doctrines and practices of religion were in the hands of all "the people," in fact they were all, in every part of the church, obliged to receive the holy sacrament at Easter; now they could not do this without knowing whether they had been previously taught to consider this as *bread and wine taken in memory of Christ,* or as the *real body and blood of Christ* himself. If they had originally held the former opinion, could they have been persuaded or dragooned into the latter, without violent opposition on their part, and violent persecution on that of their clergy? Again, they could not assist at the religious services performed at the funerals of their relations, or on the festivals of the saints, without recollecting whether they had previously been instructed to pray for the former, and to invoke the prayers of the latter. If they had not been so instructed, would they, one and all, at the same time, and in every country, have quietly yielded to the first imposters who preached up such supposed superstitions to them; as, in this case, we are sure they must have done? In a word, there is but one way of accounting for the alleged alterations in the doctrine of the church, that mentioned by the learned Dr. Bailey;* which is to suppose that, on some one night, all the Christians of the world went to sleep sound Protestants, and awoke the next morning rank Papists!

IV. I now come to consider the benefits derived from the Catholic rule or method of religion. The first part of this rule conducts us to the second part; that is to say, tradition conducts us to Scripture. We have seen that Protestants, by their own confession, are obliged to build the latter upon the former; in doing which they act most inconsistently: whereas Catholics, in doing the same thing, act with perfect consistency. Again, Protestants in building Scripture, as they do, upon tradition, as a mere human testimony, not as a *rule of faith,* can only form an act of *human faith,* that is to say, *an opinion* of its being inspired;† whereas Catholics, believing in the tradition of the church, as a *divine rule,* are enabled to believe, and do believe in the Scriptures with a *firm faith,* as the certain Word of God. Hence the Catholic church requires her pastors, who are to preach and expound the Word of God, to study this second part of her rule no less than the first part, with unremitting diligence; and she encourages those of her flock, who are properly qualified and disposed, to read it for their edification.

In perusing the books of the Old Testament, some of the most striking passages are those which regard the prerogatives

---

* He was son of the bishop of Bangor, and becoming a convert to the Catholic church, wrote several works in her defence; and among the rest, one under the title of these Letters, and another called A Challenge.

† Chillingworth in his Religion of Protestants, chap. ii. expressly teaches, that "The books of Scripture are not the objects of our faith," and that "a man may be saved, who should not believe them to be the Word of God."

of the future kingdom of the Messiah, namely, the extent, the visibility, and indefectibility of the church: in examining the New Testament, we find in several of its clearest passages, the strongest proofs of its being an *infallible guide* in the way of salvation. The texts alluded to have been already cited. Hence we look upon the church with increased veneration, and listen to her decisions with redoubled confidence.—But here I think it necessary to refute an objection which, I believe, was first started by Dr. Stillingfleet, and has since been adopted by many other controvertists. They say to us, *you argue, in what logicians call, a vicious circle: for you prove Scripture by your church, and then your church by Scripture. This is like John giving a character to Thomas, and Thomas a character to John.* True it is, that I prove the *inspiration* of Scripture by the tradition of the church, and that I prove the *infallibility* of the church by the testimony of Scripture; but you must take notice, that independently of, and prior to, the testimony of Scripture, I knew from tradition, and the general arguments of the credibility of Christianity, that the church is an illustrious society, instituted by Christ, and that its pastors have been appointed by him to guide me in the way of salvation. In a word, it is not every kind of mutual testimony which runs in a *vicious circle:* for the Baptist bore testimony to Christ, and Christ bore testimony to the Baptist.

V. The advantage, and even necessity, of having a living, speaking authority for preserving peace and order in every society is too obvious to be called in question. The Catholic church has such an authority; the different societies of Protestants, though they claim it, cannot effectually exercise it, as we have shown, on account of their opposite fundamental principle of private judgment. Hence when debates arise among Catholics concerning points of faith (for as to scholastic and other questions, each one is left to defend his own opinion,) the pastors of the church, like judges in regard of civil contentions, fail not to examine them by the received rule of faith, and to pronounce an authoritative sentence upon them. The dispute is thus quashed, and peace is restored: for *if any party will not hear the church, he is,* of course, regarded as *a heathen and a publican.* On the other hand, dissensions in any Protestant society, which adheres to its fundamental rule of religious liberty, must be irremediable and endless.

VI. The same method which God has appointed to keep peace in his church, he has also appointed to preserve it in the breasts of her several children. Hence while other Christians, who have no rule of faith but their own fluctuating opinions, *are carried about by every wind of doctrine,* and are agitated

K

by dreadful doubts and fears, as to the safety of the road they are in; Catholics, being moored to the rock of Christ's church, never experience any apprehension whatsoever on this head. The truth of this may be ascertained by questioning pious Catholics, and particularly those who have been seriously converted from any species of Protestantism: such persons are generally found to speak in raptures of the peace and security they enjoy in the communion of the Catholic church, compared with their doubts and fears before they embraced it. Still the death-bed is evidently the best situation for making this inquiry. I have mentioned, in my former letter, that great numbers of Protestants, at the approach of death, seek to be reconciled to the Catholic church; many instances of this are notorious, though many more, for obvious reasons, are concealed from public notice: on the other hand, a challenge has frequently been made by Catholics (among the rest by sir Toby Mathews, Dean Cressy, F. Walsingham, Molines dit Flechiere, and Ulric, duke of Brunswick, all of them converts) to the whole world to name a single Catholic, who, at the hour of death, expressed a wish to die in any other communion than his own!

I have now, dear sir, fully proved what I undertook to prove, that the rule of faith professed by rational Protestants, that of *Scripture as interpreted by each person's private judgment,* is no less fallacious than the rule of fanatics, who imagine themselves to be directed by an *individual, private inspiration.* I have shown that this rule is evidently *unserviceable to infinitely the greater part of mankind;* that it is *liable to lead* men into error, and that it *has actually led vast numbers of them into endless errors and shocking impieties.* The proof of these points was sufficient, according to the principles I laid down at the beginning of our controversy, to disprove the rule itself: but I have, moreover, demonstrated that our divine Master, Christ, did not establish this rule, nor his apostles follow it: that the Protesant churches, and that of England, in particular, were not founded according to this rule: and that individual Protestants have not been guided by it in the choice of their religion: finally, that the adoption of it leads to uncertainty and uneasiness of mind in life, and more particularly at the hour of death.—On the other hand, I have shown that the Catholic rule, that of the entire word of God, unwritten as well as written, together with the authority of the living pastors of the church in explaining it, was appointed by Christ:—was followed by the apostles:—was maintained by the holy fathers:—has been resorted to from necessity, in both particulars, by the Protestant congregations, though with the worst success, from the impossibility of uniting private judgment with it:—that tradition lays a firm ground for divine faith in Scripture: that these two united together as one rule, and each bearing testimony to the living, speaking authority of the church in expounding that rule, the latter is preserved in peace and union through all ages and nations:*—and, in short, that Catholics, by adhering to this rule and authority, live and die in peace and security, as far as regards the truth of their religion.

It remains for you, dear sir, and your religious friends, who have called me into this field of controversy, to determine which of the two methods you will follow, in settling your religious concerns for time and FOR ETERNITY. Were it possible for me to err in following the Catholic method, with such a mass of evidence in its favour, methinks I could answer at the judgment seat of Eternal Truth, with a pious writer of the middle ages: "Lord, if I have been deceived, thou art the author of my error."† Whereas should you be found to have mistaken the right way, by depending upon your own private opinion, contrary to the directions of your authorized guides, what would you be able to allege in excuse for such presumption?—Think of this while you have time, and pray humbly and earnestly for God's holy grace to enlighten and strengthen you.

I am, Dear Sir, &c.

J. M

———

LETTER XII.

TO JAMES BROWN, Esq. &c.

OBJECTIONS ANSWERED.

DEAR SIR,

I AM not forgetful of the promise I made in my last letter but one, to answer the contents of those which I had then received from yourself, Mr. Topham, and Mr. Askew. Within these few days I have received other letters from yourself and

* "Domicillium pacis et unitatis"—S. Cyp. Ep. 46.
† Hugh of St. Victor.

Mr. Topham, which, equally with the former, call for my attention to their substance. However, it would take up a great deal
of time to write separate answers to each of these letters, and,
as I know, that they are arguments, and not formalities, which
you expect from me, I shall make this letter a general reply to
the several objections contained in them all, with the exception
of such as have been answered in my last to you. Conceiving,
also, that it will contribute to the brevity and perspicuity of
my letter, if I arrange the several objections, from whomsoever
they came, under their proper heads; and if, on this occasion,
I make use of the scholastic instead of the epistolary style,
I shall adopt both these methods. I must, however, remark,
before I enter upon my task, that most of the objections appear
to have been borrowed from the bishop of London's book called
a *Brief Confutation of the Errors of Popery.* This was extracted from archbishop Secker's Sermons on the same subject;
which, themselves, were culled out of his predecessor Tillotson's pulpit controversy. Hence you may justly consider your
arguments as the strongest which can be brought against the
Catholic rule and religion. Under this persuasion the work in
question has been selected for gratuitous distribution, by your
tract societies, wherever they particularly wish to restrain or
suppress Catholicity.

Against the Catholic rule it is objected that Christ referred
the Jews to the Scriptures : *Search the Scriptures; for in them
ye think ye have eternal life: and they are they which testify of
me.* John v. 35. Again, the Jews of Berea are commended by
the sacred penman, *in that they search the Scriptures daily,
whether these things were so.* Acts xvii. 11.

Before I enter on the discussion of any part of Scripture,
with you or your friends, I am bound, dear sir, in conformity
with my rule of faith, as explained by the fathers, and particularly by Tertullian, to protest against your or their right to argue from Scripture, and, of course, to deny any need there is
of my replying to any objection which you may draw from it.
For I have reminded you that, *No prophecy of Scripture is of
any private enterpretation;* and I have proved to you that the
whole business of the Scriptures belongs to the church: she has
preserved them, she vouches for them, and, she alone, by confronting them, and by the help of tradition, authoritatively explains them. Hence it is impossible that the real sense of Scripture should ever be against her and her doctrine; and hence,
of course, I might quash every objection which you can draw
from any passage in it by this short reply, *The church understands the passage differently from you; therefore you mistake its meaning.* Nevertheless, as *charity beareth all things
and never faileth,* I will, for the better satisfying of you and

,your friends, quit my vantage ground for the present, and answer distinctly to every text not yet answered by me, which any of you, gentlemen, or which Dr. Porteus himself, has brought against the Catholic method of religion.

. By way of answering your first objection, let me ask you, whether Christ, by telling the Jews to *search the Scriptures* intimated that they were not to believe in his *unwritten 'Word*, which he was then preaching, nor to hear *his apostles and their successors*, with whom he promised to *remain forever?* I ask, secondly, on what *particular* question Christ referred to the Scripture, namely, the Old Scripture? (for no part of the New was then written) was it on any question that has been or might be agitated among *Christians?* No, certainly: the sole question between him and the *infidel Jews*, was, whether he was or was not the Messiah: in proof that he was the Messiah, he adduced the ordinary motives of credibility, as they have been detailed by your late worthy rector, Mr. Carey, the miracles he wrought, and the prophecies in the Old Testament that were fulfilled in him, as likewise the testimony of St John the Baptist. The same is to be said of the commendations bestowed by St Luke on the Bereans; they searched the ancient prophecies, to verify that the Messiah was to be born at such a time, and in such a place, and that his life and his death were to be marked by such and such circumstances. We still refer Jews and other Infidels to the same proofs of Christianity, without saying any thing yet to them about our rule or judge of controversies.

Dr. Porteus objects what St Luke says, at the beginning of his Gospel: *It seemed good to me also, having had perfect understanding of all things from the very first, to write unto thee in order, most excellent Theophilus, that thou mightest know the certainty of those things wherein thou hast been instructed.* Again St. John says, c. xx. *These things are written that ye might believe that Jesus is the Christ, the Son of God; and that believing ye might have life through his name.*

Answer. It is difficult to conceive how his lordship can draw an argument from these texts against the Catholic rule. Surely he does not gather from the words of St. Luke, that Theophilus *did not believe* the articles in which he *had been instructed by word of mouth* till he read this Gospel! or that the evangelist gainsayed the authority given by Christ to his disciples: *He that heareth you heareth me*, which he himself records, *Luke* x. 16. . In like manner the prelate cannot suppose that this testimony of St. John sets aside other testimonies of Christ's divinity, or that our belief in this single article without other conditions, will ensure eternal life.

Having quoted these texts, which appear to meinconclusive, the bishop adds, by way of proving that *Scripture* is sufficiently intelligible, "Surely the apostles were not worse writers, with divine assistance, than others commonly are without it."*

I will not here repeat the arguments and testimonies already brought† to show the great obscurity of a considerable portion of the Bible, particularly with respect to the bulk of mankind, because it is sufficient to refer to the clear words of St. Peter, declaring that there are in the Epistles of St. Paul, *some things hard to be understood, which the unlearned and unstable wrest, as they do all the other Scriptures, unto their own destruction,* (2 Peter iii. 16,) and to the instances, which occur in the Gospels, of the very apostles frequently misunderstanding the meaning of their divine Master.

The learned prelate says, elsewhere,‡ "The New Testament supposes them (the generality of the people) capable of judging for themselves, and accordingly requires them not only to *try the spirits whether they be of God,* 1 John iv. 1, but to *prove all things and hold fast that which is good.* 1 Thess. v. 21."

Answer. True: St. John tells the Christians, to whom he writes to *try the spirits whether they are of God, because,* he adds, many *false prophets are gone out into the world.* But then he gives them *two rules* for making trial: *Hereby ye know the spirit of God. Every spirit that confesseth that Jesus Christ is come in the flesh, is of God. And every spirit that confesseth not that Jesus is come in the flesh,* (which was denied by the heretics of that time, the disciples of Simon and Cerinthus) *is not of God.* In this, the apostle tells the Christians to see whether the doctrine of these spirits was or was not *conformable to that which they had learnt from the church.* The second rule was, *He that knoweth God, heareth us; he that is not of God, heareth not us. Hereby know we the spirit of truth and the spirit of error:* namely, he bid them observe whether these teachers did or did not listen to the divinely-constituted pastors of the church. Dr. P. is evidently here quoting Scripture *for* our rule, not *against* it. The same is to be said of the other text. Prophesy was exceedingly common at the beginning of the church; but, as we have just seen, there were false prophets as well as true prophets: hence, while the apostle defends this supernatural gift in general, *Despise not prophesyings,* he admonishes the Thessalonians to *prove them:* not certainly by their private opinions, which would be the source of endless discord; but, by the established rules of the church, and particularly by that which he tells them to *hold fast,* 2 Thess. ii. 15, namely, tradition.

* P. 4.   † Letter ix.   ‡ P 19

Dr. P. in another place,* urges the exhortation of St. Paul to Timothy, 'Continue thou in the things which thou hast learned and hast been assured of, knowing of whom thou hast learned them: and that from a child thou hast known the holy Scriptures, which are able to make thee wise unto salvation, through faith in Christ Jesus. All Scripture is given by inspiration of God, and is profitable for doctrine, for reproof,'&c. 2 Tim. iii.

Answer. Does, then, the prelate mean to say, that the *form of sound words* which Timothy *had heard* from St. Paul. and which he was commanded to *hold fast*, 2 Tim. i. 13, was all contained in the Old Testament, the only Scripture which he could have read in his childhood? Or that, in this he could have learned the mysteries of the Trinity and the incarnation, or the ordinances of baptism and the eucharist? The first part of the question is a general commendation of tradition, the latter of Scripture.

Against tradition, Dr. P. and yourself quote† Mark vii, where the Pharisees and Scribes asked Christ, *Why walk not thy disciples according to the tradition of the elders, but eat bread with unwashed hands? He answered and said to them, In vain do they worship me, teaching FOR‡ doctrines the commandments of men. For, laying aside the commandments of God, ye hold the tradition of men, as the washing of pots and cups, &c.*

Answer. Among the traditions which prevailed at the time of our Saviour, some were *divine*, such as the inspiration of the books of Moses and the other prophets, the resurrection of the body, and the last judgment, which assuredly Christ did not condemn, but confirm. There were others, merely *human*, and of a recent date, introduced, as St. Jerome informs us, by Sammai, Killel, Achiba, and other Pharisees, from which the Talmud is chiefly gathered. These, of course, were never obligatory. In like manner, there are among Catholics *divine traditions*, such as the inspiration of the Gospels, the divine, observation of the Lord's day, the lawfulness of invoking the prayers of the saints, and other things not clearly contained in Scripture; and there are among many Catholics, historical and even fabulous traditions.§ Now, it is the former, as avow-

---

* P. 69. † P. 11.

‡ This particle FOR, which in some degree affects the sense, is a corrupt interpolation a s appears from the original Greek.

N. B. The texts which Dr. P. refers to I quote from the common Bible; his citations, of it are frequently inaccurate.

§ Such are the acts of several saints condemned by Pope Gelasius; such also was the opinion of Christ's reign upon earth for a thousand years.

10*

ed to be divine by the church, that we appeal: of the others, every one may judge as he thinks best.

You both, likewise, quote Coloss. ii. 8. *Beware lest any man spoil* (cheat) *you through philosophy and vain deceit, after the tradition of men, after the rudiments of the world, and not after Christ.*

Answer. The apostle himself informs the Collossians what kind of traditions he here speaks of, where he says, *Let no man therefore judge you in meat or drink, or in respect of any holiday, or of the new moon, or of the Sabbath days.* The ancient fathers and ecclesiastical historians inform us, that, in the age of the apostles, many Jews and Pagan philosophers professed Christianity, but endeavoured to allay with it their respective superstitions and vain speculations, absolutely inconsistent with the doctrine of the Gospel. It was against these St. Paul wrote, not against those traditions which he commanded his converts to *hold fast to, whether they had been taught by word or by Epistle,* 2 Thess. ii. 15; nor those traditions which he commended his other converts *for keeping,* 1 Cor. xi. 2.* Finally, the apostles, in that passage, did not abrogate this his awful sentence, *now we command you, brethren, in the name of our Lord Jesus Christ, that ye withdraw yourselves from every brother that walketh disorderly, and not after the tradition which he received of us.* 2 Thess. iii. 6.

Against the infallibility of the church in deciding questions of faith, I am referred to various other arguments made use of by Dr. Porteus; and, in the first place, the following: " Romanists themselves own that men must use their eyes, to find this guide; why then must they put them out, to follow him ?"† I answer by the following comparisons. Every prudent man makes use of his reason, to find out an able physician to take care of his health, and an able lawyer to secure his property: but having found these, to his full satisfaction, does he dispute with the former about the quality of medicines, or with the latter about forms of law ? Thus the Catholic makes use of his reason, to observe which, among the rival communions, is the church that Christ established and promised to remain with : having ascertained that, by the plain acknowledged marks which this church bears, he trusts his soul to her unerring judgment, in preference to his own fluctuating opinion.

Dr. Porteus adds, " Ninety-nine parts in every hundred of their (the Catholic) communion, have no other rule to follow, but what a few priests and private writers tell them."‡ Ac

* The English Testament puts the word *ordinance* here for *traditions*, contrary to the sense of the original Greek, and even the authority of Beza

† P. 19   ‡ Ibid.

cording to this mode of reasoning, a loyal subject does not make any act of the legislature the rule of his civil conduct, because, perhaps, he learns it only from a printed paper, or the proclamation of the bell-man. Most likely the Catholic peasant learns the doctrine of the church from his parish priest; but then he knows that the doctrine of this priest must be conformable to that of his bishop, and that otherwise he will soon be called to an account for it. He knows also that the doctrine of the bishop himself must be conformable to that of the other bishops and the Pope, and that it is a fundamental maxim with them all, never to admit of any tenet but such as is believed by all the bishops, and was believed by their predecessors up to the apostles themselves.

The prelate gives a "rule for the unlearned and ignorant in religion, (that is to say of ninety-nine in every hundred of them,) which is this; Let each man improve his own judgment, and increase his own knowledge as much as he can; and be fully assured that God will expect no more."—What? If *Christ has given some apostles, and some prophets, and some evangelists and some pastors and teachers; for the perfecting the saints, for the work of the ministry*, Ephes. iv. 11, does he not expect that Christians should hearken to them, and obey them? The prelate goes on: "In matters, *for which he must rely on authority*," (mere Scripture then, and private judgment, according to the bishop himself, are not always a sufficient rule, even for Protestants, but they must in some matters rely on church authority,) "let him rely on the authority of that church which God's providence has placed him under," (that is to say, whether Catholic, Protestant, Socinian, Antinomian, Jewish, &c.) "rather than another which he hath nothing to do with," (every Christian has, or ought to have, something to do with Christ's true church,) and "trust to those, who, by encouraging free inquiry, appear to love truth; rather than such as, by requiring all their doctrines to be implicitly obeyed, seem conscious that they will not bear to be fairly tried." What, my lord, would you have me trust those men, who have just now deceived me, by assuring me that I should not stand in need of guides at all, rather than those who told me, from the first, of the perplexities in which I find myself entangled! Again, do you advise me to prefer these conductors, who are forced to confess that they may mislead me, to those others who assure me, and this upon such strong grounds that they will conduct me with perfect safety!

Our Episcopal controvertist finishes his admonition "to the ignorant and unlearned," with an address, calculated for the stupid and bigoted. He says, "Let others build on fathers and Popes, on traditions and councils, what they will: let us continue firm, as we are, on the foundation of the apostles and prophets, Jesus Christ himself being the chief corner-stone." *Ephes.* ii. What empty declamation! Do then the fathers, Popes, and councils, profess or attempt to build religion on any other foundation than the revelation made by God to the apostles and prophets? His lordship knows full well that they do not, and that the only questions at issue are these three: First, Whether this revelation has not been made and conveyed by the unwritten as well as by the written Word of God? Secondly, Whether Christ did not commit this Word to his apostles and their successors, till the end of the world, for them to preserve and announce it? Lastly, Whether, independently of this commission, it is consistent with common sense, for each Protestant ploughman and mechanic to persuade himself that he, individually, (for he cannot, according to his rule, build on the opinion of other Protestants, though he could find any whose faith exactly tallied with his own,) that he, I say, individually, understands the Scriptures better than all the doctors and bishops of the church, who now are, or ever have been since the time of the apostles!*

One of your Salopian friends, in writing to me, ridicules the idea of infallibility being lodged in any mortal man, or number of men. Hence, it is fair to conclude, that he does not look upon himself to be infallible: now nothing short of a man's conviction of his own infallibility, one might think, would put him on preferring his own judgment, in matters of religion, to that of the church of all ages and all nations. Secondly, if this objection were valid, it would prove that the apostles themselves were not infallible. Finally, I could wish your friend to form a right idea of this matter. The infallibility, then, of our church, is not a power of telling all things past, present, and to come, such as the Pagans ascribed to their oracles; but merely the aid of God's holy spirit, to enable her truly to decide what her faith is, and ever has been, in such articles as have been made known to her by Scripture and tradition. This definition

* The great Bossuet obliged the minister, Claude, in his conference with him, openly to avow this principle; which, in fact, every consistent Protestant must avow, who maintains his private interpretation of the Bible to be the only rule of his faith.

furnishes answers to diverse other objections and questions of Dr. P. The church does not decide the controversy concerning the conception of the Blessed Virgin, and several other disputed points, because she sees nothing absolutely clear and certain concerning them, either in the written or the unwritten Word; and therefore leaves her children to form their own opinions concerning them. She does not dictate an exposition of the whole Bible, because she has no tradition concerning a very great proportion of it, as for example, concerning the *prophecy of Enoch*, quoted by *Jude*, 14, and the *baptism for the dead*, of which St. Paul makes mention, 1 *Cor.* xv. 29, and the chronologies and genealogies in Genesis. The prelate urges that the words of St. Paul, where he declares that, *The church of God is the pillar and ground of truth*, 1 Tim. iii. 15, may be translated a different way from that received.—True : they may, but not without altering the original Greek, as also the common Protestant version. He says, it was ordained in the Old Law that every controversy should be decided by the priests and Levites, *Deut.* xvii. 8, and yet that these avowedly erred in rejecting Christ.—True: but the Law had then run its destined course, and the divine assistance failed the priests in the very act of their rejecting the promised Messiah, who was then before them. He adds, that St. Paul in his Epistle to the church of Rome bids her *not be high minded, but fear; for* (he adds) *if God spared not the Jews, take heed lest he also spare not thee*, Rom. xi.—Supposing the quotation to be accurate, and that the threat is particularly addressed to the Christians of Rome; what is that to the present purpose? We never supposed the promises of Christ to belong to them or their successors more than to the inhabitants of any other city. Indeed it is the opinion of some of our most learned commentators, that before the end of the world, Rome will relapse into its former Paganism.* In a word, the promises of our Saviour, that *hell's gates shall not prevail against his church*—that his *Holy Spirit shall lead it into all truth*—and that he himself *will remain with it for ever*, were made to the church of all nations, and all times, in communion with St. Peter and his successors, the bishops of Rome: and as these promises have been fulfilled, during a succession of eighteen centuries, contrary to the usual and natural course of events, and by the visible protection of the Almighty, so we rest assured that he will continue to fulfil them, till the

* See Cornel. a Lapid. in Apocalyp.

church militant shall be wholly transformed into the church triumphant in the heavenly kingdom.

Finally, his lordship, with other controvertists, objects against the infallibility of the Catholic church, that its advocates are not agreed where to lodge this prerogative; some ascribing it to the Pope, others to a general council, or to the bishops dispersed throughout the church. True, schoolmen discuss some such points: but let me ask his lordship, whether he finds any Catholic who denies or doubts that a general council, with the Pope at its head, or that the Pope himself, issuing a doctrinal decision, which is received by the great body of Catholic bishops, is secure from error? Most certainly not: and hence he may gather where all Catholics agree in lodging infallibility. In like manner, with respect to our national constitution; some lawyers hold that a royal proclamation, in such and such circumstances, has the force of a law, others that a vote of the house of lords, or of the commons, or of both houses together, has the same strength; but all subjects acknowledge that an act of the king, lords, and commons, is binding upon them; and this suffices for all practical purposes.

But when, dear sir, will there be an end of the objections and cavils of men, whose pride, ambition, or interest, leads them to deny the plainest truths! You have seen those which the ingenuity and learning of the Porteus's, Seckers, and Tillotsons have raised against the unchangeable Catholic rule and interpreter of faith: say, is there any thing sufficiently clear and certain in them to oppose to the luminous and sure principles, on which the Catholic method is placed? Do they afford you a sure footing, to support you against all doubts and fears on the score of your religion, especially under the apprehension of approaching dissolution? If you answer affirmatively, I have nothing more to say; but if you cannot so answer, and, if you justly dread undertaking your voyage to eternity on the presumption of your private judgment, a presumption which you have clearly seen has led so many other rash Christians to certain shipwreck, follow the example of those who have happily arrived at the port which you are in quest of: in other words, listen to the advice of the holy patriarch to his son: *Then Tobias answered his father—I know not the way, &c.:—then his father said—Seek thee a faithful guide.* Tob. v. You will no sooner have sacrificed your own wavering judgment, and have submitted to follow the guide, whom your heavenly Father has provided for you, than you will feel a deep conviction that you are in the right and secure way; and very soon you will be enabled to join with the happy converts of ancient and modern times,* in this hymn of praise : " I give thee thanks O God, my enlightener and deliverer; for that thou hast opened the eyes of my soul to know thee.   Alas ! too late have I known thee, O ancient and eternal truth ! too late have I known thee."

I am, Dear Sir, yours, &c.

J. M.

* St. Austin's Soliloquies, c. 33, quoted by Dean Cressy, Exomol. p. 655.

THE END

OF

RELIGIOUS CONTROVERSY.

——

PART II.

——

LETTER XIII.

To JAMES BROWN, Esq. &c.

ON THE TRUE CHURCH.

Dear Sir,

The Letters which I have received from you, and some others of your religious society, satisfy me that I have not altogether lost my labour in endeavouring to prove to you, that the *private interpretation of holy Scripture* is not a more certain rule of faith, than an imaginary *private inspiration* is; and, in short, that *the church of Christ* is the only sure expounder of the doctrine of Christ. Thus much you, sir, in particular, candidly acknowledge: but you ask me, on the part of some of your friends as well as yourself, why, in case you " must rely on authority," as bishop Porteus confesses " the unlearned must," that *is* to say, the great bulk of mankind, you should not, as he advises you, " rely on the authority of that church, which God's providence hath placed you under, rather than that of another which you have nothing to do with,"* and why you may not trust to the church of England, in particular, to guide you in your road to heaven, with equal security as to the church of Rome?—Before I answer you, permit me to congratulate with you on your advance towards the clear sight of the whole truth of revelation. As long as you professed to hunt out the several articles of this, one by one, through the several books of Scripture, and under all the difficulties and uncertainties which I have clearly shown to attend this study, your task was interminable, and your success hopeless: whereas, now, by taking the church of God for

* Confutation of Errors of Popery, p. 20.

your guide, you have but one simple inquiry to make : *Which
is this church?* a question that admits of being solved by *men
of good will* with equal certainty and facility. I say, there is
but one inquiry to be made : *Which is the true church?* because
if there is any one religious truth more evident than the rest
from reason, from the Scriptures, both Old* and New,† from
the apostles' creed,‡ and from constant tradition, it is this, that
" the Catholic church preserves the true worship of the Deity ;
she being the fountain of truth, the house of faith, and the temple of God," as an ancient father of the church expresses it.§
Hence it is as clear as the noon-day light, that by solving this
one question, *Which is the true church?* you will at once solve
every question of religious controversy that ever has, or that
ever can be agitated. You will not need to spend your life in
studying the sacred Scriptures in their original languages, and
their authentic copies, and in confronting passages with each
other, from Genesis to Revelation, a task by no means calculated, as is evident, for the bulk of mankind : you will only
have to hear what the church teaches upon the several articles
of her faith, in order to know with certainty what God revealed
concerning them. Neither need you hearken to contending
sects, and doctors of the present, or of past times : you will need
only to hear the *church*, which, indeed, Christ commands you
to hear under pain of being treated *as a heathen* or *a publican*.
Matt. xviii. 17. '

I now proceed, dear sir, to your question ; *why, admitting
the necessity of being guided by the church, may not you and your
friends submit to be guided by the church of England, or any
other Protestant church to which you respectively belong ?*—My
answer is ; because no such church professes, nor, consistently
with the fundamental Protestant rule of private judgment, can
profess to be *a guide* in matters of religion. If you admit, but

---

* Speaking of the future church of the Gentiles, the Almighty promises, by
Isaiah : *Sing, O barren, thou that didst not bear, &c. : as I have sworn that the
waters of Noah should no more go over the earth, so I have sworn that I would not
be wroth with thee, nor rebuke thee. For the mountains shall depart and the hills
be removed, but my kindness shall not depart from thee,* &c. liv. See also lix. lx.
lxiii. *Jerem.* xxxiii. *Ezech.* xxxvii. *Dan.* ii. *Psalm* lxxxix.

† *Upon this rock I will build my Church, and the gates of hell shall not prevail
against it.* Matt. xvi. 18. *I am with you all days even until* THE END OF
THE WORLD. Matt. xxviii. 20. *I will pray the Father and he will give you
another comforter, that he may abide with you* FOR EVER, *even the Spirit of
Truth—he will teach you* ALL TRUTH, John xiv. 16. &c. *The House of God,
which is the Church of the living God,* THE PILLAR AND GROUND OF
TRUTH. 1 Tim. iii. 14.

‡ I BELIEVE IN THE HOLY CATHOLIC CHURCH. Art. ix.

§ Lactan, De Divin. Instit. l. 4.

11

for an instant, church authority, then Luther, Calvin, and Cranmer, with all the other founders of Protestantism, were evidently heretics, by rebelling against it. In short, no other. church but the Catholic can claim to be a religious guide, because evidently she alone is *the true church of Christ.* This assertion leads me to the proof of what I asserted above, respecting the facility and certainty with which persons of good will may solve that most important question : *Which is the true church?*

Luther,[*] Calvin,[†] the church of England,[‡] assign as the characteristics, or marks of the true church of Christ, *Truth of doctrine, and the right administration of the sacraments.* But to follow this method of finding out the true church, would be to throw ourselves back into those endless controversies concerning the true doctrine, and the right discipline, which it is my present object to put an end to, by demonstrating, at once, *which is the true church.* To show the inconsistency of the Protestant method, let us suppose that some stranger were to inquire, at the levee of his neighbour, *which of the personages present is the Prince Regent?* and that he was to receive for answer, *it is the king's eldest son :* would this answer, however true, be of any use to the inquirer? Evidently not. Whereas, if he were told that the prince wore such and such clothes and ornaments, and was seated in such and such a place, these exterior marks would, at once, put him in possession of the information he was in search of. Thus we Catholics, when we are asked, *which are the marks of the true church?* point out certain exterior, visible marks, such as plain, unlearned persons can discover, if they will take ordinary pains for this purpose, no less than persons of the greatest abilities and literature, at the same time that they are the very marks of this church, which, as I said above, natural reason, the Scriptures, the creeds, and the fathers, assign and demonstrate to be the true marks of it. Yes, my dear sir, these marks of the true church are so plain in themselves, and so evidently point it out, that *fools cannot err,* as the prophet foretold, *Isai.* xxxv. 8, in their road to it. They are the *flaming beacons,* which for ever shine on *the mountain at the top of the mountains of the Lord's house.* Isai. ii. 2. In short, the particular motives for credibility, which point out the *true church of Christ,* demonstrate this with no less certitude and evidence, than the general motives of credibility demonstrate the *truth of the Christian religion.*

The chief marks of the true church, which I shall here assign,

---

* De Concil. Eccles.   † Instit. l. 41.   ‡ Art. 19.

are not only conformable to reason, Scripture, and tradition, but, which is a most fortunate circumstance, they are such as the church of England, and most other respectable denominations of Protestants, acknowledge and profess to believe in, no less than Catholics. Yes, dear sir, they are contained in those *Creeds* which you recite in your daily prayers, and proclaim in your solemn worship. In fact, what do you say of the church you believe in, when you repeat the Apostles' Creed? You say, I BELIEVE IN THE HOLY CATHOLIC CHURCH. Again, how is this church more particularly described in the Nicene Creed, which makes part of your public liturgy? In this you say, I BELIEVE IN ONE CATHOLIC AND APOSTOLIC CHURCH.* Hence it evidently follows that the church which you, no less than we, profess to believe in, is possessed of these four marks: UNITY, SANCTITY, CA-THOLICITY, and APOSTOLICITY. It is agreed upon, then, that all we have to do, by way of discovering the true church, is to find out which of the rival churches, or communions, is peculiarly ONE—HOLY—CATHOLIC—and APOSTO-LIC. Thrice happy, dear sir, I deem it, that we agree together, by the terms of our common creeds, in a matter of such infinite importance for the happy termination of all our controversies, as are these qualities, or characters of the true church, which ever that may be found to be! Still, notwithstanding this agreement in our creeds, I shall not omit to illustrate these characters, or marks, as I treat of them, by arguments from reason, Scripture, and the ancient fathers.

I am, dear sir, &c.

J. M.

---

* Order of Administration of the Lord's Supper.

M

LETTER XIV.

To JAMES BROWN, Esq &c.

UNITY OF THE CHURCH.

Dear Sir,

Nothing is more clear to natural reason, than that God cannot be the author of different religions; for being the Eternal Truth, he cannot reveal contradictory doctrines, and, being at the same time, *the Eternal Wisdom*, and the *God of Peace*, he cannot establish *a kingdom divided against itself.* Hence it follows, that the church of Christ must be strictly ONE; one in *doctrine*, one in *worship*, and one in *government.* This mark of unity in the true church, which is so clear from reason, is still more clear from the following passages of Holy Writ. Our Saviour, then, speaking of himself, in the character of the good shepherd, says, *I have other sheep* (the Gentiles) *which are not of this fold; them also I must bring, and they shall hear my voice, and there shall be ONE FOLD, and one shepherd*, John x. 16. To the same effect addressing his heavenly Father, previously to his passion, he says, *I pray for all that shall believe in me, that THEY MAY BE ONE, as thou Father, art in me and I in thee*, John xvii. 20, 21. In like manner St. Paul emphatically inculcates the unity of the church, where he writes, *We, being many, are ONE BODY in Christ, and every one members one of another*, Rom. xii. 5. Again he writes, *There is ONE BODY and one spirit, as you are called in one hope of your calling; one Lord, ONE FAITH, and one baptism.* Ephes. iv. 4, 5. Conformably to this doctrine, respecting the necessary unity of the church, this apostle reckons HERESIES among the sins which exclude *from the kingdom of God*, Gal. v. 20. and he requires that *a man who is a heretic, after the first and second admonition, be rejected.* Tit. iii. 10.

The apostolical fathers, St. Polycarp and St. Ignatius, in their published Epistles, hold precisely the same language on this subject, with St. Paul, as does also their disciple St. Irenæus, who writes thus, " No reformation can be so advantageous as the evil of schism is pernicious."[*] The great light of the third century, St. Cyprian, has left us a whole book on the

---

[*] De Hær. l. i. c. 3.

unity of the church, in which, among other similar passages, he writes as follows : " There is but one God, and one Christ, and one faith, and a people joined in one solid body with the cement of concord.   This unity cannot suffer a division, nor this one body bear to be disjointed.—He cannot have God for his father, who has not the church for his mother. If any one could escape the deluge out of Noah's ark, he who is out of the church may also escape. To abandon the church is a crime, which blood cannot wash away. Such a one may be killed, but he cannot be crowned."*   In the fourth century, the illustrious St. John Chrysostom, writes thus : " We know that salvation *belongs to the church alone*, and that no one can partake of Christ, *nor be saved out of the Catholic church and faith*."† The language of St. Augustin, in the fifth century, is equally strong on this subject, in numerous passages. Among others the Synodical epistle of the council of Zerta, in 412, drawn up by this saint, tells the Donatist schismatics, " *Whoever is separated from this Catholic church*, however innocently he may think he lives, for this crime alone, that he is separated from the unity of Christ, will not have life, but *the anger of God remains upon him*."‡   Not less emphatical to the same effect, is the testimony of St. Fulgentius and St. Gregory the Great, in the sixth century, in various passages of their writings ; I shall content myself with citing one of them. " Out of this church," says the former father, " neither the name of Christian avails, nor does baptism save, nor is a clean sacrifice offered, nor is there forgiveness of sins, nor is the happiness of eternal life to be found."§   In short, such has been the language of the fathers and doctors of the church in all ages, concerning her essential unity, and the indispensable obligation of being united to her. Such also have been the formal declarations of the church herself in those decrees, by-which she has condemned and ana-

* Cypr. de Unit. Oxon, p. 109.

† Hom. 1. in Pasc.   ‡ Concil. Labbe, tom. ii. p. 1520.

§ Lib. de Remiss. Peccat. c. 23.—N. B. This doctrine concerning the unity of the church, and the necessity of adhering to it, under pain of damnation, which appears so rigid to modern Protestants, was almost universally taught by their predecessors ; as, for example, by Calvin, l. iv. Instit. 1. and Beza, Confess. Fid. c. v. ; by the Huguenots, in their Catechism ; by the Scotch, in their Profession of 1568 ; by the church of England, Art. 18 ; by the celebrated bishop Pearson, &c. The last named writes thus : " Christ never appointed two ways to heaven ; nor did he build a church, to save some, and make another institution for other men's salvation. As none were saved from the deluge but such as were within the ark of Noah—so none shall ever escape the eternal wrath of God, which belong not to the church of God."—Exposit. of Creed, p. 349.   11*

thematized the several heretics and schismatics that have dog-
matized in succession, whatever has been the quality of their
errors, or the pretext for their disunion.

I am, dear sir, &c.

J. M.

LETTER XV.

To JAMES BROWN, Esq. &c.

PROTESTANT DISUNION.

Dear Sir,

In the inquiry I am about to make respecting the church or
society of Christians, to which this mark of unity belongs, it
will be sufficient for my purpose to consider, that of Protestants, on one hand, and that of Catholics on the other. To speak
properly, however, it is an absurdity to talk of the *church or
society of Protestants ;* for the term PROTESTANT expresses
nothing positive, much less any union or association among
them : it barely signifies one who *protests* or declares against
some other person or persons, thing or things ; and in the present instance it signifies those who *protest against the Catholic
church.* Hence there may be, and there are, numberless sects
of Protestants, divided from each other in every thing, except
in opposing their true mother, the Catholic church. St. Austin
reckons up ninety heresies which had protested against the
church before his time, that is, during the first four hundred
years of her existence; and ecclesiastical writers have counted
about the same number, who rose up since that period, down
to the era of Luther's protestation, which took place early in
the sixteenth century : whereas, from the last mentioned era, to
the end of the same century, Staphylus and cardinal Hosius
enumerated two hundred and seventy different sects of Protestants : and, alas ! how have Protestant sects, beyond reckoning
and description, multiplied, during the last two hundred years !
Thus has the observation of the above cited holy father been
verified in modern, no less than it was in former ages, where
he exclaims : "Into how many morsels have those sects been
broken who have divided themselves from the unity of the

church !"* You are not ignorant that the illustrious Bossuet has written two considerable volumes on the *Variations of the Protestants ;* chiefly on those of the Lutheran and the Calvinistic pedigrees. Numerous other variations, dissensions, and mutual persecutions, even to the extremity of death,† which have taken place among them, I have had occasion to mention in my former letters and other works.‡ I have also quoted the lamentations of Calvin, Dudith, and other heads of the Protestants, on the subject of these divisions. You will recollect, in particular, what the latter writes concerning those differences; " Our people are carried away by every wind of doctrine. If you know what their belief is to-day, you cannot tell what it will be to-morrow. Is there one article of religion, in which these churches, who are at war with the Pope, agree together ? If you run over all the articles, from the first to the last, you will not find one which is not held by some of them to be an article of faith, and rejected by others, as an impiety."§

With these and numberless other historical facts of the same nature before his eyes, would it not, dear sir, I appeal to your own good sense, be the extremity of folly for any one to lay the least claim to the mark of unity in favour of Protestants, or to pretend that they who are united in nothing but their hostility towards the Catholic church, can form *the one church* we profess to believe, in the creed ! Perhaps, however, you will say, that the mark of unity, which is wanting among the endless divisions of Protestants in general, may be found in the church to which you belong, the established church of England. I

---

* St. Aug. contra Petolian.

† Luther pronounced the Sacramentarians, namely, the Calvinists, Zuinglians, and those Protestants in general, who denied the real presence of Christ in the sacrament, *heretics,* and *damned souls, for whom it is not lawful to pray.* Epist. ad Arginten. Catech. Parv. Comment in Gen. His followers persecuted Bucer, Melancthon's nephew, with imprisonment, and Crellius to death, for endeavouring to soften their master's doctrine in this point. Mosheim by Maclaine, vol. iv. p. 341—353. Zuinglius, while he deified Hercules, Theseus, &c. condemned the Anabaptists to be drowned, pronouncing this sentence on Felix Mans : " *Qui iterum mergunt mergantur ;*" which sentence was accordingly executed at Zurich. Limborch. Introd. 71. Not content with anathematizing and imprisoning those reformers who dissented from his system, John Calvin caused two of them, Servetus and Gruet, to be put to death. The Presbyterians of Holland and New-England were equally intolerant with respect to other denominations of Protestants. The latter hanged four Quakers, one of them a woman, on account of their religion. In England itself, frequent executions of Anabaptists and other Protestants took place, from the reign of Edward VI. till that of Charles I.; and other less sanguinary persecutions till the time of James II.

‡ LETTERS TO A PREBENDARY, &c.

§ Epist. ad Capiton. inter. Epist. Bezæ.

grant, dear sir, that your communion 'has better pretentions to this, and the other marks of the church, than any other Protestant society has. She is, as our controversial poet sings, " The least *deform'd* because *reform'd* the least."* You will recollect the account I have given, in a former letter,† of the material changes which this church has undergone, at different times, since her first entire formation in the reign of the last Edward, and which place her at variance with herself. You will also remember the proofs I brought of *Hoadlyism,* in other words, of *Socinianism,* that *damnable and cursed heresy,* as this church termed it in her last synod,‡ against some of her most illustrious bishops, archdeacons, and other dignitaries of modern times. These teach, in official charges to the clergy, in consecration sermons, and in publications addressed to the throne, that the church herself is nothing more than a voluntary association of certain people for the benefit of social worship ; that they themselves are in no other sense *ministers of God* than civil officers are ; that Christ has left us no exterior means of grace, and that, of course, baptism and the Lord's Supper (which are declared *necessary for salvation* in the Catechim) produce no spiritual effect at all ; in short, that all mysteries, and among the rest those of the trinity and incarnation, (for denying which, the prelates of the church of England have sent so many Arians to the stake, in the reigns of Edward, Elizabeth, and James I.) are mere nonsense.§ When I had occasion to expose this fatal system, (the professors of which Cranmer and Ridley would have sent, at once, to the stake,) I hoped it was of a local nature, and that defending, as I was in this point, the Articles and Liturgy of the established church as well as my own, I should, thus far, be supported by its dignitaries and other learned members : I found, however, the contrary to be generally the case,‖ and that the irreligious infection was infinitely more extensive than I apprehended. In fact, I found the most celebrated professors of divinity in the universities delivering Dr. Balguy's doctrine to the young clergy in their public lectures, and the

* Dryden, Hind and Panther. 　　　　　　 † Letter viii.

‡ Constitutions and Canons, A. D. 1640. Sparrow's Collect. p. 355.

§ See extracts from the Sermons of Bishop Hoadley, Dr. Balguy, and Dr. Sturges, in Letters to a Prebendary, Let. viii. The most perspicuous and nervous of these preachers, unquestionably, was Dr. Balguy. See his Discourses and Charges preached on public occasions, and dedicated to the king. Lockyer Davis, 1785.

‖ That great ornament of the Episcopal bench, Dr. Horsley, bishop of St. Asaph's, does not fall under this censure ; as he protected the present writer, both in and out of parliament.

most enlightened bishops publishing it in their pastorals and other works.

Among these, the Norrisian professor of theology at Cambridge carries his deference to the archdeacon of Winchester so far, as to tell his scholars : " As I distrust my own conclusions more than his, (Dr. Balguy's,) if you judge that they are not reconcileable, I must exhort you to confide in him rather than me."* In fact, his ideas concerning the mysteries of Christianity, particularly the trinity and our redemption by Christ, and indeed concerning most other theological points, perfectly agree with those of Dr. Balguy. He represents the difference between the members of the established church and the Socinians to consist in nothing but " a few unmeaning words ;" and asserts, that " they need never be upon their guard against each other."† Speaking of the *custom*, as he calls it, " in the Scripture, of mentioning *Father, Son, and Holy Ghost together*, on the most solemn occasions, of which baptism is one," he says, " Did I pretend to understand what I say, I might be a Tritheist or an Infidel, but I could not worship the one true God, and acknowledge Jesus Christ to be Lord of all."‡ Another learned professor of divinity, who is also a bishop of the established church, teaches his clergy " Not to esteem any particular opinion concerning *the trinity, satisfaction*, and original sin, necessary to salvation."§ Accordingly, he equally absolves the *Unitarian* from *impiety* in refusing divine honour to our Blessed Saviour, and " the worshipper of Jesus," as he expresses himself, from *idolatry* in paying it to him, on the score of their common *good intention.*‖ This sufficiently shows what the bishop's own belief was concerning the adorable trinity, and the divinity of the second person of it. I have given, in a former letter, a remarkable passage from the above quoted charge, where bishop Watson, speaking of the doctrines of Christianity, says to his assembled clergy, " I think it *safer* to tell you *where* they are contained than *what they are.* They are contained in the Bible ; and if, in reading that book, your sentiments should be different from those of your neighbour, or *from those of the church*, be persuaded that infallibility appertains as little to you as it does to the church." I have elsewhere exposed the complete Socinianism of bishop Hoadley

---

* Lectures in Divinity, delivered in the university of Cambridge, by J. Hey, D. D. as Norrisian professor, in four volumes, 1797. Vol. ii. p. 104.

† Vol. ii. p. 41.   ‡ Vol. ii. pp. 250, 251.

§ Dr. Watson, bishop of Landaff's Charge, 1795.

‖ Collect. of Theol. Tracts, Pref. p. 17.

and his scholars,* among whom we must reckon bishop Shipley in the first rank.

Another celebrated writer, who was himself a dignitary of the establishment,† arguing, as he does most powerfully, against the consistency and efficacy of public confessions of faith, among Protestants of every denomination, says, that out of a hundred ministers of the establishment, who, every year, subscribe the Articles made " to prevent diversity of opinions," he has reason to believe " that above one-fifth of this number do not subscribe or assent to these Articles in one uniform sense."‡ He also quotes a Right Rev. author who maintains that " No two thinking men ever agreed exactly in their opinion, even with regard to any one article of it."§ He also quotes the famous bishop Burnet, who says, that " The requiring of subscription to the Thirty-nine Articles is a great imposition,‖ and that the greater part of the clergy subscribe the Articles, without ever examining them, and others do it because they must do it, though they can hardly satisfy their consciences about some things in them."¶ He shows that the advocates for subscription, Doctors Nichols, Bennet, Waterland, and Stebbing, all vindicated it on opposite grounds; and he is forced to confess the same thing, with respect to the enemies of subscription, with whom he himself ranks. Dr. Clark pretends there is a salvo in the subscription, namely, *I assent to the articles in as much as they are agreeable to scripture,*** though the judges of England have declared the contrary.†† Dr. Sykes alleges that the Articles were either purposely or negligently made *equivocal*.‡‡ Another writer, whom he praises, undertakes to explain how " these Articles may be subscribed, and consequently believed, by a Sabellian, an orthodox Trinitarian, a Tritheist, and an Arian, so called." After this citation, Dr. Blackburn shrewdly adds : " One would wonder what idea this writer had of *peace*, when he supposed it might be kept by the act of subscription among men of these different judgments."§§ If you will look into Overton's *True Churchman Ascertained*, you will meet with additional proofs of the repugnance of many other dignitaries and distinguished churchmen to the articles of their own church, as well as of their disagreement in faith among themselves. Hence you will not wonder that a numerous body of them should, some years ago, have

---

* Letters to a Prebendary.
† Dr. Blackburn, archdeacon of Cleaveland, author of the Confessional.
‡ Confess. 3 Ed. p. 45. § Dr. Clayton, bishop of Clogher.
‖ Confess. p. 83. ¶ P. 91. ** P. 222. †† P. 183.
‡‡ P. 237. §§ P. 239.

petitioned the legislature to be relieved from the *grievance*, as they termed it, of subscribing these Articles ;* and that we should continually hear of the mutilation of the liturgy by so many of them, to avoid sanctioning those doctrines of their church, which they disbelieve and reject, particularly the Athanasian Creed and the absolution.†

I might disclose a still wider departure from their original confessions of faith, and still more signal dissensions among the different dissenters, and particularly among the old stock of the Presbyterians and Independents, if this were necessary. Most of these, says Dr. Jortin, are now Socinians, though we all know, they heretofore persecuted that sect with fire and sword. The renowned Dr. Priestly not only denied the divinity of Christ, but with horrid blasphemy, accused him of numerous errors, weaknesses, and faults :‡ and when the authority of Calvin, in burning Servetus, was objected to him, he answered, " Calvin was a great man, but, if a little man be placed on the shoulders of a giant, he will be enabled to see farther than the giant himself." The doctrine now preached in the fashionable Unitarian chapels of the metropolis, I understand, greatly resembles that of the late Theophilanthropists of France, instituted by an Infidel, one of the five directors.

The chief question, however, at present is, whether the church of England can lay any claim to the first character or mark of the true church, pointed out in our common creed, that of UNITY ? On this subject I have to observe, that in addition to the dissensions among its members, already mentioned, there are whole societies, not communicating with the ostensible church of England, who make very strong and plausible pretensions to be, each of them, the real church of England. Such are the Non-jurors, who maintain the original doctrine of this church, contained in the Homilies concerning passive obedience and non-resistance, and who adhere to the first ritual of Edward VI.§ Such are the evangelical preachers and their disciples, who insist upon it that pure Calvinism is the creed of

* Particularly in 1772.
† The omission of the Athanasian Creed, in particular, so often took place in the public service, that an act of parliament has just passed, among other things, to enforce the repetition of it. But if the clergymen alluded to really believe that Christ is not God, what is the Legislature doing in forcing them to worship him as God?
‡ Theolog. Reposit. vol. 4.
§ To this church belonged Ken, and the other six bishops, who were deposed at the revolution. Leslie, Collier, Hicks, Bret, and many other chief ornaments of the church of England.

the established church.*　Finally, such are the Methodists, whom professor Hey describes as forming *the old church of England*.†　And, even now, it is notorious that many clergymen preach in the churches in the morning, and in the meeting houses in the evening; while their opulent patrons are purchasing as many church-livings as they can, in order to fill them with incumbents of the same description.　Tell me now, dear sir, whether, from this view ·of the state of the church of England, or from any other fair view which can be taken of it, you will venture to ascribe to it that first mark of the *true church*, which you profess to belong to her, when, in the face of heaven and earth, you solemnly declare, *I believe in ONE Catholic Church?*　Say, is there any single mark or principle of real *unity* in it?　I anticipate the answers your candour will give to these questions.

I am, &c.

J. M

LETTER XVI.

To JAMES BROWN, Esq. &c.

CATHOLIC UNITY.

Dear Sir,

We have now to see whether that first mark of the true church, which we confess in our creeds, but which we have found to be wanting to the Protestant societies, and even to the most ostensible and orderly of them, the established church of England, does or does not appear in that principal and primeval stock of Christianity, called *the Catholic church.*　In case this church, spread, as it is, throughout the various nations of the earth, and subsisting, as it has done, through all ages, since that of Christ and his apostles, should have maintained that religious *unity*, which the modern sects, confined to a single peo-

---

* It is clear from the Articles and Homilies, and still more from the persecution of the assertors of free-will in this country, that the church of England was Calvinistic till the end of the reign of James I. in the course of which he sent Episcopal representatives from England and Scotland to the great Protestant Synod of Dort.　These, in the name of their respective churches, signed that "the faithful who fall into atrocious crimes, do not forfeit justification, or incur damnation."

† Vol. ii. p. 73.

ple, have been unable to preserve, you will allow that it must have been framed by a consummate Wisdom, and protected by an omnipotent Providence.

Now, sir, I maintain it, as a notorious fact, that this original and great church is, and ever has been, strictly ONE in all the above-mentioned particulars, and first in her faith and terms of communion. The same creeds, namely, the Apostles' Creed, the Nicene Creed, the Athanasian Creed, and the Creed of Pope Pius IV. drawn up in conformity with the definitions of the Council of Trent, are every where recited and professed, to the strict letter; the same articles of faith and morality are taught in all our catechisms; the same rule of faith, namely, the revealed Word of God, contained in Scripture and tradition, and the same expositor and interpreter of this rule, the Catholic church speaking by the mouth of her pastors, are admitted and proclaimed by all Catholics throughout the four quarters of the globe, from Ireland to Chili, and from Canada to India. You may convince yourself of this any day, at the Royal Exchange, by conversing with intelligent Catholic merchants, from the several countries in question. You may satisfy yourself respecting it, even by interrogating the poor illiterate Irish, and other Catholic foreigners, who traverse the country in various directions. Ask them their belief as to the fundamental articles of Christianity, the unity and trinity of God, the incarnation and death of Christ, his divinity, and atonement for sin by his passion and death, the necessity of baptism, the nature of the blessed sacrament; question them on these and other such points, but with kindness, patience, and condescension, particularly with respect to their language and delivery, and, I will venture to say, you will not find any essential variation in the answers of most of them; and much less such as you will find by proposing the same questions to an equal number of Protestants, whether learned or unlearned, of the self-same denomination. At all events, the Catholics, if properly interrogated, will confess their belief in one comprehensive article; namely, this, *I believe whatever the holy Catholic church believes and teaches.*

Protestant divines, at the present day, excuse their dissent from the Articles which they subscribe and swear to, by reason of their alleged antiquity and obsoleteness,* though none of them are yet quite two centuries and a half old,† and they

* Dr. Hey's Lectures on Divinity, vol. ii. pp. 49, 50, 51, &c.
† The 39 Articles were drawn in 1562, and confirmed by the queen and the sishops in 1571.

12

feel no difficulty in avowing that "a tacit reformation," since
the first pretended reformation, has taken place among them.[*]
This alone is a confession that their church *is not one and the
same;* whereas all Catholics believe as firmly in the doctrinal
decisions of the council of Nice, passed fifteen hundred years
ago, as they do in those of the council of Trent, confirmed in
1564, and other still more recent decisions; because the Catholic church, like its divine Founder, *is the same yesterday, to-day,
and for ever.* Heb. xiii. 8.

Nor is it in her *doctrine* only, that the Catholic church is
one and the same; she is also uniform in whatever is essential
in her *liturgy.* In every part of the world, she offers up the
same unbloody sacrifice of the holy mass, which is her chief act
of divine worship; she administers the same seven sacraments,
provided by infinite wisdom and mercy for the several wants of
the faithful; the great festivals of our redemption are kept
holy on the same days, and the apostolical fast of Lent is every
where proclaimed and observed. In short, such is the unity of
the Catholic church, that when Catholic priests or laymen,
landing at one of the neighbouring ports, from India, Canada,
or Brazil, come to my chapel,[†] I find them capable of joining
with me in every essential part of the divine service.

Lastly, as a regular, uniform, ecclesiastical constitution and
government, and a due subordination of its members, are requisite to constitute a uniform church, and to preserve unity of
doctrine and liturgy in it, so these are undeniably evident in the
Catholic church, and in her alone. She is, in the language of
St. Cyprian, "The habitation of peace and unity,"[‡] and in
that of the inspired text, *like an army in battle array.*§ Spread,
as the Catholics are, over the face of the earth, according to
my former observation, and disunited, as they are in every
other respect, they form one uniform body in the order of religion. Whether roaming in the plains of Paraguay, or confined in the palaces of Pekin, each simple Catholic, in point of
ecclesiastical economy, is subject to his pastor; each pastor
submits to his bishop, and each bishop acknowledges the supremacy of the successor of St. Peter, in matters of faith, morality,
and spiritual jurisdiction. In case of error, or insubordination,
which, from the frailty and malice of the human heart, must,
from time to time, disturb her, there are found canons and ec
clesiastical tribunals, and judges, to correct and put an end to

* Hey, p. 48.
† At Winchester, where the writer resided when this letter was written.
‡ "Domicilium pacis et unitatis." St. Cyp.　　　　　§ Cent. vi. 4.

the evil, while similar evils in other religious societies are found to be interminable.

I have said little or nothing of the varieties of Protestants in regard to their liturgies and ecclesiastical governments, because these matters being very intricate and obscure, as well as diversified, would lead me too far a-field for my present plan. It is sufficient to remark, that the numerous Protestant sects expressly disclaim any union with each other in these points. That a great proportion of them reject every species of liturgy and ecclesiastical government whatever, and that, in the church of England herself, very many of her dignitaries, and other distinguished members, express their pointed disapprobation of certain parts of her liturgy, no less than of her Articles,* and that none of them appear to stand in awe of any authority, except that which is enforced by the civil power. Upon a review of the whole matter of *Protestant disunion* and *Catholic unity*, I am forced to repeat with Tertullian, " It is the character of error to vary; but when a tenet is found to be one and the same among a great variety of people, it is to be considered not as an error but as a divine tradition."†

I am, dear sir, &c.

J. M.

---

* Archdeacon Paley very naturally complains, that " the doctrine of the Articles of the church of England," which he so pointedly objects to, " are interwoven, with much industry, into her forms of public worship." I have not met with a Protestant bishop, or other eminent divine, from archbishop Tillotson down to the present bishop of Lincoln, who approves altogether of the Athanasian Creed, which, however, is appointed to be said or sung on thirteen chief festivals in the year.

† De Præscrip. contra Hær. The famous bishop Jewel, in excuse for the acknowledged variations of his own church, objects to Catholics that there are varieties in theirs; namely, some of the friars are dressed in black, and some in white, and some in blue: that some of them live on meat, and some on fish, and some on herbs: they have also disputes in their schools, as Dr. Porteus also remarks; but they both omit to mention, that these disputes are not about articles of faith.

LETTER XVII.

From JAMES BROWN, Esq. &c.

OBJECTIONS TO THE CLAIM OF EXCLUSIVE SALVATION.

Reverend Sir,

I am too much taken up myself with the present subject of your letters, willingly to interrupt the continuation of them: but some of the gentlemen, who frequent New Cottage, having communicated your three last to a learned dignitary who is upon a visit in our neighbourhood, and he having made certain remarks upon them, I have been solicited by those gentlemen to forward them to you. The terms of our correspondence render an apology from me unnecessary, and still more the conviction that I believe you entertain of my being, with sincere respect and regard,

Rev. Sir, &c.
JAMES BROWN.

Extract of a Letter from the Rev. N. N. Prebendary of N. to Mr. N.

It is well known to many Roman Catholic gentlemen, with whom I have lived in habits of social intercourse, that I was always a warm advocate for their emancipation, and that, so far from having any objections to their religion, I considered their hopes of future bliss as well founded as my own. In return, I thought I saw in them a corresponding liberality and charity. But these letters which you have sent me from the correspondent of your society at Winchester, have quite disgusted me with their bigotry and uncharitableness. In opposition to the Chrysostomes and Augustines, whom he quotes so copiously, for his doctrine of exclusive salvation, I will place a modern bishop of my church, no way inferior to them, Dr. Watson, who says, " Shall we never be freed from the narrow-minded contentions of bigots, and from the insults of men who *know not what spirit they are of,* when they stint the Omnipotent in the exercise of his mercy, and bar the doors of heaven against every sect but their own? Shall we never learn to think more humbly of ourselves and less despicably of others ; to believe that the Father of the Universe accommodates not his judgments to the wretched wranglings of pedantic theologues; but that every one, who, with an honest intention, and to the best of his abilities, seeketh truth, whether he findeth it or not, and worketh righteousness, will be accepted of by him?"* These, sir, are exactly my sentiments, as they were those of the illustrious Hoadley, in his celebrated sermon, which had the effect of stifling most of the remaining bigotry in the established church.† There is not any prayer which I more frequently or fervently repeat than that of the liberal minded poet, who himself passed for a Roman Catholic, particularly the following stanza of it :

> " Let not this weak and erring hand
> Presume thy bolts to throw,
> And deal damnation round the land
> On each I judge thy foe."‡

I hope your society will require its Popish correspondent, before he writes any more letters to it on other subjects, to answer what our prelate and his own poet have advanced against the bigotry and uncharitableness of excluding Christians of any denomination from the mercies of God and everlasting happiness. He may assign whatever marks he pleases of the true church, but I, for my part, shall ever consider charity as the only sure mark of this, conformably with what Christ says : *By this shall all know that ye are my disciples, if ye have love one to another.* John xiii. 35.

LETTER XVIII.

To *JAMES BROWN*, Esq. &c.

OBJECTIONS ANSWERED.

DEAR SIR,

In answer to the objections of the Reverend prebendary to my letters on the mark of *unity* in the true church, and the ne-

* Bishop Watson's Theolog. Tracts, Pref. p. 17.
† Bishop Hoadley's Sermon *on the Kingdom of Christ*. This made the choice of religions a thing indifferent, and subjected the whole business of religion to the civil power. Hence sprung the famous Bangorian Controversy, which, when on the point of ending in a censure upon Hoadley from the Convocation, the latter was interdicted by ministry, and has never since, in the course of a hundred years, been allowed to meet again.
‡ Pope's Universal Prayer.

cessity of being incorporated in this church, I must observe, in the first place, that nothing disgusts a reasoning divine more than vague charges of *bigotry* and *intolerance,* inasmuch as they have no distinct meaning, and are equally applied to all sects and individuals, by others, whose religious opinions are more lax than their own. These odious accusations which your churchmen bring against Catholics, the Dissenters bring against you, who are equally loaded with them by Deists, as these are, in their turn, by Atheists and Materialists. Let us then, dear sir, in the serious discussions of religion, confine ourselves to language of a defined meaning, leaving vague and tinsel terms to poets and novelists.

It seems, then, that bishop Watson, with the Rev. N. N. and other fashionable latitudinarians of the day, are indignant at the idea of " stinting the Omnipotent in the exercise of his mercy, and barring the doors of heaven against any sect," however heterodox or impious. Nevertheless, in the very passage which I have quoted, they themselves *stint* this mercy to those who " work righteousness," which implies a restraint on men's passions. Methinks I now hear some epicure Dives or elegant libertine retorting on these liberal, charitable, divines, in their own words, *Pedantic theologues, narrow minded bigots, who stint the Omnipotent in the exercise of his mercy, and bar the doors of heaven* against me, for following the impulse which he himself has planted in me ! The same language may, with equal justice, be put into the mouth of Nero, Judas Iscariot, and of the very demons themselves. Thus, in pretending to magnify God's mercy, these men would annihilate his justice, his sanctity, and his veracity ! Our business, then, is, not to form arbitrary theories concerning the divine attributes, but to attend to what he himself has revealed concerning them and the exercise of them. What words can be more express than those of Christ, on this point, *He that believeth and is baptized shall be saved ; but he that believeth not shall be damned ! *Mark xvi. 16, or than those of St. Paul : *Without faith it is impossible to please God,* Heb. xi. 6. Conformably to this doctrine, the same apostle classes *heresies* with *murder and adultery ;* concerning which he says, *they who do such things shall not inherit the kingdom of God,* Gal. v. 20, 21. Accordingly, he orders that *a man, who is a heretic,* shall be *rejected,* Tit. iii. 10, and the apostle of charity, St. John, forbids the faithful to *receive him into their houses ;* or even to *bid him God speed who bringeth not this doctrine of Christ,* 2 John i. 10. This apostle acted up to his rule, with respect to the treatment of persons out of the church, when he hastily withdrew from a public building, in which he met the heretic Cerinthus, " lest," as he said, " it should fall down upon him."*

I have given, in a former letter, some of the numberless passages in which the holy fathers speak home to the present point, and, as these are far more expressive and emphatical than what I myself have said upon it, I presume they have chiefly contributed to excite the bile of the Rev. prebendary. However he may slight these venerable authorities, yet, as I am sure that you, sir, reverence them, I will add two more such quotations, on account of their peculiar appositeness to the present point, from the great doctor of the fifth century, St. Augustine. He says : " All the assemblies, or rather. divisions, who call themselves churches of Christ, but which, in fact, have separated themselves from the congregation of unity, do not belong to the true church. They might indeed belong to her, if the Holy Ghost could be divided against himself : but as this is impossible, they do not belong to her."† In like manner, addressing himself to certain sectaries of his time, he says : " If our communion is the church of Christ, yours is not so : for *the church of Christ is one, whichsoever she is;* since it is said of her, *My dove, my undefiled is one; she is the only one of her mother.*" Cantic. vi. 9.

But, setting aside Scripture and tradition, let us consider this matter, as bishop Watson and his associates affect to do, on the side of natural reason alone. These modern philosophers think it absurd to suppose that the Creator of the Universe concerns himself about what we poor mortals do or do not believe ; or, as the bishop expresses himself, that he " accommodates his judgments to the wrangling of pedantic theologues." With equal plausibility certain ancient philosophers have represented it as unworthy the Supreme Being to busy himself about the actions of such reptiles as we are in his sight ; and thus have opened a door to an unrestrained violation of his eternal and immutable laws ! In opposition to both these schools, I maintain, as the clear dictates of reason, that as God is the author, so he is necessarily the supreme Lord and Master of all beings, with their several powers and attributes, and therefore of those noble and distinguishing faculties of the human soul, *reason* and *free will;* that he cannot divest himself of this supreme dominion, or render any being or any faculty independent of himself or of his high laws, any more than he can cease to

* S. Iren. l. iii. Euseb. Hist. l. iii.　　† De Verb. Dom. Serm. ii.

O

be God ; that, of course, he does and must require our reason to believe in his divine revelations, no less than our will to submit to his supreme commands ; that he is just, no less than he is merciful, and therefore that due atonement must be made to him for every act of disobedience to him, whether by disbelieving what he has said, or by disobeying what he has ordered. I advance a step further, in opposition to the Hoadley and Watson school, by asserting, as a self-evident truth, that there being a more deliberate and formal opposition to the Most High, in saying, *I will not believe what thou hast revealed*, than in saying, *I will not practice what thou hast commanded*, so, *cæteris paribus*, WILFUL infidelity and heresy involve greater guilt than immoral frailty.

You will observe, dear sir, that in the preceding passage, I have marked the word *wilful ;* because Catholic divines and the holy fathers, at the same time that they strictly insist on the necessity of adhering to the doctrine and communion of the Catholic church, make an express exception in favour of what is termed *invincible ignorance*, which occurs, when persons out of the true church are sincerely and firmly resolved, in spite of all worldly allurements on one hand, and opposition to the contrary on the other, to enter into it, if they could find it out, and when they use their best endeavours for this purpose. This exception, in favour of the *invincibly ignorant*, is made by the same St. Austin who so strictly insists on the general rule. His words are these : " The apostle has told us *to reject a man that is a heretic :* but those who defend a false opinion, without pertinacious obstinacy, especially if they have not themselves invented it, but have derived it from their parents, and who seek the truth with anxious solicitude, being sincerely disposed to renounce their error as soon as they discover it, such persons are not to be deemed heretics."[*] Our great controvertist, Bellarmine, asserts, that such Christians, " in virtue of the disposition of their hearts, belong to the Catholic church."[†]

Who the individuals, exteriorly of other communions, but by the sincerity of their dispositions, belonging to the Catholic church, who, and in what numbers they are, it is for the Searcher of hearts, our future Judge, alone to determine : far be it from me, and from every other Catholic, to " deal damnation" on any person in particular : still thus much, on the grounds already stated, I am bound, not only in truth, but also in charity, to say and to proclaim, that nothing short of the sincere dis-

---

[*] Epist. ad Episc. Donat.   [†] Controv. tom. ii. lib. iii. c. 0.

position in question, and the actual use of such means as Providence respectively affords for discovering the true church to those who are out of it, can secure their salvation; to say nothing of the Catholic sacraments and other helps for this purpose, of which such persons are necessarily deprived.

I just mentioned the virtue of charity; and I must here add, that on no one point are latitudinarians and genuine Catholics more at variance than upon this. The former consider themselves charitable, in proportion as they pretend to open the gate of heaven to a greater number of religionists of various descriptions: but, unfortunately, *they are not possessed of the keys of that gate;* and when they fancy they have opened the gate as wide as possible, it still remains as *narrow*, and the *way to it as strait*, as our Saviour describes these to be in the Gospel, *Mat.* vii. 14. Thus they lull men into a fatal indifference about the truths of revelation, and a false security as to their salvation. Genuine Catholics, on the other hand, are persuaded, that as there is but *one God, one faith, and one baptism*, Ephes. iv. 5. so there is but ONE SHEEP-FOLD, namely, ONE CHURCH. Hence, they omit no opportunity of alarming their wandering brethren on the danger they are in, and of bringing them into this *one fold of the one Shepherd*, John x. 16. To form a right judgment in this case, we need but ask, Is it charitable or uncharitable in the physician, to warn his patient of his danger in eating unwholesome food? Again, is it charitable or uncharitable in the *watchman who sees the sword coming to sound the trumpet of alarm?* Ezech. xxxiii. 6.

But to conclude, the Rev. prebendary, with most modern Protestants, may continue to assign his latitudinarianism, which admits all religions to be right, thus dividing *truth*, that is essentially indivisible, as a mark of the truth of his sect; in the meantime, the Catholic church ever will maintain, as she ever has maintained, that there is only *one faith* and *one true church*, and that this her uncompromising firmness, in retaining and professing this unity, is the first mark of her being this church. The subject admits of being illustrated by the well known judgment of the wisest of men. Two women dwelt together, each of whom had an infant son; but, one of these dying, they both contended for possession of the living child, and carried their cause to the tribunal of Solomon. He, finding them equally contentious, ordered the infant they disputed about to be cut in two, and one-half of it to be given to each of them; which order the *pretended mother* agreed to, exclaiming, *Let it be neither mine nor thine, but divide it. Then spake the woman, whose the*

*living child was, unto the king; for her bowels yearned upon
her son, and she said, O, my lord, give her the living child, and
in no wise slay it.   Then the king answered and said, Give her
the living child, and in no wise slay it ; SHE IS THE MO-
THER THEREOF!*   1 Kings iii. 26, 27.

I am, Dear Sir, &c.

J. M.

LETTER XIX.

To JAMES BROWN, Esq. &c.

ON SANCTITY OF DOCTRINE.

Dear Sir,

THE second mark by which you, as well as I, describe the
church in which you believe, when you repeat the Apostles'
Creed, is that of SANCTITY : we, each of us, say, *I believe
in the HOLY Catholic church.*   Reason itself tells us, that the
God of purity and sanctity could not institute a religion destitute of this character ; and the inspired apostle assures us, that
*Christ loved the church, and gave himself for it ; that he might
sanctify and cleanse it, with the washing of water, by the Word ;
that he might present it to himself a glorious church, not having
spot or wrinkle.*   Ephes. v. 25. 27.   The comparison which I
am going to institute between the Catholic church and the
leading Protestant societies in the article of *sanctity,* will be
made on these four heads : 1st. The *doctrine* of holiness ; 2dly.
The *means* of holiness ; 3dly. The *fruits* of holiness ; and,
lastly, The *divine testimony* of holiness.

To consider, first, the doctrine of the chief Protestant communions : this is well known to have been originally grounded
in the pernicious and impious principles, that God is the author
and necessitating cause, as well as the everlasting punisher, of
sin ; that man has no free will to avoid sin ; and that justification and salvation are the effects of an enthusiastic *persuasion,* under the name of *faith,* that the person is actually
justified and saved, without any real belief in the revealed
truths, without hope, charity, repentance for sin, benevolence to our fellow-creatures, loyalty to our king and country, or any other virtues, all which were censured by the first
reformers, as they are by the strict Methodists still, under the

name of *works*, and by many of them declared to be even hurtful to salvation. It is asserted, in the *Harmony of Confessions*, a celebrated work, published in the early times of the Reformation, that "all the confessions of the Protestant churches teach this primary article (of justification) ,with a holy consent;" which seems to imply, says archdeacon Blackburn, " that this was the single article in which they all did agree."* Bishop Warburton expressly declares, that " Protestantism was built upon it :"† and yet, " what impiety can be more execrable," we may justly exclaim with Dr. Balguy, " than to make God a tyrant !"‡ And what lessons can be taught more immoral, than that men are not required to repent of their sins to obtain their forgiveness, nor to love either God or man to be sure of their salvation !

To begin with the father of the Reformation, Luther teaches that " God works the evil in us as well as the good," and that " the great perfection of faith consists in believing God to be just, although, *by his own will, he necessarily renders us worthy of damnation, so as to seem to take pleasure in the torments of the miserable.*"§ Again he says, and repeats it, in his work *De Servo Arbitrio*, and his other works, that " free will is an empty name ;" adding, " If God foresaw that Judas would be a traitor, Judas *necessarily* became a traitor : nor was it in his power to be otherwise."‖ " Man's will is like a horse : if God sit upon it, it goes as God would have it ; if the devil ride it, it goes as the devil would have it : nor can the will choose its rider, but each of them strives which shall get possession of it."¶ Conformably to this system of necessity he teaches, " Let this be your rule in interpreting the Scriptures ; whenever they command any good work, do you understand that they forbid it, because you cannot perform it."** " Unless faith be without the least good work, it does not justify : it is not faith."†† " See how rich a Christian is, since he cannot lose his soul, do what he will, unless he refuses to believe : for no sin can damn him but unbelief."‡‡ Luther's favourite disciple and bottle companion, Amsdorf, whom he made bishop of Nauburg, wrote a book, expressly to prove that good works are not only *unnecessary*, but that they are *hurtful* to salvation ; for which doctrine

* Archdeacon Blackburn's Confessional, p. 16.
† Doctrine of Grace, cited by Overton, p. 31.
‡ Discourses, p. 59.
§ Luth. Opera, ed. Wittemb. tom. ii. fol. 437.
‖ De Serv. Arbit. fol. 460.   ¶ Ibid. tom. ii.
** Ibid. tom. iii. fol. 171.   †† Ibid. tom. i. fol. 391.
‡‡ De Captiv. Babyl. tom. ii. fol. 74.

he quotes his master's works at large.* Luther himself made so great account of this part of his system which denies free will, and the utility and possibility of good works, that, writing against Erasmus upon it, he affirms it to be the *hinge* on which the whole turns, declaring the questions about the Pope's supremacy, purgatory, and indulgences, to be trifles, rather than subjects of controversy.† In a former letter I quoted a remarkable passage from this patriarch of Protestantism, in which he pretends to prophesy that this article of his, shall subsist for ever, in spite of all the emperors, Popes, kings, and devils; concluding thus : " If they attempt to weaken this article, may hell-fire be their reward ; let this be taken for an inspiration of the Holy Ghost, made to me, Martin Luther."

However, in spite of these prophecies and curses of their father, the Lutherans in general, as I have before noticed, shocked at the impiety of this his primary principle, soon abandoned it, and even went over to the opposite impiety of Semi-pelagianism, which attributes to man the *first motion*, or cause of conversion and sanctification. Still it will always be true to say, that Lutheranism itself originated in the impious doctrine described above.‡ As to the second branch of the Reformation, Calvinism, where it has not sunk into Latitudinarianism or Socinianism,§ it is still distinguished by this impious system. To give a few passages from the works of this second patriarch of Protestants, Calvin says : " God requires nothing of us but faith ; he asks nothing of us, but that we believe."‖ " I do not hesitate to assert that the will of God makes all things necessary."¶ " It is plainly wrong to seek for any other cause of damnation than the hidden counsels of God."** " Men, by the free will of God, without any demerit of their own, are predestinated to eternal death."†† It is useless to cite the disciples of Calvin, Beza, Zanchius, &c. as they all stick close to the doctrine of their master, still I will give the following remarkable passage from the works of the renowned Beza : " Faith is peculiar to the elect, and consists in an absolute dependence each one has on the certainty of his election, which implies an assurance of his perseverance. Hence we have it in our power to

<hr>

* See Brierley's Protest. Apol. 393. See also Mosheim and Maclaine, Eccles. Hist. vol. vi. pp. 324, 328.

† See the passage, extracted from the work *De Servo Arbitrio*, in Letters to a Prebendary, Letter V.

‡ Bossuet's Variat. l. viii. pp. 23, 54, &c. Mosheim and Maclaine, vol. v. p. 446, &c.   § Ibid. p. 458.

‖ Calv. in Joan. vi. Rom. i. Galat. ii.

¶ Instit. l. iii. c. 23.   ** Ibid.   †† Ibid.

would have greatly strengthened the system of Calvinism; whereas it is from the termination of it, which corresponds with the concluding part of the reign of James I. that we are to date the decline of it, especially in England.* Still greater numbers of its adherents, under the name of Calvinists, and professing, not without reason, to maintain the original tenets of the church of England, subsist in this country, and their ministers arrogate to themselves the title of *Evangelical Preachers.* In like manner the numerous and diversified societies of Methodists, whether Wesleyans or Whitfieldites, Moravians or Revivalists, New Itinerants or Jumpers,† are all partisans of the impious and immoral system of Calvin. The founder of the first mentioned branch of these sectaries witnessed the follies and crimes which flowed from it, and tried to reform them by means of a laboured but groundless distinction.‡

After all, the first and most sacred branch of holy doctrine consists in those articles which God has been pleased to reveal concerning his own divine nature and operations, namely, the articles of *the unity and trinity of the Deity*, and of *the incarnation, death, and atonement of the consubstantial Son of God*. It is admitted, that these mysteries have been abandoned by the Protestants of Geneva, Holland, and Germany. With respect to Scotland, a well informed writer says : " It is certain that Scotland, like Geneva, has run from high Calvinism to almost as high Arianism or Socinianism : the exceptions, especially in the cities, are few." It will be gathered from many passages, which I have cited in my former letters, how widely extended throughout the established church is that "*tacit reform*," which a learned professor of its theology signifies to be the same thing with Socinianism. A judgment may also be formed of the prevalence of this system, by the act of July 21, 1813, exempting the professors of it from the penalties to which they were before subject. And yet this system, as I have before observed, is pronounced by the church of England, in her last made canons. " damnable and cursed heresy, being a complication of many former heresies and contrariant to the articles of religion now established in the church of England."§ I say nothing of the numerous Protestant victims, who have been burnt at the stake in this country, during the reigns of Edward VI. Elizabeth, and James I. for the errors in question, except to censure the incon-

---

* Moshiem and Maclaine, vol. v. pp. 369, 389.
† See Evans's Sketch of all Religions.
‡ Postscript, p. 56.
§ Constit. and Can. A. D. 1640.

sistency and cruelty of the proceeding : all that I had occasion
to show was, that most Protestants, and, among the rest, those
of the English church, instead of uniformly maintaining at all
times the same *holy doctrine*, heretofore abetted an impious and
immoral system, namely, Calvinism, which they have since been
constrained to reject, and that they have now compromised with
impieties, which formerly they condemned as " damnable heresies," and punished with fire and faggot.

But it is time to speak of the doctrine of the Catholic church.
If this was once *holy*, namely, in the apostolic age, it is *holy*
still ; because the church never changes her doctrine, nor suf-
fers any persons in her communion to change it, or to question
any part of it. Hence, the adorable mysteries of the trinity,
the incarnation, &c. taught by Christ and his apostles, and defined by the four first general councils, are now as firmly believed by every real Catholic, throughout her whole communion, as they were when those councils were held. Concerning
the article of man's justification, so far from holding the impious
and absurd doctrines imputed to her by her unnatural children,
(who sought for a pretext to desert her,) she rejects, she condemns, she anathematizes them ! It is then false, and notoriously false, that Catholics believe, or in any age did believe, that
they could justify themselves by their own proper merits ; or
that they can do the least good, in the order of salvation, without the grace of God, merited for them by Jesus Christ ; or that
we can deserve this grace, by any thing we have the power of
doing ; or that leave to commit sin, or even the pardon of any
sin, which has been committed, can be purchased of any person
whomsoever ; or that the essence of religion and our hopes of
salvation consist in forms and ceremonies, or in other exterior
things. These, and such other calumnies, or rather blasphemies,
however frequently or confidently repeated in popular sermons
and controversial tracts, there is reason to think are not really
believed by any Protestant of learning.* In fact, what ground
is there for maintaining them ? Have they been defined by our
councils ? No : they have been condemned by them, and particularly by that of Trent. Are they taught in our catechisms,

* The Norrisian Professor, Dr. Hey, says: " The reformed have departed
so much from the rigour of their doctrine about faith, and the Romanists from
theirs about good works, that there seems very little difference between them."
Lect. vol. iii. p. 262. True, most of the reformers, after building their religion
on *faith alone*, have now gone into the opposite heresy of *Pelagianism*, or at
least *Semi-Pelagianism :* but Catholics hold exactly the same tenets regarding
good works, which they ever held, and which were always very different from
what Dr. Hey describes them to have been. Vol. iii. p. 261.

such as the *Catechismus ad Parochos,* the *General Catechism* of Ireland, the *Douay Catechism;* or in our books of devotion, for example, those written by an à Kempis, a Sales, a Granada, and a Challoner? No: the contrary doctrine is, in these, and in our other books, uniformly maintained. In a word, the Catholic church teaches, and ever has taught, her children to trust for mercy, grace and salvation, to the merits of Jesus Christ; nevertheless she asserts that we have free will, and that this being prevented by divine grace, can and must co-operate to our justification by faith, sorrow for our sins, and other corresponding acts of virtue, which God will not fail to bestow upon us, if we do not throw obstacles in the way of them. Thus is all honour and merit ascribed to the Creator, and every defect and sin attributed to the creature. The Catholic church inculcates moreover, the indispensable necessity of humility as a virtue, by which, says St. Bernard, "from a thorough knowledge of ourselves we become little in our own estimation," as the ground-work of all other virtues. I mention this Catholic lesson, in particular, because however strongly it is enforced by Christ and his disciples, it seems to be quite overlooked by Protestants, insomuch that they are perpetually *boasting* in their speeches and writings of the opposite vice, *pride.* In like manner, it appears from the above mentioned catechisms and spiritual works, what pains our church bestows in regulating the interior no less than the exterior of her children, by repressing every thought or idea, contrary to religion or morality; of which matter, I perceive little or no notice is taken in the catechisms and tracts of Protestants. Finally, the Catholic church insists upon the necessity of being *perfect even as our heavenly Father is perfect,* Mat. v. 48, by such an entire subjugation of our passions and conformity of our will with that of God, that *our conversation may be in heaven,* while we are yet living here on earth. *Philip.* v. 20.

I am, &c.

J. M.

POSTSCRIPT TO LETTER XIX.

[The Life of the late Rev. John Wesley, founder of the Methodists, which has been written by Dr. Whitehead, Dr. Coke, and others of his disciples, shows, in the clearest light, the errors and contradictions to which even a sincere and religious

13*

mind is subject, that is destitute of the clue to revealed truth, the living authority of the Catholic church, as also the impiety and immorality of Calvinism. At first, that is to say, in the year 1729, Wesley was a modern church of England man, distinguished from other students at Oxford by nothing but a more strict and methodical form of life. Of course his doctrine then was the prevailing doctrine of that church; this he preached in England and carried with him to America, whither he sailed to convert the Indians. Returning, however, to England in 1738, he writes as follows: " For many years I have been tossed about by various winds of doctrine," the particulars of which, and of the different schemes of salvation, which he was inclined to trust in, he details. Falling, at last, however, into the hands of Peter Bohler and his Moravian brethren, who met in Fetter-lane, he became a warm proselyte to their system, declaring at the same time, with respect to his past religion, that *hitherto he had been a Papist without knowing it.* We may judge of his ardour by his exclamation when Peter Bohler left England: " O what a work hath God begun since his (Bohler's) coming to England; such a one as shall never come to an end till heaven and earth shall pass away." To cement his union with this society, and to instruct himself more fully in its mysteries, he made a journey to Hernhuth in Moravia, which is the chief seat of the United Brethren. It was whilst he was a Moravian, namely, " on the 24th of May, 1738, a quarter of an hour before nine in the evening," that John Wesley, by his own account, was " saved from the law of sin and death." This all important event happened " at a meeting house, in Aldergate-street, while a person was reading Luther's Preface to the Galatians." Nevertheless, though he had professed such deep obligations to the Moravians, he soon found out and declared that theirs was not the right way to heaven. In fact he found them, and " nine parts in ten of the Methodists" who adhered to them, " swallowed up in the dead sea of stillness, opposing the ordinances, namely, prayer, reading the Scripture, frequenting the sacrament and public worship, selling their Bibles, &c. in order to rely more fully ' on the blood of the Lamb.' " In short, Wesley abandoned the Moravian connexion, and set up that which is properly his own religion, as it is detailed by Nightingale, in his *Portrait of Methodism.* This happened in 1740, soon after which he broke off from his rival Whitfield: in fact they maintained quite opposite doctrines on several essential points: still the tenet of instantaneous justification, without repentance, charity, or other good works, and the actual feeling and certainty of this and of everlasting happiness, continued to be the essential and vital principles of Wesley's sysem, as they are of the Calvinistic sects in general; till having witnessed the horrible impieties and crimes to which it conducted, he, at a conference or synod of his preachers, in 1744, declared that he and they had " leaned too much to Calvinism and Antinomianism." In answer to the question " What is Antinomianism?" Wesley, in the same conference, answers, " The doctrine which makes void the law through faith. Its main pillars are that Christ abolished the moral law ; that, therefore, Christians are not obliged to keep it ; that Christian liberty, is liberty from obeying the commands of God ; that it is bondage to do a thing because it is commanded, or forbear it because it is forbidden ; that a believer is not obliged to use the ordinances of God, or to do good works, that a preacher ought not to exhort to good works," &c. See here the essential morality of the religion which Wesley had hitherto followed and preached, as drawn by his own pen, and which still continues to be preached by the other sects of Methodists ! We shall hereafter see in what manner he changed it. The very mention, however, of a change in this ground-work of Methodism, inflamed all the Methodist connexions : accordingly, the Hon. and Rev. Mr. Shirley, chaplain to lady Huntingdon, in a circular letter, written at her desire, declared against the *dreadful heresy* of Wesley, which, as he expressed himself, " *injured the foundation of Christianity.*" He, therefore, summoned another conference, which severely censured Wesley. On the other hand, this patriarch was strongly supported, and particularly by Fletcher of Madeley, an able writer, whom he had destined to succeed him, as the head of his connexion. Instead of being offended at his master's change, Fletcher says, " I admire the candour of an old man of God, who, instead of obstinately maintaining an old mistake, comes down like a little child, and acknowledges it before his preachers, whom it is his interest to secure." The same Fletcher published seven volumes of *Checks to Antinomianism*, in vindication of Wesley's change in this essential point of his religion. In these he brings the most convincing proofs and examples of the impiety and immorality, to which the enthusiasm of Antinomian Calvinism had conducted the Methodists. He mentions a highwayman, lately executed in his neighbourhood, who vindicated his crimes upon this principle. He mentions other more odious instances of wickedness, which, to his knowledge, had flowed from it. All these, he says, are represented by their preachers to be " damning sins in Turks

and Pagans, but only spots in God's children." He adds
" There are few of our celebrated pulpits, where more has not
been said *for sin* than *against it !*" He quotes an Hon. M. P.
" once my brother," he says, " but now my opponent," who, in
his published treatise, maintains that " murder and adultery do
not hurt the pleasant children, (the elected,) but even work for
their good :" adding, " My sins may displease God, my person
is always acceptable to him. Though I should outsin Manasses himself, I should not be less a pleasant child, because God
always views me in Christ. Hence, in the midst of adulteries,
murders and incests, he can address me with, *Thou* art all
fair, my love, my undefiled; there is not a spot in thee.
It is a most pernicious error of the schoolmen to distinguish
sins *according to the fact*, not according to the person. Though
I highly blame those who say, *let us sin that grace may abound;*
yet adultery, incest and murder, shall, upon the whole, make
me holier on earth and merrier in heaven !" It only remains
to show in what manner Wesley purified his religious system,
as he thought, from the defilement of Antinomianism. To be
brief, he invented a two-fold mode of justification, one without
repentance, the love of God, or other works; the other, to
which these works were essential: the former was for those who
die soon after their pretended experience of saving faith, the
latter for those who have time and opportunity of performing
them. Thus, to say no more of the system, according to it a
Nero and a Robespierre might have been established in the
grace of God, and in a right to the realms of infinite purity,
without one act of sorrow for their enormities, or so much as an
act of their belief in God !]

LETTER XX.

To JAMES BROWN, Esq.

ON THE MEANS OF SANCTITY.

Dear Sir,

The *efficient cause* of justification, or sanctity, according to the Council of Trent,* is the mercy of God through the merits of Jesus Christ; still, in the usual economy of his grace, he makes use of certain instruments or means, both for conferring and increasing it. The principal and most efficacious of these are THE SACRAMENTS. Fortunately, the established church agrees in the main sense with the Catholic and other Christian churches, when she defines a sacrament to be " an outward and visible sign of an inward and spiritual grace, given unto us, and ordained by Christ himself, as a means whereby we receive the same, and a pledge to assure us thereof."† But, though she agrees with other Protestant communions in reducing the number of these to two, *baptism* and *the Lord's Supper*, she differs with all others, namely, the Catholic, the Greek, the Russian, the Armenian, the Nestorian, the Eutychian, the Coptic, the Ethiopian, &c. all of which firmly maintain, and ever have maintained, as well since as before their respective defections from us, the whole collection of the *seven sacraments*.‡ This fact alone refutes the airy speculations of Protestants concerning the origin of the five sacraments, which they reject, and thus demonstrates that they are deprived of as many divinely instituted instruments or means of sanctity. As these seven channels of grace, though all supplied from the same fountain of Christ's merits, supply, each of them, a separate grace, adapted to the different wants of the faithful, and as each of them furnishes matter of observation for the present discussion, so I shall take a cursory view of them.

The first sacrament, in point of order and necessity, is bap-

---

* Sess. vi. cap. 7.

† Catechism in Com. Prayer.—N. B. The last clause in this definition is far too strong, as it seems to imply, that every person who is partaker of the outward part of a sacrament, necessarily receives the grace of it, whatever may be his dispositions; an impiety which the bishop of Lincoln calumniously attributes to the Catholics. Elements of Theol. vol. ii. p. 436.

‡ This important fact is incontrovertibly proved, in the celebrated work *La Perpetuité de la Foi*, from original documents, procured by Louis XIV. and preserved in the king's library at Paris.

tism.   In fact, no authority can be more express than that of
the Scripture, as to this necessity.   *Except a man be born of
water and of the spirit*, says Christ, *he cannot enter into the
kingdom of God.* John iii. 5.   *Repent*, cries St. Peter, *and be
baptized every one of you, in the name of Jesus, for the remission
of sins.* Acts ii. 38.   *Arise*, answered Ananias to St. Paul, *and
be baptized, and wash away thy sins.* Acts xxii. 16.   This *necessity* was heretofore acknowledged by the church of England,
at least, as appears from her Articles, and still more clearly
from her liturgy,* and the works of her eminent divines.†
Hence, as baptism is valid, by whomsoever it is conferred, the
English church may be said to have been upon an equal footing with the Catholic church, as much as concerns this instrument or means of holiness : but the case is different now, since
that *tacit reformation*, which is acknowledged to have taken
place in her.   This has nearly swept out of her both the belief
of original sin, and of its necessary remedy, baptism.   " That
we are born guilty," the great authority, Dr. Balguy, says, " is
either unintelligible or impossible."   Accordingly, he teaches,
that " the rite of baptism is no more than a *representation* of
our entrance into the church of Christ."   Elsewhere, he says,
" The sign (of a sacrament) is *declaratory*, not *efficient*.‡" Dr.
Hey says, the negligence of the parent, with respect to procuring baptism, " *may* affect the child : to say it *will* affect
him, is to run into the error I am condemning."§   Even the
bishop of Lincoln calls it " an unauthorized principle of Papists, that no person whatsoever can be saved who has not been
baptized."∥   Where the doctrine of baptism is so lax, we may
be sure the practice of it will not be more strict ; accordingly,
we have abundant proofs that, from the frequent and long de-
lays, respecting the administration of this sacrament, which occur in the establishment, very many children die without receiving it ; and that, from the negligence of ministers, as to the
right matter and form of words, many more children receive it
invalidly.   Look, on the other hand, at the Catholic church :
you will find the same importance still attached to this sacred
rite, on the part of the people and the clergy, which is observ-

* Common Prayer.
† See B. Pearson on the Creed. Art. x.   Hooker, Eccl. Polit. B. v. p. 60.
‡ Charge vii. pp. 298, 300.   § Lectures in Divinity, vol. iii. p. 182.
∥ Vol. ii. p. 470.   The learned prelate can hardly be supposed ignorant that
many of our martyrs, recorded in our Martyrology and our Breviary, are expressly declared not to have been *actually* baptized ; or that our divines unanimously teach, that not only the baptism of blood by martyrdom, but also a sincere desire of being baptized, suffices, where the means of baptism are wanting.

able in the Acts of the apostles and in the writings of the holy
fathers; the former being ever impatient to have their children
baptized, the latter equally solicitous to administer it in due
time, and with the most scrupulous exactness. Thus, as matters stand now, the two churches are not upon a level with respect to this first and common means of sanctification : the
members of one have a much greater moral certainty of the remission of that sin in which we were all born, and of their having been heretofore actually received into the church of Christ,
than the members of the others have. It would be too tedious
a task to treat of the tenets of other Protestants on this and the
corresponding matters. Let it suffice to say, that the famous
Synod of Dort, representing all the Calvinistic states of Europe, formerly decided that the children of the elect are includ-
ed in the covenant made with their parents, and thus are exempt from the necessity of baptism, as likewise of faith and
morality; being thus ensured, themselves and all their posterity, till the end of time, of their justification and salvation !*

Concerning the second channel of grace or means of sanctity,
confirmation, there is no question. The church of England,
which, among the different Protestant societies, alone, I believe, lays claim to any part of this rite, under the title of *the
ceremony of laying on of hands*, expressly teaches, at the same
time, that it is *no sacrament*, as not being *ordained by God*, or
an effectual sign of grace.† But the Catholic church, instructed by the solicitude of the apostles to *strengthen* the faith of
those her children who had received it in baptism,‡ and by the
lessons of Christ himself, concerning the importance of receiving that holy spirit, which is communicated in this sacrament,§
religiously retains and faithfully administers it to them, for
the self-same purpose, through all ages. In a word, those who
are true Christians, by virtue of baptism, are not made perfect
Christians, except by virtue of the sacrament of confirmation,
which none of the Protestant societies so much as lays a claim
to.

Of the third sacrament, indeed, *the Lord's Supper*, as they
call it, the Protestant societies, and particularly the church of
England, in her Prayer Book, say great things : nevertheless,
what is it, after all, upon her own showing ? Mere bread and
wine, received in memory of Christ's passion and death, in order to excite the receiver's faith in him : that is to say, it is a

---

* Boesuet, Variat. Book xiv. p. 46.

† Art. xxv.　　　‡ Acts viii. 14.—xix. 2.　　　§ John xvi.

bare *type* or *memorial* of Christ.　Any thing may be instituted
to be the type or memorial of another thing; but certainly the
Jews, in their paschal lamb, had a more lively figure of the
death of Christ, and so have Christians in each of the four
evangelists, than eating bread and drinking wine can be.
Hence, I infer that the communion of Protestants, according to
their belief and practice in this country, cannot be more than a
feeble excitement to their devotion, and an inefficient help to
their sanctification.　But if Christ is to be believed upon his
own solemn declaration, where he says, *Take ye and eat; this
is my body:—drink ye all of this; for this is my blood*, Mat. xxvi.
26.—*My flesh is meat indeed, and my blood is drink indeed*,
John vi. 56.　Then the holy communion of Catholics is, beyond all expression and all conception, not only the most powerful stimulative to our faith, our hope, our love, and our contrition; but also the most efficacious means of obtaining these
and all other graces from the divine bounty.　Those Catholics
who frequent this sacrament with the suitable dispositions, are
the best judges of the truth of what I here say: nevertheless,
many Protestants have been converted to the Catholic church,
from the ardent desire they felt of receiving their Saviour
Christ himself into their bosoms, instead of a bare memorial of
him, and from a just conviction of the spiritual benefits they
would derive from this intimate union with him.

The four remaining instruments of grace, *penance, extreme
unction, order,* and *matrimony*, Protestants, in general, give up
to us, no less than confirmation.　The bishop of Lincoln,* Dr.
Hey,† and other controvertists, pretend that it was Peter Lombard, in the 12th century, who made sacraments of them.　True
it is, that this industrious theologian collected together the different passages of the fathers, and arranged them, with proper
definitions of each subject, in their present scholastic order, not
only respecting the sacraments, but likewise the other branches
of divinity, on which account he is called *the master of the sentences;* but this writer could as soon have introduced Mahometanism into the church as the belief of any one sacrament which
it had not before received as such.　Besides, supposing him to
have deceived the Latin church into this belief, I ask by what
means were the schismatical Greek churches fascinated into it?
In short, though these holy rites had not been endued by Christ
with a sacramental grace, yet, practised as they are in the Ca-

---

* Elem. vol. ii. p. 414.　　　　† Lect. vol. iv. p. 190.

tholic church, they would still be great helps to piety and
Christian morality.

What I have just asserted concerning these five sacraments,
in general, is particularly true, with respect to the sacrament of
penance.   For what does this consist of? and what is the preparation for it, as set forth by all our councils, catechisms, and
prayer books?   There must first be fervent prayer to God for
his light and strength; next an impartial examination of the
conscience, to acquire that most important of all sciences, the
knowledge of ourselves; then true sorrow for our sins, with a
firm purpose of amendment, which is the most essential part of
the sacrament.   After this there must be a sincere exposure of
the state of the interior to a confidential, and at the same time,
a learned, experienced, and disinterested director.   If he could
afford no other benefit to his penitents, yet how inestimable are
those of his making known to them many defects and many duties, which their self-love had probably overlooked, of his
prescribing to them the proper remedies for their spiritual maladies, and of his requiring them to make restitution for every
injury done to each injured neighbour!   But we are well assured that these are far from being the only benefits which the
minister of this sacrament can confer upon the subject of it:
for it was not an empty compliment which Christ paid to his
apostles, when, *Breathing on them, he said to them: Receive ye
the Holy Ghost, whose sins you shall remit, they are remitted,
and whose sins you shall retain, they are retained.*   John xx. 22,
23.   O sweet balm of the wounded spirit! O sovereign restora-
tive of the soul's life and vigour! best known to those who
faithfully use thee, and not unattested by those who neglect and
blaspheme thee!*

It might appear strange, if we were not accustomed to similar
inconsistencies, that those who profess to make Scripture, in its
plain obvious sense, the sole rule of their faith and practice,
should deny *extreme unction* to be a sacrament, the external
sign of which, *anointing the sick*, and the spiritual effect of
which, the *forgiveness of sins*, are so expressly declared by St.
James, in his Epistle v. 14.   Martin Luther, indeed, who had
taken offence at this Epistle, for its insisting so strongly on
good works,† rejected the authority of this Epistle, alleging
that it was " not lawful for an apostle to institute a sacra-

* See the form of ordaining priests in bishop Sparrow's Collect. p. 158, also
the form of absolution, in the visitation of the sick, in the Common Prayer.

† Luther, in the original Jena edition of his works, calls this Epistle "a dry
and chaffy Epistle, unworthy an apostle."

14

ment."*   But, I trust, that you, dear sir, and your conscientious society, will agree with me, that it is more incredible that an apostle of Christ should be ignorant of what he was authorized by him to say and do, than that a profligate German friar should be guilty of blasphemy. Indeed, the church of England, in the first form of her Common Prayer in Edward's reign, enjoined the unction of the sick, as well as the prayer for them.† It was evidently well worthy the mercy and bounty of our divine Saviour, to institute a special sacrament for purifying and strengthening us at the time of our greatest need and terror. Owing to the institution of this, and the two other sacraments penance and the real body and blood of our Lord, it is a fact, that few, very few Catholics die without the assistance of their clergy; which assistance the latter are bound to afford, at the expense of ease, fortune, and life itself, to the most indigent and abject of their flock, who are in danger of death, no less than to the rich and the great: while, on the other hand, very few Protestants, in that extremity, partake at all of the cold rites of their religion; though one of them is declared, in the Catechism, to be " necessary for salvation!"

It is equally strange that a clergy, with such high claims and important advantages as those of the establishment, should deny that the orders of bishops, priests, and deacons, are sacramental, or that the Episcopal form of church government, and of ordaining the clergy, is in preference to any other required by Scripture. In fact, this is telling the legislature and the nation that, if they prefer the less expensive ministry of the Presbyterians or Methodists, there is nothing divine or essential in the ministry itself, which will be injured by the change; and that clergymen may be as validly ordained by the town-crier with his bell, as by the metropolitan's imposition of hands! Nevertheless, this is the doctrine, not only of Hoadley's Socinian school, as I have elsewhere demonstrated,‡ but also of those modern divines and dignitaries, who are the standard of orthodoxy.§ Thus are the clergy of the English church, as well as all other Protestant ministers, by their own confession, destitute of all sacramental grace for performing their functions holily and beneficially.‖ But we know, conformably to the doctrine of St. Paul, in both his Epistles to Timothy, 1 *Tim.* IV.

---

* Luther's works, Jena edition.
† See Collier's Eccles. Hist. vol. ii. p. 257.
‡ Dr. Balguy, Dr. Hey, &c.
§ The bishop of Lincoln's Elem. of Theol. vol. ii. pp. 370, 396.
‖ See Letters to a Prebendary, Letter VIII.

14. 2 *Tim.* i. 6. with the constant doctrine of the Catholic church, and of all other ancient churches, that this grace is conferred on those who are truly ordained and in fit dispositions to receive it. We know, moreover, that the persuasion which the faithful entertain of the divine character and grace of their clergy, gives a great additional weight to their lessons and ministry.—In like manner, with respect to *matrimony*, which the same apostle expressly calls a *sacrament, Ephes.* v. 32, independently of its peculiar grace, the very idea of its sanctity, is a preparation for entering into that state with religious dispositions.

Next to the sacraments of the Catholic church, as helps to holiness and salvation, I must mention her public service. We continually hear the advocates of the establishment crying up the beauty and perfection of their liturgy ;* but, they have not the candour to inform the public that it is all, in a manner, borrowed from the Catholic Missal and Ritual. Of this any one may satisfy himself who will compare the prayers, lessons and Gospels, in these Catholic books, with those in the *Book of Common Prayer.* But, though our service has been thus purloined, it has, by no means been preserved entire : on the contrary, we find it, in the latter, eviscerated of its noblest parts ; particularly with respect to the principal and essential worship of all the ancient churches, the holy mass, which, from a true propitiatory sacrifice, as it stands in all their Missals, is cut down to a mere verbal worship in *The Order for Morning Prayer.* Hence, our James I. pronounced of the latter, that it is *an ill-said mass.* The servants of God had, by his appointment, SACRIFICE both under the law of nature and the written law; it would then be extraordinary, if under the law of grace they were left destitute of this the most sublime and excellent act of religion, which man can offer to his Creator. But we are not left destitute of it : on the contrary, that prophecy of Malachy is fulfilled, *Mal.* i. 11. *In every place from the rising to the setting of the sun, sacrifice is offered and a pure oblation,* even Christ himself, who is really present and mystically offered on our altars in the sacrifice of the mass.

I pass over the solemnity, the order and the magnificence of our public worhip and ritual in Catholic countries, which most candid Protestants, who have witnessed them, allow to be exceedingly impressive, and great helps to devotion, and which,

* Dr. Rennel calls the church liturgy " the most perfect of human compositions and the sacred legacy of the first reformers." Disc. p. 237.

certainly, in most particulars, find their parallel in the worship
and ceremonies of the Old Law, ordained by God himself.
Nevertheless, it is a gross calumny to assert that the Catholic
church does, or ever did make the essence of religion to consist in these externals; and we challenge them to our councils
and doctrinal books in refutation of the calumny. In like manner, I pass over the many private exercises of piety which are
generally practised in regular Catholic families and by individuals, such as daily meditation and spiritual reading, evening
prayers and examination of the conscience, &c. These, it will
not be denied, must be helps to obtain sanctity for those who
are desirous of it.—But I have said more than enough to convince your friends in which of the rival communions the means
of sanctity are chiefly to be found.

I am, Dear Sir, &c.

.   J. M.

———◆———

LETTER XXI.

To JAMES BROWN, Esq.

ON THE FRUITS OF SANCTITY.

DEAR SIR,

THE fruits of sanctity are the virtues practised by those who
are possessed of it. Hence the present question is, whether
these are to be found, for the most part, among the members of
the ancient Catholic church, or among the different innovators,
who undertook to reform it in the sixteenth and seventeenth
centuries? In considering the subject, the first thing which
strikes me is, that all the saints, and even those who are recorded as such in the calendar of the church of England, and in
whose names their churches are dedicated, lived and died strict
members of the Catholic church, and zealously attached to her
doctrine and discipline.* For an example, in this calendar, we
meet with a Pope Gregory, March 12, the zealous assertor of

---

* I must except king Charles I. who is rubricated as a martyr on Jan. 30:
nevertheless, it is confessed that he was far from possessing either the purity of
a saint or the constancy of a martyr: for he actually gave up Episcopacy, and
other essentials of the established religion, by his last treaty in the Isle of Wight.

the papal supremacy,* and other Catholic doctrines; a St.
Benedict, March 21, the patriarch of the western monks and
nuns; a St. Dunstan, May 19, the vindicator of clerical celibacy; a St. Augustine of Canterbury, May 26, the introducer
of the whole system of Catholicity into England, and a venerable Bede, May 27, the witness of this important fact. It is
sufficient to mention the names of other Catholic saints, for
example, David, Chad, Edward, Richard, Elphege, Martin,
Swithun, Giles, Lambert, Leonard, Hugh, Etheldreda, Remi-
gius, and Edmund, all of which are inserted in the calendar,
and give names to the churches of the establishment. Besides
these, there are very many of our other saints, whom all learned
and candid Protestants unequivocally admit to have been such,
for the extraordinary purity and sanctity of their lives. Even
Luther acknowledges St. Anthony, St. Bernard, St. Dominic,
St. Francis, St. Bonaventure, &c. to have been saints, though
avowed Catholics, and defenders of the Catholic church against
the heretics and schismatics of their times. But, independently
of this and of every other testimony, it is certain that the supernatural virtues and heroical sanctity of a countless number
of holy personages of different countries, ranks, professions,
and sexes, have illustrated the Catholic church in every age,
with an effulgence which cannot be disputed or withstood.
Your friends, I dare say, are not much acquainted with the
histories of these brightest ornaments of Christianity: let me
then invite them to peruse them; not in the legends of obsolete
writers, but in a work which, for its various learning and luminous criticism, was commended even by the Infidel Gibbon.
I mean *The Saints' Lives*, in twelve octavo volumes, written by
the late Rev. Alban Butler, president of St. Omer's college
Protestants are accustomed to paint in the most frightful colours
the alleged depravity of the church, when Luther erected his
standard, in order to justify him and his followers' defection
from it: but to form a right judgment in the case, let them read
the works of the contemporary writers, an à Kempis, a Gerson,
an Antoninus, &c. or let them peruse the lives of Vincent Ferrer,
St. Laurence Justinian, St. Francis Paula, St. Philip Neri, St.
Cajetan, St. Teresa, St. Francis Xavier, and of those other
saints, who illuminated the church about the period in question;

* Many Protestant writers pretended that St. Gregory disclaimed the supremacy, because he asserted against John of C. P. that neither he nor any
other prelate ought to assume the title of *Universal Bishop*; but that he claimed and exercised the supremacy, his own works and the history of Bede incontrovertibly demonstrate.

or let them, from the very accounts of Protestant historians, compare, as to religion and morality, archbishop Cranmer with his rival bishop Fisher; protector Seymour with chancellor More, Ann Bullen with Catharine of Arragon, Martin Luther and Calvin with Francis Xavier and cardinal Pole, Beza with St. Francis of Sales, queen Elizabeth with Mary queen of Scots; these contrasted characters having more or less relation with each other. From such a comparison, I have no sort of doubt what the decision of your friends will be concerning them, in point of their respective holiness.

I have heretofore been called upon to consider the virtues and merits of the most distinguished reformers;* and certainly we have a right to expect from persons of this description finished models of virtue and piety. But instead of this being the case, I have shown that patriarch Luther was the sport of his unbridled passions,† pride, resentment, and lust; that he was turbulent, abusive, and sacrilegious, in the highest degree; that he was the trumpeter of sedition, civil war, rebellion, and desolation; and finally, that by his own account, he was the scholar of Satan, in the most important article of his pretended Reformation.‡ I have made out nearly as heavy a charge against his chief followers, Carlostad, Zuinglius, Ochin, Calvin, Beza, and Cranmer. With respect to the last named, who under Edward VI. and his fratricide uncle, the duke of Somerset, was the chief artificer of the Anglican church, I have shown that, from his youthful life in a college, till his death at the stake, he exhibited such a continued scene of libertinism, perjury, hypocrisy, barbarity, (in burning his fellow Protestants,) profligacy, ingratitude, and rebellion, as is, perhaps, not to be matched in history. I have proved that all his fellow-labourers and fellow-sufferers were rebels like himself, who would have been put to death by Elizabeth, if they had not been executed by Mary. I adduced the testimony not only of Erasmus and other Catholics, but also of the gravest Protestant historians, and of the very reformers themselves, in proof that the morals of the people, so far from being changed for the better, by embracing the new religion, were greatly changed for the worse.§ The pretended Reformation, in foreign countries, as

---

* Reflections on Popery, by Dr. Sturges, L. L. D. &c.
† Letters to a Preb. Let. V. p. 178.
‡ Ibid. p. 183, where Satan's conference with Luther, and the arguments by which he induced this reformer to abolish the mass, are detailed, from Luther's works. Tom. vii. p. 228.
§ Letters to a Prebendary, Letter V.

in Germany, the Netherlands, at Geneva, in Switzerland, France, and Scotland, besides producing popular insurrections, sackages, demolitions, sacrileges, and persecution beyond description, excited also open rebellions and bloody civil wars.* In England, where our writers boast of the orderly manner in which the change of religion was carried on, it, nevertheless, most unjustly and sacrilegiously seized upon, and destroyed, in the reign of Henry VIII. six hundred and forty-five monasteries, ninety colleges, and one hundred and ten hospitals, besides the bishopric of Durham; and, under Edward VI. or rather his profligate uncle, it dissolved two thousand three hundred and seventy-four colleges, chapels, or hospitals, in order to make princely fortunes of their property for that uncle and his unprincipled comrades, who, like banditti, quarrelling over their spoils, soon brought each other to the block. Such were the fruits of sanctity, every where produced by this Reformation!

I am, &c.

J. M.

* The Huguenots in Dauphiny alone, as one of their writers confesses, burnt down 900 towns or villages, and murdered 378 priests or religious, in the course of one rebellion. The number of churches destroyed by them throughout France, is computed at 20,000. The history of England's reformation (though this was certainly more orderly than that of other countries) has caused the conversion of many English Protestants: it produced this effect on James II. and his first consort, the mother of queen Mary, and queen Ann. The following is the account which the latter has left of this change, and which is to be found in Dodd's last volume, and in the Fifty Reasons of the duke of Brunswick. " Seeing much of the devotion of the Catholics, I made it my constant prayer that if I were not, I might, before I died, be in the true religion. I did not doubt but that I was so till November last, when, reading a book called *The History of the Reformation, by Dr. Heylin,* which I had heard very much commended, and had been told, if ever I had any doubts in my religion that would settle me: instead of which I found it the description of the horridest sacrileges in the world; and could find no cause why we left the church, but for three, the most abominable ones: 1st, Henry VIII. renounced the Pope, because he would not give him leave to part with his wife and marry another: 2dly, Edward VI. was a child and governed by his uncle, who made his estate out of the church lands: 3dly, Elizabeth not being lawful heiress to the crown, had no way to keep it but by renouncing a church which would not suffer so unlawful a thing. I confess I cannot think the Holy Ghost could ever be in such councils."

R

LETTER XXII.

To Mr. J. TOULMIN.

OBJECTIONS ANSWERED.

DEAR SIR,

I HAVE received your letter, animadverting upon mine to our common friend, Mr. Brown, respecting the fruits of sanctity, as they appear in our respective communions. I observe, you do not contest my general facts or arguments, but resort to objections which have been already answered in these, or in my other letters now before the public. You assert, as a notorious fact, that for several ages, prior to the Reformation, the Catholic religion was sunk into ceremonies and pageantry, and that it sanctioned the most atrocious crimes. In refutation of these calumnies, I have referred to our councils, to our most accredited authors of religion and morality, and to the lives and deaths of our most renowned saints, during the ages in question. I grant, sir, that you hold the same language on this subject that other Protestant writers do; but I maintain that none of them make good their charges, and that their motive for advancing them is to find a pretext for excusing the irreligion of the pretended Reformation. You next extol the alleged sanctity of the Protestant sufferers, called martyrs, in the unhappy persecution of queen Mary's reign. I have discussed this matter at some length in *The Letters to a Prebendary*, and have shown, in opposition to John Fox and his copyists, that some of these pretended martyrs were alive when he wrote the history of their death;* that others of them, and the five bishops in particular, so far from being saints, were notoriously deficient in the ordinary duties of good subjects and honest men ;† that others again were notorious assassins, as Gardener, Flower, and Rough ; or robbers, as Debenham, King, Marsh, Cauches, Gilbert, Massey, &c.‡ while not a few of them retracted their errors, as Bilney, Taylor, Wassalia, and died, to all appearance, Catholics. To the whole ponderous folio of Fox's falsehoods I have opposed the genuine and edifying *Memoirs of Missionary Priests and other Catholics, who suffered death for their Religion* during the reigns of Elizabeth and the Stuarts. Finally, you reproach me with the scandalous lives of some of

* See Letter IV. on Persecution.
† See Letter V. on the Reformation.   ‡ Letter IV.

our Popes, during the middle ages, and of very many Catholics of different descriptions, throughout the church at the present day; and you refer me to the edifying lives of a great number of Protestants, now living, in this country.

My answer, dear sir, in brief, to your concluding objections, is that I, as well as Baronius, Bellarmin, and other Catholic writers, have unequivocally admitted that some few of our pontiffs have disgraced themselves by their crimes, and given just cause of scandal to Christendom;* but I have remarked that the credit of our cause is not affected by the personal conduct of particular pastors, who succeed one another in a *regular way,* in the manner that the credit of yours is by the behaviour of your founders, who professed to have received *extraordinary commission from God to reform religion.*† I acknowledge, with the same unreservedness, that the lives of a great proportion of Catholics in this and other parts of the church, is a disgrace to that *holy* Catholic church which they profess to believe in. Unhappy members of the true religion, *by whom the name of God* (and his holy church) *is blasphemed among the nations!* Rom. ii. 24. Unhappy Catholics, who *live enemies of the cross of Christ, whose end is destruction, who mind only earthly things!* Philip iii. 18. But, *it must needs be that scandals should come : nevertheless, wo to that man by whom the scandal cometh!* Mat. xviii. 7. In short, I bear a willing testimony to the public and private worth of very many of my Protestant countrymen, of different religions, as citizens, as subjects, as friends, as children, as parents, as moral men, and as Christians, in the general sense of the word; still I must say that I find the best of them far short of the *holiness,* which is prescribed in the Gospel and is exemplified in the lives of those saints, whom I have mentioned. On this subject I will quote an authority which I think you will not object to. Dr. Hey says : " In England, I could almost say, we are too little acquainted with contemplative religion.' The monk painted by Sterne, may give us a more favourable idea of it, than our prejudices generally suggest. I once travelled with a *recolet,* and conversed with a *minim* at his convent : and they both had that kind of character which Sterne gives to his monk : that refinement of body and mind; that pure glow of meliorated passion, that polished piety and humanity."‡ In a former letter to your society, I have stated that sincere humility, by which, from a

* See Letter II. on Supremacy.　　　　　　　† Ibid.
‡ Lectures in Divinity, vol. i. p. 364.

thorough knowledge of our sins and misery, we become little in
our own eyes, and try to avoid, rather than to gain the praise
and notice of others, is the very groundwork of all other Christian virtues.   It has been objected to Protestants, ever since the
defection of their arrogant patriarch, Luther, that they have
said little, and have appeared to understand less, of this essential virtue.   I might say the same with respect to the necessity
of an entire subjugation of our other congenial passions, avarice,
lust, anger, intemperance, envy, and sloth, as I have said of
pride and vain glory; but I pass over these, to say a few words
of certain maxims expressly contained in Scripture.   It cannot
then be denied that our Saviour said to the rich young man, *If
thou wilt be perfect, go sell all thou hast and give to the
poor, and thou shalt have treasures in heaven;* or that he declared, on another occasion, *There are eunuchs who have made
themselves eunuchs* (continent) *for the kingdom of heaven's sake.
He that is able to receive it, let him receive it.* Mat. xix. 12.
Now it is notorious that this life of voluntary poverty and perpetual chastity, continues to be vowed and observed by great
numbers of both sexes in the Catholic church; while it is nothing more than a subject of ridicule to the best of Protestants.
Again: " that we ought to fast, is a truth more manifest than it
should here need be proved."   I here use the words of the
church of England, in her Homily iv. p. 11; conformably
with which doctrine, your church enjoins, in her Common
Prayer Book, the same days of fasting and abstinence as the
Catholic church does, namely, the forty days of Lent, the em-
ber days, all the Fridays in the year, &c.; nevertheless, where
is the Protestant to be found, who will submit to the mortifica-
tion of fasting, even to obey his own church?   I may add, that
Christ enjoins *constant prayer,* Luke xviii. 1; conformably to
which injunction, the Catholic church requires her clergy, at
least, from the subdeacon up to the Pope, daily to say the seven
canonical hours, consisting chiefly of Scriptural psalms and
lessons, and which take up in the recital, near an hour and a
half, in addition to their other devotions : now what pretext had
the Protestant clergy, whose pastoral duties are so much lighter than ours, to lay aside these inspired prayers, except in devotion? Luther himself said his office, for some time after his
apostasy.—But to conclude, as it is of so much importance to
ascertain which is *the holy church,* mentioned in your creed;
and as you can follow no better rule for this purpose than to
judge of the tree by its fruits, so let me advise you and your
friends to make use of every means in your power to compare

regular families, places of education, and especially ecclesiastical establishments of the different communions, with each other,
as to morality and piety, and to decide for yourselves according
to what you observe in them.

I am, &c.

J. M.

— ◆ —

LETTER XXIII.

To JAMES BROWN, Esq. &c.

ON DIVINE ATTESTATION OF SANCTITY.

Dear Sir,

Having demonstrated the distinctive holiness of the Catholic
church, in her *doctrine*, her *practices*, and her *fruits* of sanctity,
I am prepared to show that God himself has borne testimony to
her holiness, and to those very doctrines and practices, which
Protestants object to as unholy and superstitious, by the many
incontestable miracles he has wrought in her and in their favour, from the age of the apostles down to the present age.

The learned Protestant advocates of revelation, such as Grotius, Abbadie, Paley, Watson, &c. in defending this common
cause against Infidels, all agree in the sentiment of the last
named, that " Miracles are the criterion of truth." Accordingly
they observe, that both Moses, *Exod.* iv. xiv. *Numb.* xvi. 29, and
Jesus Christ, *John* 37, 38.—xiv. 12.—xv. 24. constantly appealed
to the prodigies they wrought, in attestation of their divine mission and doctrine.   Indeed the whole history of God's people,
from the beginning of the world down to the time of our Blessed Saviour, was nearly a continued series of miracles.*   The
latter, so far from confining the power of working them to his
own person or time, expressly promised the same, and even a
greater power of this nature to his disciples, *Mark* xvi. 17.
John xiv. 12.   For both the reasons here mentioned, namely,
that the Almighty was pleased to illustrate the society of his
chosen servants, both under the law of nature and the written
law, with frequent miracles, and that Christ promised a con-

---

* To say nothing of the Urim and Thummim, the Water of Jealousy, and the
superabundant harvest of the sabbatical year, it is incontestable, from the Gospel of St. John v. 2, that the probatical pond was endowed by an angel with a
miraculous power of healing every kind of disease, in the time of Christ.

tinuance of them to his disciples under the new law, we are led
to expect that the true church should be distinguished by miracles, wrought in her, and in proof of her. Accordingly the
fathers and doctors of the Catholic church, among other proofs
in her favour, have constantly appealed to miracles, by which
she is illustrated, and reproached their contemporary heretics
and schismatics with the want of them. Thus St. Irenæus, a
disciple of St. Polycarp, who himself was a disciple of St. John
the Evangelist, reproaches the heretics, against whom he writes,
that they could not give sight to the blind, hearing to the deaf,
cast out devils, or raise the dead to life, as he testifies was frequently done in the true church.* Thus also his contemporary,
Tertullian, speaking of the heretics, says: " I wish to see the
miracles they have wrought."† St. Pacian, in the fourth century, writing against the schismatic Novatus, scornfully asks:
" Has he the gift of tongues or prophecy? Has he restored the
dead to life?"‡ The great St. Augustin, in various passages
of his works, refers to the miracles wrought in the Catholic
church, in evidence of her veracity.§ St. Nicetas, bishop of
Treves, in the sixth century, advises queen Clodosind, in order
to convert her husband, Alboin, king of the Lombards, from
Arianism, to induce him to send confidential messengers to witness the miracles wrought at the tombs of St. Martin, St. Germanus, or St. Hilary, in giving sight to the blind, speech to the
dumb, &c.; adding: " Are such things done in the churches of
the Arians?"‖ About the same time, Levigild, king of the
Goths in Spain, an Arian, who was converted, or nearly so, by
his Catholic son, St. Hermengild, reproached his Arian bishops
that no miracles were wrought among them, as was the case,
he said, among the Catholics.¶ The seventh century was illustrated by the miracles of our apostle St. Augustin, of Canterbury, wrought in confirmation of the doctrine which he
taught, as was recorded on his tomb;** and this doctrine, by

---

* Lib. ii. contra Hær. c. 31.   † Lib. De Præscr.

‡ Ep. ii. ad Symphor.

§ " Dubitamus nos ejus Ecclesiæ condere gremio, quæ usque ad confessionem
generis humani ad Apostolica sede, per successionem Episcoporum (frustra
hæreticis circumlatrantibus, et partim plebis ipsius judicio, partim Conciliorum
gravitate, partim etiam *Miraculorum majestate* damnatis) culmen auctoritatis obtinuit."—De Utilit. Cred. c. iv.

‖ Labbe's Concil. tom v. p. 835.   ¶ Greg. Turon. l. ix. c. 15.

** " Hic requiescit D. Augustinus, &c. qui operatione miraculorum suffultus,
Edelberthum Regem ac gentem illius ab idolorum cultu ad fidem Christi con-
vertit."—Bed. Eccles. Hist. l. ii. c. 3. See, in particular, the account of this
saint's restoring sight to a blind man in confirmation of his doctrine. Ibid. c. 2.

the confession of the learned Protestants, was purely the Roman Catholic.* In the eleventh century, we hear a celebrated doctor, speaking of the proofs of the Catholic religion, exclaim thus : " O Lord ! if what we believe is an error, thou art the author of it, since it is confirmed amongst us by those signs and prodigies which could not be wrought but by thee."† In short, St. Bernard, St. Dominic, St. Xavier, &c. all appealed to the miracles, which God wrought by their hands in proof of the Catholic doctrine. I need not mention the controversial works of Bellarmin and other modern schoolmen; nevertheless, I cannot help observing, that even Luther, when the Anabaptists, adopting his own principles, had proceeded to excesses of doctrine and practice which he disapproved of, required them to prove their authority for their innovations by the performance of miracles !‡ You will naturally ask, dear sir, how Luther himself got rid of the argument implied by this requisition, which it is evident, bore as strongly against him, as against the Anabaptists? On one occasion, he answered thus : " I have made an agreement with the Lord not to send me any visions, or dreams, or angels,"§ &c. On another occasion, he boasts of his visions as follows : " I also was in spirit," and, " if I must glory in what belongs to me, I have seen more spirits than they (the Swinkfeldians, who denied the real presence) will see in a whole year."‖

Such has been the doctrine of the fathers and Catholic writers concerning miracles in general, as divine attestations in favour of that church in which God is pleased to work them. I will now mention, or refer to a few particular miraculous events of unquestionable evidence, which have illustrated this church, during the eighteen centuries of her existence.

No Christian questions the miracles and prophecies of the apostles ; and if they do not, why should any Christian question the vision and prophecy of the apostolic saint Polycarp, the angel of the church of Smyrna, *Rev.* ii. 8, concerning the manner of his future martyrdom, namely, by fire ?¶ or the testimony of his episcopal correspondent, who was likewise a disciple of the apostles, St. Ignatius bishop of Antioch, who testifies that the wild beasts, let loose upon the martyrs, were frequently restrained by a divine power from hurting them? In conse

* The Centuriators of Magdeburg, Sæc. 6. Bale. In Act. Rom. Pont. Humphrey's Jesuit, &c.
† Ric. a S. Vict. de Trinit. l. i.   ‡ Sleidan.
§ Manlius in loc. commun. See Brierley's Apology, p. 448.
‖ Luth. ad Senat. Civil. Germ.   ¶ Genuine Acts, by Ruinart.

quence of this he prayed that it might not be the case with
him.* St. Irenæus, bishop of Lyons, was the disciple of St.
Polycarp, and like him, an illustrious martyr: shall we then
call in question his testimony, when he declares, as I have noticed above, that miracles, even to the revival of the dead, frequently took place in the Catholic church, but never among the
heretics?† Or shall we disbelieve that of the learned Origen,
in the next century, who says that it was usual with the Christians of his time to drive away devils, heal the sick, and foretel
things to come: adding, " God is my witness, I would not recommend the religion of Jesus by fictitious stories, but only by
clear and certain facts."‡ One of Origen's scholars was St.
Gregory, bishop of Neocesarea, surnamed *Thaumaturgus*, or
Wonderworker, for the numerous and astonishing miracles
which God wrought by his means. Many of these, even to the
stopping the course of a flood, and the moving of a mountain,
are recorded by the learned fathers, who, soon after, wrote his
life.§ St. Cyprian, the great ornament of the third century,
recounts several miracles which took place in it, some of which
prove the blessed eucharist to be a *sacrifice*, and the lawfulness
of receiving it *under one kind*. In the middle of the fourth
century happened that wonderful miracle, when the emperor
Julian the Apostate, attempting to rebuild the temple of Jerusalem, in order to disprove the prophecy of Daniel, concerning
it, *Dan.* ix. 27, tempests, whirlwinds, earthquakes, and fiery
eruptions convulsed the scene of the undertaking, maiming or
blasting the thousands of Jews and other labourers employed in
the work, and, in short, rendering the completion of it utterly
impossible. In the mean time a luminous cross, surrounded
with a circle of rays, appeared in the heavens, and numerous
crosses were impressed on the bodies and garments of the persons present. These prodigies are so strongly attested by almost all the authors of the age, Arians and Pagans, no less than
Catholics,‖ that no one but a downright sceptic can call them in
question. They have accordingly been acknowledged by the
most learned Protestants.¶ Another miracle, which may vie

* Ep. ad Roman.   † Contra Hær. l. ii. c. 31.
‡ Contra Cels. l. i.
§ Greg. Nyss. Euseb. l. vi. St. Basil, St. Jerom.
‖ Besides the testimony of the Fathers, St. Gregory Nazianzen, St. Chrysostom, St. Ambrose, and of the historians Socrates, Sozomen Theodoret, &c. these
events are also acknowledged by Philostorgius the Arian, Ammianus Marcellinus the Pagan, &c.
¶ Bishop Warburton published a book, called Julian, in proof of these miracles. They are also acknowledged by Bishop Halifax, Disc. p. 23.

with the above mentioned, for the number and quality of its
witnesses, took place in the following century, at Typassus in
Africa; where a whole congregation of Catholics being assembled to perform their devotions, contrary to the orders of the
Arian tyrant, Hunnerick, their right hands were chopped off, and
their tongues cut out to the roots, by his command: nevertheless
they continued to speak as perfectly as they did before this
barbarous act.* I pass over numberless miracles recorded by
SS. Basil, Athanasius, Jerom, Chrysostom, Ambrose, Augustin,
and the other illustrious fathers and church historians, who
adorned the fourth, fifth, and sixth centuries of Christianity;
and shall barely mention one miracle, which both the last mentioned holy bishops relate, as having been themselves actual
witnesses of it, that of restoring sight to a blind man, by the
application to his eyes of a cloth which had touched the relics
of SS. Gervasius, and Protasius.† The latter saint, one of the
most enlightened men who ever handled a pen, gives an account, in the work to which I have just referred,‡ of a great
number of miracles, wrought in Africa, during his episcopacy,
by the relics of St. Stephen, and among the rest, of seventy
wrought in his own diocese of Hippo, and some of them in his
own presence, in the course of two years; among these was the
restoration of three dead bodies to life.

From this notice of the great St. Augustin of Hippo, in the
fifth century, I proceed to observe, concerning St. Augustin of
Canterbury, at the end of the sixth, that the miracles wrought
by him, were not only recorded on his tomb, and in the history
of the venerable Bede and other writers, but that an account of
them was transmitted, at the time they took place, by St. Gregory to Eulogius, patriarch of St. Alexandria, in an Epistle,
still extant, in which this Pope compares them with those performed by the apostles.§ The latter saint wrote likewise an
Epistle to St. Augustin himself, which is still extant in his
works, and in Bede's history, cautioning him against being
elated with vain glory, on the occasion of these miracles, and

---

* The vouchers for this miracle are Victor Vitensis, Hist. Persec. Vandal. l.
ii. the emperor Justinian, who declares that he had seen some of the sufferers,
Codex Just. Tit. 27, the Greek historian Procopius, who says he had conversed
with them, L. i. de Bell. Vand. c. 8. Æneas of Geza, a Platonic philosopher,
who having examined their mouths, protested that he was not so much surprised
at their being able to talk as at their being able to live. De Immort. Anim. Victor.
Turon. Isid. Hispal. Greg. Magn. &c. The miracle is admitted by Abbadie,
Dodwell, Mosheim, and other learned Protestants.

† Aug. De Civit. Dei, l. xxii. p. 8. ‡ Ibid. l. xxii.
§ Epist. S. Greg. l. vii.

reminding him that God had bestowed the power of working
them, not on his own account, but for the conversion of the
English nation.* On the supposition that our apostle had
wrought no miracles, what farces must these Epistles have exhibited among the first characters of the Christian world.

Among the numberless and well attested miracles which the
histories of the middle ages present to our view, I stop at those
of the illustrious abbot St. Bernard, in the twelfth century, to
whose sanctity the most eminent Protestant writers have borne
high testimony.† This saint, in the life of his friend, St. Malachy of Armagh, among other miracles, mentions the cure of
the withered hand of a youth, by the application of his friend's
dead hand to it.‡ But this, and all the miracles which St.
Bernard mentions of other saints, quite disappear, when compared with those wrought by himself; which for their splendour
and publicity, never were exceeded. All France, Germany,
Switzerland, and Italy bore testimony to them; and prelates,
princes, and the emperor himself were often the spectators of
them. In a journey which the saint made into Germany, he
was followed by Philip, archdeacon of Liege, who was sent by
Sampson, archbishop of Rheims, to observe his actions.§ This
writer, accordingly, gives an account of a vast number of instantaneous cures, which the holy abbot performed on the
lame, the blind, the paralytic, and other diseased persons, with
all the circumstances of them. Speaking of those wrought at
Cologne, he says: " They were not performed in a corner;
but the whole city was witness to them. If any one doubts or
is curious, he may easily satisfy himself on the spot, especially
as some of them were wrought on persons of no inconsiderable
rank and reputation." || A great number of these miracles were
performed in express confirmation of the Catholic doctrine
which he defended. Thus preaching at Sarlat against the impious and impure Henricians, a species of Albigenses, he took
some loaves of bread and blessed them: after which he said
" By this you shall know that I preach to you the true doc
trine, and the heretics a false doctrine: *all your sick, who shall
eat of this bread, shall recover their health;*" which prediction

---

* Ibid. et Hist. Bed, l. i. c. 31.
† Luther, Calvin, Bucer, Œcolompadius, Jewel, Whitaker, Mosheim, &c.
‡ Vita Malach. inter Oper. Bern.
§ St. Bernard's Life was written by his three contemporaries, William, abbot of St. Thierry, Arnold, abbot of Bonevaux, and Geoffery, the saint's secretary, and by other early writers: his own eloquent Epistles, and other works
furnish many particulars.
|| Published by Mabillon.

was confirmed by the event.* St. Bernard himself, in the most celebrated of his works,† addressed to Pope Eugenius III. refers to the miracles, which God enabled him to work, by way of justifying himself for having preached up the second crusade ;‡ and, in his letter to the people of Thoulouse, he mentions his having detected the heretics among them, not only by words, but also by miracles.§

The miracles of St. Francis Xavier, the apostle of India, who was cotemporary with Luther, in number, splendour, and publicity, may vie with St. Bernard's. They consisted in foretelling future events, speaking unknown languages, calming tempests at sea, curing various maladies, and raising the dead to life ; and though they took place in remote countries, yet they were verified in the same, soon after the saint's death, by virtue of a commission from John III. king of Portugal, and they were generally acknowledged, not only by Europeans of different religions in the Indies,‖ but also by the native Mahometans and Pagans.¶ At the same time with this saint lived the holy contemplative St. Philip Neri, in proof of whose miracles three hundred witnesses, some of them persons of high rank, were juridically examined.** The following century was illustrated by the shining virtues and attested miracles, even to the resurrection of the dead, of St. Francis of Sales,†† as it was also by those of St. John Francis Regis, concerning which, twenty-two bishops of Languedoc wrote thus to Pope Clement XI : " We are witnesses that, before the tomb of F. J. F. Regis, the blind see, the lame walk, the deaf hear, the dumb speak."‡‡ You will understand, dear sir, that I mention but a few of the saints, and with respect to these, but a few of their miracles, as my object is to prove the single fact that God has illustrated the Catholic church, chiefly by means of his saints, with undeniable miracles, in the different ages of her existence. What now will you, dear sir, and your friends say to the evidence, here adduced ? Will you say that all the holy fathers, up to the apostolic age, and that all the ecclesiastical writers down to the Reformation, and, since this period, that all Catholic authors, prelates and officials, have been in a league to deceive

---

* Geof. in Vit. Bern.
† De Consideratione.   ‡ De Consid. l. ii. ‖ Ad Tolos. Ep. 241.
‖ See the testimonies of Hackluyt, Baldeus, and Tavernier, all Protestants, in Bouhour's Life of St. Xavier, translated by the poet Dryden.
¶ Ibid.   ** See Butler's Saints' Lives, May 26.
†† See Marsollier's Life of St. F. de Sales, translated by Dr. Coombes.
‡‡ See his Life by Daubenton, which is abridged by Butler, June 16.

mankind? In short, that they are all liars and impostors alike? Such, in fact, is the absurd and horrible system, which, to get rid of the DIVINE ATTESTATION, in favour of the Catholic church, the celebrated Dr. Conyers Middleton has declared for; as have most Protestant writers who have handled the subject, since the publication of his *Free Inquiry*. This system, however, which is *a libel on human nature*, does not only lead to general scepticism in other respects, but also undermines the credit of the Gospel itself. For if all the ancient fathers and other writers are to be disbelieved, respecting the miracles of their times, and even those which they themselves witnessed, upon what grounds are we to believe them, in their report of the miracles which they had heard of Christ and his apostles, those main props of the Gospel and our common Christianity? Who knows but they may have forged all the contents of the former, and the whole history of the latter? It was impossible these consequences should escape the penetration of Middleton.: but a worse consequence, in his opinion, which would follow from admitting the veracity of the holy fathers, namely, a *divine attestation of the sanctity of the Catholic church*, banished his dread of the former. Let him now speak to this point for himself, in his own flowing periods. He begins with establishing an important fact, which I also have been labouring to prove, where he says: "It must be confessed that the claim to a miraculous power was universally asserted and believed in all Christian countries and in all ages of the church, till the time of the Reformation: for ecclesiastical history makes no difference between one age and another, but carries on the succession of its miracles, as of all other common events, through all of them indifferently to that memorable period.* As far as church historians can illustrate any thing, there is not a single point, in all history, so constantly, explicitly, and unanimously affirmed by them as the continual succession of those powers, through all ages, from the earliest father, who first mentions them, down to the Reformation; which same succession is still further deduced by persons of the same eminent character for probity, learning and dignity, in the Romish church, to this very day; so that the only doubt which can remain with us is, whether church historians are to be trusted or not: for if any credit be due to them in the present case, it must reach to all or none: because the reason for believing them in any one age will be found to be of equal force in all, as far as it depends on the character of

<hr>

* *Free Inquiry, Introduct. Diso. p. xlv.*

the persons attesting, or on the thing attested."* We shall now hear Dr. Middleton's decision on this weighty matter, and upon what grounds it is formed. He says: " The prevailing opinion of Protestants, namely, of Tillotson, Marshal, Dodwell, &c. is, that miracles continued during the three first centuries. Dr. Waterland brings them down to the fourth, Dr. Beriman to the fifth. These unwarily betrayed the Protestant cause into the hands of its enemies: for it was in those primitive ages, particularly in the third, fourth, and fifth, those flourishing times of miracles, in which the chief corruptions of Popery, monkery, the worship of relics, invocation of saints, prayers for the dead, superstitious use of images and of sacraments were introduced."† " We shall find, after the conversion of the Roman empire, the greater part of their boasted miracles were wrought either by monks, or relics, or the sign of the cross, &c.: wherefore, if we admit the miracles, we must admit the rites for the sake of which they were wrought: they both rest on the same bottom."‡ " Every one may see *what a resemblance the principles and practice of the fourth century, as they are described by the most eminent fathers of that age, bear to the present rites of the Popish church.*"§ " When we reflect on the surprising confidence with which the fathers of the fourth age affirmed, as true, what they themselves had forged, or knew to be forged, it is natural to suspect that so bold a defiance of truth could not be acquired or become general at once, but must have been gradually carried to that height by the example of former ages."‖ Such are the grounds on which this shameless declaimer accuses all the most holy and learned men, whom the world has produced during 1800 years, of forgery and a combination to cheat mankind. He does not say a word to show that the combination itself is either probable or possible; all he advances is, that this libel on human nature, is *necessary for the support of Protestantism;* for he says, and this with evident truth : " By granting the Romanists but a single age of miracles, after the time of the apostles, we shall be entangled in a series of difficulties, whence we can never fairly extricate ourselves, till we allow the same powers also to the present age."¶

Methinks I hear some of your society thus asking me, *Do you then pretend that your church possesses the miraculous powers at*

---

* Ibid. Preface, p. xv.   † Introd. p. li.
‡ Introd. p. lxvi.   § Ibid. lxv.
‖ Ibid. p. lxxxiv.   ¶ Ibid. p. xcvi.

the present day? I answer, that the church never possessed miraculous powers in the sense of most Protestant writers, so as to be able to effect cures or other supernatural events at her mere pleasure: for even the apostles could not do this, as we learn from the history of the lunatic child, *Mat.* xvii. 16: but this I say, that the Catholic church, being always the beloved *spouse of Christ*, Rev. xxi. 9, and continuing at all times to bring forth children of heroical sanctity, God fails not in this, any more than in past ages, to illustrate her and them by unquestionable miracles: accordingly in those processes which are constantly going on, at the apostolical See, for the canonization of new saints,* fresh miracles of a recent date continue to be proved with the highest degree of evidence, as I can testify from having perused, on the spot, the official printed account of some of them.† For the further satisfaction of your friends, I will inform them that I have had satisfactory proof that the astonishing catastrophe of Louis XVI. and his queen, in being *beheaded on a scaffold*, was foretold by a nun of Fougeres, Sœur Nativite, twenty years before it happened, and that the banishment of the French clergy from their country, long before it happened, was predicted by the holy French pilgrim, Benedict Labre, whose miracles caused the conversion of the late Rev. Mr. Thayer, an American clergyman, who being at Rome, witnessed several of them. With respect to miraculous cures of a late date, I have the most respectable attestation of several of them, and I am well acquainted with four or five persons who have experienced them. The following facts are respectfully attested, but at much greater length, by the Rev. Thomas Sadler, of Trafford, near Manchester, and the Rev. J. Crathorne, of Garswood, near Wigan :—Joseph Lamb, of Eccles, near Manchester, now twenty-eight years old, on the 12th of August, 1814, fell from a hay-rick, four yards and a half high, by which accident it was conceived the spine of his back was broken. Certain it is, that he could neither walk nor stand without crutches, down to the second of October, and that he described himself as feeling the most exquisite pain in his back. On that day, having prevailed with much difficulty upon

---

* Among the late canonizations are those, in 1807 and 1808, of S. F. Caraccíolo, founder of the Regular Clerks; of St. Angela de Mercia, foundress of the Ursuline Nuns, of St. Mary of the Incarnation, Mlle. Acarie, &c. One of the latest beatifications is that of B. Alfonso Liguori, bishop of St. Agata de Goti.

† One of these, proved in the process of the last mentioned saint, consisted in the cure and *restoration of an amputated breast* of a woman, who was at the point of death from a cancer.

his father, who was then a Protestant, to take him in a cart with
his wife and two friends, Thos. Cutler and Eliz. Dooley, to
Garswood, near Wigan, where the hand of F. Arrowsmith, one
of the Catholic priests who suffered death at Lancaster, for the
exercise of his religion, in the reign of Charles I. is preserved,
and has often caused wonderful cures, he got himself conveyed
to the altar rails of the chapel, and there to be signed, on his
back, with the sign of the cross, by that hand; when, feeling *a
particular sensation and total change in himself,* as he expressed
it, he exclaimed to his wife, *Mary, I can walk;* this he did without any help whatever, walking first into an adjoining room and
thence to the cart which conveyed him home. With his debili-
ty, his pains also left him, and his back has continued well ever
since.* These particulars, as tney were respectively witnesses
of them, the above named persons, all now living, are ready to
declare upon oath. I have attestations of incurable cancers and
other disorders being suddenly remedied by the same instrument
of God's bounty; but it would be a tedious work to transcribe
them, or the other attestations in my possession of a similar nature.

Among those of my personal acquaintance who have experienced supernatural cures, I will mention Mary Wood, now living at Taunton Lodge, where several other witnesses of the
facts I am going to state live with her. "On March 15, 1809,
Mary Wood, in attempting to open a sash window, pushed her
left hand through a pane of glass, which caused a very large
and deep transverse wound in the inside of the left arm, and divided the muscles and nearly the whole of the tendons that lead
to the hand; from which accident, she not only suffered, at
times, the most acute pain, but was from the period I first saw
her (March 16) till some time in July, totally deprived of the
use of her hand and arm."† What passed between the latter
end of July, when, as the surgeon elsewhere says, "he left his
patient," having no hopes of restoring her, till the 6th of August, on the night of which she was perfectly and miraculously
cured, I shall copy from a letter to me, dated Nov. 19, 1809
by her amanuensis, Miss Maria Hornyold. "The surgeon
gave little or no hopes of her ever again having the use of her
hand, which, together with the arm, seemed withered and some-
what contracted; only saying, *in some years,* nature might give

* The Rev. Mr. Sadler's letter to me is dated Aug. 6, 1817.
† This account is copied from a letter to Miss F. T. Bird, dated Sept. 30,
1809, by Mr. Woodford, an eminent surgeon of Taunton, who attended Mary
Wood.

her some little use of it, which was considered by her superiors as a mere delusive comfort. Despairing of further human assistance towards her cure, she determined, with the approbation of her said superiors, to have recourse to God, through the intercession of St. Winefrid, by a Novena.* Accordingly on the 6th of August she put a piece of moss, from the saint's well, on her arm, continuing recollected and praying, &c.; when, to her great surprise, the next morning she found she could dress herself, put her arm behind her and to her head, having regained the free use and full strength of it. In short, she was perfectly cured!" In this state I myself saw her and examined her hand, a few years afterwards, and in the same state she still continues, at the above named place, with many other highly credible vouchers who are ready respectively to attest these particulars. "On the 16th of the month, the surgeon was sent for; and, being asked his opinion concerning Mary Wood's arm, he gave *no hope of a perfect cure*, and very little of her ever having *even the least use of it;* when she being introduced to him and showing him the arm, which he thoroughly examined and tried, he was so affected at the sight and the recital of the manner of the cure, as to shed tears, and exclaim, it was a special interposition of Divine Providence."

I shall say little of the miraculous cure of Winefrid White, a young woman of Wolverhampton, on the 28th of June, 1805, at Holywell, having published a detailed account of it, soon after it happened, which work has been republished in England and in Ireland.† Let it suffice to say; 1st, that the disease was one of the most alarming topical ones which are known, namely, a *curvature of the spine*, as her physician and surgeon ascertained, who treated it accordingly, by making two great issues, one on each side of the spine, of which the patient's back still bears the marks; 2dly, that, besides the most acute pains, throughout the whole nervous system, and particularly in the brain, this disease of the spine produced a *hemiplegia* or palsy on one side of the patient, so that when she could feebly crawl, with the help of a crutch under her right arm, she was forced to drag her left leg and arm after her, just as if they made no part of her; 3dly, that her disorder was of long continuance, namely, of three years standing; though not in the same degree, till the latter part of that time, and that it was publicly

* Certain prayers continued during nine days.

† By Ceating and Brown, Duke-street, Grosvenor-square, London; Coyne, Dublin.

known to all her neighbours and a great many others; 4thly, that having performed the acts of devotion which she felt herself called to undertake, and having bathed in the fountain, she, *in one instant* of time, on the 28th of June, 1805, found herself freed from all her pains and disabilities, so as to be able to walk, run and jump, like any other young person, and to carry a greater weight with the left arm than she could with the right; 5thly, that she has continued in this state these twelve years down to the present time; lastly, that all the above-mentioned circumstances have been ascertained by me in the regular examination of the several witnesses of them; being persons of different religions, situations in life and countries, in the places of their respective residence, namely, in Staffordshire, Lancashire, and Wales, the authentic documents of which are contained in the work referred to above. Several of the witnesses are still living, as is Winefrid White herself.

I am, &c.
J. M

LETTER XXIV

To JAMES BROWN, Esq. &c.

OBJECTIONS ANSWERED.

DEAR SIR,

I SUBSCRIBE to the objection, which you say has been suggested to you by your learned friend, on the subject of miracles. Namely, I admit that a vast number of incredible and false miracles, as well as other fables, have been forged by some, and believed by other Catholics in every age of the church, including that of the apostles.* I agree with him and you in rejecting the *Legenda Aurea* of Jacobus de Voragine, the *Speculum* of Vincentius Belluacensis, the *Saints' Lives* of the Patrician, Metaphrastes, and scores of similar legends, stuffed as they are, with relations of miracles of every description. But, sir, are we to deny the truth of all history, because there are number-

---

* St. Jerom, in rejecting certain current fables concerning St. Paul and St. Thecla, mentions a priest who was deposed by St. John the Evangelist, for inventing similar stories. De Script. Apost.—Pope Gelasius, in the 5th century, condemned several Apochryphal Gospels and Epistles, and legends of saints, and among the latter the common ones of St. George.

T

less false histories ? Are we to question the four evangelists, because there have been several fabricated Gospels ? Most certainly not : but we must make the best use we can of the discernment and judgment which God has given us, to distinguish false accounts of every kind from those which are true ; and we ought, I allow, to make use of double diligence and caution, in examining alleged revelations and events contrary to the general laws of nature.

Your friend's second objection, which impeaches the diligence, integrity and discernment of the cardinals, prelates, and other ecclesiastics at Rome, appointed to examine into the proofs of the miracles there published, shows that he is little acquainted with the subject he talks of. In the first place, then, a juridical examination of each reported miracle must be made in the place where it is said to have happened, and the depositions of the several witnesses must be given upon oath ; this examination is generally repeated two or three different times at intervals. In the next place, the examiners at Rome are unquestionably men of character, talents and learning, who, nevertheless, are not permitted to pronounce upon any cure or other effect in nature, till they have received a regular report of physicians and naturalists upon it. So far from being precipitate, it employs them whole years to come to a decision, on a few cases, respecting each saint ; this is printed and handed about among indifferent persons, previously to its being laid before the Pope. In short, so strict is the examination, that, according to an Italian proverb : *It is next to a miracle to get a miracle proved at Rome.* It is reported by F. Daubenton that an English Protestant gentleman, meeting, in that city, with a printed process of forty miracles, which had been laid before the Congregation of Rites, to which the examination of them belonged, was so well satisfied with the respective proofs of them, as to express a wish that Rome would never allow of any miracles, but such as were as strongly proved, as these appeared to be ; when to his great surprise, he was informed that every one of these had been rejected by Rome as not sufficiently proved !

Nor can I admit of the third objection of your friend, by which he rejects our miracles, on the alleged ground, that there was no sufficient cause for the performance of them ; for not to mention that many of them were performed for the conversion of infidels, I am bound to cry out with the apostle : *Who hath known the mind of the Lord, or who hath been his counsellor !* Rom. xi. 34. Thus much is certain from Scripture, that the same Deity who preserved Jonas in the whale's belly, to preach repentance to the Ninivites, created a gourd to shelter his head from the heat of the sun, *Jonas* iv. 6, and that as he sent fire from heaven to save his prophet Elias, so he caused iron to swim, in order to enable the son of a prophet to restore the axe which he had borrowed, 2 *Kings* vi. 6. In like manner, we are not to reject miracles, sufficiently proved, under pretext that they are mean, and unworthy the hand of Omnipotence; for we are assured, that God equally turned the dust of Egypt into lice, as he turned the waters of it into blood, *Exod.* viii.

Having lately perused the works of several of the most celebrated Protestant writers, who, in defending the Scripture miracles, endeavour to invalidate the credit of those they are pleased to call *Popish miracles*, I think it just, both to your cause and my own, to state the chief arguments they make use of, and the answers which occur to me, in refutation of them. On this head, I cannot help expressing my surprise and concern that writers of character, and some of them of high dignity, should have published several *gross falsehoods*; not, I trust, intentionally, but from the blind precipitancy and infatuation which a panic fear of Popery generally produces. The late learned bishop of Salisbury, Dr. J. Douglas, has borrowed from the infidel Gibbon what he calls " A most satisfying proof that the miracles ascribed to the Romish saints are *forgeries* of an age posterior to that they lay claim to."* The latter says: " It may seem remarkable, that Bernard of Clairvaux, who records so many miracles of his friend St. Malachy, *never takes notice* of his own, which in their turn, however, are carefully related by his companions and disciples. In the long series of ecclesiastical history, does there occur a single instance of a saint asserting that he himself possessed the gift of miracles?"† Adopting this objection, the bishop of Salisbury says: " I think I may safely challenge the admirers of the Romish saints to produce any writing of any of them, in which a power of working miracles is claimed."‡ Elsewhere he says: " From Xavier himself (namely, from his published letters) we are furnished, not only with a negative evidence against his having any miraculous power, but also with a positive fact, which is the strongest possible presumption against it."§ Nevertheless, in spite of the confident assertions of these celebrated authors, it is certain (though

* The Criterion, or Rules by which the true Miracles of the New Testament are distinguished from the spurious Miracles of Pagans and Papists, by John Douglas, D. D. lord bishop of Salisbury, p. 71, note.
† Hist. of Decline and Fall, chap. xv.
‡ Criterion, p. 369.   § Ibid. p. 76.

the last thing which true saints choose to speak of are their own
supernatural favours) that several of them, when the occasion
required it, have spoken of the miracles, of which they were the
instruments;* and among the rest, those two identical saints,
St. Bernard and St. Francis Xavier, whom Gibbon and Dr.
Douglas instance, to prove their assertion. I have already referred to the passages in the works of St. Bernard, where he
speaks of his miracles as of notorious facts; and I here again
insert them in a note.† With respect to St. Xavier, he not only
mentions, in those very letters which Dr. Douglas appeals to, a
miraculous cure, which he wrought upon a dying woman in the
kingdom of Travancor; but he expressly calls it A MIRACLE,
and affirms that it caused the conversion of the whole village in
which she resided.‡

A second palpable falsehood is thus confidently advanced by
the capital enemy of miracles, Dr. Middleton; " I might risk
the merit of my argument upon this single point, that, after the
apostolic times, there is not, in all history, one instance, either
well attested, or *even so much as mentioned*, of any particular
person who had ever exercised that gift (of tongues) or pretended to exercise it, in any age or country whatsoever."§ In
case your learned friend is disposed to take up the cause ot
Middleton, I beg to refer him to the history of St. Pacomius,
the Egyptian abbot, and founder of the Cenobites, who,
" though he never learned the Greek or Latin languages, yet
sometimes miraculously spoke them," as his disciple and biographer reports,‖ and to that of the renowned preacher, St.
Vincent Ferrer, who, having the gift of tongues, preached indifferently to Jews, Moors, and Christians, in their respective languages, and converted incredible numbers of each of these des-

---

* The great St. Martin acknowledged his own miracles, since, according to
his friend and biographer, Sulpicius, Dialogue 2, he used to say, that he was not
endowed with so great a power of working them, after he was a bishop, as he
had been before.

† Addressing himself to P. Eugenius III. in answer to his enemies, who reproached him with the ill success of the second crusade, he says, " Sed dicunt for-
sitan isti: *Unde scimus quod a Domino sermo egressus sit? Quæ signa tu facis ut
credamus tibi?* non est quod ad ista ipse respondeam: parcendum verecundiæ
meæ: responde tu pro me et pro te ipso, secundum ea quæ vidisti et audisti."
De Consid. l. ii. c. 1. In like manner, writing to the people of Thoulouse, of his
miracles wrought there, he says: " Mora quidem brevis apud vos sed non in-
fructuosa: veritate nimirum per nos manifestatâ, non solum in sermone sed etiam *in virtute.*" Ep. 241.

‡ Epist. S. F. Xav. L. 1. Ep. iv.
§ Inquiry into Mirac. Powers, p. 120, &c.
‖ Tillemont, Mem. Ecc. tom. vii.

cripcions.* In like manner, the bull of the canonization of St. Lewis Bertrand, A. D. 1671, declares that he possessed the gift of tongues, by means of which he converted as many as ten thousand Indians of different tribes in South America, in the space of three years.† Lastly, let your friend peruse the history of the great apostle of the East Indies, St. Xavier, who, though he ordinarily studied the languages of the several nations he announced the word of God to, yet, on particular occasions, he was empowered to speak those he had not learned.‡ This was the case in Travancor, as his companion Vaz testified, so as to be enabled to convert and instruct there ten thousand infidels, all of whom he baptized with his own hand. This was the case again at Amanguchi, where he met with a number of Chinese merchants. Finally, the bull of St. Xavierius's canonization by Urban VIII. proclaims to the world, that this saint was illustrated with the *gift of tongues:* so false is the bold assertion of Middleton, adopted in part by bishop Douglas and other Protestants, that " there is not, in all history, one instance, either well attested, or so much as mentioned, of any person who had ever exercised the gift of tongues, or pretended to exercise it."

Nor is there more truth in what the bishop of Salisbury, Dr. Paley, &c. maintain, namely, that " the Popish miracles," as they insultingly call them, were not wrought to confirm any truth, and that no converts were made by them !§ In refutation of this, I may again refer to the epitaph of our apostle, St. Augustin, and to the miracles of St. Bernard at Sarlat, mentioned above. To these instances, I may add the prodigy of St. Dominic, who, to prove the truth of the Catholic doctrine, threw a book containing it into the flames, in which it remained unconsumed, at the same time challenging the heretics, whom he was addressing, to make the same experiment on their creed.‖ In like manner, St. Xavier, on a certain occasion, finding his words to have no effect on his Indian auditory, requested them to open the grave of a corpse that had been buried the day before, when falling on his knees, he besought God to restore it to life for the conversion of the infidels present; upon which, the

* See his Life by Lanzano, Bishop of Lucca, also Spondanus ad An. 1403.
† See Alban Butler's Saints' Lives, Oct. 9.
‡ See Bouhour's Life of St. Xavier, translated by Dryden, &c.
§ Criterion, p. 369.   View of Evidences, by Dr. Paley, vol. i. p. 346.
‖ Petrus Vallis Cern. Hist.   Alb. Butler's Saint's Lives, Aug. 4.

dead man was instantly restored to life and perfect health, and
the country round about received the faith.*

It is chiefly through the sides of the apostle of India, that the
author of The Criterion endeavours to wound the credit of the
other saints and the Catholic church, on the point of miracles.
Hence in the application of his three laboured rules of criticism,
he objects, that the alleged miracles of St. Xavier were performed in the extremities of the East; that the accounts of them
were published, not on the spot, but in Europe, at an immense
distance; and this not till thirty-five years after the saint's
death.† A single document, of the most public nature, at once
overturns all the three rules in regard of this saint. He died at
the end of 1552, and on the 28th of March, 1556, a letter was
sent from Lisbon by John III. king of Portugal, to his viceroy
in India, Don Francisco Barretto, " enjoining him to take depositions upon oath, in all parts of the Indies, where there is a
probability of finding witnesses, not only concerning the life and
manners of Francis Xavier, and of all the things commendably
done by him, for the salvation and example of men, but also
concerning the *miracles*, which he has wrought, both living and
dead. You shall send these authentic instruments, with all the
evidences and proofs, signed with your handwriting, and sealed
with your ring, by three different conveyances."‡

But the author of The Criterion, it seems, has more positive,
and what he calls " conclusive evidence, that during this time,
(thirty-five years from his death,) Xavier's miracles had not been
heard of. The evidence," he says, " I shall allege, is that of
Acosta, (namely, Joseph Acosta,) who himself had been a missionary among the Indians. His work, *De Procuranda Indo-
rum Salute*, was printed in 1589, that is, above thirty-seven
years after the death of Xavier, and in it we find an express acknowledgment, that no miracles had ever been performed by
missionaries among the Indians. Acosta was himself a Jesuit,
and therefore, from his silence, we may infer unexceptionably,
that between thirty and forty years had elapsed before Xavier's

* This was one of the miracles referred to by the Paravas of Cape Comorin,
when the Dutch sent a minister from Batavia, to proselyte them to Protestantism. On this occasion, they answered the minister's discourse thus : *The great
father* (St. Xavier) *raised to life five or six dead persons ; do you raise twice as
many ; do you cure all our sick, and make the sea twice as productive of fish as it
now is, and then we will listen to you.* Du Halde's Recueil, voi. v. Berault
Bercastel's Hist. Ecc. tom. xxiii. p. 454.   † Criter. p. 78, 81, &c.

‡ This letter is extant in Tursellinus, but had been published several years
before by Emanuel Acosta, in his *Rerum in Oriente Gestarum*. Dilingen, 1571.
Paris, 1572.

miracles were thought of."* The argument has been thought
so conclusive, that Mr. Le Mesurier,† Hugh Farmer,‡ the Rev.
Peter Roberts,§ and other Protestant writers on miracles, have
adopted it with exultation, and it has probably contributed as
much to the author's title of *Detector Douglas*, as his exposure
of the two impostors, Lauder and Archibald Bower. But what
will the admirers of this *Detector* say, if it should appear that
Acosta barely says, that " there was not *the same faculty* or *facility* of working miracles among the missionaries, which there
was among the apostles ?"|| Or rather, what will they say, if
this same Acosta, in the very work which Doctor Douglas
quotes, expressly asserts, that *signs and miracles* too numerous
to be related, accompanied the preaching of the Gospel both in
the East and the West Indies, *in his own time !*¶ And yet further, with respect to this same " Blessed Master Francis," as he
calls him, " being a man of an apostolical life, that so many
and such great signs have been reported of him by numerous
and credible witnesses, that hardly more in number or greater
in magnitude are read of any one, except the apostles ?"** Now
all this I affirm Acosta does say, in the very work quoted by
bishop Douglas, a copy of which I beg leave to inform your
learned friend, (and through him, other learned men,) is to be
found in the Bodleian library at Oxford, under the title which
I insert below.†† The author of *The Criterion* is hardly entitled to more mercy for his cavils on what Ribadeneira says of
the miracles of St. Ignatius, than for those on what Acosta says
of the miracles of St. Xavier. The fact is, the Council of
Trent, having recently prohibited the publication of any new miracles, until they had been examined and approved of by the
proper ecclesiastical authority, Ribadeneira, in the first edition of his life of St. Ignatius, observed due caution in speaking of this saint's miracles; however, in that very edition, he

* Criterion, p. 73.   † Bampton Lectures, p. 238.
‡ Dissertation on Miracles, p. 205.   § Observations on a Pamphlet.
|| " Altera causa in nobis est cur apostolica prædicatio institui omnino non
possit apostolice, quod miraculorum nulla *facultas* sit, quæ apostoli plurima per-
petrarunt."—Acosta, De Proc. l. ii. c. 8.
¶ " Et quidem dona Spiritus *signa* et *miracula*, quæ fidei prædicatione innotuer-
unt, *his etiam temporibus*, quando charitas usque adeo refrixit, ennumerare longum
esset, tum in Orientali illa India, tum in hac Occidentali."—De Procur. l. i. c.
8, p. 141.
** Convertamus oculos in nostri sæculi hominem, B. Magistrum Franciscum,
virum Apostolicæ vitæ, cujus tot et tam magna signa referuntur per plurimos,
eosque idoneos, testes ut vix de alio exceptis Apostolis, plura legantur. Quid
Magister Gaspar aliique socii, &c."—De Procur. Ind. Salut. l. ii. c. 10, p. 226.
†† The book is to be inquired for at the Bodleian library by the following
quaint description; *Johanna Papissa toti Orbi manifestata. 8*°· c 29. *Art. Seld.*

16*

declared that many such had been wrought by him : but these having subsequently been juridically proved in the process of the saint's canonization, his biographer published them without scruple, as he candidly and satisfactorily informs his readers in that third edition ; which edition now stands in his folio work of *The Saints' Lives.**

I shall close this very long letter, with a very few words respecting a work which has lately appeared, animadverting on my account of *The Miraculous Cure of Winefrid White.*† The writer sets out with the system of Dr. Middleton, by admitting none except Scripture miracles; but very soon he undermines these miracles also, where he says : " An independent and express divine testimony is that alone, which can assure us whether effects are miraculous or not, except in a few cases." He thus reverses the proofs of Christianity, as its advocates and its divine Founder himself have laid them down. He adds : " No mortal ought to have the presumption to say, a thing is or is not contrary to the established laws of nature." Again he says : " To prove a miracle, there must be a proof of the particular divine agency." According to this system we may say, No one knows but the motion of the funeral procession, or some occult quality of nature, raised to life the widow of Naim's son ! Mr. Roberts will have no difficulty in saying so, as he denies that the resurrection of the murdered man from the touch of the prophet Elisha's bones, 2 *Kings* xiii, was a miracle ! Possessed of this opinion, the author can readily persuade himself, that a curvated spine and hemiplegia, or any other disease whatever, may be cured, in an instant, by immersion in cold water, or by any thing else; but as it is not likely that any one else will adopt it, I will say no more of his physical arguments on this

---

* " Mihi tantum abest ut ad vitam Ignatii illustrandam miracula deesse videantur, ut multa eaque præstantissima judicem in media luce versari." The writer proceeds to mention several cures, &c. edit. 1572.——I cannot close this article without protesting against the disingenuity of several Protestant writers in reproaching Catholics with the impositions practised by the Jansenists at the tomb of Abbé Paris. In fact, who detected those impositions, and furnished Dr. Campbel, Dr. Douglas, &c. with arguments against them, except our Catholic prelates and theologians? In like manner Catholics have reason to complain of these and other Protestant writers, for the manner in which they discuss the stupendous miracle that took place at Saragossa in 1640, on one Michael Pellicer, whose leg, having been amputated, he, by his prayers, obtained a new, natural leg, just as if this miracle rested on no better foundation than the slight mention which cardinal Retz makes of it in his *Memoirs*. In fact, we might have expected that learned divines would have known that this miracle had been amply discussed, soon after it happened, between Dr. Stillingfleet and the Jesuit Edward Worsley, in which discussion, the latter produced such attestations of the fact as it seems impossible not to credit.—See Reason and Religion, p. 328.

† By the Rev. Peter Roberts, rector of Llanarmon, &c.

subject. He next proceeds to charge W. White and her friends with a studied imposition; in support of which charge, he asserts, that " the church of Rome had not announced a miracle for many years." This only proves that his ignorance of what is continually going on in the church, is equal to his bigotry against it. The same ignorance and bigotry are manifested in the ridiculous story concerning Sixtus V. which he copies from the unprincipled Leti, as also in his account of the exploded and condemned book, the *Taxæ Cancellariæ, &c.* * Towards the conclusion of his work, he expresses a doubt whether I have read bishop Douglas's Criterion, though I have so frequently quoted it; because, he says, if I had read it, I must have known that Acosta proves that St. Xavier wrought no miracles among the Indians, and that the same thing appears from the saint's own letters. Now the only thing, dear sir, which these assertions prove, is, that Mr. Roberts himself, no more than bishop Douglas, ever read either Acosta's work, or St. Xavier's Letters, notwithstanding they so frequently refer to them; for this is the only way of acquitting them of a far heavier charge.

I am, &c.

J. M

LETTER XXV.

To JAMES BROWN, Esq. &c.

ON THE TRUE CHURCH BEING CATHOLIC.

Dear Sir,

In treating of this third mark of the true church, as expressed in our common creed, I feel my spirits sink within me, and I am almost tempted to throw away my pen, in despair. For what chance is there of opening the eyes of candid Protestants to the other marks of the church, if they are capable of keeping them shut to this? Every time that each of them addresses the God of Truth, either in solemn worship or in private devotion, he fails not to repeat, *I believe in THE CATHOLIC church:* and yet if I ask him the question, *Are you a CATHOLIC?* he is sure to answer me, *No, I am a PROTESTANT!* Was

* Euseb. Eccles. Hist. L. iv. c. 15.

U

there ever a more glaring instance of inconsistency and self-con demnation among rational beings!

At the first promulgation of the Gospel, its followers were distinguished from the Jews by the name of *Christians*, as we learn from Scripture, *Acts* xi. 26. Hence the title of Catholic did not occur in the primitive edition of the apostles' Creed;[*] but no sooner did heresies and schisms arise, to disturb the peace of the church, than there was found to be a necessity of discriminating the main stock of her faithful children, to whom the promises of Christ belonged, from those self-will *choosers* of their articles of belief, as the word *heretic* signifies, and those disobedient *separatists*, as the word *schismatic* means. For this purpose the title of CATHOLIC, or *universal*, was adopted, and applied to the true church and her children. Accordingly we find it used by the immediate disciples of the apostles, as a distinguishing *mark of the true church*. One of these was the illustrious martyr St. Ignatius, bishop of Antioch, who, writing to the church of Smyrna, expressly says, that " Christ is where the *Catholic* church is." In like manner, the same church of Smyrna, giving a relation of the martyrdom of their holy bishop St. Polycarp, who was equally a disciple of the apostles, addresses it to " The *Catholic* churches."[†] This characteristical title of the true church continued to be pointed out by the succeeding fathers in their writings and the acts of their councils.[‡] St. Cyril, bishop of Jerusalem, in the fourth century, gives the following directions to his pupils : " If you go into any city, do not ask merely, *Where is the church, or house of God?* because the heretics pretend to have this; but ask, *Which is the Catholic church?* because this title belongs alone to our holy mother."[§] " We," says a father of the fifth century, " are called *Catholic* Christians."[||] His contemporary, St. Pacian, describes himself as follows : " *Christian* is my name, *Catholic* is my sirname : by the former I am called, by the latter I am distinguished. By the name of *Catholic*, our society is distinguished from all *heretics*."[¶] But there is not one of the fathers or doctors of antiquity, who enlarges so copiously or so pointedly on this title of the true church, as the great St. Augustin, who died at the end of the fifth century. " Many things," he says, " detain me in the bosom of the Ca-

---

tholic church—the very name of CATHOLIC detains me in it, which she has so happily preserved amidst the different heretics; that whereas they are all desirous of being called *Catholics,* yet, if any stranger were to ask them, *Which is the assembly of the Catholics?* none of them would dare to point out his own place of worship."* To the same purpose, he says elsewhere: " We must hold fast the communion of that church which is called *Catholic,* not only by her own children, but also by all her enemies. For heretics and schismatics, whether they will or· not, when they are speaking of the Catholic church with strangers, or with their own people, call her by the name of *Catholic ;* inasmuch as they would not be understood, if they did not call her by the name by ·which all the world calls her."† In proportion to their affection for the glorious name of *Catholic,* is the aversion of these primitive doctors, to every ecclesiastical name or title derived from particular persons, countries, or opinions. " What new heresy," says St. Vincent of Lerins, in the sixth century, " ever sprouted up, without bearing the name of its founder, the date of its origin ?" &c.‡ St. Justin, the philosopher and martyr, had previously made the same remark in the second century, with respect to the Marcionite, Valentinian, and other heretics of his time.§ Finally, the nervous St. Jerom lays down the following rule on this subject: "We must live and die in that church, which, having been founded by the apostles, continues down to the present day. If, then, you should hear of any Christians not deriving their name from Christ, but from some other founder, as the Marcionites, the Valentinians, &c. be persuaded that they are not of Christ's society, but of Antichrist's."||

I now appeal to you, dear sir, and to the respectable friends who are accustomed to deliberate with you on religious subjects, whether these observations and arguments of the ancient fathers are not as strikingly true in this nineteenth century, as they were during the six first centuries, in which they wrote? Is there not, among the rival churches, one exclusively known and distinguished by the name and title of THE CATHOLIC CHURCH, as well in England, Holland, and other countries, which *protest* against this church, as in those which adhere to it ? Does not this effulgent mark of the true religion so incontestably belong to us, in spite of every effort to obscure it, by

* Contra Epist. Fundam. c. 1.   † De Ver. Relig. c. 7.
‡ Common. Advers. Hær. c. 34.   § Advers. Tryphon.
|| Advers. Luciferan.

the nick-names of *Papists, Romanists,* &c.* that the rule of St.
Cyril and St. Augustin is as good and certain now, as it was in
their times?　What I mean is this: if any stranger in London,
Edinburgh, or Amsterdam, were to ask his way to the *Catholic
chapel,* I would risk my life for it, that no sober Protestant inhabitant would direct him to any other place of worship than
to ours.　On the other hand, it is notorious, that the different
sects of Protestants, like the heretics and schismatics of old, are
denominated either from their founders, as the *Lutherans,* the
Calvinists, the *Socinians,* &c. or from the countries in which
they prevail, as the *church of England,* the *Kirk of Scotland,*
the *Moravians,* &c. or from some novelty in their belief or practice, as the *Anabaptists,* the *Independents,* the *Quakers,* &c.
The first father of Protestants was so sensible that he and they
were destitute of every claim to the title of *Catholic,* that in
translating the apostles' Creed into Dutch, he substituted the
word *Christian* for that of *Catholic.*　The first Lutherans did
the same thing in their catechism, for which they are reproached by the famous Fulke, who, to his own confusion, proves that
the true church of Christ must be *Catholic in name,* as well as
in *substance.*†

I am, &c.

J. M.

LETTER XXVI.

To JAMES BROWN, Esq. &c.

ON THE QUALITIES OF CATHOLICITY.

Dear Sir,

　To proceed now, from the name *Catholic,* to the signification
of that name: this is to be gathered from the etymology of the
word itself, and from the sense in which the apostolical fathers
and other doctors of the church have constantly used it.　It is
derived from the Greek word Καθολικος, which means *universal;*
and, accordingly, it has ever been employed by those writers to
discriminate the great body of Christians, under their legiti-

---

* St. Gregory of Tours, speaking of the Arians, and other contemporary heretics of the 6th century, says: "Romanorum nomiue vocitant nostræ religionis
homines."　Hist. l. xvii. c. 25.
† On the New Testament, p. 378.

late pastors, and subsisting in all nations and all ages, from those comparatively small bodies of Christians, who, in certain places and at certain times, have been separated from it. "The Catholic church," says St. Augustin, " is so called, because it is spread throughout the world."[*] " If your church," adds he, addressing certain heretics, "is Catholic, show me that it spreads its branches throughout the world; for such is the meaning of the word Catholic."[†] " The Catholic or universal doctrine," writes St. Vincent of Lerins, " is that which remains the same through all ages, and will continue so till the end of the world. He is a true Catholic who firmly adheres to the faith which he knows the Catholic church has universally taught from the days of old."[‡] It follows, from these and other testimonies of the fathers, and from the meaning of the term itself, that the true church is *Catholic* or Universal in three several respects, as to *persons*, as to *places*, and as to *time*. It consists *of the most numerous body of Christians;* it is more or less *diffused wherever Christianity prevails:* and it has *visibly existed ever since the time of the apostles.* Hence, dear sir, when you hear me glorying in the name of *Catholic*, you are to understand me as equivalently proclaiming thus :—I am not a Lutheran, nor a Calvinist, nor a Whitfieldite, nor a Wesleyan; I am not of the church of England, nor of the Kirk of Scotland, nor of the consistory of Geneva; I can tell the place *where* and the time *when* each of these sects began; and I can describe the *limits* within which they are respectively confined; but I am a member of that great Catholic church, which was planted by Christ and his apostles, and has been spread throughout the world, and which still constitutes the *main stock of Christianity;* that to which all the fathers of antiquity and the saints of all ages have belonged on earth, and still belong in the bright regions above; that which has endured and overcome the persecutions and heresies of eighteen centuries; in short, that against which *the gates of hell have not prevailed*, and we are assured, *never shall prevail.* All this is implied by my title of *Catholic.*

But to form a more accurate opinion of the number and diffusiveness of Catholics, compared with any sect of Protestants, it is proper to make a slight survey of their state in the four quarters of the world. In Europe, then, notwithstanding the

---

[*] Epist. 170. ad S. Sever.   [†] Contra Gaudent. l. iii. c. 1.
[‡] Commonit. The same father briefly and accurately defines the Catholic doctrine to be that which has been believed *Semper et ubique et ab omnibus.*

revolutionary persecution which the Catholic religion has endured and is enduring, it is still the religion of the several states of Italy, and most of the Swiss Cantons, of Piedmont, o. France, of Spain, of Portugal, and of the islands in the Mediterranean, of three parts in four of the Irish, of far the greater part of the Netherlands, Poland, Bohemia, Germany, Hungary, and the neighbouring provinces; and, in those kingdoms and states in which it is not the established religion, its followers are very numerous, as in Holland, Russia, Turkey, the Lutheran and Calvinistic states of Germany and England. Even in Sweden and Denmark several Catholic congregations, with their respective pastors, are to be found. The whole vast continent of South America, inhabited by many millions of converted Indians, as well as by Spaniards and Portuguese, may be said to be Catholic. The same may be said of the empire of Mexico, and the surrounding kingdoms in North America, including California, Cuba, Hispaniola, &c. Canada and Louisiana are chiefly Catholic; and throughout the United Provinces, the Catholic religion, with its several establishments, is completely protected, and unboundedly propagated. To say nothing of the islands of Africa inhabited by Catholics, such as Malta, Madeira, Cape Verd, the Canaries, the Azores, Mauritius, Goree, &c. there are numerous churches of Catholics, established, and organized under their pastors, in Egypt, Ethiopia, Algiers, Tunis, and the other Barbary states on the northern coast; and thence, in all the Portuguese settlements along the western coast, particularly at Angola and Congo. Even on the eastern coast, especially in the kingdom of Zanquebar and Monomotapa, are numerous Catholic churches. There are also numerous Catholic priests and many bishops, with numerous flocks, throughout the greater part of Asia. All the Maronites about Mount Libanus, with their bishops, priests and monks, are Catholics, so are many of the Armenians, Persians, and other Christians, of the surrounding kingdoms and provinces.* In whatever islands or states the Portuguese or Spanish power does prevail, or has prevailed, most of the inhabitants, and in some all of them have been converted. The whole population of the Philippine islands, consisting of two millions of souls, is all Catholic. The diocese of Goa contains four hundred thousand Catholics. In short, the number of Catholics is so great throughout all the peninsula of India within the Ganges, notwithstanding the power and influence of Britain, as

---

* See Sir R. Steel's account of the Catholic Religion throughout the world.

to excite the jealousy and complaints of the celebrated Protestant missionary, Dr. Buchanan.* In a late parliamentary record, it is stated that in Travancor and Cochin is a Catholic archbishopric and two bishoprics, one of which contains thirty-five thousand *communicants.*† There are numerous Catholic flocks, with their priests and even bishops, in all the kingdoms and states beyond the Ganges, particularly in Siam, Cochin-china, Tonquin, and the different provinces of the Chinese empire. I must add, on this subject, that, whereas, none of the great Protestant sects was ever much more numerous or widely spread than it is at present, the Catholic church, heretofore, prevailed in all the countries which they now collectively inhabit. The same may be said with respect to the Greek schismatics, and in a great measure to the Mahometans. It is in this point of view that the Right Rev. Dr. Marsh ought to institute his comparison between the church of England and the church of Rome;‡ or rather the *Catholic church, in communion with the See of Rome.* In the mean time, we are assured by his fellow prelate, the bishop of Lincoln, that " The articles and liturgy of the church of England do not correspond with the sentiments of the eminent reformers on the continent, or with the creeds of any Protestant churches there established."§ And with respect to this very church, nothing would be more inconsistent than to ascribe the greater part of the population of our two islands to it. For if the Irish Catholics, the Scotch Presbyterians, the English Methodists and other Dissenters, together with the vast population who neither are nor profess to be of any religion at all, are subtracted, to what a comparatively small number would the church of England be reduced! And, how utterly absurd would it be for her to pretend to be the *Catholic church!* Nor are these the only subtractions to be made from her numbers, and indeed from those of all other Christian societies, divided from the true church; since, there being but *one baptism,* all the young children who have been baptized in them, and all invincibly ignorant Christians, who exteriorly adhere to them, really belong to the Catholic church, as I have shown above.

In finishing this subject, I shall quote a passage from St. Augustin, which is as applicable to the sectaries of this age as it

---

* See Christian Researches in Asia, p. 131. Mem. Eccl.

† Dr. Kerr's Letter, quoted in the late parliamentary Report on the Catholic Question, p. 487.

‡ See his Comparative View of the Churches of England and Rome!

§ Charge, in 1803.

17

was to those of the age in which he lived. "There are heretics every where, but not the same heretics every where. For there is one sort in Africa, another sort in the East, a third sort in Egypt, and a fourth sort in Mesopotamia, being different in different countries, though all produced by the same mother, namely, pride. Thus also the faithful are all born of one common mother, the Catholic church; and though they are every where dispersed, they are every where the same."*

But it is still more necessary that the true church should be *Catholic* or *Universal* as to *time* than as to numbers or to place. If there ever was a period since her foundation, in which she has failed, by teaching or promoting error or vice, then the promises of the Almighty in favour of the seed of David and the kingdom of the Messiah, in the Book of Psalms,† and in those of Isaiah, Jeremiah, and Daniel, have failed;‡ then the more explicit promises of Christ, concerning this church and her pastors have failed;§ then the Creed itself, which is the subject of our present discussion, has been false.‖ On this point, learned Protestants have been wonderfully embarrassed, and have involved themselves in the most palpable contradictions. A great proportion of them have maintained that the church, in past ages, totally failed, and became the synagogue of satan, and that its head pastor, the bishop of Rome, was and is the *man of sin*, the identical *Antichrist:* but they have never been able to settle among themselves, when this most remarkable of all revolutions since the world began, actually took place; or who were the authors, and who the opposers of it; or by what strange means the former prevailed on so many millions of people of different nations, languages, and interests, throughout Christendom, to give up the supposed pure religion, which they had learned from their fathers, and to embrace a pretended new and false system, which its adversaries now call *Popery!* In a word, there is no way of accounting for the pretended change of religion, at whatever period this may be fixed, but by supposing, as I have said, that the whole collection of Christians, on some one night, went to bed Protestants, and awoke the next morning Papists!

That the church in communion with the See of Rome is the original, as well as the most numerous church, is evident in

---

* Lib. de Pact. c. 8.　　　　† Ps. lxxxviii. alias lxxxix. &c.
‡ Is. c. liv. lix. Jerem. xxxi. 31. Dan. ii. 44.
§ Mat. xvi. 18.—xxviii. 19, 20.
‖ I believe in the holy Catholic church.

several points of view. *The stone cries out of the wall*, as the prophet expresses it,* in testimony of this. I mean that our venerable cathedrals and other stone churches, built by Catholic hands and for the Catholic worship, so as to resist, in some sort, that which is now performed in them, proclaim that ours is the ancient and original church. This is still more clear from the ecclesiastical historians of our own as well as other nations. Venerable Bede, in particular, bears witness,† that the Roman missionary, St. Augustin of Canterbury, and his companions, converted our Saxon ancestors, at the end of the sixth century, to the belief of the Pope's supremacy, transubstantiation, the sacrifice of the mass, purgatory, the invocation of saints, and the other Catholic doctrines and practices, as learned Protestants in general agree.‡ Now, as these missionaries were found to be of the same faith and religion, not only with the Irish, Picts, and Scots, who were converted almost two centuries before them, but also with the Britons or Welsh, who became Christians in the second century, so as only to differ from them about the time of keeping Easter and a few other unessential points, this circumstance alone proves the Catholic religion to have been that of the church in the aforesaid early age. Still the most demonstrative proofs of the antiquity and originality of our religion are gathered from comparing it with that contained in the works of the ancient fathers. An attempt was made, during a certain period, by some eminent Protestants, especially in this country, to press the fathers into their service. Among these, bishop Jewel of Sarum, was the most conspicuous. He not only boasted that those venerable witnesses of the primitive doctrine were generally on his side, but also published the following challenge to the Catholics : " Let them show me but one only father, one doctor, one sentence, two lines, and the field is theirs."§ However, this his vain boasting, or rather deliberate impugning of the known truth, only served to scandalize sober and learned Protestants, and among others, his biographer, Dr. Humphreys, who complains that he thereby " Gave a scope to the Papists, and spoiled himself and the Protestant church."‖ In fact, this hypocrisy, joined with his shameful falsification of the fathers, in quoting them, occasioned the conversion of a beneficed clergyman, and one of the

---

* Habak. ii. 11.   † Hist. Eccles.
‡ Bishop Bale. Humphreys the Centur. of Magdeb. &c.
§ Jewel's Sermon at St. Paul's Cross ; likewise his Answers to Dr. Cole.
‖ Life of Jewel, quoted by Walsingham, in his invaluable *Search into Matters of Religion*, p. 172.

ablest writers of his age, Dr. W. Reynolds.[*]   Most Protestant
writers of later times[†] follow the late Dr. Middleton, and Luther himself, in giving up the ancient fathers to the Catholics
without reserve, and thereby the faith of the Christian church
during the six first centuries, of which faith these fathers were
the witnesses and the teachers.   Among other passages to this
purpose, the above named doctor writes as follows : " Every
one must see what a resemblance the principles and practice of
the fourth century bear to the present rites of the Popish
church."[‡]   Thus, by the confession of her most learned adversaries our church is not less CATHOLIC or *Universal*, as to
time, than she is with respect to *name, locality*, and *numbers*.

I am, &c.

J. M.

LETTER XXVII.

To JAMES BROWN, Esq.

OBJECTIONS ANSWERED.

DEAR SIR,

I HAVE received the letter written by your visiter, the Rev.
Joshua Clark, B. D. at the request, as he states, of certain members of your society, animadverting on my last to you ; an answer to which letter I am requested to address to you.   The
Reverend gentleman's arguments are by no means consistent
one with another; for like other determined controvertists, he
attacks his adversary with every kind of weapon that comes to
his hand, in the hopes *per fas et nefas* of demolishing him.   He
maintains, in the first place, that, though Protestantism was not
visible before it was unveiled by Luther, it subsisted in the
hearts of the true faithful, ever since the days of the apostles,
and that the believers in it constituted the real primitive Catholic church.   To this groundless assumption I answer, that an
invisible church is no church at all; that the idea of such a
church is at variance with the predictions of the prophets respecting Jesus Christ's future church, where they describe it as

---

[*] Dodd's Church Hist. vol. ii.
[†] See the acknowledgment, on this head, of the learned Protestants, Obrecht,
Dumoulin, and Causabon.
[‡] *Inquiry into Miracles*, Introd. p. 45.

a *mountain on the top of mountains*, Is. ii. 2. Mic. iv. 2. and as a city, whose *watchmen shall never hold their peace*, Is. lxii. 6. and, indeed, with the injunction of our Lord himself, *to tell the church*, Mat. xviii. 17, in a certain case, which he mentions. It is no less repugnant to the declaration of Luther, who says of himself, " At first I stood alone :"* and to that of Calvin, who says, " The first Protestants were obliged to break off from the whole world ;"† as also to that of the church of England in her Homilies, where she says, " Laity and clergy, learned and unlearned, all ages, sects and degrees, have been drowned in abominable idolatry, most detested by God and damnable to man, for eight hundred years and more."‡ As to the argument in favour of an invisible church, drawn from 1 *Kings* xix. 18. where the Almighty tells Elijah, *I·have left me seven thousand in Israel, whose knees have not been bowed to Baal;* our divines fail not to observe, that however invisible the church of the Old Law was in the schismatical kingdom of Israel, at the time here spoken of, it was most conspicuous and flourishing in its proper seat, the kingdom of Judah, under the pious king Josaphat. Mr. Clark's second argument is borrowed from Dr. Porteus, and consists in a mere quibble. In answer to the question; " Where was the Protestant religion before Luther?" this prelate replies, " It was just where it is now : only that then it was corrupted with many sinful errors, from which it is now reformed."§ But this is to fall back into the refuted system of an invisible church; it is also to contradict the Homilies, or else it is to confess the real truth, that Protestancy had no existence at all before the sixteenth century.

The Reverend gentleman next maintains, on quite opposite grounds, that there have been large and *visible* societies of *Protestants*, as he calls them, who have stood in opposition to the church of Rome, in all past ages. True, there have been heretics and schismatics of one kind or other during all that time, from Simon Magus, down to Martin Luther; many sects of whom, such as the Arians, the Nestorians, the Eutychians, the Monotholites, the Albigenses, the Wickliffites, and the Hussites, have been exceedingly numerous and powerful in their turns, though most of them now have dwindled away to nothing : but observe, that none of the ancient heretics held the doctrines of any description of modern Protestants, and all of them maintained doctrines and practices which modern Protestants repro-

---

* Opera. Pref. † Epist. 171. ‡ Perils of Idolatry, p. lii.
§ Confut. p. 79.
17*

bate, as much as Catholics do. Thus the Albigenses were real Manicheans, holding two First Principles, or Deities, attributing the Old Testament, the propagation of the human species, to Satan, and acting up to these diabolical maxims.* The Wickliffites and Hussites were the levelling and sanguinary Jacobins of the times and countries in which they lived ;† in other respects these two sects were Catholics, professing their belief in the seven sacraments, the mass, the invocation of saints, purgatory, &c. If, then, your Reverend visiter is disposed to admit such company into his religious communion, merely because they protested against the supremacy of the Pope, and some other Catholic tenets, he must equally admit Jews, Mahometans, and Pagans into it, and acknowledge them to be equally *Protestants* with himself.

Your Reverend visiter concludes his letter with a long dissertation, in which he endeavours to show, that however we Catholics may boast of the antiquity and perpetuity of our church in past times, our triumphs must soon cease by the extinction of this church, in consequence of the persecution now carrying on against it in France, and other parts of the continent,‡ and also from the preponderance of the Protestant power in Europe, and particularly that of our own country, which, he says, is nearly as much interested in the extirpation of Popery as of Jacobinism. My answer is this: I see and bewail the anti-Catholic persecution which has been, and is carried on in France and its dependent states, where to decatholicize is the avowed order of the day. This was preceded by the less sanguinary, though equally anti-Catholic persecution of the emperor Joseph II. and his relatives in Germany and Italy. I hear the exultations and menaces on this account, of the Wranghams, De Coetlegons, Towsons, Bichenos, Ketts, Fabers, Daubenys, and a crowd of other declamatory preachers and writers, some of whom proclaim that the Romish Babylon is on the point of falling, and others that she is actually fallen. In the mean time, though more living branches of the mystical vine should be cut off by the sword, and more rotten branches should fall off, from their own decay,§ I am not at all fearful for the life of the tree itself;

---

* See an account of them, and the authorities on which this rests, in *Letters to a Prebendary*, Letter IV.　　　　　　　† Ibid.

‡ Namely, in 1802.

§ Since the present letter was written, many circumstances have occurred to show the *mistaken* politics of our rulers, in endeavouring to weaken and supplant the religion of their truly loyal and conscientious Catholic subjects. Among other measures for this purpose, may be mentioned the late instructions sent to

since the divine veracity is pledged for its safety, *as long as the sun and moon shall endure*, Ps. lxxxix. ; and since the experience of eighteen centuries has confirmed our faith in these divine promises. During this long interval, kingdoms and empires have risen and fallen, the inhabitants of every country have been repeatedly changed; in short, every thing has changed except the doctrine and jurisdiction of the Catholic church, which are precisely the same now as Christ and his apostles left them. In vain did Pagan Rome, during three centuries, exert its force to drown her in her own blood; in vain did Arianism and other heresies sap her foundations, during two centuries more; in vain did hordes of barbarians, from the north, and of Mahometans, from the south, labour to overwhelm her; in vain did Luther swear that he himself would be her death :* she has survived these, and numerous other enemies equally redoubtable; and she will survive even the fury and machinations of anti-christian philosophy, though directed against her exclusively : for not a drop of Protestant blood has been shed in this impious persecution. Nor is that church which, in a single kingdom, the very head quarters of infidelity, could at once furnish twenty-four thousand martyrs and sixty thousand voluntary exiles, in defence of her faith, so likely to sink under external violence, or internal weakness, as your Rev. visiter supposes. Alluding to the then recent attempt of the emperor Julian to falsify the prophecy of Daniel by rebuilding the Jewish temple, St. John Chrysostom exclaimed, " Behold the temple of Jerusalem; God has destroyed it, and have men been able to restore it ? Behold the church of Christ; God

---

the governor of Canada, which Catholic province alone remained faithful at the time of trial, when all the Protestant provinces abjured their allegiance. To the same intent may be cited the letter of Dr. Kerr, senior chaplain of fort St. George, quoted in the late Parliamentary Report. By this it appears that the Catholics in that province generally converted about three hundred Infidels to Christianity every year, and that there was a prospect of their converting many of the Hindoo chiefs, but that *our government set its face against these conversions.* Thus is the infamous worship of Juggernaut itself preferred to the religion which converted and civilized our ancestors. Juggernaut, as Dr. Buchanan informs us, is a huge idol, carved with the most obscene figures round it, and publicly worshipped before hundreds of thousands with obscene songs and unnatural rites, too gross to be described. It is placed on a carriage, under the wheels of which great numbers of its votaries are encouraged to throw themselves in order to be crushed to death by them. Now this infernal worship is *not barely permitted,* but even supported by our government in India, as it takes a tribute from each individual who is present at it, and likewise *defrays the expense of it,* to the amount, says Dr. Buchanan, of 8,700*l.* annually, including the keep of the prostitutes, &c.

* Luther ordered this epitaph to be engraved on his tomb : *Pestis eram vivens, moriens ero mors tua, Papa.*

has built it, have men been able to destroy it?"　Should the Almighty permit such a persecution to befall any of the Protestant communions, as we have beheld raging against the Catholic church on the continent, does your visiter really believe they will exhibit the same constancy, in suffering for their respective tenets, that she has shown in defence of hers?　In fact; for what tenets should their members suffer exile and death, since, without persecution, they have all, in a manner, abandoned their original creeds, from the uncertainty of their rule of faith, and their own natural mutability? Human laws and premiums may preserve the exterior appearance, or *mere carcass of a church*, as one of your divines expresses it; but, if the pastors and doctors of it should demonstrate by their publications that they no longer maintain her original fundamental articles, can we avoid subscribing to the opinion, expressed by a late dignitary, that " the church in question, properly so called, is not in existence ?"*

I am, &c.
J. M.

LETTER XXVIII.

To JAMES BROWN, Esq.

ON THE APOSTOLICITY OF THE CATHOLIC CHURCH.

Dear Sir,

THE last of the four marks of the church, mentioned in our common Creed, is APOSTOLICITY.　We each of us declare, in our solemn worship, *I believe in one, holy, Catholic and APOS-TOLICAL church.*　Christ's last commission to his apostles was this: *Go teach all nations, baptizing them in the name of the Father, and of the Son, and of the Holy Ghost. and lo! I am with you always, even unto THE END OF THE WORLD.* Mat. xxviii. 20.　Now the event has proved, as I have already observed, that the apostles, themselves, were only to live the ordinary term of man's life; therefore, the commission of preaching and ministering, together with the promise of the Divine assistance, regards the successors of the apostles, no less than the apostles themselves.　This proves that there must

---

* Confessional, p. 244.

have been an uninterrupted series of such successors of the apostles in every age since their time, that is to say, successors to their *doctrine*, to their *jurisdiction*, to their *orders*, and to their *mission*. Hence it follows that no religious society whatever, which cannot trace its succession, in these four points, up to the apostles, has any claim to the characteristic title, APOSTOLICAL.

Conformably with what is here laid down, we find the fathers and ecclesiastical doctors of every age referring to this mark of *apostolical succession*, as demonstrative of their belonging to *the true church of Christ*. St. Irenæus of Lyons, the disciple of St. Polycarp, who himself appears to have been consecrated by St. John the evangelist, repeatedly urges this argument against his contemporary heretics. "We can count up," he says, "those who were appointed bishops in the churches by the apostles and their successors down to us, none of whom taught this doctrine. But as it would be tedious to enumerate the succession of Bishops in the different churches, we refer you to the tradition of that greatest, most ancient, and universally known church, founded at Rome by St. Peter and St. Paul, and which has been preserved there through the succession of its bishops down to the present time." He then recites the names of the several Popes down to Eleutherius, who was then living.* Tertullian, who also flourished in the same century, argues in the same manner, and challenges certain heretics, in these terms: "Let them produce the origin of their church; let them display the succession of their bishops, so that the first of them may appear to have been ordained by an *apostolic man*, who persevered in their communion." He then gives a list of the pontiffs in the Roman See, and concludes as follows: "Let the Heretics feign any thing like this."† The great St. Augustin, who wrote in the fifth century, among other motives of credibility in favour of the Catholic religion, mentions the one in question: "I am kept in this church," he says, "by the succession of prelates from St. Peter, to whom the Lord committed the care of his sheep, down to the present bishop."‡ In like manner St. Optatus, writing against the Donatists, enumerates all the Popes from St. Peter down to the then living Pope, Siricius, "with whom," he says, "we and all the world are united in communion. Do you, Donatists, now give the history

---

* Lib. iii. advers. Hær. c. iii.
† " Fingant tale aliquid hæretici." Præscript.
‡ Contra Epist. Fundam.

of your episcopal ministry."* In fact, this mode of proving
the Catholic church to be *apostolical* is conformable to common
sense and constant usage. If a prince is desirous of showing
his title to a throne, or a nobleman or gentleman his claim to
an estate, he fails not to exhibit his genealogical table, and to
trace his pedigree up to some personage whose right to it was
unquestionable. I shall adopt the same precise method on the
present occasion; by sending your society a slight sketch of our
apostolical tree, by which they will see, at a glance, an abridgment of the succession of our chief bishops in the apostolical
See of Rome, from St. Peter up to the present edifying pontiff,
Pius VII, as likewise that of other illustrious doctors, prelates
and saints, who have defended the apostolical doctrine by their
preaching and writings, or who have illustrated it by their lives.
They will also see the fulfilment of Christ's injunction to the
apostles and their successors in the conversion of nations and
people to his faith and church. Lastly, they will behold the
unhappy series of heretics and schismatics, who, in different
ages, have fallen off from the doctrine or communion of the
apostolic church. But as it is impossible, in so narrow a compass as the present sheet, to give the names of all the Popes, or
to exhibit the other particulars here mentioned in the distinct
and detailed manner which the subject seems to require, I will
try to supply the deficiency by the subjoined copious note.†

* Contra Parmen. lib. ii.

† Within the first century from the birth of Christ, this long expected Messiah founded the kingdom of his holy church in Judæa, and chose his apostles to
propagate the same throughout the earth, over whom he appointed Simon, as the
centre of union and *head pastor;* charging him to feed his whole flock, sheep as
well as lambs, giving him the keys of the kingdom of heaven, and changing his
name into that of PETER, or ROCK; adding, *on this rock I will build my
church.* Thus dignified, St. Peter first established his See at Antioch, the head
city of Asia, whence he sent his disciple St. Mark to establish and govern the See
of Alexandria, the head city of Africa. He afterwards removed his own See to
Rome, the capital of Europe and the world. Here, having, with St. Paul, sealed the Gospel with his blood, he transmitted his prerogative to St. Linus, from
whom it descended in succession to St. Cletus and St. Clement. Among the
other illustrious doctors of this age are to be reckoned, first, the other apostles,
then SS. Mark, Luke, Barnaby, Timothy, Titus, Hermas, Ignatius, bishop of
Antioch, and Polycarp of Smyrna. From the few remaining writings of these
may be gathered the necessity of unity and submission to bishops, tradition, the
real presence, the sacrifice of the mass, veneration for relics, &c. In this age,
churches were founded, besides the above-mentioned places, in Samaria,
throughout lesser Asia, in Armenia, India, Greece, Egypt, Ethiopia, Italy,
Spain, and Gaul; in this apostolical age, also, and as it were under the eyes of
the apostles, different proud innovators pretended to *reform* the doctrine which
they taught. Among these were Simon the Magician, Hymeneus and Philetus,
the incontinent Nicolaites, Cerinthus, Ebion, and Meander.

I do not, dear sir, pretend to exhibit a history of the church, nor even a regular epitome of it, in the present note, any more

CENT. II.

The succession of chief pastors in the chair of Peter was kept up through this century by the following Popes, who were also, for the most part, martyrs: Anacletus, Evaristus, Alexander I, Xystus I, Telesphorus, Hyginus, Pius I, Anicetus, Soter, Eleutherius, who sent Fugatius and Damianus to convert the Britons, and Victor I, who exerted his authority against certain Asiatic bishops for keeping Easter at an undue time. The truth of Christianity was defended, in this age, by the apologists Quadratus, Aristides, Melito, and Justin, the philosopher and martyr; and the rising heresies of Valentinian, Marcion, and Carpocrates, were confounded by the bishops Dionysius of Corinth, and Theophylus of Antioch, in the east, and by St. Irenæus and Tertullian, in the west. In the mean time, the Catholic church was more widely spread, through Gaul, Germany, Scythia, Africa, and India, besides Britain.

CENT. III.

The Popes who presided over the church, in the third age, were all eminent for their sanctity, and almost all of them martyrs. Their names are Zephyrinus, Calixtus I, Urban I, Pontianus, Antherus, Fabian, Cornelius, Lucius, Stephen I, Xystus II, Dionysius, Felix I, Etuychian, Caius, and Marcellinus. The most celebrated doctors of this age were St. Clement of Alexandria, Origen, Minutius Felix, St. Cyprian, St. Hypolitus, both martyrs, and St. Gregory, bishop, surnamed for his miracles Thaumaturgus. At this time Arabia, the Belgic Provinces, and many districts of Gaul, were almost wholly converted: while Paul of Samosata, for denying the divinity of Christ, Sabellus, for denying the distinction of persons in the B. Trinity, and Novatus, for denying the power of the church to remit sins, with Manes, who believed in two deities, were cut off as rotten branches from the Apostolic tree.

CENT. IV.

St. Marcellus, the first Pope in this century, died through the hardships of imprisonment for the faith. After him came Eusebius, Melchiades, Silvester, under whom the Councils of Arles, against the Donatists, and of Nice, against the Arians, were held, Marcus Julius, in whose time the right of appeal to the Roman See was confirmed, Liberius, and Damasus. The church, which hitherto had been generally persecuted by the Roman emperors, was, in this age, alternately protected and oppressed by them. In the mean time, her numbers were prodigiously increased by conversions throughout the Roman empire, and also in Armenia, Iberia, and Abyssinia, and her faith was invincibly maintained by St. Athanasius, St. Hilary, St. Gregory Nazianzen, St. Basil, St. Ambrose of Milan, &c. against the Arians, who opposed the divinity of Christ, the Macedonians, who opposed that of the Holy Ghost, the Aerians, who impugned episcopacy, fasting and prayers for the dead, and other new heretics and schismatics.

CENT. V.

During this age, the perils and sufferings of the church were great; but so also were the resources and victories by which her Divine Founder supported her. On one hand the Roman empire, that fourth great Dynasty, compared by Daniel to iron, was broken to pieces by numberless hordes of Goths, Vandals, Huns, Burgundians, Franks and Saxons, who came pouring in upon the civilized world, and seemed to be on the point of overwhelming arts, sciences, laws, and religion, in one undistinguished ruin. On the other hand, various classes of powerful and subtil heretics strained every nerve to corrupt the apostolical doc-

Y

than in the apostolical tree ; nevertheless, either of these will give you and your respectable society, a sufficient idea of the

trine, and to interrupt the course of the apostles' successors. Among these, the Nestorians denied the union of Christ's divine and human natures; the Eutychians confounded them together; the Pelagians denied the necessity of divine grace, and the followers of Vigilantius scoffed at celibacy, prayers to the saints, and veneration for their relics.   Against these innovators a train of illustrious pontiffs and holy fathers opposed themselves, with invincible fortitude and decided success.   The Popes were Innocent I, Zosimus, Boniface I, Celestin I, who presided by his legates in the Council of Ephesus, Xystus III, Leo the Great, who presided in that of Chalcedon, Hilarius, Simplicius, Felix III, Gelasius I, Anastacius II, and Symachus.   Their zeal was well seconded by some of the brightest ornaments of orthodoxy and literature who ever illustrated the church, St. John Chrysostom, St. Jerom, St. Augustin, St. Gregory of Nyssa, &c. By their means, and those of other apostolic Catholics, not only were the enemies of the church refuted, but also her bounds greatly enlarged by the conversion of the Franks, with their king, Clovis, of the Scotch and the Irish.   The apostle of the former was St. Palladius, and of the latter St. Patrick, both commissioned by the See of Rome.

CENT. VI.

The church had to combat with infidels, heretics, and worldly politicians, in this as in other ages; but failed not to receive the accustomed proofs of the divine protection, amidst her dangers. The chief bishops succeeded each other in the following order : Hormisdas, St. John I, who died a prisoner for the faith, Felix IV, Boniface II, John II, Agapetus I, St. Silverius, who died in exile for the unity of the church, Vigilius, Pelagius I, John III, Benedict I, Pelagius II, and St. Gregory the Great, a name which ought to be engraved on the heart of every Englishman who knows how to value the benefits of Christianity, since it was he who first undertook to preach the Gospel to our Saxon ancestors, and, when he was prevented by force from doing this, sent his deputies, St. Augustin and his companions, on this apostolical errand.   Other beneficial lights of this age were St. Fulgentius of Ruspa, Cesarius of Arles, Lupus, Germanus, Severus, Gregory of Tours, our venerable Gildas, and the great patriarch of the monks, St. Benedict. The chief heretics who disturbed the peace of the church were the Acephali and Jacobites, both branches of Eutychianism, the Tritheists, the powerful supporters of the Three Chapters, Severus, Eleurus, Mongus, Athimius, and Acacius.   A more terrible scourge, however, than these, or than any other which the church had yet felt, God permitted in this age to fall upon her, in the rapid progress of the impostor Mahomet; what however she lost in some quarters, was made up to her in others, by the suppression of Arianism among the Visigoths of Spain and among the Ostrogoths of Italy, and by the conversion of the Lazes, Axumites, and Southern English.

CENT. VII.

The Popes in this century are most of them honoured for their sanctity, namely, Sabinianus, Boniface III, Boniface IV, Deusdedit, Boniface V, Honorius I, Severinus, John IV, Theodorus, Martin I, who died an exile, in defence of the faith, Eugenius I, Vitalianus, Domnus I, Agatho, who presided, by his legates, in the sixth General Council, held against the Monotholites, Leo II, Benedict II, John V, Conon, and Sergius I. Other contemporary doctors and saints were St. Sophronius and St. John the almoner, bishops, and St. Maximus, martyr, in the East. SS. Isidore, Ildefonsus and Eugeinus, in Spain, SS. Amand, Eligius, Omer and Owen, in France, and SS. Paulinus, Wilfrid, Birinus, Felix, Chad, Aidan and Cuthbert, in England. The East, at this time, was distracted by the

uninterupted succession of supreme pastors, which has subsisted in the See of Rome from St. Peter, whom Christ made head of

Monotholite heretics, and in some parts, by the Paulicians, who revived the detestable heresy of the Manicheans, but most of all by the sanguinary course of the Mahometans, who overran the most fertile and civilized countries of Asia and Africa, and put a stop to the apostolical succession in the primitive Sees of the East. To compensate for these losses, the church spread her roots wide in the northern regions. The whole Heptarchy of England became Christian, and diffused the sweet odour of Christ throughout the West. Hence issued SS. Willibord and Swibert to convert Holland and Frizeland, and the two brothers, of the name of Ewald, who confirmed their doctrine with their blood. The martyr St. Killian, who converted Franconia, was an Irishman; but all these apostolical men received their commission from the chair of St. Peter.

CENT. VIII.

The apostolic succession of the See of Rome was kept up in this age by John VI, John VII, Sisinnius, Constantine, Gregory II, Gregory III, Zacharias, Stephen II, Stephen III, Paul I, Adrian I, who presided by his legates in the seventh general council against the Iconoclasts, and Leo III. The Saracens now crossed the straits of Gibraltar and nearly overran Spain, making numerous martyrs; while Felix and Elipand broached errors in the West, nearly resembling those of Nestorius. The most signal defenders of the orthodox doctrine were St. Germanus Patriarch, St. John Damascene, Paul the deacon, Ven. Bede, St. Aldhelm, St. Willibald, Alcuin, St. Boniface, bishop and martyr, and St. Lullus. Most of these were Englishmen, and, by their means, Hessia, Thuringia, Saxony, and other provinces, were added to the Catholic church.

CENT. IX.

The apostolic tree, in this age, was agitated by storms more violent than usual; but, being refreshed with the dew of grace from above, held fast by its roots. Claudius of Turin, united in one system the heresies of Nestorius, Vigilantius, and the Iconoclasts, while Gotescalc laboured to infect the church with predestinarianism. A more severe blow, to her, however, was the Greek schism, occasioned by the resentment and ambition of the hypocrite, Photius. But the greatest danger of all arose from the overbearing power of the Antichristian musselmen, who now carried their arms into Sicily, France, and Italy, and became masters, for a time, of the holy See itself. The succession of its bishops, however, continued uninterrupted, in the following order: Stephen V, Pascal I, Eugenius II, Valentin, Gregory IV, Sergius II, Leo IV, Benedict III, Nicholas I, Adrian II, who presided by his legates in the eighth general council, John VIII, Marinus, Adrian III, Stephen VI, Formosus, Stephen VII, and Romanus. Other props of the church, in this age, were Theodore the Studite, St. Ignatius, the legitimate patriarch of C. P. Rabanus, Hincmar, and Agobard, French bishops, together with our countrymen, St. Swithun, Neot, Grimbald, Alfred, and Edmund. In this age St. Ansgarius converted the people of Holstein, and SS. Cyril and Methodius the Sclavonians, Moravians, and Bohemians, by virtue of a commission from Pope Adrian II.

CENT. X.

The several Popes during this century were Theodore II, John IX, Benedict IV, Leo V, Christopher, Sergius III, Anastasius, Lando, John X, Leo VI, Stephen VIII, John XI, Leo VII, Stephen IX, Martin II, Agapetus II, John XII, Benedict V, John XIII, Domnus II, Benedict VII, John XIV, John XV, and Gregory V. This age is generally considered as the least enlightened by piety

his church, up to the present Pope, Pius VII.   And this attribute of perpetual succession, you are, dear sir, to observe, is

and literature of the whole number. Its greatest disgrace, however, arose from the misconduct of several of the above-mentioned pontiffs, owing to the prevalence of civil factions at Rome, which obstructed the freedom of canonical election: yet, in this list of names, there are ten or twelve, which do honour to the papal calendar, and even those who disgraced it by their lives, performed their public duty, in preserving the faith and unity of the church, irreproachably. In the mean time a crowd of holy bishops and other saints, worthy the age of the apostles, adorned most parts of the church, which continued to be augmented by numerous conversions. In Italy SS. Peter Damian, Romuald, Nilus, and Rathier, bishop of Verona adorned the church with their sanctity and talents, as did the holy prelates, Ulric Wolfgang, and Bruno, in Germany, and Odo, Dunstan, Oswald, and Ethelwold, in England. At this time St. Adelbert, bishop of Prague, converted the Poles by his preaching and his blood; the Danes were converted by St. Poppo, the Swedes, by St. Sigifrid, an Englishman, the people of lesser Russia by SS. Bruno and Boniface, and the Muscovites by missionaries sent from Greece, but at a time when that country was in communion with the See of Rome.

CENT. XI.

During this age the vessel of Peter was steered by several able and virtuous pontiffs. Silvester II was esteemed a prodigy of learning and talents. After him came John XVIII, John XIX, Sergius IV, Benedict VIII, John XX, Benedict IX, Gregory VI, Clement II, Damascus II, Leo IX, who has deservedly been reckoned among the saints, Victor II, Stephen X, Nicholas II, Alexander II, Gregory VII, who is also canonized, Victor III, and Urban II.   Other defenders of virtue and religion, in this age, were St. Elphege and Lanfranc, archbishops of Canterbury, the prelates Burcard of Worms, Fulbert and Ivo of Chartres, Odilo an abbot, Alger a monk, Guitmund and Theophylactus. The crown, also, was now adorned with saints equally signal for their virtue and orthodoxy. In England shone St. Edward the confessor; in Scotland, St. Margaret; in Germany, St. Henry, Emperor; in Hungary, St. Stephen. The cloister also was now enriched with the Cisterchian order, by St. Robert; the Carthusian order was founded by St. Bruno; and the order of Valombroso, by St. John Gualbert. While, on one hand, a great branch of the apostolic tree was lopped off, by the second defection of the Greek church, and some rotten boughs were cut off from it, in the new Manicheans, who had found their way from Bulgaria into France, as likewise in the followers of the innovator Berengarius; it received fresh strength and increase from the conversion of the Hungarians, and of the Normans and Danes, who before had desolated England, France, and the two Sicilies.

CENT. XII.

In this century heresy revived with fresh vigour, and in a variety of forms, though mostly of the Manichean family. Mahometanism also again threatened to overwhelm Christianity. To oppose these, the Almighty was pleased to raise up a succession of as able and virtuous Popes as ever graced the Tiara, with a proportionable number of other Catholic champions to defend his cause. These were Paschal II, Gelasius II, Calixtus II, Honorius II, Innocent II, who held the second general council of Lateran, Celestin II, Lucius II, Eugenius III, Anastasius IV, Adrian IV, an Englishman, Alexander III, who held the third Lateran council, Lucius III, Urban III, Gregory VIII, Clement III, and Celestin III. The doctors of note were, in the first place, the mellifluous Bernard, a saint, however, who was not more powerful in word than in work; likewise the venerable

peculiar to the See of Rome : for in all the other churches, founded by the apostles, as those of Jerusalem, Antioch, Alex-

Peter, abbot of Clugni, St. Anselm and St. Thomas, archbishops of Canterbury, Peter Lombard, master of the sentences, St. Otto, bishop of Bamberg, St. Norbert of Magdeburg, St. Henry of Upsal, St. Malachy of Armagh, St. Hugh of Lincoln, and St. William of York. The chief heresies, alluded to, were those propagated by Marsilius of Padua, Arnold of Brescia, Henry of Tholouse, Tanchelm, Peter Bruis, the Waldenses, or disciples of Peter Waldo, and the Bogomilians, Patarins, Cathari, Puritans, and Albigenses, all the latter being different sects of Manicheans. To make up for the loss of these, the church was increased by the conversion of the Norwegians and Livonians, chiefly through the labours of the above named Adrian IV, then an apostolic missionary, called Nicholas Breakspeare. Courland was converted by St. Meinard, and even Iceland was engrafted in the apostolic tree by the labours of Catholic missionaries.

CENT. XIII.

The successors of St. Peter in this age were Innocent III, who held the fourth Lateran council, at which four hundred and twelve bishops, eight hundred abbots, and ambassadors from most of the Christian sovereigns were present, for the extinction of the impious and infamous Albigensian or Manichean heresy. Honorius III, Gregory IX, Celestin IV, who held the first general council of Lyons, Alexander IV, Urban IV, Gregory X, who held the second council of Lyons, in which the Greeks renounced their schism, though they soon fell back into it, Innocent V, Adrian V, John XXI, Nicholas III, Martin IV, Honorius IV, Nicholas IV, Celestin V, who abdicated the pontificate and was afterwards canonized, and Boniface VIII. The most celebrated doctors of the church were St. Thomas of Aquin, St. Bonaventure, St. Anthony of Padua, and St. Raymond of Pennafort. Other illustrious supporters and ornaments of the church, were St. Lewis, king of France, St. Elizabeth, queen of Hungary, St. Hedwidge of Poland, St. Francis of Assisium, St. Dominic, St. Edmund, archbishop of Canterbury, St. Thomas of Hereford, and St. Richard of Chichester. The chief heretics were the Beguardi and Fratricelli, whose gross immoralities Mosheim himself confesses. In the mean time Spain was, in a great measure, recovered to the Catholic church from the Mahometan impiety ; Courland, Gothland, and Estonia, were converted by Baldwin, a zealous missionary : the Cumani, near the mouths of the Danube, were received into the church, and several tribes of Tartars, with one of their emperors, were converted by the Franciscan missionaries, whom the Pope sent among them, not, however, without the martyrdom of many of them.

CENT. XIV.

Still did the promise of Christ, in the preservation of his church, contrary to all opposition, and beyond the term of all human institutions, continue to be verified. The following were the head pastors, who successively presided over it ; Benedict XI, Clement V, who held the general council of Vienna, John XXII, Clement VI, Innocent VI, Urban V, Gregory XI, Urban VI, and Boniface IX. Among the chief ornaments of the church, in this age, may be reckoned St. Elizabeth, queen of Portugal, St. Bridget of Sweden, Count Elzear and his spouse Delphina, St. Nicholas of Tolentino, St. Catharine of Sienna, John Rusbrock, Peter, bishop of Autun, &c. The Manichean abominations maintained and practised by the Turlupins, Dulcinians and other sects, continued to exercise the vigilance and zeal of the Catholic pastors, and the Lollards of Germany, together with the Wickliffites of England, whose errors and conduct were levelled at the foundations of society, as well as of religion, were opposed by all true Catholics in their respective stations. The chief conquests of the church

andria, Corinth, Ephesus, Smyrna, &c. owing to internal dissensions and external violence, the succession of their bishops

in this century were in Lithuania, the prince and people of which received her faith, and in Great Tartary, where the archbishopric of Cambalu and six suffragan bishoprics were established by the Pope. Odoric, the missionary, who furnished the account of these events, is known himself to have baptized twenty thousand converts.

CENT. XV.

The succession of Popes continued through this century, though among numerous difficulties and dissensions, in the following order: Innocent VII, Gregory XII, Alexander V, John XXII, Martin V, Eugenius IV, who held the general council of Florence, and received the Greeks, once more, into the Catholic communion, Nicholas V, Calixtus III, Pius II, Paul II, Sixtus IV, Innocent VIII, and Alexander VI. In this age flourished St. Vincent Ferrer, the Wonder-worker, both in the order of grace and in that of nature, St. Francis of Paula, whose miracles were not less numerous or extraordinary, St. Laurence Justinian, Patriarch of Venice, St. Antonius, archbishop of Florence, St. Casimir, Prince of Poland, the Venerable Thomas à Kempis, Dr. John Gerson, Thomas Waldensis, the learned English Carmelite, Alphonsus Tostatus, Cardinal Ximenes, &c. At this period the Canary Islands were added to the church, as were, in a great measure, the kingdoms of Congo and Angola, with other large districts in Africa and Asia, wherever the Portuguese established themselves. The Greek schismatics also, as I have said, together with the Armenians and Monotholites of Egypt, were, for a time, engrafted on the apostolic tree. These conquests, however, were dampt by the errors and violence of the various sects of Hussites, and the immoral tenets and practices of the Adamites, and other remnants of the Albigenses.

CENT. XVI.

This century was distinguished by that furious storm from the north, which stripped the apostolic tree of so many leaves and branches in this quarter. That arrogant monk, Martin Luther, vowed destruction to the tree itself, and engaged to plant one of those separated branches instead of it; but the attempt was fruitless; for the main stock was sustained by the arm of Omnipotence, and the dissevered boughs splitting into numberless fragments, withered, as all such boughs had heretofore done. It would be impossible to number up all these discordant sects; the chief of them were, the Lutherans, the Zuinglians, the Anabaptists, the Calvinists, the Anglicans, the Puritans, the Family of Love, and the Socinians. In the mean time, on the trunk of the apostolic tree grew the following Pontiffs; Pius III, Julius II, who held the fifth Lateran Council, Leo X, Adrian VI, Clement VII, Paul III, Julius III, Marcellus II, Paul IV, Pius IV, who concluded the Council of Trent, where 281 prelates condemned the novelties of Luther, Calvin, &c., St. Pius V, Gregory XIII, Sixtus V, Urban VII, Gregory XIV, Innocent IX, and Clement VIII. Other supporters of the Catholic and apostolic church against the attacks made upon her, were, Fisher, bishop of Rochester, Sir Thomas More, Chancellor, Cuthbert Maine, and some hundreds more of priests and religious who were martyred under Henry VIII and Elizabeth, in this cause; also the Cardinals Pole, Hosius, Cajetan and Allen, with the writers Eckius, Cochleu, Erasmus, Campion, Parsons, Stapleton, &c. together with that constellation of great saints which then appeared, SS. Charles Borromeo, Cajetan, Philip Neri, Ignatius, F. Xavier, F. Borgia, Teresa, &c. In short, the damages sustained from the northern storm were amply repaid to the church, by innumerable conversions in the new eastern and western worlds. It is computed that St. Xavier alone preached the faith in 52 kingdoms

has, at different times, been broken and confounded. Hence
the See of Rome is emphatically and for a double reason call-

or independent states, and baptized a million of converts with his own hand, in
India and Japan. St. Lewis Bertrand, Martin of Valentia, and Bartholomew
Las Casas, with their fellow missionaries, converted most of the Mexicans, and
great progress was made in the conversion of the Brazilians, though not without
the blood of many martyred preachers in these and the other Catholic missions.
David, emperor of Abyssinia, with many of his family and other subjects, were
now reclaimed to the church, and Pulika, patriarch of the Nestorians in Assyria,
came to Rome, in order to join the numerous churches under him to the centre of
unity and truth.

CENT. XVII.

The sects, of which I have been speaking, were, at the beginning of this century, in their full vigour; and though they differed in most other respects, yet
they combined their forces, under the general name of Protestants, to overthrow
Christ's everlasting church. These attempts, however, like the waves of the
troubled ocean, were dashed to pieces against the rock on which he had built
it. On the contrary, they weakened themselves by civil wars and fresh divisions. The Lutherans split into Diaphorists and Adiaphorists, the Calvinists
into Gomarists and Arminians, and the Anglicans into Episcopalians, Presbyterians, Independents, and Quakers. A vain effort was now set on foot, through
Cyril Lucaris, to gain over the Greek churches to Calvinism, which ended in
demonstrating their inviolable attachment to all the controverted doctrines of
Catholicity. Another more fatal attempt, was made to infect several members
of the church itself with the distinguishing error of Calvinism, under the name
of Jansenism. But the successors of St. Peter continued, through the whole of
the century, equally to make head against Protestant innovations, Jansenistical
vigour, and casuistical laxity. Their names, in order, were these, Leo XI,
Paul V, Gregory XV, Urban VIII, Innocent X, Alexander VII, Clement IX,
Clement X, Innocent XI, Alexander VIII, and Innocent XII. Their orthodoxy
was powerfully supported by the Cardinals Bellarmin, Baronius and Perron,
with the bishops Huetius, Bossuet, Fenelon, Richard Smith, and the divines
Petavius, Tillemont, Pagi, Thomassin, Kellison, Cressy, &c. Nor were the canonized saints of this age fewer in number or less illustrious than those of the
former, namely, St. Francis of Sales, St. Frances Chantal, St. Camillus, St. Fidelis Martyr, St. Vincent of Paul, &c. Finally, the church continued to be
crowded with fresh converts, in Peru, Chili, Terra Firma, Canada, Louisiana,
Mingrelia, Tartary, India, and many islands both of Africa and Asia. She had
also the consolation of receiving into her communion the several Patriarchs of
Damascus, Aleppo, and Alexandria, and also the Nestorian archbishops of Chaldæa and Meliapore, with their respective clergy.

CENT. XVIII.

At length we have mounted up the apostolic tree to our own age. In this
heresy having sunk, for the most part, into Socinian indifference, and Jansenism into philosophic infidelity, this last waged as cruel a war against the Catholic church, [and O glorious mark of truth! against her alone] as Decius and
Dioclesian did heretofore: but this has only proved her internal strength of constitution, and the protection of the God of heaven. The Pontiffs, who have
stood the storms of this century, were Clement XI, Innocent XIII, Benedict XIV,
Clement XIII, Clement XIV, Pius VI, as at the beginning of the present century Pius VII has done. Among other modern supporters and ornaments of the
church, may be mentioned the Cardinals Thomasi and Quirina, the bishops
Languet, La Motte, Beaumont, Challoner, Hornyold, Walmesley, Hay and

18*

ed THE APOSTOLICAL SEE, and being the head See and centre of union of the whole Catholic church, furnishes the first claim to its title of THE APOSTOLICAL CHURCH. But you also see, in the sketch of this mystical tree, an uninterrupted series of other bishops, doctors, pastors, saints, and pious personages, of different times and countries, through these eighteen centuries, who have, in their several stations, kept up the perpetual succession, those of one century having been the instructors of those who succeeded them in the next, all of them following the same two-fold rule, Scripture and tradition; all of them acknowledging the same expositor of this rule, the Catholic church, and all of them adhering to the main trunk or centre of union, the apostolic See. Some of the general councils or synods likewise appear, in which the bishops from different parts of the church, under the authority of the Pope, assembled, from time to time, to define its doctrine and regulate its discipline. The size of the sheet did not admit of all the councils being exhibited. Again you behold, in this tree, the continuation of the apostolical work, the conversion of nations, which, as it was committed by Christ to the Catholic church, so it has never been blessed by him with success in any hands but in hers. This exclusive miracle, in the order of grace, like those in the order of nature, which I treated of in a former letter is itself a divine attestation on her behalf. Speaking of the conversion of nations, I must not fail, dear sir, to remind your society. that this our country has twice been reclaimed from Paganism, and each time by the apostolic labours of missionaries, sent hither by the See of Rome. The first conversion took

Moylan. Among the writers are Calmet, Muratori, Bergier, Feller, Gother, Manning, Hawarden, and Alban Butler; and among the personages distinguished by their piety, the *Good* Dauphin, his sister Louisa the Carmelite nun, his heroical daughter Elizabeth, his other daughter Clotilda, whose beatification is now in progress, as those of bishop Liguori, and Paul of the cross, founder of the Passionists; as also FF. Surenne, Nolhac and L. Enfant, with their fellow-martyrs and the venerable Labre, &c. Nor has the apostolical work of converting Infidels been neglected by the Catholic church, in the midst of such persecutions. In the early part of the century, numberless souls were gained by Catholic preachers in the kingdoms of Madura, Cochinchina, Tonquin, and in the empire of China, including the peninsula of Corea. At the same time numerous savages were civilized and baptized among the Hurons, Miamis, Illinois, and other tribes of North America. But the most glorious conquest, because the most difficult and most complete, was that gained by the Jesuits in the interior of South America over the wild savages of Paraguay, Uraguay and Parona, together with the wild Canisians, Moxos and Chiquites, who, after shedding the blood of some hundreds of their first preachers, at length opened their hearts to the mild and sweet truths of the Gospel, and became models of piety and morality, nor less so of industry, civil order, and polity.

place in the second century, when Pope Eleutherius sent Fugatius and Duvianus for this purpose, to the ancient Britons, or
Welsh, under their king or governor, Lucius, as Bede and other
historians relate.   The second conversion was that of our immediate ancestors, the English Saxons and Angles, by St. Augustin and his companions, at the end of the sixth century, who
were sent from Rome, on this apostolical errand, by Pope Gregory the Great. Lastly, you see in the present sketch, a series
of unhappy children of the church, who, instead of *hearing* her
doctrines, as it was their duty to do, have pretended to *reform*
them ; and thus, losing the vital influx of their parent stock,
have withered and fallen off from it as mere dead branches.

I am, &c.

J. M.

LETTER XXIX.

To JAMES BROWN, Esq. &c.

ON THE APOSTOLICITY OF THE CATHOLIC MINISTRY.

Dear Sir,

In viewing *the apostolical tree*, you are to consider it as representing an uninterrupted succession of pontiffs and prelates,
who derive not barely their *doctrine*, but also, in a special manner, their *ministry*, namely their *holy orders* and the *right* or
jurisdiction to exercise those orders in a right line, from the
apostles of Jesus Christ. In fact, the Catholic church, in all
past ages, has not been more jealous of the sacred deposite of
orthodox doctrine, than of the equally sacred deposites of *legitimate ordination*, by bishops who themselves had been rightly
ordained and consecrated, and of *valid jurisdiction* or *divine
mission*, by which she authorizes her ministers to exercise their
respective functions in such and such places, with respect to
such and such persons, and under such and such conditions, as
she, by the depositaries of this jurisdiction, is pleased to ordain.
Thus, my dear sir, every Catholic pastor is authorized and enabled to address his flock as follows : *The word of God which I
announce to you, and the holy sacraments which I dispense to
you, I am* QUALIFIED *to announce and dispense by such a
Catholic bishop, who was consecrated by such another Catholic*

Z

bishop, and so on, in a series, which reaches to the apostles themselves: and I am AUTHORIZED *to preach and minister to you, by such a prelate, who received authority, for this purpose, from the successor of St. Peter, in the apostolic See of Rome.* Heretofore, during a considerable time, the learned and conscientious divines of the church of England held the same principles, on both these points, that Catholics have ever held, and were no less firm in maintaining the *divine right* of episcopacy and the ministry than we are. This appears from the works of one who was, perhaps, the most profound and accurate amongst them, the celebrated Hooker. He proves, at great length, that the ecclesiastical ministry is a divine function, instituted by God, and deriving its authority from God, " in a very different manner from that of princes and magistrates :" that it is " a wretched blindness not to admire so great a power as that, which the clergy are endowed with, or to suppose that any but God can bestow it :" that " it consists in a power over the *mystical body* of Christ by the *remission of sins,* and over his *natural body* in the *sacrament,* which antiquity doth call *the making of Christ's body.*"* He distinguishes between the power of orders and the authority of *mission* or *jurisdiction,* on both which points he is supported by the canons and laws of the establishment. Not to speak of prior laws; the act of uniformity,† provides that no minister shall hold any living, or officiate in any church, who has not received episcopal ordination. It also requires that he shall be approved and *licensed* for his particular place and *function.* This is also clear from the form of induction of a clerk into any cure.‡ In virtue of this system, when Episcopacy was re-established in Scotland, in the year 1662, four Presbyterian ministers having been appointed by the king to that office, the English bishops refused to consecrate them, unless they consented to be previously ordained deacons and priests, thus renouncing their former ministerial character, and acknowledging that they had hitherto been mere laymen.§ In like manner, on the accession of king William, who was a Dutch Calvinist, to the throne, when a commission of ten bishops and twenty divines was appointed to modify the articles and liturgy of the established church, for the purpose of form-

---

* Ecclesiast. Politic. B. v. Art. 77.   † Stat. 13 and 14 Car. 2, c. 4.
‡ " Curam et regimen animarum parochianorum tibi committimus."
§ Collier's Eccl. Hist. Vol. ii. p. 887. It appears from the same history that four other Scotch ministers, who had formerly permitted themselves to be consecrated bishops, were, on that account, excommunicated and degraded by the kirk. Records, N. cxlii.

ing a coalition with the dissenters, it appeared that the most lax among them, such as Tillotson and Burnet, together with chief baron Hales and other lay lords, required that the dissenting ministers should, at least be *conditionally ordained*,* as being thus far mere laymen. In a word, it is well known to be the practice of the established church, at the present day, to ordain all dissenting Protestant ministers of every description, who go over to her, whereas, she never attempts to re-ordain an apostate Catholic priest, who offers himself to her service, but is satisfied with his taking the oaths prescribed by law.† This doctrine of the establishment, evidently *unchurches*, as Dr. Heylin expresses it, all other Protestant communions; as it is an established principle that, *No ministry no church*,‡ and with equal evidence, it *unchristians* them also; since this church unanimously resolved, in 1575, that baptism cannot be performed by any person but a·lawful minister.§

But dismissing these uncertain and wavering opinions, we know what little account all other Protestants, except those of England, have made of apostolical succession and episcopal ordination. Luther's principles on these points are clear from his famous *Bull against the* FALSELY CALLED *order of bishops*,‖ where he says, "Give ear now, you bishops, or rather you visors of the devil: Dr. Luther will read you a Bull and a Reform, which will not sound sweet in your ears. Dr. Luther's Bull and Reform is this, whoever spend their labour, persons and fortunes, to lay waste your episcopacies, and to extinguish the government of bishops, they arc the beloved of God, true Christians, and opposers of the devil's ordinances. On the other hand, whoever support the government of bishops, and willingly obey them, they are the devil's ministers," &c. True it is, that afterwards, namely, in 1542, this arch reformer, to

* Life of Tillotson by Dr. Birch, pp. 42. 176.

† Notwithstanding these proofs of the doctrine and practice of the established church, a great proportion of her modern divines consent, at the present day, to sacrifice all her pretensions to divine authority and uninterrupted succession. It has been shown in *The Letters to a Prebendary*, that in the principles of the celebrated Dr. Balguy, a priest or a bishop can as well be made by the town crier, if commissioned by the civil power, as by the metropolitan. To this system, Dr. Sturges, Dr. Hey, Dr. Paley, and a crowd of other learned theologians subscribe their names. Even the bishop of Lincoln, in maintaining Episcopacy to be an apostolical institution, denies it to be binding on Christians to adopt it: which, in fact, is to reduce it to a mere civil and optional practice. Elem. Vol. ii. Art. 23.

‡ "Ubi nullus est Sacerdos nulla est Ecclesia." St. Jerom, &c.
§ Elem. of Theol. Vol. ii. p. 471.
‖ Adversus falso Nomin. Tom. ii. Jen. A. D. 1525.

gratify his chief patron, the Elector of Saxony, took upon himself to consecrate his bottle companion, Amsdorf, bishop of Naumburgh :* but, then, it is notorious, from the whole of his conduct, that Luther set himself above all law, and derided consistency and decency.   Nearly the same may be said of another later reformer, John Wesley, who, professing himself to be a *Presbyter of the church of England*, pretended to ordain Messrs. Whatcoat, Vesey, &c. priests, and to consecrate Dr. Coke *a bishop !*† With equal inconsistency, the elders of Hernhuth in Moravia, profess to consecrate bishops for England and other kingdoms.   On the other hand, how averse the Calvinists, and other dissenters, are to the very name as well as the office of bishops, all modern histories, especially those of England and Scotland, demonstrate.   But, in short, by whatever name, whether of bishops, priests, deacons, or pastors, these ministers respectively call themselves, it is undeniable, that they are all *self-appointed*, or, at most, they derive their claim from other men, who themselves were *self-appointed*, fifteen, sixteen, or seventeen hundred years subsequent to the time of the apostles.

The chief question which remains to be discussed concerns the ministry of the church of England; namely, whether the first Protestant bishops, appointed by queen Elizabeth, when the Catholic bishops were turned out of their Sees, did or did not receive valid consecration from some other bishop, who, himself, was validly consecrated?   The discussion of this question has filled many volumes, the result of which is, that the orders are, to say the least, exceedingly doubtful.   For, first, it is certain that the doctrine of the fathers of this church was very loose, as to the necessity of consecration and ordination.   Its chief founder, Cranmer, solemnly subscribed his name to the position, that princes and governors, no less than bishops, can make priests, and that no consecration is appointed by Scripture to make a bishop or priest.‡   In like manner, Barlow, on the validity of whose consecration that of Mathew Parker and of all succeeding Anglican bishops chiefly rests, preached openly that

---

* Sleidan, Comment. L. 14.

† Dr. Whitehead's Life of Charles and John Wesley. It appears that Charles was horribly scandalized at this step of his brother John, and that a lasting schism among the Wesleyan Methodists was the consequence of it.

‡ Burnet's Hist. of Reform.   Records, B. iii. N. 21.   See also his Rec. Part ii. N. 2, by which it appears that Cranmer and the other complying prelates took out fresh commissions on the death of Henry VIII, from Edward VI, to govern their dioceses, *durante beneplacito*, like mere civil officers.

the king's appointment, without any orders whatsoever, suffices to make a bishop.* This doctrine seems to have been broached by him to meet the objection that he himself had never been consecrated: in fact, the record of such a transaction has been hunted for in vain, during these two hundred years. Secondly, it is evident, from the books of controversy, still extant, that the Catholic doctors, Harding, Bristow, Stapleton, and Cardinal Allen, who had been fellow-students and intimately acquainted with the first Protestant bishops, under Elizabeth, and particularly with Jewel, bishop of Sarum, and Horne, bishop of Winton, constantly reproached them, in the most pointed terms, that they never had been consecrated at all, and that the latter, in their voluminous replies, never accepted of the challenge or refuted the charge, otherwise than by ridiculing the Catholic consecration. Thirdly, it appears that after an interval of fifty years from the beginning of the controversy, namely in the year 1613, when Mason, chaplain to archbishop Abbot, published a work, referring to an alleged Register at Lambeth, of archbishop Parker's consecration by Barlow, assisted by Coverdale and others, the learned Catholics universally exclaimed that the Register was a forgery, unheard of till that date, and asserted, among other arguments, that, admitting it to be true, it was of no avail, as the pretended consecrator of Parker, though he had sat in several Sees, had not himself been consecrated for any of them.†

These, however, are not the only exceptions which Catholic divines have taken to the ministerial orders of the church of England. They have argued, in particular, against the *form* of them, as theologians term it; in fact, according to the ordinal of Edward VI, restored by Elizabeth, priests were ordained by the power of *forgiving sins*,‡ without any power of *offering up sacrifice*, in which the essence of the *sacerdotium*, or *priesthood* consists; and, according to the same ordinal, bishops were consecrated without the communication of any fresh power whatsoever, or even the mention of episcopacy, by a *form* which might be used to a child, when confirmed or baptized.§ This

* Collier's Eccl. Hist. Vol. ii. p. 135.

† Richardson, in his notes on Godwin's Commentary, is forced to confess as follows: " Dies consecrationis ejus (Barlow) nondum apparet." p. 642.

‡ " Receive the Holy Ghost : whose sins thou dost forgive, they are forgiven; and whose sins thou dost retain, they are retained. and be thou a faithful dispenser of the word of God, and of his Holy Sacraments." Bishop Sparrow's Collection, p. 158.

§ " Take the Holy Ghost, and remember that thou stir up the grace of God, which is in thee by the imposition of hands."—Ibid. p. 164.

was agreeable to the maxims of the principal author of that ordinal, Cranmer, who solemnly decided that " bishops and priests were no two things, but one and the same office."[*]   On this subject our controvertists urge, not only the authority of all the Latin and Greek ordinals, but also the confession of the above-mentioned Protestant divine, Mason, who says, with evident truth, " Not every form of words will serve for this institution (conveying orders) but such as are significant of the power conveyed by the order."[†]   In short, these objections were so powerfully urged by our divines, Dr. Champney, J. Lewgar, S. T. B.[‡] and others, that almost immediately after the last named had published his work containing them, called *Erastus Senior* namely, in 1662, the convocation, being assembled, it *altered the form* of ordaining priests and consecrating bishops, in order to obviate these objections.[§]   But admitting that these alterations are sufficient to obviate *all* the objections of our divines to the ordinal, which they are not, they came above a hundred years too late for their intended purpose; so that if the priests and bishops of Edward's and Elizabeth's reigns were invalidly ordained and consecrated, so must those of Charles II.'s reign, and their successors, have been also.

However long I have dwelt on this subject, it is not yet exhausted : the case is, there is the same necessity of an apostolical succession of *mission* or authority, to execute the functions of holy orders, as there is of the holy orders themselves.   This *mission*, or authority, was imparted by Christ to his apostles, when he said to them, *As the Father hath sent me, I also send you*, Mat. xx. 21, and of this St. Paul also speaks, where he says of the apostles, *How can they preach unless they are sent?* Rom. x. 15.   I believe, sir, that no regular Protestant church, or society, admits its minister, to have, by their ordination or appointment, unlimited authority in every place and congregation : certain it is, from the ordinal and articles of the establish-

[*] Burnet's Hist. of Reform. vol. i. Record, b: iii. n. 21, quest. 10.
[†] Ibid. B. ii. c. 16.
[‡] Lewgar was the friend of Chillingworth, and by him converted to the Catholic faith, which, however, he refused to abandon, when the latter relapsed into Latitudinarianism.
[§] The form of ordaining a priest was thus altered : " Receive the Holy Ghost for the office and work of a priest in the church of God, now committed to thee by the imposition of our hands: Whose sins thou shalt forgive, they are forgiven," &c.—The form of consecrating a bishop was thus enlarged : " Receive the Holy Ghost for the office and work of a bishop in the church of God, now committed unto thee by the imposition of our hands, in the name of the Father, and of the Son, and of the Holy Ghost ; and remember, that thou stir up the grace of God, which is in thee."

ed church, that she confines the jurisdiction of her ministers to " the congregation to which they shall be appointed."* Conformably to this, Dr. Berkley teaches, that " a defect in the *mission* of the ministry, invalidates the sacraments, affects the purity of public worship, and therefore deserves to be investigated by every sincere Christian."† To this archdeacon Daubeny adds, that " Regular mission only subsists in the churches which have preserved apostolical succession." I moreover believe that in all Protestant societies the ministers are persuaded that the authority by which they preach and per form their functions is, some how or another, *divine.* But, on this head, I must observe to you, dear sir, and your society, that there are only two ways by which divine mission or authority can be proved or communicated; the one *ordinary,* the other *extraordinary.* The former takes place when this authority is transmitted in regular succession from those who originally received it from God; the other, when the Almighty interposes, in an extraordinary manner, and immediately commissions certain individuals to make known his will to men. The latter mode evidently requires indisputable miracles to attest it; and accordingly Moses and our Saviour Christ, who were sent in this manner, constantly appealed to the prodigies they wrought in proof of their divine mission. Hence, even Luther, when Muncer, Storck, and their followers, the Anabaptists, spread their errors and devastations through Lower Germany, counselled the magistrates to put these questions to them, (not reflecting that the questions were as applicable to himself as to Muncer,) " Who *conferred upon you the office* of preaching? And who *commissioned you* to preach? If they answer, *God,* then let the magistrates say, *prove this to us* by some evident miracle: for so God makes known his will, when he changes the institutions, which he had before established."‡ Should this advice of the first reformer to the magistrates be followed in this age and country, what swarms of sermonizers and expounders of the Bible would be reduced to silence! For, on one hand, it is notorious, that they are *self-appointed* prophets, who *run without being sent;* or, if they pretend to a commission, they derive it from other men, who themselves had received none, and who did not so much as claim any, by regular succession from the apostles. Such was Luther himself; such also were Zuinglius, Calvin, Muncer, Menno, John Knox,

---

* Article 23. Form of ordering priests and deacons.
† Serm. at Consecr. of bishop Horne. ‡ Sleidan. De Stat. Relig. L ▾

19

George Fox, Zinzendorf, Wesley, Whitfield, and Swedenborg.
None of these preachers, as I have signified, so much as pretended to have received their mission from Christ in *the ordinary way*, by uninterrupted succession from the apostles.   On
the other hand, they were so far from undertaking to work real
miracles, by way of proving they have received *an extraordinary mission from God*, that, as Erasmus reproached them, they
could not so much as cure a lame horse, in proof of their divine
legation.

Should your friend, the Rev. Mr. Clark, see this letter, he
will doubtless exclaim, that, whatever may be the case with
dissenters, the church of England, at least, has received her
mission and authority, together with her orders, by regular
succession from the apostles, through the Catholic bishops, in
the ordinary way.   In fact, this is plainly asserted by the bishop of Lincoln.*   But take notice, dear sir, that though we
were to admit of an apostolical succession of *orders* in the established church, we never could admit of an apostolical succession of *mission, jurisdiction*, or right to exercise those orders
in that church : nor can its clergy, with any consistency, lay
the least claim to it.   For, first, if the Catholic church, that is
to say, its " Laity and clergy, all sects and degrees, were
drowned in abominable idolatry, most detested of God and
damnable to man, for the space of eight hundred years," as the
Homilies affirm,† how could she retain this divine mission and
jurisdiction, all this time, and employ them in commissioning
her clergy all this time to preach up this " detestable idolatry ?"   Again, was it possible for the Catholic church to give
jurisdiction and authority, for example, to archbishop Parker,
and the bishops Jewel and Horne, to preach against herself ?
Did ever any insurgents against an established government, except the regicides in the grand rebellion, claim authority from that
very government to fight against it, and destroy it?   In a word, we
perfectly well know, from history, that the first English Protestants did not profess, any more than foreign Protestants, to derive
any mission or authority whatsoever from the apostles, through
the existing Catholic church.   Those of Henry's reign preached and ministered in defiance of all authority, ecclesiastical and
civil.‡   Their successors in the reign of Edward and Elizabeth
claimed their whole right and mission to preach and to minis-

* Elem. of Theol. vol. ii. p. 400.   † Against the Perils of Idolatry, P. iii.
‡ Collier's Hist. vol. ii. p. 81.

ter from the civil power only.* This latter point is demonstratively evident from the act and the oath of supremacy, and
from the homage of the archbishops and bishops to the said
Elizabeth, in which the prelate elect " acknowledges and confesses, that he holds his bishopric, as well in *spirituals* as in
temporals, from her alone and the crown royal." The same
thing is clear from a series of royal ordinances respecting the
clergy in matters purely spiritual, such as the *pronouncing on
doctrine,* the *prohibition of prophesying,* the *inhibition of all
preaching,* the *giving and suspending of spiritual faculties,* &c.
Now, though I sincerely and cheerfully ascribe to my sovereign
all the *temporal and civil power,* jurisdiction, rights, and authority, which the constitution and laws ascribe to him, I cannot believe that Christ appointed any temporal prince to *feed
his mystical flock,* or any part of it, or to exercise *the power of
the keys of the kingdom of heaven* at his discretion. It was foretold by bishop Fisher in Parliament, that the royal ecclesiastical supremacy, if once acknowledged, might pass to a child or
to a woman,† as, in fact, it soon did to each of them. It was
afterwards transferred, with the crown itself, to a foreign Calvinist, and might have been settled, by a lay assembly, on a
Mahometan. All, however, that is necessary for me here to
remark is, that the acknowledgment of a royal ecclesiastical
supremacy " in all spiritual and ecclesiastical things or
causes,"‡ (as when the question is, who shall preach, baptize,
&c. and who shall not; what is sound doctrine, and what is not,)
is decidedly a renunciation of Christ's commission given to his
apostles, and preserved by their successors in the Catholic
apostolic church. Hence it clearly appears that there is and
can be no *apostolical* succession of ministry in the established
church more than in the other congregations or societies of
Protestants. All their preaching and ministering, in their
several degrees, is performed by *mere human authority.*§ On
the other hand, not a sermon is preached, nor a child baptized,
nor a penitent absolved, nor a priest ordained, nor a bishop

* Archbishop Abbot having incurred suspension by the canon law, for acci-
dentally shooting a man, a royal commission was issued to restore him. On another occasion he was suspended by the king himself, for refusing to license a
book. In Elizabeth's reign, the bishops approved of *prophesying,* as it was called,
the queen disapproved of it, and she obliged them to condemn it.

† See his Life by Dr. Bailey : also Dodd's Eccles. Hist. vol. i.

‡ Oath of supremacy, Homage of bishops, &c.

§ It is curious to see in queen Elizabeth's Injunctions, and in the 37th Article,
the disclaimer of her " *actually ministering the Word and the Sacrament.*" The
question was not about this, but about the *jurisdiction* or *mission* of the ministry.

consecrated, throughout the whole extent of the Catholic church, without the minister of such function being able to show his authority from Christ for what he does, in the commission of Christ to his apostles: *All power in heaven and on earth is given to me: Go therefore, teach all nations, baptizing them, &c.* Mat. xxviii. 19; and without being able to prove his claim to that commission of Christ, by producing the table of his uninterrupted succession from the apostles. I will not detain you by entering into a comparison, in a religious point of view, between a ministry, which officiates by *divine authority*, and others which act by *mere human authority*; but shall conclude this subject by putting it to the good sense and candour of your society, whether, from all that has been said, it is not as evident, which, among the different communions, is THE APOSTOLIC CHURCH we profess to believe in, as which is THE CATHOLIC CHURCH?

I am, &c.

J. M.

LETTER XXX.

To JAMES BROWN, Esq.

OBJECTIONS ANSWERED.

Dear Sir,

I find that your visiter, the Rev. Mr. Clark, had not left you at the latter end of last week; since it appears, by a letter which I have received from him, that he had seen my two last letters, addressed to you at New Cottage. He is much displeased with their contents, which I am not surprised at; and he uses some harsh expressions against them and their author, of which I do not complain, as he was not a party to the agreement entered into at the beginning of our correspondence, by the tenor of which I was left at full liberty to follow up my arguments to whatever lengths they might conduct me, without any person of the society being offended with me on that account. I shall pass over the passages in the letter which seem to have been dictated by too warm a feeling, and shall confine my answer to those which contain something like argument against what I have advanced.

The Reverend gentleman, then, objects against the claim of our pontiffs to the apostolic succession; that in different ages this succession has been interrupted, by the contentions of rival Popes; and that the lives of many of them have been so criminal, that according to my own argument, as he says, it is incredible that such pontiffs should have been able to preserve and convey the commission and authority given by Christ to his apostles. I grant, sir, that, from the various commotions and accidents to which all sublunary things are subject, there have been several vacancies, or interregnums in the Papacy; but none of them have been of such a lengthened duration as to prevent a moral continuation of the Popedom, or to hinder the execution of the important offices annexed to it. I grant also, that there have been rival Popes and unhappy schisms in the church, particularly one great schism, at the end of the fourteenth and the beginning of the fifteenth century: still the true Pope was always clearly discernible at the times we are speaking of, and in the end was acknowledged even by his opponents. Lastly, I grant that a few of the Popes, perhaps a tenth part of the whole number, swerving from the example of the rest, have, by their *personal vices*, disgraced their holy station: but even these Popes always fulfilled their *public duties* to the church by maintaining the *apostolical doctrine*, moral as well as speculative, the *apostolical orders*, and the *apostolical mission;* so that their misconduct chiefly injured their own souls, and did not essentially affect the church. But if what the Homilies affirm were true, that the whole church had been " drowned in idolatry for eight hundred years," she must have taught and commissioned all those, whom she ordained to teach this horrible apostasy, which she never could have done, and at the same time retained Christ's commission and authority to teach all nations the Gospel. This demonstrates the inconsistency of those clergymen of the establishment, who accuse the Catholic church of apostasy and idolatry, and at the same time boast of having received, *through her*, a spiritual jurisdiction and ministry from Jesus Christ.

, Your visiter next expatiates, in triumphant strains, on the exploded fable of Pope Joan; for *exploded* it certainly may be termed, when such men as the Calvinist minister Blondel, and the infidel Bayle, have abandoned and refuted it. But the circumstances of the fable themselves sufficiently refute it. According to these. in the middle of the ninth century, an *English*

19*

woman, born at Mentz, in *Germany*,* studied philosophy at
Athens, where there was no school of philosophy in the ninth
century, more than there is now, and taught divinity at *Rome*.
·It is pretended that, being elected Pope, on the death of Leo
IV in 855, she was *delivered of a child*, as she was walking in
a *solemn procession* near the Colliseum, and *died* on the spot;
and moreover, that a *statue of her* was there erected in memory
· of the *disgraceful event!* There have been great debates
among the learned concerning the first author of this absurd
tale, and concerning the interpolations in the copies of the first
chronicles which mention it.† At all events, it was never heard
of for more than two hundred years after the period in question :
and in the mean time, we are assured, from the genuine works
of *contemporary writers* and distinguished prelates, some of
whom then resided at Rome, such as Anastasius the librarian,
Luitprand, Hincmar, archbishop of Rheims, Photius of C. P.
Lupis Ferrar, &c. that Benedict III. was canonically elected
Pope in the said year 855, only three days after the death of
Leo IV, which evidently leaves no interval for the pontificate
of the fabulous Joan.

From the warfare of attack, my Reverend antagonist
passes to that of defence, as he terms it. In this he heavily
complains of my not having done justice to the Protestants,
particularly in the article of *foreign missions*. On this head,
he enumerates the different societies, existing in this country,
for carrying them on, and the large sums of money which they
annually raise for this purpose. The societies, I learn from
him, are the following : 1st, the Society for promoting Christian Knowledge, called the Bartlet Building Society, which,
though strictly of the Establishment, employs missionaries in
India to the number of six, all Germans, and it should seem, all
Lutherans. 2dly, There is the Society for propagating Christianity in the English colonies; but I hear nothing of its doings. 3dly, There is another for the conversion of negro
slaves, of which I can only say, ditto. 4thly, There is another
for sending missionaries to Africa and the East, concerning
which we are equally left in the dark. 5thly, There is the
London Missionary Society, which sent out the ship Duff, with
certain preachers and their wives, to Otaheite, Tongabatoo, and
the Marquesas, and published a journal of the voyage, by

* Ita Pseudo Martinus Polonus, &c.
† See Breviarium Historico—Chronologico—criticum Pontif. Roman. studio
R. F. Pagi, tom. ii. p. 72.

which it appears that they are strict Calvinists, and Independents. 6thly, The Edinburgh Missionary Society fraternizes with the last mentioned. 7thly, There is an Arminian Missionary Society under Dr. Coke, the head of the Wesleyan Methodists. 8thly, There is a Moravian Missionary Society, which appears more active than any others, particularly at the Cape and in Greenland and Surinam. To these, your visiter says, must be added, the Hibernian Society for diffusing Christian knowledge in Ireland; as also, and still more particularly, the Bible Society, with all its numerous ramifications. Of this last named, he *speaks glorious things*, foretelling that it will, in its progress, purify the world from infidelity and wickedness.

In answer to what has been stated, I have to mention several marked differences between the Protestant and the Catholic missionaries. The former preached various discordant religions; for what religions can be more opposite than the Calvinistic and the Arminian? And how indignant would a churchman feel, if I were to charge him with the impiety and obsceuity of Zinzendorf and his Moravians? The very preachers of the same sect, on board of the Duff, had not agreed upon the creed they were to teach, when they were within a few days sail of Otaheite.* Whereas the Catholic missionaries, whether Italians, French, Portuguese, or Spaniards, taught and planted precisely the same religion in the opposite extremities of the globe. Secondly, the envoys of those societies had no commission or authority to preach, but what they derived from the men and women, who contributed money to pay for their voyages and accommodations. *I have not sent these prophets*, says the Lord, *yet they ran; I have not spoken to them, yet they prophesied*, Jer. xxiii. 21. On the other hand, the apostolical men, who, in ancient and in modern times, have converted the nations of the earth, all derived their mission and authority from the centre of the apostolic tree, the See of Peter. Thirdly, I cannot but remark the striking difference between the Protestant and the Catholic missionaries, with respect to their qualifications and method of proceeding. The former were, for the most part, mechanics and laymen, of the lowest order, without any learning infused or acquired, beyond what they could pick up from the English translation of the Bible; they were frequently incumbered with wives and children, and arm-

---

* " By the middle of January, the Committee of eight (among the 30 missionaries) had nearly finished *the articles of faith*. Two of the number dissented, but gave in."—Journal of the Duff.

ed with muskets and bayonets, to kill those whom they could not convert.* Whereas the Catholic missionaries have always been priests, or ascetics, trained to literature and religious exercises, men of continency and self-denial, who have had no other defence than their breviary and crucifix, no other weapon than *the sword of the spirit, which is the word of God*, Ephes. vi. 17. Fourthly, I do not find any portion of that lively faith and heroical constancy, in braving poverty, torments, and death, for the Gospel, among the few Protestant converts, or even among their preachers, which have so frequently illustrated the different Catholic missions. Indeed, I have not heard of a single martyr of any kind, in Asia, Africa, or America, who can be considered as the fruit of the above-named societies, or of any other Protestant mission whatsoever. On the other hand, few are the countries in which the Christian religion has been planted by Catholic priests, without being watered with some of their own blood and of that of their converts. To say nothing of the martyrs of a late date in the Catholic missions of Turkey, Abyssinia, Siam, Tonquin, Cochinchina, &c., there has been an almost continual persecution of the Catholics in the empire of China, for about a hundred years past, which, besides confessors of the faith, who have endured various tortures, has produced a very great number of martyrs, native Chinese as well as Europeans; laity as well as priests and bishops.† Within these two years,‡ the wonderful apostle of the great Peninsula of Corea, to the east of China, James Ly, with as many as one hundred of his converts, has suffered death for the faith. In the islands of Japan, the anti-christian persecution, excited by the envy and avarice of the Dutch, raged with a fury unexampled in the records of Pagan Rome. It began with the crucifixion of twenty-six martyrs, most of them missionaries. It then proceeded to other more horrible martyrdoms, and it concluded with putting to death as many as eleven

---

* The eighteen preachers who remained at Otaheite "took up arms *by way of precaution.*"—Ibid. It appears, from subsequent accounts, that the preachers made use of their arms, to protect their wives from the men whom they came to convert. Of the nine preachers destined for Tongabatoo, six were for carrying fire arms on shore, and three against it.—Journal.

† Hist. de l'Eglise par Berault Bercastel, tom. 22, 23. Butler's Lives of the Saints, Feb. 5. Mem. Eccles. pour le 18 Siéc.

‡ Namely, in 1801. While this work is in the press, we receive an account of the martyrdom of Mgr. Dufresse, bishop of Tabraca, and Vicar apostolic of Sutchuen, in China, who was beheaded there Sept. 14, 1815, and of F. J. de Frior, missionary in Chiensi. who. after various torments, was strangled, Feb. 13, 1816.

hundred thousand Christians.* Nor were those numerous and splendid victories of the Gospel in the provinces of South America achieved without torrents of Catholic blood. Many of the first preachers were slaughtered by the savages to whom they announced the Gospel, and not unfrequently devoured by them, as was the case with the first bishop of Brazil. In the last place, the Protestant missions have never been attended with any great success. Those heretofore carried on by the Dutch, French, and American Calvinists, seemed to have been more levelled at the destruction of the Catholic missions, than at the conversion of the Pagans.† In later times, the zealous Wesley went on a mission to convert the savages of Georgia, but returned without making one proselyte. His companion Whitfield afterwards went to the same country on the same errand, but returned without any greater success. Of the missionaries who went out in the Duff, those who were left at the Friendly Islands and the Marquesas abandoned their posts in despair, as did eleven of the eighteen left at Otaheite. The remaining seven had not, in the course of six years, baptized a single Islander. In the mean time, the depravity of the natives in killing their infants and other abominations increased so fast, as to threaten their total extinction. In the Bengal government, extending over from thirty to forty millions of people, with all its influence and encouragement, not more than eighty converts have been made by the Protestant missionaries in seven years, and those were almost all Chandalas or outcasts from the Hindoo religion, who were glad to get a pittance for their support,‡ "for the perseverance of several of whom,"

* Berault Bercastel says two millions, tom. 20.

† It is generally known, and not denied by Mosheim himself, that the extermination of the flourishing missions in Japan is to be ascribed to the Dutch. When they became masters of the Portuguese settlements in India, they endeavoured, by persecution as well as by other means, to make the Christian natives abandon the Catholic religion to which St. Xavier and his companions had converted them. The Calvinist preachers having failed in their attempt to proselyte the Brazilians, it happened that one of their party, James Sourie, took a merchant vessel at sea with forty Jesuit missionaries, under F. Azevedo, on board of it, bound to Brazil, when, in hatred to them and their destination, he put them all to death. The year following, F. Diaz, with eleven companions, bound on the same mission, and falling into the hands of the Calvinists, met with the same fate. Incredible pains were taken by the ministers of New England to induce the Hurons, Iroquois, and other converted savages, to abandon the Catholic religion, when the latter answered them: " You never preached the word to us while we were Pagans; and now that we are Christians, you try to deprive us of it."

‡ Extract of a Speech of C. Marsh, Esq. in a committee of the H. of C. July 1, 1815. See also Major Waring's remarks on Oxford Sermons.

their instructors say, " they tremble."*   How different a scene
do the Catholic missions present!   To say nothing of ancient
Christendom, all the kingdoms and states of which were reclaimed from Paganism and converted to Christianity by Catholic preachers, and not one of them by preachers of any other
description : what extensive and populous islands, provinces and
states, were wholly, or in a great part reclaimed from idolatry,
in the East and in the West, soon after Luther's revolt, by Catholic missionaries !   But to come still nearer to our own time:
F. Bouchet, alone, in the course of his twelve years labours in
Madura, instructed and baptized twenty thousand Indians,
while F. Britto, within fifteen months only, converted and re-
generated eight thousand, when he sealed his mission with his
blood.   By the latest returns which I have seen from the Eastern missionaries to the directors of the French *Missions Etran-
geres*, it appears that in the western district of Tonquin, during
the five years preceding the beginning of this century, four
thousand one hundred and one adults, and twenty-six thousand
nine nundred and fifteen children, were received into the church
by baptism, and that in the lower part of Cochinchina, nine
hundred grown persons had been baptized in the course of two
years, besides vast numbers of children.   The empire of China
contains six bishops and some hundreds of Catholic priests.   In
a single province of it, Sutchuen, during the year 1796, fifteen
hundred adults were baptized, and two thousand five hundred
and twenty-seven Catechumens were received for instruction.
By letters of a later date from the above mentioned martyr
Dufresse, bishop of Tabraca and Vic. Ap. of Sutchuen, it appears, that during the year 1810, in spite of a severe persecution, nine hundred and sixty-five adults were baptized, and during 1814, though the persecution increased, eight hundred and
twenty-nine, without reckoning infants, received baptism.   Bishop Lamote, Vic. Ap. of Fokien, testifies that, in his district,
during the year 1810, ten thousand three hundred and eighty-
four infants, and one thousand six hundred and seventy-seven
grown persons, were baptized, and two thousand six hundred
and seventy-four Catechumens admitted.   From this short
specimen, I trust, dear sir, it will appear manifest to you, on
which Christian society God bestows his grace to execute the
work of the apostles, as well as to preserve their *doctrine*, their
orders and their *mission*.

   As to the wonderful effects which your visiter expects from

* Transact. of Prot. Miss. quoted in Edinb. Review, April, 1808.

the Bible Society, and the three score and three translations into foreign tongues of the English translation of the Bible, in the conversion of the Pagan world, I beg leave to ask him, who is to vouch to the Tartars, Turks, and idolaters, that the Testaments and Bibles, which the society is pouring in upon them, were inspired by the Creator? Who is to answer for these translations, made by officers, merchants, and merchants' clerks, being accurate and faithful? Who is to teach these barbarians to read, and, after that, to make any thing like a connected sense of the mysterious volumes? Does Mr. C. really think that an inhabitant of Otaheite, when he is enabled to read the Bible, will extract the sense of the 39 Articles or of any other Christian system whatever from it? In short, has the Bible Society, or any of the other Protestant societies, converted a single Pagan or Mahometan by the bare text of Scripture? When such a convert can be produced, it will be time enough for me to propose to him those further gravelling questions which result from my observations on the Sacred Text in a former letter to you. In the mean time let your visiter rest assured, that the Catholic church will proceed in the old and successful manner, by which she has converted all the Christian people on the face of the earth; the same, which Christ delivered to his apostles and their successors: *Go ye into all the world and preach the Gospel to every creature.* Mark. xvi. 15. On the other hand, how illusory the gentleman's hopes are, that the depravity of this age and country will be reformed by the efforts of the Bible Society, has been victoriously proved by the Rev. Dr. Hook, who, with other clear sighted churchmen, evidently sees that the grand principle of Protestantism, strictly reduced to practice, would undermine their establishment. One of his brethren, the Rev. Mr. Gisborne, had publicly boasted, that in proportion to the opposition, which the Bible Society had met with, its annual income had increased, till it reached near a hundred thousand pounds in a year: Dr. Hook, in return, showed, by lists of the convictions of criminals during the first seven years of the society's existence, that the wickedness of the country, instead of being diminished, had almost been doubled!* Since that period up to the pre-

---

* List of capital convictions, in London and Middlesex, in the following years, from Dr. Hook's Charge, and the London Chronicle:—

In the year	1808	1809	1810	1811	1812	1813	1814	1815	1616	1817
Convictions	798	863	884	872	998	1012	1027	[illegible]	[illegible]	[illegible]

sent year, it has increased three-fold and four-fold, compared
with its state before the society began.

————

POSTSCRIPT.

I HAVE now, dear sir, completed the second task which I undertook, and therefore proceed to sum up my evidence.   Having then proved in my twelve former letters, the rough copies
of which I have preserved, that the two alleged rules of faith,
that of *private inspiration* and that of *private interpretation of
Scripture*, are equally fallacious, and that there is no certain
way of coming to the truth of divine revelation but by *hearing
that church* which Christ *built on a rock* and promised to *abide
with for ever;* I engaged, in this my second series of letters, to
demonstrate, which, among the different societies of Christians,
is the church that Christ founded and still protects.   For this
purpose I have had recourse to the principal *characters* or *marks
of Christ's church*, as they are pointed out in Scripture and
formally acknowledged by Protestants of nearly all descriptions, no less than by Catholics, in their articles and in those
creeds, which form part of their private prayers and public
liturgy, namely, *unity, sanctity, Catholicity* and *apostolicity*. In
fact, this is what every one acknowledges who says in the apostles' Creed, *I believe in the holy Catholic church;* and, in the
Nicene Creed,* *I believe one Catholic and apostolic church.*
Treating of the first mark of the true church, I proved from
natural reason, Scripture, and tradition, that *unity* is essential
to her; I then showed that there is no union or principle of
union among the different sects of Protestants, except their common *protestation* against their mother church, and that the
church of England, in particular, is *divided against itself* in
such manner, that one of its most learned prelates has declared
himself *afraid to say, what is its doctrine.*   On the other hand.

Capital convictions in England and Wales, during the former seven years, from
Dr. Hook's Charge :—

|2723|3238|3158|3163|3913|4422|4025|

N. B. To the convictions, during the three last years, in London and Middlesex,
are added those of Surry, in the London Chronicle, March 9, 1818.
* See the Communion Service, in Com. Prayer.

I have shown that the Catholic church, spread as she is over the whole earth, is one and the same in her *doctrine*, in her *liturgy*, and in her *government;* and, though I detest religious persecution, I have, in defiance of ridicule and clamour, vindicated her unchangeable doctrine, and the plain dictate of reason, as to the indispensable obligation of believing what God teaches; in other words, of a right faith: I have even proved that her adherence to this tenet is a proof both of the *truth* and the *charity* of the Catholic church. On the subject of *holiness*, I have made it clear that the pretended Reformation every where originated in the pernicious doctrine of *salvation by faith alone, without good works;* and that the Catholic church has ever taught the necessity of them both; likewise that she possesses many peculiar *means of sanctity*, to which modern sects do not make a pretension, likewise that she has, in every age, produced the genuine *fruits of sanctity;* while the fruits of Protestantism have been of quite an *opposite nature:* finally, that *God himself has bore witness to the sanctity of the Catholic church*, by undeniable *miracles*, with which he has illustrated her in every age. It did not require much pains to prove that the Catholic church possesses, exclusively, the name of CA-THOLIC, and not much more to demonstrate that she alone has the *qualities* signified by that name. That the Catholic church is also APOSTOLICAL, by descending in a right line from the apostles of Christ, is as evident as that she is Catholic. However, to illustrate this matter, I have sketched out a genealogical, or, as I call it, *the apostolical tree*, which, with the help of a note subjoined, shows the uninterrupted succession of the Catholic church in her chief pontiffs and other illustrious prelates, doctors, and renowned saints, from the apostles of Christ, during eighteen centuries, to the present period; together with the continuation in her of the apostolical work of converting nations and people. It shows also a series of unhappy heretics and schismatics, of different times and countries, who, refusing to hear her inspired voice and to obey her divine authority, have been separated from her communion and have withered away, like branches, cut off from a vine, which are fit for no human use. *Ezek.* xv. Finally, I have shown the necessity of an uninterrupted succession from the apostles, of *holy orders* and *divine mission*, to constitute an apostolical church, and have proved that these, or at least the latter of them, can only be found in the holy Catholic church. Having demonstrated all this in the foregoing letters, I am justified, dear sir, in affirming that the *motives of credibility*, in favour of the Chris-than religion, in general, are not one whit more clear and certain than those in favour of the Catholic religion in particular. But without inquiring into the *degree of evidence* attending the latter motives, it is enough for my present purpose that they are *sufficiently evident* to influence the conduct of dispassionate and reasonable persons, who are acquainted with them, and who are really in earnest to save their souls. Now, in proof, that these motives are at least so far clear, I may again appeal to the conduct of Catholics on a death bed, who, in that awful situation, never wish to die in any religion but their own: I may also appeal to the conduct of so many Protestants in the same situation, who seek to reconcile themselves to the Catholic church. Let us, one and all, my dear sir, as far as is in our power, adopt these sentiments in every respect now, which we shall entertain, when the transitory scene of this world is closing to our sight, and during the countless ages of eternity. O the length, the breadth, and the depth of the abyss of ETERNITY! *"No security,"* says a holy man, *"can be too great where eternity is at stake."**

I am, &c.
J. M.

* " Nulla satis magna securitas ubi periclitatur Æternitas."

THE END

OF

RELIGIOUS CONTROVERSY.

PART III.

LETTER XXXI.

From JAMES BROWN, Esq. to the Rev. J. M.
D. D. F. S. A.

INTRODUCTION.

REVEREND SIR,

The whole of your letters have again been read over in our
society; and they have produced important though diversified
effects on the minds of its several members. For my own part,
I am free to own, that, as your former letters convinced me in
the truth of your rule of faith, namely the entire Word of God,
and of the right of the true church to expound it in all questions
concerning its meaning; so your subsequent letters have satisfied me that the characters or marks of the true church, as they
are laid down in our common creeds, are clearly visible in the
Roman Catholic church, and not in the collection of Protestant churches, nor in any one of them. This impression was, at
first, so strong upon my mind that I could have answered you
nearly in the words of king Agrippa, to St. Paul: *almost thou
persuadest me to become a* Catholic, *Acts* xxvi. 28. The same
appear to be the sentiments of several of my friends : but when,
on comparing our notes together, we considered the heavy
charges, particularly of superstition and idolatry, brought
against your church by our eminent divines, and especially by
the bishop of London (Dr. Porteus,) and never, that we have
heard of, refuted or denied, we cannot but tread back the steps
we have taken towards you, or rather stand still, where we are,

in suspense, till we hear what answer you will make to them : I speak of those contained in the bishop's well known treatise called *A Brief Confutation of the Errors of the Church of Rome.* With respect to certain other members of our society, I am sorry to be obliged to say, that, on this particular subject, I mean the arguments in favour of your religion, they do not manifest the candour and good sense, which are natural to them, and which they show on every other subject. They pronounce, with confidence and vehemence, that Dr. Porteus's charges are all true, and that you cannot make any rational answer to them; at the same time, that several of these gentlemen, to my knowledge, are very little acquainted with the substance of them. In short, they are apt to load your religion and the professors of it, with epithets and imputations too gross and injurious for me to repeat, convinced as I am of their falsehood. I shall not be surprised to hear that some of these imputations have been transmitted to you by the persons in question, as I have declined making my letters the vehicle of them ; it is a justice, however, which I owe them, to assure you, Rev. sir, that it is only since they have understood the inference of your arguments to be such as to imply an obligation on them of renouncing their own respective religions, and embracing yours, that they have been so unreasonable and violent. Till this period they appeared to be nearly as liberal and charitable with respect to your communion as to any other.

I am, Rev. Sir, &c.
JAMES BROWN.

LETTER XXXII.

To JAMES BROWN, Esq.

ON THE CHARGES AGAINST THE CATHOLIC CHURCH.

Dear Sir,

I should be guilty of deception were I to disguise the satisfaction I derive from your and your friends, near approach to the *house of unity and peace*, as St. Cyprian calls the Catholic church: for such I must judge your situation to be from the tenour of your last letter, by which it seems to me, that your entire reconciliation with this church depends on my refuting Bp. Porteus's objections against it: and yet, dear sir, if I were to insist on the strict rules of reasoning, I might take occasion of complaining of you from the very concessions which afford me so much pleasure. In fact, if you admit that the church of God, is, by his appointment, *the interpreter of the entire Word of God*, you ought to pay attention to her doctrine on every point of it, and not to the suggestions of Dr. Porteus or your own fancy in opposition to it. Again, if you are convinced that the *one, holy, Catholic* and *apostolical* church is the *true* church of God, you ought to be persuaded that it is utterly impossible she should inculcate idolatry, superstition, or any other wickedness, and, of course, that those who believe her to be thus guilty are and must be in a fatal error. I have proved from reason, tradition, and holy Scripture, that, as individual Christians cannot of themselves judge with certainty of matters of faith, God has therefore provided them with an unerring guide, in his holy church ; and hence that Catholics, as Tertullian and St. Vincent of Lerins emphatically pronounce, cannot strictly and consistently, be required by those who are not Catholics, to vindicate the particular tenets of their belief, either from Scripture or any other authority: it being sufficient for them to show that they hold the doctrine of the true church which all Christians are bound to hear. Nevertheless, as it is my duty, after the example of the apostle, to *become all things to all men*, I Cor. ix. 22, and as we Catholics are conscious of being able to meet our opponents on their own ground, as well as on ours, I am willing, dear sir, for your and your friends' satisfaction, to enter on a brief discussion of the leading points of controversy which are agitated between the Catholics and the Protestants, particularly those of the church of England. I must however

20*

previously stipulate with you for the following conditions, which I trust you will find perfectly reasonable.

1st. I require that Catholics should be permitted to *lay down their own principles* of belief and practice, and, of course, to distinguish between their *articles of faith* in which they must all agree, and mere *scholastic opinions*, of which every individual may judge for himself; as, likewise, between the *authorized liturgy and discipline of the church* and the *unauthorized devotions and practices of particular persons*. I insist upon this preliminary, because it is the constant practice of your controversialists to dress up a hideous figure, composed of their own misrepresentations, or else of those undefined opinions and unauthorized practices, which they call *Popery;* and then to amuse their readers or hearers with exposing the deformity of it and pulling it to pieces; and I have the greater right to insist upon this preliminary, because our creeds and professions of faith, the acts of our councils and our approved expositions and Catechisms, containing the principles of our belief and practice, from which no real Catholic in any part of the world can ever depart, are before the public and upon constant sale among booksellers.

2dly. It being a notorious fact that certain individual Christians, or bodies of Christians, have departed from the faith and communion of the church of all nations, under pretence that they had authority for so doing, it is necessary that their alleged authority should be express, and incontrovertible. Thus, for example, if texts of Scripture are brought for this purpose, it is evidently necessary that such texts should be *clear* in themselves and *not contrasted* by any other texts seemingly of an opposite meaning. In like manner, when any doctrine or practice appears to be undeniably sanctioned by a father of the church, for example, of the third or the fourth century, without an appearance of contradiction from any other father, or ecclesiastical writer, it is unreasonable to affirm that he or his contemporaries were the authors of it, as Protestant divines are in the habit of affirming. On the contrary, it is natural to suppose that such father has taken up this with the other points of his religion from his predecessors, who received them from the apostles. This is the sentiment of that bright luminary St. Augustin, who says, " Whatever is found to be held by the Universal church, and not to have had its beginning in bishops and councils, must be esteemed a tradition from those by whom the church itself was founded."[*]

You judged right in supposing that I have received some letters, containing virulent and gross invectives against the Catholic religion, from certain members of your society. These do not surprise or hurt me, as the writers of them have probably not yet had an opportunity of knowing much more of this religion than what they could collect from fifth of November, and other sermons of the same tendency, and from circulated pamphlets expressly calculated to inflame the population against it and its professors; but what truly surprises and afflicts me is, that so many other personages in a more elevated rank of life, whose education and studies enable them to form a more just idea of the religious and moral principles of their ancestors, benefactors, and founders, in short of their acknowledged fathers and saints, should combine to load these fathers and saints with calumnies and misrepresentations which they must know to be utterly false. But, a bad cause must be supported by bad means; they are unfortunately implicated in a revolt against the true church; and not having the courage and self-denial to acknowledge their error and return to her communion, they endeavour to justify their conduct by interposing a black and hideous mask before the fair countenance of this true mother, Christ's spotless spouse. This is so far true, that when, as it often happens, a Protestant is, by dint of argument, forced out of his errors and prejudices against the true religion, if he be pressed to embrace it, and wants grace to do it, he is sure to fly back to those very calumnies and misrepresentations which he had before renounced. The fact is, he must fight with these, or yield himself unarmed to his Catholic opponent.

That you and your friends may not think me, dear sir, to have complained without just cause of the publications and sermons of the respectable characters I have alluded to, I must inform you that I have now lying before me a volume called *Good Advice to the Pulpits*, consisting of the foulest and most malignant falsehoods against the Catholic religion and its professors, which tongue or pen can express, or the most envenomed heart conceive. It was collected from the sermons and treatises of prelates and dignitaries, by that able and faithful writer, the Rev. John Gother, soon after the gall of calumnious ink had been mixed up with the blood of slaughtered Catholics; a score of whom were executed as traitors for a pretended plot

* Lib. ii. De Bapt.

to murder their friend and proselyte, Charles II; a plot which was hatched by men who themselves were soon after convicted of a real assassination plot against the king. At that time, the parliaments were so blinded as repeatedly to vote the reality o. the plot in question: hence it is easy to judge with what sort of language the pulpits would resound against the poor devoted Catholics at that period. But without quoting from former records, I need only refer to a few of the publications of the present day to justify my complaint. To begin with some of the numberless slanders contained in the *No Popery* Tract of the bishop of London, Dr. Porteus: he charges Catholics with "senseless idolatry to the infinite scandal of religion;"* with trying "to make the ignorant think that indulgences deliver the dead from hell;"† and that by means of "zeal for holy church, the worst man may be secured from future misery:"‡ and the bishop of St. Asaph, Dr. Halifax, charges Catholics with "Antichristian idolatry,§ the worship of demons,‖ and idol mediators."¶ He, moreover, maintains it to be the doctrine of the church of Rome, that "pardon for every sin, whether committed or designed, may be purchased for money.**" The bishop of Durham, Dr. Shute Barrington, accuses them of "idolatry, blasphemy, and sacrilege."†† The bishop of Landaff, Dr. Watson, impeaches the Catholic priests, martyrologists, and monks, without exception, of the "hypocrisy of liars;"‡‡ and he lays it down, as the moral doctrine of Catholics, that "humility, temperance, justice, the love of God and man, are not laws for all Christians, but only counsels of perfection."§§ He elsewhere says, "that the Popish religion is the Christian religion, is a false position."‖‖ He has, moreover, adopted and republished the sentiments of some of his other mitred brethren to the same purpose. One of these asserts, that, "instead of worshipping God through Christ, they (the Catholics) have substituted the doctrine of demons."¶¶ "They have contrived numberless ways to make a holy life needless, and to assure the most abandoned of salvation, without repentance, provided they will sufficiently pay the priest for absolution."*** "They have consecrated murders, &c."††† "The Papists stick fast in filthy mire—by the affection they

---

* Confutation, p. 39, edit. 1796. † Ibid. p. 53. ‡ Ibid. p. 53.
§ Warburton's Lectures, p. 191. ‖ Ibid. p. 355. ¶ Ibid. p. 358.
** Ibid. p. 347. †† Charge, p. 11. ‡‡ Letter II. to Gibbon.
§§ Bishop Watson's Tracts, vol. I. ¶ Ibid. vol. v. Contents.
¶¶ Bishop Benson's Tracts, vol. v. p. 272. *** Ibid. p. 273.
††† Ibid. p. 282.

near to other lusts, which their errors are fitted to gratify."* "It is impossible that any sincere person should give an implicit assent to many of their doctrines : but, whoever can practice upon them, can be nothing better than a most shamefully debauched and immoral wretch."† Another prelate, of later promotion, gives a comprehensive idea of Catholics, where he calls them " Enemies of all law, human and divine."‡ If such be the tone of the Episcopal bench, it would be vain to expect more moderation from the candidates for it : but I must contract my quotations in order to proceed to more important matter. One of these, who, while he was content with an inferior dignity, acted and preached as the friend of Catholics, since he has arrived at the verge of the highest, proclaims " Popery to be idolatry and Antichristianism;" maintaining, as does also the bishop of Durham, that it is " the parent of Atheism, and of that antichristian persecution" (in France) of which it was *exclusively* the victim.§ Another dignitary of the same cathedral, taking up Dr. Sparke's calumny, seriously declares that the Catholics are *Antinomians,*‖ which is the distinctive character of the Jumpers, and other rank Calvinists. Finally, the celebrated city preacher, C. De Coetlogon, among similar graces of oratory, pronounces that " Popery is calculated only for the meridian of hell. To say the best of it that can be said, Popery is a most horrid compound of idolatry, superstition, and blasphemy."¶ " The exercise of Christian virtues is not at all necessary in its members, nay, there are many heinous crimes, which are reckoned virtues among them, such as perjury and murder, when committed against heretics."** And is such then, dear sir, the real character of the great body of Christians throughout the world? Is such a true picture of our Saxon and English ancestors? Were such the clergy from whom these modern preachers and writers derive their liturgy, their ritual, their honours and benefices, and from whom they boast of deriving their orders and mission also? But, after all, do these preachers and writers themselves seriously believe such to be the true character of their Catholic countrymen, and the primitive religion? No, sir, they do not seriously believe it :††

* Bishop Fowler, vol. vi. p. 386. † Ibid. p. 387.
‡ Dr. Sparke, Bishop of Ely, *Concio. ad Synod.* 1807.
§ Discourses of Dr. Rennel, dean of Winchester, p. 140, &c.
‖ Charge of Dr. Hook, archdeacon, &c. p. 5, &c.
¶ Seasonable Caution against the abominations of the Church of Rome, Pref
p. 5. ** Ibid. p. 14.
†† This may be exemplified by the conduct of Dr. Wake, archbishop of Canterbury. Few writers had misrepresented the Catholic religion more foully than he

but being unfortunately engaged, as I said before, in an here
ditary revolt against the church, which shines forth conspicuous,
with every feature of truth in her countenance, and wanting the
rare grace of acknowledging their error, at the expense of
temporal advantages, they have no other defence for themselves
but clamour and calumny, no resource for shrouding those
beauteous features of the church, but by placing before them
the hideous mask of misrepresentation!

Before I close this letter, I cannot help expressing an earnest
wish that it were in my power to suggest three most important
considerations to all and every one of the theological calumniators in question. I pass over their injustice and cruelty towards
us; though this bears some resemblance with the barbarity of
Nero towards our predecessors, the first Christians of Rome,
who disguised them in the skins of wild beasts, and then hunted
them to death with dogs. But Christ has warned us as follows:
*It is enough for the disciple to be as his master; if they have
called the master of the house Beelzebub: how much more them
of his household.* In fact, we know that those our above-mentioned predecessors were charged with worshipping the head of
an ass, and of killing and eating children, &c.

The first observation which I am desirous of making to these
controvertists, is, that their charges and invectives against Catholics never unsettle the faith of a single individual amongst
us; much less do they cause any Catholic to quit our communion. This we are sure of, because, after all the pains and ex-

had done in his controversial works: even in his commentary on the Catechism,
he accuses it of *heresy, schism,* and *idolatry:* but, having entered into a correspondence with Dr. Dupin, for the purpose of uniting their respective churches, he assures the Catholic divine, in his last letter to him, as follows: " In dogmatibus,
prout a te candide proponuntur, non admodum dissentimus: in regimine eccle-
siastico minus; in fundamentalibus, sive doctrinam, sive disciplinam spectemus
vix omnino." Append. to Mosheim's Hist. vol. vi. p. 121. The present writer
has been informed, on good authority, that one of the bishops, whose calumnies
are here quoted, when he found himself on his deathbed, refused the proffered
ministry of the primate, and expressed a great wish to die a Catholic. When
urged to satisfy his conscience, he exclaimed: *What then will become of my lady
and my children!* Certain it is that very many Protestants, who had been the most
violent in their language and conduct against the Catholic church, as for example,
John, Elector of Saxony, Margaret, Queen of Navarre, Cromwell, Lord Essex,
Dudley, Earl of Northumberland, king Charles II, the late Lords Montague, Nu-
gent, Dunboyne, &c. did actually reconcile themselves to the Catholic church in
that situation. The writer may add, that another of the calumniators here quoted,
being desirous of stifling the suspicion of his having written an anonymous No-
Popery publication, when first he took part in that cause, privately addressed himself to the writer in these terms: *How can you suspect me of writing against your
religion, when you so well know my attachment to it!* In fact, this modern Luther,
among other similar concessions, has said thus to the writer: *I sucked in a love for
the Catholic religion with my mother's milk.*

penses of the Protestant societies to distribute Dr. Porteus's *Confutation of Popery*, and other tracts, in the houses and cottages of Catholics, not one of the latter ever comes to us, their pastors, to be furnished with an answer to the accusations contained in them; the truth is, they previously know from their catechisms, the falsehood of them. Sometimes, no doubt, a dissolute youth, from " libertinism of principles and practice," as one of the above-mentioned lords loudly proclaimed of himself, on his deathbed; and sometimes an ambitious or avaricious nobleman or gentleman, to get honour or wealth; finally, sometimes a profligate priest, to get a wife, or a living, forsakes our communion; but, I may challenge Dr. Porteus to produce a single proselyte from Popery throughout the dioceses of Chester and London, who has been gained by his book against it: and I may say the same with respect to the bishop of Durham's *No Popery* Charges, throughout the dioceses of Sarum and Durham.

A second point of still greater importance for the consideration of these distinguished preachers and writers is, that their flagrant misrepresentation of the Catholic religion, is constantly an occasion of the conversion of several of their own most upright members to it. Such Christians, when they fall into company with Catholics, or get hold of their books, cannot fail of inquiring whether they are really those monsters of idolatry, irreligion and immorality, which those divines have represented them to be; when, discovering how much they have been deceived in these respects, by misrepresentation; and, in short, viewing now the fair face of the Catholic church, instead of the hideous mask which had been placed before it, they seldom fail to become enamoured of it, and, in case religion is their chief concern, to become our very best Catholics.

The most important point, however, of all others for the consideration of these learned theologues, is the following: *We must all appear before the judgment seat of Christ,* to be examined on our observance of that commandment, among the rest, *thou shalt not bear false witness against thy neighbour;* supposing then these their clamorous charges against their Catholic neighbours, of idolatry, blasphemy, perfidy, and thirst of blood, should then appear, as they most certainly will appear, to be calumnies of the worst sort, what will it avail their authors that these have answered the temporary purpose of preventing the emancipation of Catholics, and of rousing the po-

pular hatred and fury against them!   Alas! what will it avail
them!

I am, Dear Sir, yours, &c.

J. M.

LETTER XXXIII.

To JAMES BROWN, Esq.

ON THE INVOCATION OF SAINTS.

DEAR SIR,

THE first and most heavy charge which Protestants bring
against Catholics, is that of idolatry.   They say, that the Catholic church has been guilty of this crime and apostasy, by
sanctioning the invocation of saints, and the worship of images
and pictures: and that on this account they have been obliged
to abandon her communion, in obedience to *the voice from heaven, saying, Come out of her, my people, that ye be not partakers
of her sins, and that ye receive not of her plagues.* Rev. xviii.
4.   Nevertheless, it is certain, dear sir, that Protestantism was
not founded on this ground either in Germany or in England:
for Luther warmly defended the Catholic doctrine in both the
aforesaid particulars, and our English reformers, particularly
king Edward's uncle, the duke of Somerset, only took up this
pretext of idolatry, as the most popular, in order to revolution-
ize the ancient religion, which they were carrying on from motives of avarice and ambition.   The same reasons, namely, that
this charge of idolatry is best calculated to inflame the ignorant
against the Catholic church, and to furnish a pretext for deserting her, have caused Protestant controvertists to keep up
the outcry against her ever since, and to vie with each other in
the foulness of their misrepresentation of her doctrine in this
particular.

. To speak first of the invocation of saints: archbishop Wake,
[who afterward, as we have seen, acknowledged to Dr. Dupin,
that there was *no fundamental difference* between his doctrine
and that of Catholics] in his popular Commentary on the

Church Catechism, maintains, that " The church of Rome has other Gods besides the Lord."* Another prelate, whose work has been lately republished by the bishop of Landaff, pronounces of Catholics, that, " Instead of worshipping Christ, they have substituted the doctrine of *demons*."† In the same blasphemous terms, Mede, and a hundred other Protestant controvertists, speak of our communion of saints. The bishop of London, among other such calumnies, charges us with " Bringing back the heathen multitude of deities into Christianity ;" that we " Recommend ourselves to some favourite saint, not by a religious life, but by flattering addresses and costly presents, and often depend much more on his intercession, than on our blessed Saviour's ;" and that, " being secure of the favour of these courtiers of heaven, we pay little regard to the King of it."‡ Such is the misrepresentation of the doctrine and practice of Catholics on this point, which the first ecclesiastical characters in the nation publish ; because, in fact, their cause has not a leg to stand on, if you take away misrepresentation! Let us now hear what is the genuine doctrine of the Catholic church in this article, as solemnly defined by the Pope, and near three hundred prelates of different nations, at the council of Trent, in the face of the whole world ; it is simply this, that " The saints reigning with Christ *offer up their prayers to God for men ; that it is good* and *useful* suppliantly to invoke them, and to have recourse to their *prayers*, help, and assistance, to obtain favours from God, *through his Son Jesus Christ our Lord*, who is *alone ur Redeemer and Saviour*."§ Hence the Catechism of the council of Trent, published in virtue of its decree,‖ by order of Pope Pius V, teaches, that " God and the saints are not to be prayed to in the same manner ; for we pray to God that *he himself would give us good things*, and *deliver us from evil things*; but we beg of the saints, because they are pleasing to God, that they *would be our advocates, and obtain from God what we stand in need of*."¶ Our first English Catechism for the instruction of children, says, " We are to honour saints and angels as God's special friends and servants, but not with the honour which belongs to God." Finally, *The Papist Misrepresented and Represented*, a work of great authority among Catholics, first published by our eminent divine Gother, and republished by our venerable bishop, Challoner, pronounces the

<hr>

* Sect. 2—3.   † Bishop Watson's Theol. Tracts, vol. v. p. 272.
‡ Brief Confut. pp. 23, 25.   § Concil. Trid. Sess. 25. de Invoc.
‖ Sess. 24. de Ref. c. 7.   ¶ Pars   Quis orandus.

following anathema against that idolatrous phantom of Catholicity, which Protestant controvertists have held up for the identical Catholic church. " Cursed is he that believes the saints in heaven to be his redeemers, that prays to them as such, or that gives God's honour to them, or to any creature whatsoever. Amen." " Cursed is every goddess worshipper, that believes the B. Virgin Mary to be any more than a creature; that worships her, or puts his trust in her more than in God, 'that believes her above her Son, or that she can in any thing command him. Amen."*

You see, dear sir, how widely different the doctrine of Catholics, as defined by our church, and really held by us, is from the caricature of it, held up by interested preachers and controvertists, to scare and inflame an ignorant multitude. So far from making gods and goddesses of the saints, we firmly hold it to be an article of faith, that, as they have no virtue or excellence but what has been gratuitously bestowed upon them by God, for the sake of his incarnate Son, Jesus Christ, so they can procure no benefit for us, but by means of their prayers to the *Giver of all good gifts*, through their and our common Saviour, Jesus Christ. In short, they do nothing for us mortals in heaven, but what they did while they were here on earth, and what all good Christians are bound to do for each other, namely, they help us by their prayers. The only difference is, that as the saints in heaven are free from every stain of sin and imperfection, and are confirmed in grace and glory, so their prayers are far more efficacious for obtaining what they ask for, than are the prayers of us imperfect and sinful mortals. In short, our Protestant brethren will not deny that St. Paul was in the practice of begging for the prayers of the churches to which he addressed his epistles, *Rom.* xv. 30, &c. and that the Almighty himself commanded the friends of Job to obtain his prayers for the pardon of their sins, *Job* xlii. 8; and moreover, that they themselves are accustomed to pray publicly for one another. Now these concessions, together with the authorized exposition of our doctrine, laid down above, are abundantly sufficient to refute most of the remaining objections of Protestants against it. In vain, for example, does Dr. Porteus quote the text of St. Paul, 1 *Tim.* ii. 5, *There is one Mediator between God and men, the man Christ Jesus;* for we grant that Christ alone is the *Mediator of salvation;* but if he argues, from thence, that there is no other *mediator of intercession*, he would condemn the con-

* Pap. Misrep. Abridg. p. 78.

duct of St. Paul, of Job's friends, and of his own church. In vain does he take advantage of the ambiguous meaning of the word *worship*, in *Mat.* iv. 10; because, if the question be about a *divine adoration*, we restrain this as strictly to God, as he can do; but if it be about merely *honouring the saints*, we cannot censure that, without censuring other passages of Scripture,* and condemning the bishop himself, who expressly says, " The saints in heaven we love and *honour*."† In vain does he quote *Revel.* xix. 10, where the angel refused to let St. John prostrate himself, and adore him; because, if the mere act itself, independently of the evangelist's mistaking him for the Deity, was forbidden, then the three angels, who permitted Abraham to *bow himself to the ground before them*, were guilty of a crime, *Gen.* xviii. 2, as was that other angel, before whom *Josuah fell on his face and worshipped*. Jos. v. 14.

The charge of *idolatry* against Catholics, for merely honouring those *whom God honours*, and for desiring them to pray to God for us, is too extravagant, to be any longer published by Protestants of learning and character; accordingly the bishop of Durham is content with accusing us of *blasphemy*, on the latter part of the charge. What he says is this: " It is blasphemy, to ascribe to angels and saints, by praying to them, the divine attribute of universal presence."‡ To say nothing of his lordship's new invented blasphemy, I should be glad to ask him, how it follows, from my praying to an angel or a saint in any place, that I necessarily believe the angel or saint to be in that place? Was Elisha really in Syria when he saw the ambush prepared there for the king of Israel? 2 *Kings* vi. 9. Again, we know that *There is joy before the angels of God over one sinner that repenteth*, Luke xv. 10. Now, is it by visual rays, or undulating sounds, that these blessed spirits in heaven know what passes in the hearts of men upon earth? How does his lordship know, that one part of the saint's felicity may not

---

* The word *worship*, in this place, is used for *supreme divine homage*, as appears by the original Greek: whereas in St. Luke xiv. 10, the English translators make use of it for the *lowest degree of respect: Thou shalt have worship in the presence of them that sit at meat with thee.* The latter is the proper meaning of the word worship, as appears by the marriage service: *With my body I thee worship*, and by the designation of the lowest order of magistrates, his worship Mr. Alderman N. Nevertheless, as the word may be differently interpreted, Catholics abstain from applying it to persons or things inferior to God: making use of the words *honour* and *veneration* in their regard; words which, so applied, even bishop Porteus approves us. Thus it appears, that the heinous charge of *idolatry* brought against Catholics for their respect towards the saints, is grounded on nothing but the mistaken meaning of a word!

† P 23.　　　　　‡ Charge 1810, p. 12

consist in contemplating the wonderful ways of God's providence with all his creatures here on earth? But, without recurring to this supposition, it is sufficient for dissipating the bishop's uncharitable phantom of *blasphemy*, and Calvin's profane jest about the length of the saint's ears, that God is able to reveal to them the prayers of Christians who address them here on earth. In case I had the same opportunity of conversing with this prelate, which I once enjoyed, I should not fail to make the following observation to him : my lord, you publicly maintain, that the act of praying to saints, ascribes to them the divine attribute of *universal presence ;* this you call blasphemy : now it appears, by the articles and injunctions of your church, that you believe in the existence and efficacy of " sorceries, enchantments, and witchcraft, invented by the devil, to procure his counsel or help,"* wherever the conjuror or witch may chance to be ; do you, therefore, ascribe the divine attribute of *universal presence* to the devil? You must assert this, or you must withdraw your charge of blasphemy against the Catholics for praying to the saints.

That it is lawful and profitable to invoke the prayers of the angels, is plain from Jacob's asking and obtaining the angel's blessing, with whom he had mystically wrestled, *Gen.* xxxii. 26, and from his invoking his own angel to bless Joseph's sons, *Gen.* xlvii. 16. The same is also sufficiently plain, with respect to the saints, from the Book of Revelations, where the four and twenty elders in heaven are said to have, *golden vials full of odours, which are the prayers of the saints.* Rev. v. 8. The church, however, derived her doctrine on this and other points immediately from the apostles, before any part of the New Testament was written. The tradition was so ancient and universal, that all those Eastern churches, which broke off from the central church of Rome, a great many ages before Protestantism was heard of, perfectly agree with us in honouring and invoking the angels and saints. I have said that the patriarch of Protestantism, Martin Luther, did not find any thing idolatrous in the doctrine or practice of the church with respect to the saints So far from this, he exclaims, " Who can deny that God works great miracles at the tombs of the saints? I therefore, with the whole Catholic church, hold that the saints are to be honoured and invocated by us."† In the same spirit he recommends

* Injunctions, A. D. 1559. Bishop Sparrow's Collection, p. 89. Articles, Ibid. p. 180.
† In Purg. quorumd. Artic. Tom. i. Germet. Ep. ad Georg. Spalat.

this devotion to dying persons, " Let no one omit to call upon the B. Virgin and the angels and saints, that they may intercede with God for them at that instant."* I may add that several of the brightest lights of the established church, such as archbishop Sheldon and the bishops Blandford,† Gunning,‡ Montague, &c. have altogether abandoned the charge of idolatry against Catholics on this head. The last mentioned of them says, " I own that Christ is not wronged in his mediation. It is no impiety to say, as they (the Catholics) do, *Holy Mary, pray for me; Holy Peter, pray for me;*"§ whilst the candid prebendary of Westminster warns his brethren " not to lead people by the nose, to believe they can prove Papists to be idolaters when they cannot."‖

In conclusion, dear sir, you will observe that the council of Trent, barely teaches that it is *good and profitable* to invoke the prayers of the saints; hence our divines infer that there is no positive law of the church, incumbent on all her children to pray to the saints :¶ nevertheless, what member of the Catholic church militant will fail to communicate with his brethren of the church triumphant? What Catholic, believing in the *communion of saints*, and that " the saints, reigning with Christ pray for us, and that it is good and profitable for us to invoke their prayers," will forego this advantage! How sublime and consoling! how animating is the doctrine and practice of true Catholics, compared with the opinions of Protestants! We hold daily and hourly converse, to our unspeakable comfort and advantage, with the angelic choirs, with the venerable patriarchs and prophets of ancient times, with the heroes of Christianity, the blessed apostles and martyrs, with the bright ornaments of it in later ages, the Bernards, the Xaviers, the Teresas, and the Sales's : they are all members of the Catholic church. Why should not you partake of this advantage? Your soul, you complain, dear sir, is in trouble; you lament that your prayers to God are not heard: continue to pray to him with all the fervour of your soul : but why not engage his friends and courtiers to add the weight of their prayers to your own? Perhaps his Divine Majesty may hear the prayers of the Jobs, when he will not listen to those of an Eliphaz, a Bildad,

* Luth. Prep. ad Mort.
† See Duchess of York's Testimony in Brunswick's 50 Reasons.
‡ Burnet's Hist. of his own Times, Vol. i. p. 437.
§ Treat. of Invoc. of Saints, p. 118.
‖ Thorndike, Just Weights, p. 10.
¶ Petavius, Suarez, Wallenburg, Muratori, Nat. Alex.

or a Zophar. *Job* xlii.   You believe, no doubt, that you have
an angel guardian, appointed by God to protect you, conformably to what Christ said of the children presented to him : *Their
angels do always behold the face of my Father who is in heaven*,
Mat. xviii. 10 : address yourself to this blessed spirit with gra-
titude, veneration, and confidence.   You believe also, that,
among the saints of God, there is one of supereminent purity
and sanctity, pronounced by an archangel to be, not only gracious, but " full of grace;" the chosen instrument of God in
the incarnation of his Son, and the intercessor with this her Son,
in obtaining his first miracle, that of turning water into wine, at
a time, when his " time" for appearing to the world by miracles,
was " not yet come." *John* ii. 4.   " It is impossible," as one
of the fathers says, " to love the son, without loving the mother :" beg of her, then, with affection and confidence, to intercede with Jesus, as the poor Canaanites did, to change the
tears of your distress into the wine of gladness, by affording
you the light and grace you so much want.   You cannot refuse to join with me in the angelic salutation : *Hail full of
grace, our Lord is with thee*,* nor in the subsequent address of
the inspired Elizabeth : *Blessed art thou among women, and
blessed is the fruit of thy womb*, Luke i. 42 : cast aside, then, I
beseech you, dear sir, prejudices, which are not only groundless but also hurtful, and devoutly conclude with me, in the
words of the whole Catholic Church, upon earth : *Holy Mary,
mother of God, pray for us sinners, now, and at the hour of our
death. Amen.*

I am, &c.

J. M.

---

* Luke i. 28.   The Catholic version is here used, as more conformable to the
Greek as well as the Vulgate than the Protestant, which renders the passage: *Hail
thou who art highly favoured.*

LETTER XXXIV.

To JAMES BROWN, Esq.

ON RELIGIOUS MEMORIALS.

DEAR SIR,

IF the Catholic church has been so grievously injured by the misrepresentation of her doctrine respecting prayers to the saints, she has been still more grievously injured by the prevailing calumnies against the respect which she pays to the memorials of Christ and his saints, namely to crucifixes, relics, pious pictures and images. This has been misrepresented, from almost the first eruption of Protestantism,* as rank idolatry, and as justifying the necessity of a Reformation. To countenance such misrepresentation in our own country, in particular, avaricious courtiers and grandees seized on the costly shrines, statues and other ornaments of all the churches and chapels, and authorized the demolition or defacing of all other religious memorials of whatever nature or materials, not only in places of worship, but also in market places and even in private houses. In support of the same pious fraud, the Holy Scriptures were corrupted in their different versions and editions,† till religious

---

* Martin Luther, with all his hatred of the Catholic church, found no idolatry in her doctrine respecting crosses and images: on the contrary, he warmly defended it against Carlostadius and his associates, who had destroyed those in the churches of Wittenberg. Epist. ad Gasp. Guttal. In the titlepages of his volumes, published by Melancthon, Luther is exhibited on his knees before a crucifix. Queen Elizabeth persisted for many years in retaining a crucifix on the altar of her chapel, till some of her Puritan courtiers engaged Patch, the fool, to break it : " no wiser man," says Dr. Heylen, (Hist. of Reform. p. 124,) " daring to undertake such a service." James I. thus reproached the Scotch bishops, when they objected to his placing pictures and statues in his chapel at Edinburgh : "You can endure Lions and Dragons *(the supporters of the royal arms)* and Devils, (Q Elizabeth's Griffins) to be figured in your churches, but will not allow the like place to patriarchs and apostles." Spotswood's History, p. 530.

† See in the present English Bible, Colos. iii, 5. *Covetousness which is idolatry :* this, in the Bibles of 1562, 1577, and 1579, stood thus : *Covetousness which is the worshipping of images.* In like manner where we read, *a covetous man, who is an idolater,* in the former editions we read, *a covetous man which is a worshipper of idols.* Instead of, *What agreement hath the temple of God with idols,* 2 Cor. vi. 16 : it used to stand, *How agreeth the temple of God with images.* Instead of, *Little children keep yourselves from idols,* 1 John v. 21 : it stood, during the reigns of Edward and Elizabeth, *Babes keep yourselves from images.* There were several other manifest corruptions in this as well as in other points in the ancient Protestant Bibles; some of which remain in the present version.

Protestants, themselves, became disgusted with them,* and loudly called for a new translation. This was accordingly made, at the beginning of the first James's reign. In short, every passage in the Bible, and every argument which common sense suggests against idolatry, was applied to the decent respect which Catholics show to the memorials of Christianity.

The misrepresentation, in question, still continues to be the chosen topic of Protestant controvertists, for inflaming the minds of the ignorant against their Catholic brethren. Accordingly, there is hardly a lisping infant, who has not been taught that *the Romanists pray to images*, nor is there a secluded peasant who has not been made to believe, that the *Papists worship wooden gods.* The Book of Homilies repeatedly affirms that our *images* of Christ and his saints are *idols ;* that we " pray and ask of *them* what it belongs to God alone to give ; and that " images have beene and bee worshipped, and so, idolatry committed to them by infinite multitudes to the great offence of God's majestie, and danger of infinite soules; that idolatrie can not possibly be separated from images set up in churches, and that God's horrible wrath, and our most dreadful danger, cannot be avoided without the destruction and utter abolition of all such images and idols out of the church and temple of Gód."† Archbishop Secker teaches that " The church of Rome has other Gods, besides the Lord," and that " there never was greater idolatry among heathens in the business of image-worshipping than in the church of Rome."‡ Bishop Porteus, though he does not charge us with idolatry, by name, yet he intimates the same thing, where he applies to us one of the strongest passages of Scripture against idol worship : *They that make them are like unto them ; and so is every one that trusteth in them. O Israel, trust thou in the Lord.* Ps. cxiii.§

Let us now hear what the Catholic church herself has solemnly pronounced on the present subject, in her general coun-

---

* See the account of what passed on this subject, at the Conference of Hampton Court, in Fuller's and Collier's Church Histories, and in Neal's History of the Puritans.

† Against the Perils of Idol. P. iii.—This admonition was quickly carried into effect, throughout England. All statues, bas-relievos, and crosses, were demolished in all the churches, and all pictures were defaced ; while they continued to hold their places, as they do still, in the Protestant churches of Germany. At length common sense regained its rights, even in this country. Accordingly, we see the cross exalted at the top of its principal church (St. Paul's,) which is also ornamented, all round it, with the statues of saints; most of the cathedrals and collegiate churches now contain pictures, and some of them, as for example, Westminster Abbey, carved images.

‡ Comment. on Ch. Catech. sect. 24.　　　　　　§ P. 31.

cil of Trent. She says, " The images of Christ, of the Virgin Mother of God, and the other saints, are to be kept and retained, particularly in the churches, and due honour and veneration is to be paid them : *not that we believe there is any divinity or power in them*, for which we respect them, or that any thing is to be asked of them, or that trust is to be placed in them, as the heathens of old trusted in their idols."* In conformity with this doctrine of our church, the following question and answer are seen in our first catechism, for the instruction of children : " Question : May we pray to relics or images? Answer : No; by no means, for they have no life or sense to hear or help us." Finally, that work of the able Catholic writers Gother and Challoner, which I quoted above, *The Papist Misrepresented and Represented*, contains the following anathema, in which I am confident every Catholic existing will readily join, " Cursed is he that commits idolatry ; that prays to images or relics, or worships them for God. Amen."

Dr. Porteus is very positive that there is no Scriptural warrant for retaining and venerating these exterior memorials, and he maintains that no other memorial ought to be admitted than the Lord's Supper.† Does he remember the ark of the covenant, made by the command of God, together with the punishment of those who profaned it, and the blessing bestowed on those who revered it ? And what was the ark of the covenant, after all ? A chest of Settim wood, containing the tables of the law and two golden pots of manna ; the whole being covered over by two carved images of cherubims ; in short, it was a memorial of God's mercy and bounty to his people. But, says the bishop, " The Roman Catholics make images of Christ and of his saints after their own fancy : before these images, and even that of the cross, they kneel down and prostrate themselves : to these they lift up their eyes, and in that posture they pray."‡ Supposing all this to be true ; has the bishop never read, that when the Israelites were smitten at Ai, *Joshua fell to the earth upon his face, before the ark of the Lord, until the even tide, he and the elders of Israel, and Joshua said, Alas, O Lord God, &c.* Jos. vii. 6. Does not he himself oblige those who frequent the above-mentioned memorial, to kneel and prostrate themselves before it, at which time it is to be supposed they lift up their eyes to the sacrament and say their prayers ? Does not he require of his people that " when the name of JESUS is pronounced in any lesson, &c. due re-

---

* Sess. xxv.   † P. 23.   ‡ Confut. p. 27

verence be made of all with lowness of courtesie ?"* And does he consider as well founded, the outcry of idolatry against the established church, on this and the preceding point, raised by the dissenters? Again, is not his lordship in the habit of kneeling to his majesty and of bowing with the other peers, to an empty chair when it is placed as his throne? Does he not often reverently kiss the material substance of printed paper and leather, I mean the Bible, because it relates to and represents the sacred word of God? When the bishop of London shall have well considered these several matters, methinks he will understand the nature of relative honour, by which an inferior respect may be paid to the sign, for the sake of the thing signified, better than he seems to do at present; and he will neither directly nor indirectly charge the Catholics with idolatry, on account of indifferent ceremonies, which take their nature from the intention of those who use them. During the dispute about pious images, which took place in the eighth century, St. Stephen of Auxence, having endeavoured in vain to make his persecutor, the emperor Copronimus, conceive the nature of relative honour and dishonour in this matter, threw a piece of money, bearing the emperor's figure, on the ground, and treated it with the utmost indignity; when the latter soon proved, by his treatment of the saint, that the affront regarded himself rather than the piece of metal.†

The bishop objects, that the Catholics " make pictures of God the Father under the likeness of a venerable old man." Certain painters indeed have represented him so, as in fact he was pleased to appear so to some of the prophets, *Isa.* vi. 1. *Dan.* vii. 9; but the council of Trent says nothing concerning that representation, which, after all, is not so common as that of a triangle among Protestants, to represent the trinity. Thus much, however, is most certain, that if any Christian were obstinately to maintain, that the divine nature resembles the human form, he would be an anthropomorphite heretic. The bishop moreover signifies, what most other Protestant controvertists express more coarsely, that to screen our idolatry we have suppressed the second commandment of the Decalogue, and to make up the deficiency, we have split the tenth commandment into two. My answer is, that I apprehend many of these disputants are ignorant enough to believe that the division of the commandments, in their Common Prayer Book, was copied,

* Injunctions, A. D. 1559, n. 52.　Canons 1603, n. 18.
† Fleury, Hist. Eoc. L. xliii. n. 41.

if not from the identical Tables of Moses, at least from his original text of the Pentateuch; but the bishop, as a man of learning, must know that in the original Hebrew, and in the several copies and versions of it, during some thousands of years, there was no mark of separation between one commandment and another; so that we have no rules to be guided by, in making the distinction, but the sense of the context, and the authority of the most approved fathers,* both which we follow. In the mean time, it is a gross calumny that we suppress any part of the Decalogue; for the whole of it appears in all our Bibles, and in all our most approved catechisms.† To be brief the words, *Thou shalt not make to thyself any graven thing*, are either a prohibition of all images, and, of course, those round the bishop's own cathedral of St. Paul, as likewise of all existing coins; which I am sure he will not agree to; or else it is a mere prohibition of images made to receive divine worship, in which we perfectly agree with him. You will observe, dear sir, that I intend to include *relies*, meaning things which have some way appertained to and been *left* by personages of eminent sanctity, among religious memorials. Indeed the ancient fathers generally call them by that name. Surely Dr. Porteus will not say that there is no warrant in Scripture for honouring these, when he recollects that, *From the body of St. Paul were brought unto the sick, handkerchiefs and aprons, and the diseases departed from them*, Acts xix. 12; and that, *When the dead man was let down and touched the bones of Elisha, he revived and stood upon his feet.* 2 Kings xiii. 21.

But to make an end of the present discussion: nothing but the pressing want of a strong pretext for breaking communion with the ancient church could have put the revolters upon so extravagant an attempt as that of confounding the inferior and relative honour which Catholics pay to the memorials of Christ and his saints, (an honour which they themselves pay to the Bible-book, to the name of JESUS, and even to the king's throne) with the idolatry of the Israelites to their golden calf, *Exod.* xxxii. 4, and of the ancient heathens to their idols, which they believed to be inhabited by their gods. In a word, the end for which pious pictures and images are made and retained by Catholics, is the same for which pictures and images are made and retained by mankind in general, to put us in mind of the

---

* St. Augustin, Quæst. in Exod. Clem. Alex. Strom. 1. vi. Hieron, in Ps. xxxii.
† Catech. Roman ad Paroch. The folio Catech. of Montpellier. Douay Catech. Abridgment of Christian Doctrine.

persons and things they represent.   They are not primarily intended for the purpose of being venerated; nevertheless, as they
bear a certain relation with holy persons and things, by representing them, they become entitled to a relative or secondary
veneration; in the manner already explained.   I must not forget one important use of pious pictures, mentioned by the holy
fathers, namely, that they help to instruct the ignorant.*   Still,
it is a point agreed upon among Catholic doctors and divines,
that the memorials of religion form no essential part of it.†
Hence, if you should become a Catholic, as I pray God you
may, I shall never ask you, if you have a pious picture or relic,
or so much as a crucifix in your possession : but then, I trust,
after the declarations I have made, that you will not account me
an idolater, should you see such things in my oratory or study,
or should you observe how tenacious I am of my crucifix, in
particular.   Your faith and devotion may not stand in need of
such memorials : but mine, alas! do.   I am too apt to forget
what my Saviour has done and suffered for me; but the sight
of his representation often brings this to my memory, and
affects my sentiments.   Hence I would rather part with most of
the books in my library, than with the figure of my crucified
Lord.

I am, &c.
J. M.

---

* St. Gregory calls pictures *Idiotorum libri.*   Epist. L. ix. 9
 † The learned Petavius says : "We must lay it down as a principle, that images
are to be reckoned among the *adiphora*, which do not belong to the substance of
religion, and which the church may retain or take away as she judges best."   L.
xv. de Incar.   Hence Dr. Hawarden, Of Images, p. 353, teaches with Delphinus,
that if in any place, there is danger of real idolatry or superstition from pictures,
they ought to be removed by the pastors ; as St. Epiphanius destroyed a certain
pious picture, and Ezechias destroyed the brazen serpent.

LETTER XXXV.

To the Rev. ROBERT CLAYTON, M. A.

OBJECTIONS ANSWERED.

Rev. Sir,

I learn by a letter from our worthy friend, Mr. Brown, as well as by your own, that I am to consider you, and not him as the person charged to make the objections, which are to be made, on the part of the church of England, against my theological positions and arguments in future. I congratulate the society of New Cottage on the acquisition of so valuable a member as Mr. Clayton, and I think myself fortunate in having so clear-headed and candid an opponent to contend with, as his letter shows him to be.

You admit, that, according to my explanation, which is no other than that of our divines, our catechisms and our councils in general, we are not guilty of idolatry in the honour we pay to saints and their memorials, and that the dispute between your church and mine upon these points, is a dispute about words rather than about things, as bishop Bossuet observes, and as several candid Protestants, before you, have confessed. You and bishop Porteus agree with us, that " the saints are to be loved and honoured; on the other hand, we agree with you, that it would be idolatrous to pay them *divine worship*, or to *pray to their memorials* in any shape whatever. Hence, the only question remaining between us is concerning the *utility* of desiring the prayers of the saints : for you say it is useless, because you think that they cannot hear us, and that, therefore, the practice is superstitious : whereas, I have vindicated the practice itself, and have shown that the utility of it no way depends on the circumstance of the blessed spirits immediately hearing the addresses made to them.

Still you complain that I have not answered *all* the bishop's objections against the doctrine and practices in question. My reply is, that I have answered the chief of them : and whereas they are, for the most part, of ancient date, and have been again and again solidly refuted by our divines, I shall send to New Cottage, together with this letter, a work of one of them, who, for depth of learning and strength of argument, has not been

22

surpassed since the time of Bellarmin.* There, Rev. sir, you will find all that you inquire after, and you will discover, in particular, that the *worship of the angels*, which St. Paul condemns in his Epistle to the Colossians, chap. ii. 18, means, that of the fallen or *wicked angels*, whom Christ *despoiled*, ver. 15, and which was paid to them by Simon the magician and his followers, as the makers of the world. As to the doctrine of Bellarmin concerning images, it is plain that his lordship never consulted the author himself, but only his misrepresenter Vitringa; otherwise, he would have gathered from the whole of this precise theologian's distinctions, that he teaches precisely the contrary to that which he is represented to teach.†

You next observe, that I have said nothing concerning the extravagant forms of prayer to the blessed Virgin and other saints, which Dr. Porteus has collected from Catholic prayer books, and which, you think, prove that we attribute an absolute and unbounded power to those heavenly citizens. I am aware, Rev. sir, that his lordship, as well as another bishop,‡ who is all sweetness of temper, except when Popery is mentioned in his hearing, and indeed a crowd of other Protestant writers, has employed himself in making such collections, but from what sources, for the greater part I am ignorant. If I were to charge his faith, or the faith of his church with all the conclusions that could logically be drawn from different forms of prayer to be met with in the books of her most distinguished prelates and divines, or from the Scriptures themselves, I fancy the bishop would strongly protest against that mode of reasoning. If, for example, an anthropomorphite were to address him : you say, my lord, in your creed, that Christ " ascended into heaven, and sitteth at the right hand of God," therefore it is plain you believe with me, that God has a human shape; or if a Calvinist were to say to him, You pray to God that he " would not lead you into temptation," therefore you acknowledge that it is God who tempts you to commit sin : in either of these cases the bishop would insist upon explaining the texts here quoted; he would argue on the nature of figures of speech, especially in the language of poetry and devotion; and would

* The true church of Christ, by Edward Hawarden, DD. S. T. P. The author was engaged in successful contests with Dr. Clark, bishop Bull, Mr. Leslie, and other eminent Protestant divines. The work has been lately republished in Dublin by Coyne.

† See De Imag. L. ii. c. 24.

‡ The bishop of Hereford, Dr. Huntingford, who has squeezed a large quantity of this irrelevant matter into his examination of the Catholic Petition.

maintain, that the belief of his church is not to be collected from these, but from her defined articles. Make but the same allowance to Catholics, and all this phantom of verbal idolatry will dissolve into air.

Lastly, you remind me of the bishop's assertion, that " neither images nor pictures were allowed in churches for the first hundred years." To this assertion you add your own opinion, that during that same period no prayers were addressed by Christians to the saints. A fit of oblivion must have overtaken Dr. Porteus when he wrote what you quoted from him, as he cannot be ignorant that it was not till the conversion of Constantine, in the fourth century, that the Christians were generally allowed to build churches for their worship, having been obliged, during the ages of persecution, to practice it in subterraneous catacombs, or other obscure recesses. We learn, however, from Tertullian, that it was usual, in his time, to represent our Saviour in the character of *the good shepherd*, on the chalices used at the assemblies of the Christians :* and we are informed by Eusebius, the father of church history, and the friend of Constantine, that he himself had seen a miraculous image of our Saviour in brass, which had been erected by the woman, who was cured by touching the hem of his garment, and also different pictures of him, and of St. Peter and St. Paul, which had been preserved since their time.† The historian Zozomen adds, concerning that statue, that it was mutilated in the reign of Julian the apostate, and that the Christians, nevertheless, collected the pieces of it, and placed it in their church.‡ St. Gregory of Nyssa, who flourished in the fourth century, preaching on the martyrdom of St. Theodore, describes his relics as being present in the church, and his sufferings as being painted on the walls, together with an image of Christ, as if surveying them.§ It is needless to carry the history of pious figures and paintings down to the end of the sixth century, at which time St. Augustin and his companions, coming to preach the Gospel to our Pagan ancestors, " carried a silver cross before them as a banner, and.a·painted picture of our Saviour Christ."‖ The above-mentioned Tertullian testifies, that at every movement and in every employment, the primitive Christians used to sign their foreheads with the sign of the cross,¶ and Eusebius and St. Chrysostom fill whole pages of their

---

* Lib. de Pudicitia, c. 10.
‡ Hist. Eccles. l. v. c. 21.
‖ Bede's Eccles. Hist. l. i. c. 25.

† Hist. l. vii. c. 18.
§ Orat. in Theod.
¶ De Coron. Milit. c. 3.

works with testimonies of the veneration in which the figure of
the cross was anciently held; the latter of whom expressly says,
that the cross was placed on the altars* of the churches.   The
whole history of the martyrs, from St. Ignatius and St. Polycarp, the disciples of the apostles, whose relics, after their execution, were carried away by the Christians, as " more valuable
than gold and precious stones,"† down to the latest martyr,
incontestibly proves the veneration which the church has ever
maintained for these sacred objects.   With respect to your own
opinion, Rev. sir, as to the earliest date of prayers to the saints,
I may refer you to the writings of St. Irenæus, the disciple of
St. Polycarp, who introduces the blessed Virgin praying for
Eve,‡ to the apology of his contemporary St. Justin the martyr,
who says, " We venerate and worship the angelic host, and the
spirits of the prophets, teaching others as we ourselves have been
taught,"§ and to the light of the fourth century, St. Basil, who
expressly refers these practices to the apostles, where he says,
" I invoke the apostles, prophets, and martyrs to pray for me,
that God may be merciful to me, and forgive me my sins.   I
honour and reverence their images, since these things have
been ordained by tradition from the apostles, and are practised
in all our churches."‖   You will agree with me, that I need not
descend lower than the fourth age of the church.

I am, &c.

J. M.

* In Orat. Quod Christus sit Deus.
† Euseb. Hist. l. iv. c. 15.   Acta Sincer. Apud Ruinart.
‡ Contra Hæres. l. v. c. 19.   § Apol. 2. prope Init.
‖ Epist. 205. t. iii. edit. Paris.

LETTER XXXVI.

To JAMES BROWN, Esq.

ON TRANSUBSTANTIATION.

DEAR SIR,

IT is the remark of the prince of modern controvertists, bishop Bossuet, that, whereas in most other subjects of dispute between Catholics and Protestants, the difference is less than it seems to be, in this of the holy eucharist or Lord's Supper, it is greater than it appears.* The cause of this is, that our opponents misrepresent our doctrine concerning the veneration of saints, pious images, indulgences, purgatory, and other articles, in order to strengthen their arguments against us; whereas their language approaches nearer to our doctrine than their sentiments do on the subject of the eucharist, because our doctrine is so strictly conformable to the words of Holy Scripture. This is a disingenuous artifice; but I have to describe two others of a still more fatal tendency; first, with respect to the present welfare of the Catholics, who are the subjects of them, and secondly, with respect to the future welfare of the Protestants, who deliberately make use of them.

The first of these disingenuous practices consists in misrepresenting Catholics as *worshippers of bread and wine* in the sacrament, and therefore as *idolaters*, at the same time that our adversaries are perfectly aware that we firmly believe, as an article of faith, that *there is no bread nor wine*, but Christ alone, true God, as well as man, present in it. Supposing, for a moment, that we are mistaken in this belief, the worst we could be charged with, is an error, in supposing Christ to be where he is not; and nothing but uncharitable calumny, or gross inattention, could accuse us of the heinous crime of idolatry. To illustrate this argument, let me suppose, that being charged with a loyal address to the sovereign, you presented it, by mistake, to one of his courtiers, or even to an inanimate figure of him, which, for some reason or other, had been dressed up in royal robes, and placed on the throne, would your heart reproach you, or would any sensible person reproach you with the guilt of treason in this case? Were the people who thought in their

---

* Exposition of the doctrine of the Catholic church, Sect. xvi.

hearts that John the Baptist was the Christ, *Luke* iii. 15, and who probably worshipped him as such, idolaters, in consequence of their error? The falsehood, as well as the uncharitableness of this calumny is too gross to escape the observation of any informed and reflecting man: yet is it upheld and vociferated to the ignorant crowd, in order to keep alive their prejudices against us, by bishop Porteus,* and the Protestant preachers and writers in general, and it is perpetuated by the legislature to defeat our civil claims!† It is not, however, true, that all Protestant divines have laid this heavy charge at the door of Catholics for worshipping Christ in the sacrament, as all those eminent prelates in the reigns of Charles I. and Charles II. must be excepted, who generally acquitted us of the charge of idolatry, and more especially the learned Gunning, bishop of Ely, who reprobated the above signified *declaration*, when it was brought into the house of lords, protesting that his conscience would not permit him to make it.‡ The candid Thorndyke, prebendary of Westminster, argues thus on the present subject: " Will any Papist acknowledge that he honours the elements of the eucharist for God? Will common sense charge him with honouring that in the sacrament, which he does not believe to be there?"§ The celebrated bishop of Down, Dr. Jeremy Taylor, reasons with equal fairness, where he says, " The object of their (the Catholics') adoration in the sacrament is the only true and eternal God, hypostatically united with his holy humanity, which humanity they believe actually present under the veil of the sacrament. And if they thought him not present, they are so far from worshipping the bread, that they profess it idolatry to do so. This is demonstration that the soul has nothing in it that is idolatrical; the will has nothing in it but what is a great enemy to idolatry."||

The other instance of disingenuity and injustice on the part of Protestant divines and statesmen consists in their overlooking the main subject in debate, namely, *whether Christ is or is not*

---

* He charges Catholics with " senseless idolatry," and with worshipping the creature instead of the Creator." Confut. P. ii. c 1.

† The *Declaration against Popery*, by which Catholics were excluded from the Houses of Parliament, was voted by them during that time of national frenzy and disgrace, when they equally voted the reality of the pretended Popish Plot, which cost the Catholics a torrent of innocent blood, and which was hatched by the unprincipled Shaftesbury, with the help of Dr. Tongue, and the infamous Oates; to prevent the succession of James II. to the crown. See Echard's Hist. North's Exam.

‡ Burnet's Hist. Own Times.
§ Just Weights and Measures, c. 19.
|| Liberty of Prophesying, Sect. 20.

really and personally present in the sacrament; and in the mean time employing all the force of their declamation and ridicule, and all the severity of the law to a point of inferior, or at least secondary consideration; namely, to *the mode* in which he is considered by one particular party *as being present.* It is well known that Catholics believe, that, when Christ took the bread and gave it to his apostles, saying, THIS IS MY BODY, he changed the bread into his body, which change is called *transubstantiation.* On the other hand, the Lutherans, after their master, hold that *the bread and the real body of Christ are united, and both truly present* in the sacrament, as iron and fire are united in a redhot bar.* This sort of presence, which would be not less miraculous and incomprehensible than transubstantiation, is called *consubstantiation:* while the Calvinists and church of England men in general (though many of the brightest luminaries of the latter have approached to the Catholic doctrine) maintain that Christ is barely present in *figure*, and received only *by faith.* Now all the alleged absurdities, in a manner, and all the pretended impiety and idolatry, which are attributed to *transubstantiation*, equally attaches to *consubstantiation* and to the *real presence* professed by those eminent divines of the established church. Nevertheless, what controversial preacher or writer ever attacks the latter opinions? What law excludes Lutherans from parliament, or even from the throne? So far from this, a chapel royal has been founded and is maintained in the palace itself for the propagation of their consubstantiation and the participation of their real presence! In short, you may say with Luther, *the bread is the body of Christ,* or with Osiander, *the bread is one and the same person with Christ,* or with bishop Cosin, that " Christ is present really and substantially by an incomprehensible mystery,"† or with Dr. Balguy, that there is no mystery at all, but a mere " federal rite, barely signifying the receiver's acceptance of the benefit of redemption;"‡ in short, you may say any thing you please concerning the eucharist, without obloquy or inconvenience to yourself, except what the words of Christ, *this is my body,* so clearly imply, namely, that *he changes the bread into his body.* In fact, as the bishop of Meaux observes, " the declarations of Christ operate what they express; when he speaks, nature obeys, and he does what he says: thus he cured the

* De Capt. Babyl. Osiander, whose sister, Cranmer married, taught *Impanation,* or an hypostatical and personal union of the bread with Christ's body, in consequence of which a person might truly say: *This bread is Christ's body.*

† Hist. of Transub. p. 44.　　　　　　　　‡ Charge vii.

ruler s son, by saying to him, *Thy son liveth;* and the crooked woman, by saying, *Thou art loosed from thy infirmity.*"[*] The prelate adds, for our further observation, that Christ did not say, *My body is here; this contains my body,* but, *this is my body: this is my blood.* Hence Zuinglius, Calvin, Beza, and the defenders of the figurative sense in general, all except the Protestants of England, have expressly confessed, that, admitting the real presence, the Catholic doctrine is far more conformable to Scripture than the Lutheran. I shall finish this letter with remarking, that, as transubstantiation, according to bishop Cosin, was the first of Christ's miracles in changing water into wine; so it may be said to have been his last, during his mortal course, by changing bread and wine into his sacred body and blood.

I am, &c.

J. M

LETTER XXXVII.

To JAMES BROWN, Esq.

ON THE REAL PRESENCE OF CHRIST IN THE B. SACRAMENT.

Dear Sir,

It is clear from what I have stated in my last letter to you, that the first and main question to be settled between Catholics and church Protestants is concerning *the real or figurative presence* of Christ in the sacrament. This being determined, it will be time enough, and, in my opinion, it will not require a long time, to conclude upon the *manner of his presence,* namely, whether by consubstantiation or transubstantiation. To consider the authorized exposition or catechism of the established church, it might appear certain that she herself holds *the real presence;* since she declares, that " The body and blood of Christ are *verily* and *indeed* taken and received by the faithful in the Lord's Supper." To this declaration I alluded, in the first place, where I complained of Protestants *disguising their real tenets,* by adopting language of a different meaning from

<hr>

[*] Variat. T. ii. p. 34.

their sentiments, and conformable to those of Catholics, in consequence of such being the language of the sacred text. In fact, it is certain and confessed, that she does *not*, after all, *believe the real* body and blood to be in the supper, but mere bread and wine, as the same catechism declares. This involves an evident contradiction; it is saying, *you receive that in the sacrament, which does not exist in the sacrament:** it is like the speech of a debtor, who should say to his creditor, *I hereby verily and indeed pay you the money I owe you; but I have not verily and indeed the money to pay you with.*

Nothing proves more clearly the fallacy of the Calvinists and other dissenters, as likewise of the established church men in general, who profess to make the Scripture, in its plain and literal sense, the sole rule of their faith, than their denial of the real presence of Christ in the sacrament, which is so manifestly and emphatically expressed therein. He explained and promised this divine mystery near one of the Paschs, John vi. 4 previous to his institution of it. He then multiplied five loaves and two fishes, so as. to afford a superabundant meal to five thousand men, besides women and children, *Mat.* xiv. 21; which was an evident sign of the future multiplication of his own body on the several altars of the world; after which he took occasion to speak of this mystery, by saying, *I am the living bread, which came down from heaven. If any man eat of*

* Dryden, in his Hind and Panther, ridicules this inconsistency as follows:
  "The literal sense is hard to flesh and blood;
  "But nonsense never could be understood."
Even Dr. Hey calls this "an unsteadiness of language and a seeming inconsistency." Lect. vol. iv. p. 338.

N. B. It is curious to trace in the Liturgy of the Established church her variations on this most important point of Christ's presence in the sacrament. The first communion service, drawn up by Cranmer, Ridley, and other Protestant bishops and divines, and published in 1548, clearly expresses the real presence, and that "the whole body of Christ is received under each particle of the sacrament." Burnet, P. ii. b. 1.

Afterwards, when the Calvinistic party prevailed, the 29th of the 42 Articles of Religion, drawn up by the same prelates and published in 1552, expressly denies the real presence, and the very possibility of Christ being in the Eucharist, since he has ascended up to heaven. Ten years afterwards, Elizabeth being on the throne, who patronized the real presence, (see Heylin, p. 124,) when the 42 Articles were reduced to 39, this declaration against the real and corporal presence of Christ was left out of the Common Prayer Book, for the purpose of comprehending those persons who believed in it, as was the whole of the former rubric, which explained that "by kneeling at the sacrament no adoration was intended to any corporal presence of Christ's natural flesh and blood." Burnet, P. ii. p. 392. So the liturgy stood for just 100 years, when, in 1662, during the reign of Charles II. among other alterations of the liturgy, which then took place, the old rubric against the real presence and the adoration of the sacrament was again restored as it stands at present!

this bread, he shall live for ever: and the bread that I will give, is my flesh, for the life of the world. John vi. 51. The sacred text goes on to inform us of the perplexity of the Jews, from their understanding Christ's words in their plain and natural sense, which he, so far from removing by a different explanation, confirms by expressing that sense in other terms still more emphatical. *The Jews therefore strove amongst themselves, saying, How can this man give us his flesh to eat? Then Jesus said unto them: Verily, verily, I say unto you: except ye eat the flesh of the son of man, and drink his blood, ye have no life in you.—For my flesh is meat indeed, and my blood is drink indeed.* Ver. 52, 53, 55. Nor was it the multitude alone who took offence at this mystery of a real and corporal reception of Christ's person, so energetically and repeatedly expressed by him, but also several of his own beloved disciples, whom certainly he would not have permitted to desert him to their own destruction, if he could have removed their difficulty by barely telling them that they were only to receive him by faith, and to take bread and wine in remembrance of him. Yet this merciful Saviour permitted them to go their ways, and he contented himself with asking the apostles, if they would also leave him. They were as incapable of comprehending the mystery as the others were, but they were assured that Christ is ever to be credited upon his word, and accordingly they made that generous act of faith, which every true Christian will also make, who seriously and devoutly considers the sacred text before us. *Many therefore of his disciples, when they had heard this, said: This is a hard saying: who can hear it? From that time many of his disciples went back and walked no more with him. Then Jesus said unto the twelve: will ye also go away? Then Simom Peter answered him: Lord, to whom shall we go? thou hast the words of eternal life.* Ver. 60, 66, 67, 68.

The apostles thus instructed by Christ's express and repeated declaration, as to the nature of this sacrament, when he promised it to them, were prepared for the sublime simplicity of his words in instituting it. For, *whilst they were at supper, Jesus took bread, and blessed it, and brake it, and gave it to the disciples, and said: take ye and eat:* THIS IS MY BODY. *And taking the chalice, he gave thanks, and gave it to them, saying: drink ye all of this;* FOR THIS IS MY BLOOD OF THE NEW TESTAMENT, WHICH SHALL BE SHED FOR MANY UNTO THE REMISSION OF SINS. *Mat.* xxvi. 26, 27, 28. This account of St. Matthew is repeated by St Mark, xiv. 22, 23, 24, and, nearly word for word, by St. Luke,

xxii. 19, 20, and St. Paul, 1 *Cor.* xi. 23, 24, 25 ; who adds :
Therefore whoever shall eat this bread, or drink the chalice of
the Lord unworthily, shall be guilty of the body and of the blood
of the Lord—and *eateth and drinketh judgment* (the Protestant
Bible says *damnation) to himself.* 1 *Cor.* xi. 27, 29.

To the native evidence of these texts I shall add but two
words. First, supposing it possible that Jesus Christ had deceived the Jews of Capharnaum, and even his disciples and his
very apostles, in the solemn asseverations which he, six times
over, repeated of his real and corporal presence in the sacrament, when he promised to institute it; can any one believe
that he would continue the deception on his dear apostles in
the very act of instituting it ? and when he was on the point of
leaving them ? in short, when he was bequeathing them the
legacy of his love ? In the next place, what propriety is there
in St. Paul's heavy denunciations of profaning Christ's person,
and of damnation, on the part of unworthy communicants, if
they partook of it only by faith and in figure ? for, after all, the
Paschal Lamb, which the people of God had, by his command,
every year eat since their deliverance out of Egypt, and which
the apostles themselves eat, before they received the blessed eucharist, was, as a mere figure, and an incitement to faith, far
more striking, than eating and drinking bread and wine are :
hence the guilt of profaning the Paschal Lamb, and the numerous other figures of Christ, would not be less heinous than profaning the sacrament, if he were not really there.

I should write a huge folio volume, were I to transcribe all
the authorities in proof of the real presence and transubstantiation which may be collected from the ancient fathers, councils
and historians, anterior to the origin of these doctrines assigned
by the bishops of London* and Lincoln. The latter, who
speaks more precisely on the subject, says, " The idea of
Christ's bodily presence in the eucharist was first started in the
beginning of the eighth century. In the twelfth century, the
actual change of the bread and wine into the body and blood of
Christ, by the consecration of the priest, was pronounced to be
a Gospel truth. The first writer who maintained it was Pascasius Radbert. It is said to have been brought into England by
Lanfranc."† What will the learned men of Europe, who are
versed in ecclesiastical literature, think of the state of this science in England, should they hear that such positions as these,
have been published by one of its most celebrated prelates ? I

have assigned the cause why I must content myself with a *few*
of the numberless documents which present themselves to me in
refutation of such bold assertions. St. Ignatius, then, an apostolical bishop of the first century, describing certain contemporary heretics, says, " They do not admit of eucharists and ob-
lations, because they do not believe the eucharist to be the flesh
of our Saviour Jesus Christ, who suffered for our sins."* I
pass over the testimonies, to the same effect, of St. Justin martyr,† St. Irenæus,‡ St. Cyprian,§ and other fathers of the
second and third centuries; but will quote the following words
from Origen, because the prelate appeals to his authority, in
another passage, which is nothing at all to the purpose. He
says, then, " Manna was formerly given, as a figure; but now,
the flesh and blood of the Son of God is specifically given, and
is real food."‖ I must omit the clear and beautiful testimonies
for the Catholic doctrine, which St. Hilary, St. Basil, St. John
Chrysostom, St. Jerom, St. Austin, and a number of other illustrious doctors of the fourth and fifth ages furnish; but I cannot pass over those of St. Cyril of Jerusalem and St. Ambrose
of Milan, because these occurring in catechetical discourses or
expositions of the Christian doctrine to their young neophytes,
must evidently be understood in the most plain and literal sense
they can bear. The former says, " S ... himself affirms
thus of the bread, *This is my body;* who is so daring as to
doubt of it? And since he affirms, *This is my blood;* who will
deny that it is his blood? At Cana of Galilee, he, by an act
of his will, turned water into wine, which resembles blood; and
is he not then to be credited when he changes wine into blood?
Therefore, full of certainty, let us receive the body and blood
of Christ: for, under the form of bread, is given to thee his
body, and, under the form of wine, his blood."¶ St. Ambrose
thus argues with his spiritual children, " Perhaps you will say,
Why do you tell me that I receive the body of Christ, when I
see quite another thing? We have this point therefore to prove.
How many examples do we produce to show you, that this is
not what nature made it, but what the benediction has consecrated it; and that the benediction is of greater force than nature, because, by the benediction, nature itself is changed!
Moses cast his rod on the ground, and it became a serpent; he
caught hold of the serpent's tail, and it recovered the nature of
a rod. The rivers of Egypt, &c. Thou hast read of the crea-

---

* Ep. ad Smyrn. † Apolog. to Emp. Antonin. ‡ L. v. c. 11.
§ Ep. 54 ad Cornel. ‖ Hom. 7. in Levit. ¶ Catech. Mystagog. 4.

tion of the world: If Christ, by his word, was able to make something out of nothing, shall he not be thought able to change one thing into another?"* But I have quoted enough from the ancient fathers to refute the rash assertions of the two modern bishops.

True it is that Pascasius Radbert, an abbot of the ninth century, writing a treatise on the eucharist, for the instruction of his novices, maintains the real corporal presence of Christ in it; but so far from teaching a novelty, he professes to say nothing but what all the world believes and professes.† The truth of this appeared, when Berengarius, in the eleventh century, among other errors, denied the real presence; for then the whole church rose up against him: he was attacked by a whole host of eminent writers, and among others by our archbishop Lanfranc; all of whom, in their respective works, appeal to the belief of all nations; and Berengarius was condemned in no less than eleven councils. I have elsewhere shown the absolute impossibility of the Christians of all the nations in the world being persuaded into a belief, of that sacrament which they were in the habit of receiving, being the living Christ, if they had before held it to be nothing but an inanimate memorial of him; though, even by another impossibility, all the clergy of the nations were to combine together for effecting this. On the other hand it is incontestible, and has been carried to the highest degree of moral evidence,‡ that all the Christians of all the nations of the world, Greeks as well as Latins, Africans as well as Europeans, except Protestants and a handful of Vaudois peasants have, in all ages, believed and still believe in the real presence and transubstantiation.

I am now, dear sir, about to produce evidence of a different nature, I mean Protestant evidence, for the main point under consideration, the real presence. My first witness is no other than the father of the pretended Reformation, Martin Luther himself. He tells us how very desirous he was, and how much he laboured in his mind to overthrow this doctrine, because, says he, (observe his motive,) " I clearly saw how much I should thereby injure Popery; but I found myself caught, without any way of escaping: for the text of the Gospel was too plain for this purpose."§ Hence he continued, till his death, to

---

* De his qui Myst. Init. c. 9.

† " Quod totus orbis credit et confitetur." See Perpetuité de la Foi.

‡ See in particular the last named victorious work, which has proved the conversion of many Protestants, and among the rest of a distinguished churchman now living. § Epist. ad Argenten. tom. 4. fol. 502. Ed. Witten.

condemn those Protestants who denied the corporal presence, employing for this purpose sometimes the shafts of his coarse ridicule,* and sometimes the thunder of his vehement declamation and anathemas.† To speak now of former eminent bishops and divines of the establishment in this country; it is evident from their works that many of them believe firmly in the real presence, such as the bishops Andrews, Bilson, Morton, Laud, Montague, Sheldon, Gunning, Forbes, Bramhall and Cosin, to whom I shall add the justly esteemed divine, Hooker, the testimonies of whom, for the real presence, are as explicit as Catholics themselves can wish them to be. I will transcribe in the margin a few words from each of the three last named authors.‡ The near, or rather close approach of these and other eminent Protestant divines to the constant doctrine of the Catholic church, on this principal subject of modern controversy, is evidently to be ascribed to the perspicuity and force of the declaration of Holy Scripture concerning it. As to the holy fathers, they received this, with her other doctrines, from the apostles, independently of Scripture: for, before even St. Matthew's Gospel was promulgated, the sacrifice of the mass was celebrated, and the body and blood of Christ distributed to the faithful throughout a great part of the known world.

In finishing this letter I must make an important remark on

---

* In one place he says, that "The Devil seems to have mocked those, to whom he has suggested a heresy so ridiculous and contrary to Scripture, as that of the Zuinglians," who explained away the words of the institution in a figurative way. He elsewhere compares these glosses with the following translation of the first words of Scripture: *In principio Deus creavit cœlum et terram:—In the beginning the cuckoo eat the sparrow and his feathers.* Def. Verb. D*om.*

† On one occasion he calls those who deny the real and corporal presence; "A damned sect, lying heretics, bread-breakers, wine-drinkers, and soul-destroyers." In Parv. Catech. On other occasions he says: "They are indevilized and super-devilized." Finally he devotes them to everlasting flames, and builds his own hopes of finding mercy at the tribunal of Christ on his having, with all his soul, condemned Carlostad, Zuinglius, and other believers in the symbolical presence.

‡ Bishop Bramhall writes thus: "No genuine son of the church (of England) did ever deny a true, real presence. Christ said: *This is my body,* and what he said we steadfastly believe. He said neither CON nor SUB nor TRANS: therefore we place these among the opinions of schools, not among articles of faith." Answer to Militiaire, p. 74.——Bishop Cosin is not less explicit in favour of the Catholic doctrine. He says: "It is a monstrous error to deny that Christ is to be adored in the eucharist. We confess the necessity of a supernatural and heavenly change, and that the signs cannot become sacraments but by the infinite power of God. If any one make a bare figure of the sacrament, we ought not to suffer him in our churches." Hist. of Transub. Lastly, the profound Hooker expresses himself thus; "I wish men would give themselves more to meditate, with silence, on what we have in the sacrament, and less to dispute of the manner *how.* Sith we all agree that Christ, by the sacrament, doth really and truly perform in us his promise, why do we vainly trouble ourselves with so fierce contentions whether by consubstantiation, or else by transubstantiation?" Eccles. Polit. B. v. 67.

the object or end of the institution of the blessed sacrament. this our divine master tells us was to communicate a new and ·special grace, or *life*, as he calls it, to us his disciples of the new law. *The bread that I will give is my flesh, for the life of the world. As the living Father hath sent me, and I live by the Father; so he that eateth me, the same shall also live by me. This is the bread that came down from heaven: not as your fathers did eat manna, and are dead: he that eateth this bread shall live for ever.* John vi. 52, 58, 59. He explains, in the same passage, the particular nature of this spiritual life, and shows in what it consists, namely, in an intimate union with him, where he says, *He that eateth my flesh, and drinketh my blood, abideth in me and I in him.* Ver. 57. Now the servants of God, from the beginning of the world, had striking figures and memorials of the promised Messiah, the participation of which, by faith and devotion, was, in a limited degree, beneficial to their souls; such were the tree of life, the various sacrifices of the patriarchs and those of the Mosaic Law, but more particularly the Paschal Lamb, the loaves of proposition, and the manna of which Christ here speaks: still, these signs, in their very institution, were so many promises, on the part of God, that he would bestow upon his people the thing signified by them; even that incarnate Deity, who is at once our victim and our food, and who gives spiritual life to the worthy communicants, not in a limited measure, but indefinitely, according to each one's preparation. The same tender love which made him shroud the rays of his divinity and *take upon himself the form of a servant, and the likeness of man*, in his incarnation; and become as a *worm and not a man, the reproach of men and the outcast of the people*, in his .... on Mount Calvary, has caused him to descend a step lower, and to conceal his human nature also, under the veils of our ordinary nourishment, that thus we may be able to salute him with our mouths and lodge him in our breasts; in order that we may thus, each one of us, *abide in him and he abide in us*, for the life of our souls. No wonder that Protestants, who are strangers to these heavenly truths, and who are still immersed in the clouds of types and figures, not pretending to any thing more in their sacrament, than what the Jews possessed in their ordinances, should be comparatively so indifferent, as to the preparation for receiving it, and, indeed, as to the reception of it at all! No wonder that many of them, and among the reat Anthony Ulric, duke of Brunswick,* should have reconciled themselves to the Catholic church, chiefly for the benefit of exchanging the figure for the substance; the bare memorial of Christ, for his adorable body and blood.

I am, &c.

J. M. .

LETTER XXXVIII.

To the Rev. ROBERT CLAYTON, M. A.

OBJECTIONS ANSWERED.

Rev. Sir,

Though I had not received the letter with which you have honoured me, it was my intention to write to Mr. Brown, by way of answering bishop Porteus's objections against the Catholic doctrine of the blessed eucharist. As you, Rev. sir, have in some manner adopted those objections, I address my answer to you.

You begin with the bishop's arguments from Scripture, and say, that the same divine personage who says, *Take, eat, this is my body*, elsewhere calls himself *a door* and *a vine:* hence you argue, that, as the two latter terms are metaphorical, so the first is also. I grant that Christ makes use of metaphors when he calls himself a door and a vine; but then he explains that they are metaphors, by saying, *I am the door of the sheep, by me if any man enter he shall be saved*, John x. 9; and again, *I am the vine, you the branches: he that abideth in me, and I in him, beareth much fruit: for without me you can do nothing.* John xv. 5. But, in the institution of the sacrament, though he was then making his last will, and bequeathing that legacy to his children which he had in his promise of it assured them should me *meat indeed, and drink indeed;* not a word falls from him to signify that his legacy is not to be understood in the plain sense of the terms he makes use of. Hence those incredulous Christians, who insist on allegorizing the texts in question, (professing at the same time to make the plain natural

---

sense of Scripture their only rule of faith,) may allegorize every other part of the Holy Writ, as ridiculously as Luther has translated the first words of Genesis; and thus gain no certain knowledge from any part of it. His lordship adds, that the apostles did not understand this institution literally, as they asked no questions, nor expressed any surprise concerning it. True, they did not: but then they had been present on a former occasion, at a scene in which the Jews, and even many of the disciples, expressed great surprise at the annunciation of this mystery, and asked, *How can this man give us his flesh to eat?* On that occasion we know that Christ tried the faith of his apostles, as to this mystery; when they generously answered, *Lord, to whom shall we go? Thou hast the words of eternal life.*

You may quote, after Dr. Porteus, Christ's answer to the murmur of the Jews on this subject: *Doth this offend you? If then you shall see the Son of Man ascend up where he was before? It is the spirit that quickeneth; the flesh profiteth nothing. The words that I have spoken to you are spirit and life.* John vi. 63, 64. To this I answer, that if there were an apparent contradiction between this passage and those others in the same chapter, in which Christ so expressly affirms, that his *flesh* is MEAT INDEED, and his *blood* DRINK INDEED, it would only prove ♦ more clearly the necessity of inquiring into the doctrine of the Catholic church concerning them. But there is no such appearance of contradiction: on the contrary, our controvertists draw an argument from the first part of this passage, in favour of the real presence.* The utmost that can be deduced from the remaining part is, that Christ's inanimate flesh, manducated, like that of animals, according to the gross idea of the Jews, would not confer the spiritual life which he speaks of: though some of the fathers understand these words, not of the body and blood of Christ, but of our unenlightened natural reason, in contradistinction to inspired faith, in which sense Christ says to St. Peter, *Blessed art thou, because flesh and blood has not revealed this to thee, but my Father who is in heaven.* Mat. xvi. 17. You add from St Luke, that Christ says in the very institution, *Do this in memory of me.* Luke xxii. 19. I answer, that neither here is there any contradiction: for the eucharist is both a memorial of Christ and the real presence of Christ. When a person stands visibly before us, we have no need of any sign to call him to our memory; but if he were present in such

---

* Verité de la Relig. Cat. prouvée par l'Ecriture, par M. Des Mahis, p. 163.
23*

manner as to be *concealed* from all our senses, without a memorial of him, we might as easily forget him, as if he were at a
great distance from us.   These words of Christ, then, which we
always repeat at the consecration, and the very sight of the
sacramental species, serve for this purpose.

The objections, however, which you, Rev. sir, and bishop
Porteus chiefly insist upon, are the testimony of our senses.
You both say, the bread and wine are seen, and touched, and
tasted, in our sacrament, the same as in yours.   " If we cannot ,
believe our senses," the bishop says, " we can believe nothing."
This was a good popular topic for archbishop Tillotson, from
whom it is borrowed, to flourish upon in the pulpit, but it will
not stand the test of Christian theology.   It would undermine
the incarnation itself.   With equal reason the Jews said of
Christ, *Is not this the carpenter's son?   Is not his mother called
Mary?* Mat. xiii. 55.   Hence they concluded that he was not
what he proclaimed himself to be, the Son of God.   In like
manner, Josuah thought he saw a man, *Josuah* v. 13, and Jacob,
that he touched one, *Gen.* xxxii. 24, and Abraham that he eat
with three men, *Gen.* xviii. 8, when in all these instances there
were no real men, but unbodied spirits, present; the different
senses of those patriarchs misleading them.   Again, were not
*the eyes of the disciples, going to Emmaus, held so that they
should not know Jesus?* Luke xxiv. 16.   Did not the same
thing happen to Mary Magdalen and the apostles? *John* xx. 15.
But independently of Scripture, philosophy and experience
show that there is no essential connexion between our sensations
and the objects which occasion them, and that, in fact, each of
our senses frequently deceives us.   How unreasonable then is
it, as well as impious, to oppose their fallible testimony to God's
infallible word !*

But, the bishop, as you remind me, undertakes to show that
there are absurdities and contradictions in the doctrine of *transubstantiation;* he ought to have said of the *real presence:* for
every one of his alleged contradictions is equally found in the
Lutheran *consubstantiation,* in the belief of which our gracious
queen was educated, and in the corporal presence, held by so

* For example, we think we see the setting sun in a line with our eyes, but phi
losophy demonstrates that a large portion of the terraqueous globe, is interposed
between them, and that the sun is 18 degrees below the horizon. As we trust
more to our feeling than to any other sense: let any person cause his neighbour
to shut his eyes, and then crossing the two first fingers of either hand, make him
rub a pea, or any other round substance between them, he will then protest that
he feels *two* such objects.

many English bishops. He accordingly asks how Christ's body can be contracted into the space of a host? How it can be at the right hand of his Father in heaven, and upon our altars at the same time? &c. I answer, first, with an ancient father, that if we insist on using this HOW of the Jews, with respect to the mysteries revealed in Scripture, we must renounce our faith in it.* 2dly, I answer that we do not know what constitutes the essence of matter and of space. I say, 3dly, that Christ *transfigured* his body, on Mount Thabor, *Mark* ix. 1, bestowing on it many properties of a spirit, before his passion, and that after he had ascended up to heaven, he appeared to St. Paul on the road to Damascus, *Acts* ix. 17, and *stood by him* in the Castle of Jerusalem, *Acts* xxiii. 11. Lastly, I answer, that God fills all space, and is whole and entire in every particle of matter; likewise, that my own soul is in my right hand and my left, whole and entire; that the bread and wine, which I eat and drink, are transubstantiated into my own flesh and blood; that this body of mine, which some years ago was of a small size, has now increased to its present bulk; that soon it will turn into dust, or perhaps be devoured by animals or cannibals, and thus become part of their substance, and that, nevertheless, God will restore it entire, at the last day. Whoever will enter into these considerations, instead of employing the Jewish HOW, will be disposed with St. Austin, to " admit that God can do much more than we can understand," and to cry out with the apostles, respecting this mystery: *Lord, to whom shall we go? Thou hast the words of eternal life.*

I am, &c.

J. M.

* Cyril. Alex. L. 4, in Joan.

LETTER XXXIX.

To JAMES BROWN, Esq.

COMMUNION UNDER ONE KIND.

DEAR SIR,

I TRUST you have not forgotten, what I demonstrated in the first part of our correspondence, that the Catholic church was formed and instructed in its divine doctrine and rites, and especially in its sacraments and sacrifice, before any part of the New Testament was published, and whole centuries before the entire New Testament was collected and pronounced by her to be authentic and inspired. Indeed, Protestants are forced to have recourse to the *tradition of the church*, for determining a great number of points which are left doubtful by the Sacred Text, particularly with respect to the two sacraments, which they acknowledge. From the doctrine and practice of the church alone, they learn, that though Christ, our pattern, was baptized in a river, *Mark* i. 9, and the Ethiopian eunuch was led by St. Philip *into the water*, Acts viii. 38, for the same purpose, the application of it by infusion or aspersion is valid, and that, though Christ says, *He that BELIEVETH and is baptized shall be saved*, Mark xvi. 16, infants are susceptible of the benefits of baptism, who are incapable of making an act of faith. In like manner respecting the eucharist, it is from the doctrine and practice of the church alone, Protestants learn, that though Christ communicated the apostles, at an evening supper, after they had feasted on a lamb, and their feet had been washed, a ceremony which he appears to enjoin on that occasion with the utmost strictness, *John* xiii. 8, 15, none of these rites are essential to that ordinance, or necessary to be practised at present. With what pretension to consistency can they reject her doctrine and practice in the remaining particulars of this mysterious institution? A clear exposition of the institution itself, and of the doctrine and discipline of the church, concerning the controversy in question, will afford the best answer to the objections raised against the latter.

It is true that our B. Saviour instituted the holy eucharist under two kinds; but it must be observed that he then made it a *sacrifice* as well as a *sacrament*, and that he ordained *priests*, namely, his twelve apostles, (for none else but they were present on the occasion) to consecrate this sacrament and offer this sacrifice. Now, for the latter purpose, namely, a sacrifice, it was requisite that a victim should be really present, and, at least, mystically immolated, which was then, and is still, performed in the mass, by the symbolical disunion, or separate consecration of the body and the blood. It was requisite, also, for the completion of the sacrifice, that the priests who had immolated the victim, by mystically separating its body and its blood, should consummate it in both these kinds. Hence it is seen, that the command of Christ, on which our opponents lay so much stress, *drink ye all of this*, regards the apostles, *as priests*, and not the laity, as communicants.* True it is, that when Christ promised this sacrament to the faithful in general, he promised, in express terms, both his body and his blood, *John* vi.: but this does not imply that they must, therefore, receive them under the different appearances of bread and wine. For as the council of Trent teaches, " He who said, *Unless you shall eat the flesh of the Son of Man and drink his blood, you shall not have life in you*, has likewise said, *If any one shall eat of this bread, he shall live for ever.* And he who has said, *Whoso eateth my flesh, and drinketh my blood, hath life everlasting*, has also said, *The bread which I will give, is my flesh, for the life of the world.* And lastly, he who has said, *He who eateth my flesh, and drinketh my blood, abideth in me and I in him :* has nevertheless said, *He who eateth this bread shall live for ever.*"†

The truth is, dear sir, after all the reproaches of the bishop of Durham concerning our alleged sacrilege, *in suppressing half a sacrament*, and the general complaint of Protestants, of our *robbing the laity of the cup* of salvation,‡ that the precious body and blood, being equally and entirely present under each species, is equally and entirely given to the faithful, whichever they receive : whereas the Calvinists and Anglicans do not so much as pretend to *communicate either the real body or the blood;* but present mere types or memorials of them. I do not deny, that, in their mere figurative system, there may be some reason for

---

* The acute Apologist of the Quakers has observed, how inconclusively Protestants argue from the words of the institution. He says: " I would gladly know now, from the words, they can be certainly resolved that these words (*Do this*) must be understood of the clergy. Take, bless, and break this bread, and give it to others; but to the laity only: Take and eat, but do not bless," &c. *Barclay's Apology, Prop.* xiii. p. 7.

† Sess. xxi. c. 1.

‡ Conformably to the above doctrine, neither our priests nor our bishops receive under more than one kind, when they do not offer up the holy sacrifice.

receiving the liquid as well as the solid substance, since the former may appear to represent more aptly the blood, and the latter the body; but to us Catholics, who possess the reality of them both, their species or outward appearance is no more than a matter of changeable discipline.

It is the sentiment of the great lights of the church, St. Chrysostom, St. Austin, St. Jerom, &c. and seems clear from the text, that when Christ, on the day of his resurrection, *took bread, and blessed and brake, and gave it* to Cleophas and the other disciple, whose guest he was at Emmaus, on his doing which *their eyes were opened, and they knew him, and he vanished out of their sight,* Luke xxiv. 30, 31, he administered the holy communion to them under the form of bread alone. In like manner, it is written of the baptized converts of Jerusalem, that, *they were persevering in the doctrine of the apostles, and in the communication of the BREAKING OF BREAD, and in prayer,* Acts ii. 42; and of the religious meeting at Troas: *on the first day of the week, when we were assembled to BREAK BREAD,* Acts xx. 7, without any mention of the other species. These passages plainly signify that the apostles were accustomed, sometimes at least, to give the sacrament under one kind alone, though bishop Porteus has not the candour to confess it. Another more important passage for communion under either kind he entirely overlooks, where the apostle says, *Whosoever shall eat this bread, OR drink the chalice of the Lord unworthily, shall be guilty of the body and the blood of the Lord.** True it is, that in the English Bible; the text is here corrupted, the conjunctive AND being put for the disjunctive OR, contrary to the original Greek, as well as to the Latin Vulgate, to the version of Beza, &c.; but as his lordship could not be ignorant of

* Ἢ πίνῃ, *or drink,* 1 Cor. xi. 27. The Rev. Mr. Grier, who has attempted to vindicate the purity of the English Protestant Bible, has nothing else to say for this alteration of St. Paul's Epistle, than that in what they falsely call " the parallel texts of Luke and Matthew," the conjunctive *and* occurs! Grier's Answer to Ward's Errata, p. 13. I may here notice the horrid and notorious misrepresentation of the Catholic doctrine concerning the Eucharist, of which two living dignitaries are guilty in their publications. The bishop of Lincoln says: " Papists contend that the *mere receiving* of the Lord's Supper merits the remission of sin, *ex opere operato,* as it were mechanically, whatever may be the character or disposition of the communicants." Elem. of Theol. vol. ii. p. 461. Dr. Hey repeats the charge in nearly the same words. Lectures, vol. iv. p. 355. What Catholic will not lift up his hands in amazement at the grossness of this calumny, knowing, as he does, from his catechism and all his books, what purity of soul, and how much greater a preparation is required for the reception of our sacrament than Protestants require for receiving theirs. See Concil. Trid. Sess. xiii. c. 7. Cat. Rom. Douay Catech. &c. .

this corruption and the importance of the genuine text, it is inexcusable in him to have passed it over unnoticed.

The whole series of ecclesiastical history proves that the Catholic church, from the time of the apostles down to the present, ever firmly believing that the whole body, blood, soul and divinity of Jesus Christ equally subsist under each of the species or appearances of bread and wine, regarded it as a mere matter of discipline, which of them was to be received in the holy sacrament. It appears from Tertullian, in the second century,[*] from St. Dennis of Alexandria[†] and St. Cyprian,[‡] in the third; from St. Basil[§] and St. Chrysostom, in the fourth, &c.[||] that the blessed sacrament, under the form of bread, was preserved in the oratories and houses of the primitive Christians, for private communion, and for the viaticum in danger of death. There are instances also of its being carried on the breast, at sea, in the orarium or neckcloth.[¶] On the other hand, as it was the custom to give the B. Sacrament to baptized children, it was administered to those who were quite infants, by a drop out of the chalice.[**] On the same principle, it being discovered, in the fifth century, that certain Manichæan heretics, who had come to Rome from Africa, objected to the sacramental cup, from an erroneous and wicked opinion, Pope Leo ordered them to be excluded from the communion entirely,[††] and Pope Gelasius required all his flock to receive under both kinds.[‡‡] It appears, that in the twelfth century, only the officiating priest and infants received under the form of wine, which discipline was confirmed at the beginning of the fifteenth by the Council of Constance,[§§] on account of the profanations, and other evils resulting from the general reception of it in that form. Soon after this, the more orderly sect of the Hussites, namely, the Calixtins, professing their obedience to the church in other respects, and petitioning the council of Basil to be in-

* Ad Uxor. l. ii.   † Apud Euseb. l. iv. c. 44.   ‡ De Lapsis.
§ Epist. ad Cesar. || Apud Soz. l. viii. c. 8.
¶ St. Ambros. In obit. Frat.—It appears also that St. Birinus, the apostle of the West Saxons, brought the blessed sacrament with him into this Island in an Orarium. Gul. Malm. Vit. Pontif. Florent. Wigorn, Higden, &c.
** St. Cypr. de Laps.   †† Sermo. lv. de Quadrag.
‡‡ Decret. Comperimus Dist. iii.
§§ Dr. Porteus, Dr. Croomber, Kemnitius, &c. accuse this council of decreeing that " *notwithstanding* (for so they express it) our Saviour ministered in both kinds, one only shall, in future, be administered to the laity:" as if the council opposed its authority to that of Christ; whereas it barely defines that *some circumstances of the institution* (namely, that it took place, *after supper*, that the apostles received *without being fasting*, and that *both species were consecrated*) are not obligatory on all Christians. See Can. xiii.

dulged in the use of the chalice, this was granted them.[*] In
like manner Pope Pius IV, at the request of the emperor Fer-
dinand, authorized several bishops of Germany to allow the use
of the cup to those persons of their respective dioceses who desired it.[†] The French kings, since the reign of Philip, have
had the privilege of receiving under both kinds, at their coro-
nation and at their death.[‡] The officiating deacon and subdeacon of St. Dennis, and all the monks of the order of Cluni,
who serve the altar, enjoy the same.[§]

From the above statement bishop Porteus will learn, if not
that the manner of receiving the sacrament under one or the
other kind, or under both kinds, is a mere matter of variable
discipline, at least that the doctrine and the practice of the Catholic church are consistent with each other. I am now going
to produce evidence of another kind, which, after all his, and
the bishop of Durham's anathemas against us, on account of
this doctrine and discipline, will demonstrate, that, conformably
with the declarations of the three principal denominations of
Protestants, the point at issue is a *mere matter of discipline*, or
else that they are utterly inconsistent with themselves.

To begin with Luther: he reproaches his disciple Carlostad,
who in his absence had introduced some new religious changes
at Wittenberg, with having " placed Christianity in things of
no account, such as *communicating under both kinds*," &c.[||]
On another occasion, he writes, " if a council did ordain or
permit *both kinds*, in spite of the council, we would take but
one, or take neither, and curse those who should take both."[¶]
Secondly, the Calvinists of France, in their synod at Poictiers
in 1560, decreed thus : " the *bread* of our Lord's Supper ought
to be administered to those who *cannot drink wine*, on their
making a protestation that they do not refrain from contempt.[**]
Lastly, by separate acts of that parliament and that king, who
established the Protestant religion in England, and by name,
communion in both kinds, it is provided that the latter should
only be *commonly so delivered and ministered*, and an exception
is made in case " *necessity* did otherwise require."[††] Now I

----

[*] Sess. ii.   [†] Mem. Granv. t. xiii. Odorhainal.
[‡] Annal. Pagi.   [§] Nat. Alex. t. i. p. 430.
[||] Epist. ad Gasp. Gustol.   [¶] Form. Miss. t. ii. pp. 384, 386.
[**] On the Lord's Supper, c. iii. p. 7.
[††] Burnet's Hist. of Reform. Part ii. p. 41. Heylin's Hist. of Reform. p. 58. For
the proclamation, see bishop Sparrow's Collection, p. 17.—N. B. The writer has
heard of *British made wine* being frequently used by Church ministers in their sacrament, for *real wine*. The missionaries, who were sent to Otaheite, used the
bread fruit for *real bread* on the like occasion. See Voyage of the ship Duff

need not observe, that, if the use of the cup were, *by the appointment of Christ*, an *essential* part of the sacrament, no necessity can ever be pleaded in bar of that appointment, and men might as well pretend to celebrate the eucharist without bread as without wine, or to confer the sacrament of baptism without water. The dilemma is inevitable. Either the ministration of the sacrament under one or under both kinds is a matter of changeable discipline, or each of the three principal denominations of Protestants has contradicted itself. I should be glad to know what part of the alternative his lordship may choose.

I am, &c.
J. M.

LETTER XL.

To JAMES BROWN, Esq.

ON THE SACRIFICE OF THE NEW LAW.

Dear Sir,

The bishop of London leads me next to the consideration of the sacrifice of the new law, commonly called THE MASS, on which, however, he is brief, and evidently embarrassed. As I have already touched upon this subject, in treating of the means of sanctification in the Catholic church, I shall be as brief upon it as I well can.

A sacrifice is an offering up and immolation of a living animal, or other sensible thing, to God, in testimony that he is the master of life and death, the Lord of us and all things. It is evidently a more expressive act of the creature's homage to his Creator, as well as one more impressive on the mind of the creature itself than mere prayer is, and therefore it was revealed by God to the patriarchs, at the beginning of the world, and afterwards more strictly enjoined by him to his chosen people, in the revelation of his written law to Moses, as the most acceptable and efficacious worship that could be offered up to his Divine Majesty. The tradition of this primitive ordinance, and the notion of its advantageousness, have been so universal, that it has been practiced, in one form or other, in every age from our first parents down to the present, and by every people whether civilized or barbarous, except modern Protestants. For when the nations of the earth *changed the glory of the incorruptible God into the likeness of the image of corruptible man, and of birds and fourfooted beasts,* Rom. i. 23, they continued the rite of sacrifice, and transferred it to these unworthy objects of their idolatry. From the whole of this I infer, that it would have been truly surprising, if, under the most perfect dispensation of God's benefits to men, the new law, he had left them destitute of sacrifice. But he has not so left them; on the contrary, that prophecy of Malachy is evidently verified in the Catholic church, spread as it is over the surface of the earth: *From the rising of the sun even to the going down thereof, my name is great among the Gentiles; and, in every place, there is sacrifice; and there is offered to my name a clean oblation.* Malac. i. 11. If Protestants say, we have the sacrifice of Christ's death; I answer, so had the servants of God under the law of nature and the written law: *for it is impossible that with the blood of oxen and goats sin should be taken away:* nevertheless, they had perpetual sacrifices of animals to represent the death of Christ, and to apply the fruits of it to their souls; in the same manner, Catholics have Christ himself really present, and mystically offered on their altars daily, for the same ends, but in a far more efficacious manner, and, of course, *a true propitiatory sacrifice.* That Christ is truly present in the blessed eucharist, I have proved by many arguments; that a mystical immolation of him takes place in the holy mass, by the separate consecration of the bread and of the wine, which strikingly represents the separation of his blood from his body, I have likewise shown: finally, I have shown you that the officiating priest performs these mysteries by command of Christ, and in memory of what he did at the last supper, and what he endured on Mount Calvary: DO THIS IN MEMORY OF ME. Nothing then is wanting in the holy mass, to constitute it the true and propitiatory sacrifice of the new law, a sacrifice which as much surpasses, in dignity and efficacy, the sacrifices of the old law, as the chief priest and victim of it, the incarnate Deity, surpasses, in these respects, the sons of Aaron, and the animals which they sacrificed. No wonder then, that, as the fathers of the church, from the earliest times, have borne testimony to the reality of this sacrifice,* so they should speak, in such lofty

* St. Justin, who appears to have been, in his youth, contemporary with St. John the Evangelist, says, that " Christ instituted a sacrifice in bread and wine, which

terms, of its awfulness and efficacy : no wonder that the church
of God should retain and revere it as the most sacred, and the
very essential part of her sacred liturgy : and I will add, no
wonder that Satan should have persuaded Martin Luther to attempt to abrogate this worship, as that which, most of all, is
offensive to him.*

The main arguments of the bishops of London and Lincoln,
and of Dr. Hey, with other Protestant controvertists, against
the sacrifice of the new law, are drawn from St. Paul's Epistle
to the Hebrews, where, comparing the sacrifice of our Saviour
with the sacrifices of the Mosaic Law, the apostle says, that
*Christ being come a high priest of the good things to come, by a
greater and more perfect tabernacle, not made with hands, that is,
not of this creation: neither by the blood of goats, or of calves,
but by his own blood, entered once into the holies, having obtained eternal redemption.* Heb. ix. 11, 12. *Nor yet that he should
offer himself often, as the high priest entereth into the holies every
year.* Ver. 25.   Again, St. Paul says, *Every priest standeth indeed daily ministering and often offering the same sacrifices,
which can never take away sins: but this man offering one sacrifice for sins, sitteth at the right hand of God.*   Chap. x. 11,
12.

Such are the texts, at full length, which modern Protestants
urge so confidently against the sacrifice of the new law;
but in which neither the ancient fathers, nor any other description of Christians, but themselves, can see any argument against
it.   In fact, if these passages be read in their context, it will
appear that the apostle is barely proving to the Hebrews (whose
lofty ideas and strong tenaciousness of their ancient rites appear from different parts of the Acts of the Apostles) how infinitely superior the sacrifice of Christ is, to those of the Mosaic
Law; particularly from the circumstance, which he repeats, in

---

Christians offer up in every place," quoting Malachy i. 19. Dialog. cum Trypbon
St. Irenæus, whose master, Polycarp, was a disciple of that Evangelist, says, that
" Christ, in consecrating bread and wine, has instituted the sacrifice of the New
Law, which the church received from the apostles, according to the prophecy of
Malachy," L. iv. 32.   St. Cyprian calls the Eucharist " A true and full sacrifice ;"
and says, that " as Melchisedech offered bread and wine, so Christ offered the
same, namely, his body and blood." Epist. 63.   St. Chrysostom, St. Austin, St.
Ambrose, &c. are equally clear and expressive on this point.   The last mentioned
calls this sacrifice by the name of *Missa* or mass, so do St. Leo, St. Gregory, our
Ven. Bede, &c.

* Luther, in his Book' De Unct. et Miss. Priv. tom. vii. fol. 228, gives an account of the motive which induced him to suppress the sacrifice of the mass among
his followers.   He says that the Devil appeared to him at midnight, and in a long
conference with him, the whole of which he relates, convinced him that the worship of the mass is idolatry.   See Letters to a Prebendary.   Let. v

different forms, namely, that there was a necessity of their sacrifices being *often repeated*, which, after all, *could not* of themselves, and independently of the one they prefigured, *take away sin*; whereas the latter, namely, Christ's death on the cross, *obliterated at once* the sins of those who availed themselves of it Such is the argument of St. Paul to the Jews, respecting their sacrifices, which in no sort militates against the sacrifice of the mass; this being the same sacrifice with that of the cross, as to the *victim* that is offered, and as to the *priest* who offers it, differing in nothing but the manner of offering;* in the one there being a real, and in the other a mystical, effusion of the victim's blood.† So far from invalidating the Catholic doctrine on this point, the apostle confirms it, in this very Epistle; where quoting and repeating the sublime Psalm of the royal prophet concerning the Messiah; *Thou art a priest for ever* ACCORDING TO THE ORDER OF MELCHISEDECH, *Ps.* 109, *alias* 110, he enlarges on the dignity of this sacerdotal patriarch, to whom Aaron himself, the high priest of the old law, paid tribute, as to his superior, through his ancestor Abraham, *Heb.* v. vii. Now in what did this *order of Melchisedech* consist? In what, I ask, did his sacrifice differ from those which Abraham himself and the other patriarchs, as well as Aaron and his sons offered? Let us consult the sacred text, as to what it says concerning this royal priest, when he came to meet Abraham, on his return from victory: *Melchisedech, the king of Salem,* bringing forth BREAD AND WINE, *for he was the priest of the most High God; blessed him.* Gen. xiv. 18. It was then in offering up *a sacrifice of bread and wine*,‡ instead of slaughtered animals, that Melchisedech's sacrifice differed from the generality of those in the Old Law, and that he prefigured the sacrifice, which Christ was to institute in the New Law, from the same elements. No other sense but this can be elicited from the Scripture as to this matter, and accordingly, the holy fathers unanimously adhere to this meaning.§

In finishing this letter, I cannot help, dear sir, making two or three short, but important observations. The first regards the deception practised on the unlearned by the above-named bishops, Dr. Hey, and most other Protestant controvertists, in

---

* Concil. Trid. Sess. xxii. cap. 2.　　　† Cat. ad Paroc. P. ii. p. 81.

‡ The sacrifice of Cain, *Gen.* iv. 3. and that ordered in *Levit.* ii. 1, of flour, oil, and incense, prove that inanimate things were sometimes of old offered in sacrifice.

§ St. Cypr. Ep. 63. St. Aug. in Ps. xxxiii. St. Chrys. Hom. 35. St. Jerom, Ep. 126, &c.

talking, on every occasion, of the *Popish mass*, and representing the. tenets of the real presence, transubstantiation, and a subsisting true propitiatory sacrifice, as peculiar to *Catholics;* whereas, if they are persons of any learning, they must know that these are and have always been held by all the Christians in the world, except the comparatively few who inhabit the northern parts of Europe. I speak of the Melchite or common Greeks of Turkey, the Armenians, the Muscovites, the Nestorians, the Eutychians or Jacobites, the Christians of St. Thomas in India, the Cophts and Ethiopians in Africa; all of whom maintain each of those articles, and almost every other on which Protestants differ from Catholics, with as much firmness as we ourselves do. Now as these sects have been totally separated from the Catholic church, some of them eight hundred and some fourteen hundred years, it is impossible they should have derived any recent doctrines or practices from her; and, divided, as they ever have been among themselves, they cannot have combined to adopt them. On the other hand, since the rise of Protestantism, attempts have been repeatedly made to draw some or other of them to the novel creed; but all in vain. Melancthon translated the Ausburg Confession of Faith into Greek, and sent it to Joseph, patriarch of C. P., hoping he would adopt it; whereas the patriarch did not so much as acknowledge the receipt of the present.* Fourteen years later, Crusius, professor of Tubigen, made a similar attempt on Jeremy, the successor of Joseph, who wrote back, requesting him to write no more on the subject, at the same time making the most explicit declaration of his belief in the seven sacraments, the sacrifice of the mass, transubstantiation, &c.† In the middle of the seventeenth century, fresh overtures being made to the Greeks by the Calvinists of Holland, the most convincing evidence of the orthodox belief of all the above-mentioned communions, on the articles in question, were furnished by them, the originals of which were deposited in the French king's library at Paris.‡ I have to remark, in the second place, on the inconsistencies of the church of England, respecting this point; she has *priests,*§ but, *no sacrifice!* She has *altars,*|| but, *no victim!* She has an *essential consecration* of the sacramental elements,¶ *without any the least effect upon them!* Not to dive

---

* Sheffmac. tom. ii. p. 7.　　　† Ibid.　　　‡ Perpetuité de la Foi.
§ See the Rubrics of the communion service.
|| See ditto in Sparrow's Collec. p. 20.
¶ " If the consecrated bread or wine be all spent, before all have communicated, the priest is to consecrate more." Rubr. N. B. Bishop Warburton and bishop
24*

deeper into this chaos, I would gladly ask bishop Porteus, what hinders a deacon, or even a layman, from consecrating the sacramental bread and wine *as validly* as a priest or a bishop can do, agreeably to his system of consecration? There is evidently no obstacle at all, except such as the mutable law of the land interposes. In the last place, I think it right to quote some of the absurd and irreligious invectives of the renowned Dr Hey against the holy mass, because they show the extreme ignorance of our religion, which generally prevails among the most learned Protestants, who write against it. The doctor first describes the mass as " blasphemous, in dragging down Christ from heaven," according to his expression; 2dly, as " pernicious, in giving men an easy way," as he pretends, " of evading all their moral and religious duties;" 3dly, as " promoting infidelity:" in conformity with which latter assertion, he maintains that " most Romanists of letters and science are infidels." He next proceeds seriously to *advise* Catholics to abandon this part of their sacred liturgy, namely, the adorable sacrifice of the New Law; and he then concludes his theological farce with the following ridiculous threats against this sacrifice: " If the Romanists will not listen to our brotherly exhortations; let them *fear our threats.* The rage of *paying for masses* will not last for ever: as *men improve, (by the French Revolution,)* it will continue to grow weaker; as philosophy *(that of Atheism)* rises, masses will *sink in price* and superstition pine away."* I wish I had an opportunity of telling the learned professor, that I should have expected, from the failure of patriarch Luther, counselled and assisted as he was by Satan himself, in his attempts to abolish the holy mass, he would have been more cautious in dealing prophetic threats against it! [In fact he has lived to see this divine worship *publicly* restored in every part of christendom, where it was proscribed, when he vented his menaces: for as to the *private celebration of mass,* this was never intermitted, not even in the depth of the gloomiest dungeons, and where no pay could be had by the Catholic priesthood. What other religious worship, I ask, could have triumphed over such a persecution! The same will be the case in the latter days; when *the man of sin shall have indignation*

Cleaver earnestly contend that the Eucharist is *a feast upon a sacrifice:* but as, in their dread of Popery, they admit no change, nor even the reality of a victim, their feast is proved to be an imaginary banquet on an ideal viand.

* Dr. Hey's Theol. Lectures, vol. iv. p. 385. The professor tells us in a note, that this lecture was delivered in the year 1792; the hey-day of that antichristian and antisocial philosophy, which attempted, through an ocean of blood, to subvert every altar and every throne.

against the covenant of the sanctuary,—and shall take away the continual sacrifice, Dan. xi. 30, 34; for even then, the mystical *woman who is clothed with the sun, and has the moon under her feet,—shall fly into the wilderness,* Rev. xii. 1, 6, and perform the divine mysteries of an incarnate Deity in caverns and catacombs, as she did in early times, till that happy day, when her heavenly spouse, casting aside those sacramental veils, under which his love now shrouds him, shall shine forth *in the glory of God the Father,* the *Judge of the living and the dead.*]

I am, &c.

J. M.

LETTER XLI.

To the Rev. ROBERT CLAYTON, M. A.

ON ABSOLUTION FROM SIN.

DEAR SIR,

I PERCEIVE that you chiefly follow B. Porteus, who mixes in the same chapter the heterogeneous subjects of the mass and the forgiveness of sins, in the selection of your objections against the church, though you adopt some others from the Tracts of bishop Watson, and even from writers of such little repute as the Rev. C. De Coetlogon. This preacher, in venting the horrid calumnies, which a great proportion of other Protestant preachers and controvertists of different sects, equally with himself, instil into the minds of their ignorant hearers and readers, expresses himself as follows: " In the church of Rome you may purchase not only pardons for sins already committed, but for those that shall be committed; so that any one may promise himself impunity, upon paying the rate that is set upon any sin he hath a mind to commit. And so truly is Popery the mother of abominations, that if any one hath wherewithal to pay, he may not only be indulged in his present transgressions, but may even be *permitted to transgress in future.*"* And are these shameless calumniators real Christians,

---

* Abominations of the church of Rome, p. 13. The preacher goes on to state the sums of money for which, he says, Catholics believe they may commit the most

who believe in a judgment to come! And do they expect to
make us Catholics renounce our religion, by representing it to
us as the very reverse of what we know it to be! It is true, bishop Porteus does not go the lengths of the pulpit-declaimer
above quoted, and of the other controvertists alluded to, in his
attack upon the Catholic doctrine of absolution and justification: still he is guilty of much gross misrepresentation of it.
As his language is confused, if not contradictory on the subject, I will briefly state what the Catholic church has ever believed, and has solemnly defined in her last general council
concerning it.

The council of Trent, then, teaches, that " All men lost their
innocence and become defiled and *children of wrath*, in the pre-
varication of Adam ; that, not only the Gentiles were unable, by
the force of nature, but that even the Jews were unable, by the
Law of Moses, to rise, notwithstanding free-will was not extinct
in them, however weakened and depraved :"* that " The heavenly Father of mercy and God of all consolation sent his Son,
Jesus Christ, to men, in order to redeem both Jews and Gentiles ;"† that " Though he died for all, yet all do not receive
the benefit of his death ; but only those to whom the merit of
his passion is communicated ;"‡ that, for this purpose, " Since
the preaching of the Gospel, baptism, or the desire of it, is necessary ;"§ that " The beginning of justification, in adult persons (those who are come to the use of reason) is to be derived
from God's preventing grace, through Jesus Christ, by which,
without any merits of their own, they are called ; so that they
who, by their sins, were averse from God, by his exciting and
assisting grace, are prepared to convert themselves to their
justification, by freely consenting to and co-operating with his

atrocious crimes; " For incest, &c. five sixpences; for debauching a virgin, six
sixpences; for perjury, ditto; for him who kills his father, mother, &c. one crown
and five groats !" This curious account is borrowed from the *Taxa Cancellariæ
Romanæ*, a book which has been frequently published, though with great variations
both as to the crimes and the prices, by the Protestants of Germany and France,
and as frequently condemned by the See of Rome. It is proper that Mr. Clayton
and his friends should know, that the Pope's Court of Chancery has no more to
do, nor pretends to have any more to do, with the *forgiveness of sins*, than his Majesty's court of chancery does. In case there ever was the least real groundwork
of this vile book, which I cannot find there was, the money paid into the papal
chancery could be nothing else but the *fees of office*, on restoring certain culprits to
the *civil privileges* which they had forfeited by their crimes. When the proceedings in doctors commons, in case of incest, are suspended (as I have known them
suspended during the whole life of one of the accused parties) fees of office are always required: but would it not be a vile calumny to say, that leave to commit
incest may be purchased in England for certain sums of money?

* Sess. vi. cap. i.　　† Cap. ii.　　‡ Cap. iii.　　§ Cap. iv.

grace :"* that, " Being excited and assisted by divine grace, and receiving faith from hearing, they are freely moved towards God, believing the things which have been divinely revealed and promised—they are excited to hope that God will be merciful to them for Christ's sake, and they begin to love him, as the fountain of all justice ; and therefore are moved to a certain hatred and detestation of sins." Lastly, " They resolve on receiving baptism, to begin a new life and keep God's commandments."† Such is the doctrine of the church concerning the justification of the adult in baptism ; with respect to the pardon of sins committed after baptism, the church teaches, that " The penance of a Christian, after his fall, is very different from that of baptism, and that it consists, not only in refraining from sins and a detestation of them, namely, *a contrite and humble heart*, but also in a sacramental confession of them, at least in desire, and, at a proper time, and the priestly absolution ; and likewise in satisfaction, by fasting, alms, prayers, and other pious exercises of a spiritual life ; not indeed for *the eternal punishment*, which, together with the crime, is remitted in the sacrament, or the desire of the sacrament, but *for the temporal punishment*, which the Scripture teaches is not always and wholly remitted, as in baptism."‡ Such is and always was the doctrine of the Catholic church, which thus ascribes the whole glory of man's justification, both in its beginning and its progress, to God, through Jesus Christ ; in opposition to Pelagians and *modern* Lutherans, who attribute the beginning of conversion to the human creature. On the other hand, this doctrine leaves man in possession of his free will, for co-operating in this great work ; and thereby rejects the pernicious tenet of the Calvinists, who deny free will, and ascribe even our sins to God. In short, the Catholic church equally condemns the enthusiasm of the Methodist, who fancies himself justified, in some unexpected instant, without faith, hope, charity, or contrition ; and the presumption of the unconverted sinner, who supposes that exterior good works and the reception of the sacrament will avail him, without any degree of the above-mentioned divine virtues. Such, I say, is the Catholic doctrine, in spite of De Coetlogon and bishop Porteus's calumnies. This prelate is chiefly bent on disproving the necessity of sacramental confession, and on depriving the sacerdotal absolution of all efficacy whatsoever. Accordingly, he maintains that when Christ *breathed upon his apostles and said to them : Receive ye the Holy Ghost :* WHOSE SINS YOU SHALL FORGIVE,

---

* Cap. v.   † Cap. vi.   ‡ John xx. 22, 23.

THEY ARE FORGIVEN TO THEM; AND WHOSE SINS YOU SHALL RETAIN, THEY ARE RETAINED, *John* xx. 22, 23, he did not give them any real power to remit sins, but only " a power of declaring who were truly penitent, and of inflicting miraculous punishments on sinners; as likewise of preaching of the word of God," &c.* And is this, I appeal to you, Rev. sir, following the plain and natural sense of the written word? But, instead of arguing the case myself, I will produce an authority against the bishop's vague and arbitrary gloss on this decisive passage, which I think he cannot object to or withstand; it is no other than that of the renowned Protestant champion, Chillingworth. Treating of this text he says, "Can any man be so unreasonable as to imagine, that, when our Saviour, in so solemn a manner, having first breathed upon his disc.ples, thereby conveying and insinuating the Holy Ghost into their hearts, renewed unto them, or rather confirmed that glorious commission, &c. whereby he delegated to them an authority of binding and loosing sins upon earth, &c.; can any one think, I say, so unworthily of our Saviour as to esteem these words of his for no better than compliment? Therefore, in obedience to his gracious will, and as I am warranted and enjoined by my holy mother, the church of England, I beseech you, that, by your practice and use, you will not suffer that commission, which Christ hath given to his ministers, to be a vain form of words, without any sense under them. When you find yourselves charged and oppressed, &c. have recourse to your spiritual physician, and freely disclose the nature and malignancy of your disease, &c. And come not to him, only with such a mind as you would go to a learned man, as one that can speak comfortable things to you; but as to one that *hath authority, delegated to him from God himself, to absolve and acquit you of your sins.*"†

Having quoted this great Protestant authority against the prelate's cavils concerning sacerdotal absolution, I shall produce one or two more of the same sort, and then return to the more direct proofs of the doctrine under consideration. The Lutherans, then, who are the elder branch of the Reformation, in their Confession of Faith and apology for that Confession, expressly teach that absolution is no less a sacrament than baptism and the Lord's Supper, that *particular absolution* is to be retained in confession, that to reject it is the error of the Novatian heretics; and that, by the power of the keys, *Mat.* xvi. 19

---

* P. 45.	† Serm. vii. Relig. pp. 408, 409.

sins are remitted, not only in the sight of the church, but also *in the sight of God.** Luther himself, in his Catechism, required that the penitent, in confession, should expressly declare that he believes " the *forgiveness of the priest* to be the *forgiveness of God.*"† What can bishop Porteus and other modern Protestants say to all this, except that Luther and his disciples were infected with Popery? Let us then·proceed to inquire into the doctrine of the church itself, of which he is one of the most distinguished heads. In *The Order of the Communion*, composed by Cranmer, and published by Edward VI, the parson, vicar or curate, is to proclaim this among other things : " If there be any of you whose conscience is troubled and grieved at any thing, lacking comfort or counsel, let him come to me, or to some other discreet and learned priest, and *confess and open his sin and grief secretly*, &c. and that of us, as a minister of God and of the church, he may *receive comfort and absolution.*"‡ Conformably with this admonition, it is ordained in *the Common Prayer Book* that when the minister visits any sick person, the latter " should be moved to make a *special confession of his sins*, if he feels his conscience troubled with any weighty matter; after which confession, the priest shall absolve him, if he humbly and heartily desire it, after this sort: *Our Lord Jesus Christ, who hath left power to his church to absolve all sinners, who truly repent and believe in him, of his great mercy, forgive thee thine offences : and, by his authority committed to me,* I ABSOLVE THEE FROM ALL THY SINS, *in the name of the Father, and of the Son, and of the Holy Ghost. Amen.*"§ I may add, that, soon after James I. became, at the same time, the member and the head of the English church, he desired his prelates to inform him, in the conference at Hampton Court, what authority this church claimed in the article of *absolution from sin*, when archbishop Whitgift began to entertain him with an account of the general confession and absolution, in the communion service; with which the king not being satisfied, Bancroft, at that time bishop of London, fell on his knees, and said, " It becomes us to deal plainly with your majesty: there is also in the book a more particular and personal absolution in *the visitation of the sick.* Not only the confession of Augusta, (Ausburg)

---

* Confess. August. Art. xi. xii. xiii. Apol.
† In Catech. Parv. See also Luther's Table Talk, c. xviii. on Auricular Confession.
‡ Bishop Sparrow's Collect. p. 20.
§ Order for the Visitation of the Sick. N. B. To encourage the secret confession of sins the church of England has made a Canon, requiring her ministers not to reveal the same. See Canones Eccles. A. D. 1692, n. 113.

Bohemia and Saxony, retain and allow it, but also Mr. Calvin doth approve both such a general and such a *private confession and absolution.*" To this the king answered, I exceedingly well approve it, being an apostolical and Godly ordinance, given in the name of Christ to one that desireth it upon the clearing of his conscience."*

I have signified that there are other passages of Scripture, besides that quoted above from *John* xx. in proof of the authority exercised by the Catholic church in the forgiveness of sin; such as *St. Mat.* xvi. 19, where Christ gives the *keys of the kingdom of heaven* to Peter; and chap. xviii. 18, where he declares to all his apostles: *Verily I say unto you; whatsoever ye shall bind on earth, shall be bound in heaven, and whatsoever ye shall loose on earth, shall be loosed in heaven.* But here also Bp. Porteus and modern Protestants distort the plain meaning of Scripture, and say, that no other power is expressed by these words, than those of inflicting *miraculous punishments*, and of *preaching the word of God!* Admitting, however, it were possible to affix so foreign a meaning to these texts, I would gladly ask the bishop, why, after ordaining the priests of his church by this very form of words, he afterwards, by a separate form, commissions them to preach the word, and to minister?† " No one," exclaims the bishop, " but God, can forgive sins." True; but as he has annexed the forgiveness of sins committed before baptism, to the reception of this sacrament with the requisite dispositions: *Do penance*, said St. Peter to the Jews, *and be baptized every one of you, in the name of Jesus Christ, for the remission of your sins*, Acts ii. 38; so he is pleased to forgive sins committed after baptism, by means of contrition, confession, satisfaction, and the priest's absolution.

Against the obligation of confessing sins, which is so evident-ly sanctioned in Scripture: *Many that believed, came and confessed, and declared their deeds*, Acts xix. 18; and so expressly commanded therein, *confess your sins one to another*, James v 16, the bishop contends that " It is not knowing a person's sins that can qualify the priest to give him absolution, but knowing he hath repented of them."‡ In refutation of this objection, I do not ask, why, then, does the English church move the dy-

---

* Fuller's Ch. Hist. B. x. p. 9. See the Defence of Bancroft's Sucessor in the See of Canterbury, Dr. Laud, who endeavoured to enforce auricular Confession, in Heylin's life of Laud, P. ii. p. 415. It appears from this writer, that Laud was Confessor to the duke of Buckingham, and from Burnet, that bishop Morley was Confessor to the Dutchess of York when a Protestant. Hist. of his own Times.
† See the Form of Ordering Priests.　　　　　　　‡ P. 46

mg man to confess his sins? but I say, that the priest, being vested by Christ with a judicial power to *bind* or to *loose,* to *forgive* or to *retain sins,* cannot exercise that power, without taking cognizance of the cause on which he is to pronounce, and without judging in particular of the dispositions of the sinner, especially as to his sorrow for his sins, and resolution to refrain from them in future: now this knowledge can only be gained from the penitent's own confession. From this may be gathered, whether his offences are those of *frailty* or of *malice,* whether they are *accidental* or *habitual;* in which latter case they are ordinarily to be retained, till his amendment gives proof of his real repentance. Confession is also necessary, to enable the minister of the sacrament to decide whether a public reparation for the crimes committed be or be not requisite; and whether there is or is not restitution to be made to the neighbour who has been injured in person, property, or reputation. Accordingly, it is well known that such restitutions are frequently made by those who make use of sacramental confession, and very seldom by those who do not use it. I say nothing of the incalculable advantage it is to the sinner in the business of his conversion, to have a confidential and experienced pastor, to withdraw the veils behind which self-love is apt to conceal his favourite passions and worst crimes, and to expose to him the enormity of his guilt, of which before he had perhaps but an imperfect notion; and to prescribe to him the proper remedies for his entire spiritual cure. After all, it is for the holy Catholic church, with whom the Word of God and the sacraments were deposited by her divine spouse, Jesus Christ, to explain the sense of the former, and the constituents of the latter. In short, this church has uniformly taught, that confession and the priest's absolution, where they can be had, are required of the penitent sinner, as well as contrition and a firm purpose of amendment. But, to believe the bishop, our church does not require contrition at all, though she has declared it to be one of the necessary parts of sacramental penance, nor " any dislike to sin or love to God,"* for the justification of the sinner. I will make no farther answer to this shameful calumny, than by referring you and your friends to my above citations from the council of Trent. In these, you have seen that she requires " a hatred and detestation of sin;" in short, " *a contrite and humble heart, which God never de-*

25   * P. 47.

pises:" and moreover, " an incipient love of God, as the fountain of all justice."

Finally, his lordship has the confidence to maintain, that " The primitive church did not hold confession and absolution of this kind to be necessary," and that " Private confession was never thought of as a command of God, for nine hundred years after Christ, nor determined to be such till after 1200."[*] The few following quotations from ancient fathers and councils, will convince our Salopian friends what sort of trust they are to place in this prelate's assertions on theological subjects. Tertullian, who lived in the age next to that of the apostles, and is the earliest Latin writer, whose works we possess, writes thus: " If you withdraw from confession, think of hell-fire, which confession extinguishes."[†]　Origen, who wrote soon after him, inculcates the necessity of confessing our most private sins, even those of thought,[‡] and advises the sinner " to look carefully about him in choosing the person to whom he is to confess his sins."[§]　St. Basil, in the fourth century, wrote thus: " It is necessary to disclose our sins to those to whom the dispensation of the divine mysteries is committed."[||]　St. Paulinus, the disciple of St. Ambrose, relates, that this holy doctor used to " weep over the penitents whose confessions he heard, but never disclosed their sins to any but to God alone."[¶]　The great St. Austin writes, " Our merciful God wills us to confess in this world, that we may not be confounded in the other;[**] and elsewhere he says, " Let no one say to himself, I do penance to God in private. Is it then in vain that Christ has said, *Whatsoever you loose on earth, shall be loosed in heaven?* Is it in vain that the keys have been given to the church?"[††]　I could produce a long list of other passages to the same effect, from fathers and doctors, and also from councils of the church, anterior to the periods he has assigned to the commencement and confirmation of the doctrine in question: but I will have recourse to a shorter, and perhaps more convincing proof, that this doctrine could not have been introduced into the church at any period whatsoever subsequent to that of Christ and his apostles. My argument is this: it is impossible it should have been at any time introduced, if it was not from the first necessary. The pride of the human heart would at all times have

---

[*] Ibid.　　[†] Lib. de Pœnit.　　[‡] Hom. 3 in Levit.
[§] Hom. 2 in Ps. xxxvii.　　[||] Rule 229　　[¶] In Vit. Ambros.
[**] Hom. 20.　　[††] Hom. 49

revolted at the imposition of such a humiliation, as that of confessing all its most secret sins, if Christians had not previously
believed that this rite is of divine institution, and even necessary
for the pardon of them. Supposing, however, that the clergy,
at some period, had fascinated the laity, kings and emperors,
as well as peasants, to submit to this yoke; it will still remain
to be accounted for, how they took it up themselves; for
monks, priests and bishops, and the Pope himself, must equally
confess their sins with the meanest of the people. And if even
this could be explained, it would still be necessary to show how
the numerous organized churches of the Nestorians and Eutychians, spread over Asia and Africa, from Bagdad to Axum, all
of whom broke from the communion of the Catholic church in
the fifth century, took up the notion of penance being a sacrament, and that confession and absolution are essential parts of
it, as they all believe at the present day. With respect to the
main body of the Greek Christians, they separated from the
Latins much about the period which our prelate has set down
for the rise of this doctrine; but though they reproached the
Latin Christians with shaving their beards, singing Allelujah
at wrong seasons, and other such like minutiæ, they never accused them of any error respecting private confession or sacerdotal absolution. To support the bishop's assertions on this
and many other points, it would be necessary to suppose, as I
have said before, that a hundred millions of Greek and Latin
Christians lost their senses on some one and the same day or
night !

In finishing this letter, I take leave, Rev. sir, to advert to the
case of some of your respectable society, who, to my knowledge, are convinced of the truth of the Catholic religion, but
are deterred from embracing it, by the dread of that sacrament
ot which I have been treating. Their pitiable case is by no
means singular: we continually find persons, who are not only
desirous of reconciling themselves to their true mother, the Catholic church, but also of laying *the sins of their youth and their
ignorances*, Ps. xxiv. alias xxv. 7, at the feet of some one or
other of her faithful ministers, convinced that thereby they
would procure ease to their afflicted souls, yet have not the
courage to do this. Let the persons alluded to humbly and
fervently pray to *the Giver of all good gifts* for his strengthening grace, and let them be persuaded of the truth of what an
unexceptionable witness says, who had experienced, while he
was a Catholic, the interior joy he describes, where, persuading
the penitent to go to his confessor " not as to one that can

speak comfortable and quieting words to him, but as to one that hath authority delegated to him from God himself, to absolve and acquit him of his sins," he goes on, " If you shall do this, assure your souls, that the understanding of man is not able to conceive that transport, and excess of joy and comfort, which shall accrue to that man's heart, who is persuaded he hath been made partaker of this blessing."* On the other hand, if such persons are convinced, as I am satisfied they are, that Christ's words to his apostles, *Receive the Holy Ghost: whose sins you shall remit, they are remitted*, mean what they express, they must know, that confession is necessary to buy off overwhelming confusion, as the fathers I have quoted signify, at the great day of manifestation, and with this never-ending punishment.

I am, &c.
J. M.

LETTER XLII.

To the Rev. ROBERT CLAYTON, M. A.

ON INDULGENCES.

Rev Sir,

I trust you will pardon me, if I do not send a special answer to the objections you have stated against my last letter to you, because you will find the substance of them answered in this and my next letter concerning indulgences and purgatory. Bishop Porteus reverses the proper order of these subjects, by treating first of the latter : indeed his ideas are much confused, and his knowledge very imperfect concerning them both. This prelate describes an indulgence to be, in the belief of Catholics, (without, however, giving any authority whatever for his description) " a transfer of the overplus of the saints' goodness, joined with the merits of Christ, &c. by the Pope, as head of the church, towards the remission of their sins, who fulfil, in their lifetime, certain conditions appointed by him, or whose

---

* Chillingworth, Sermon vii. p. 409.

friends will fulfil them, after their death."*   He speaks of it as
" a method of making poor wretches believe that wickedness
here may become consistent with happiness hereafter—that repentance is explained away or overlooked among other things
joined with it, as saying so many prayers and paying so much
money."†   Some of the bishop's friends have published much
the same description of indulgences, but in more perspicuous
language.   One of them, in his attempt to show that each
Pope, in succession, has been the *man of sin*, or Antichrist,
says, " Besides their own personal vices, by their indulgences,
pardons, and dispensations, which they claim a power from
Christ of granting, and which they have sold in so infamous
a manner, they have encouraged all manner of vile and
wicked practices.   They have contrived numberless methods of making a holy life useless, and to assure the most
abandoned of salvation, provided they will sufficiently pay
the priests for absolution."‡   With the same disregard of
charity and truth, another eminent divine speaks of the matter
thus, " the Papists have taken a notable course to secure men
from the fear of hell, that of penances and indulgences.   To
those, who will pay the price, absolutions are to be had for the
most abominable and not to be named villanies, and license
also for not a few wickednesses."§   In treating of a subject,
the most intricate of itself among the common topics of controversy, and which has been so much confused and perplexed by
the misrepresentations of our opponents, it will be necessary,
for giving you, Rev. sir, and my other Salopian friends, a clear
and just idea of the matter, that I should advance, step by step,
in my explanation of it.   In this manner I propose showing
you, first, what an indulgence is not, and, next, what it really
is.

I. An indulgence, then, never was conceived by any Catholic
to be a leave to commit a sin of any kind, as De Coetlogon,
bishop Fowler, and others charge them with believing.   The
first principles of natural religion must convince every rational
being that God himself cannot give leave to commit sin.   The
idea of such a license takes away that of his sanctity, and, of
course, that of his very being.   II. No Catholic ever believed
it to be a pardon for future sins, as Mrs. Hannah More, and a
great part of other Protestant writers represent the matter.

* P. 53.
† P. 54, Benson on the Man of Sin, republished by bishop Watson, Tracts, vol
v. p. 273.
‡ Bishop Fowler's Design of Christianity, Tracts, vol. vi. p. 382.
§ Benson on the Man of Sin, Collect.

25*

This lady describes the Catholics as " procuring indemnity for future gratifications by temporary abstractions and indulgences, purchased at the court of Rome."* Some of her fraternity, indeed, have blasphemously written, " Believers ought not to mourn for sin, because it was pardoned before it was commit·ted ;"† but every Catholic knows that Christ himself could not pardon sin before it was committed, because this would imply that he forgave the sinner without repentance. III. An indulgence, according to the doctrine of the Catholic church, is not, and does not include the pardon of any sin at all, little or great, past, present, or to come, or the eternal punishment due to it, as all Protestants suppose. Hence, if the pardon of sin is mentioned in any indulgence, this means nothing more than the remission of the *temporary punishments* annexed to such sin. IV. We do not believe an indulgence to imply any exemption from repentance, as B. Porteus slanders us; for this is always enjoined or implied in the grant of it, and is indispensably necessary for the effect of every grace ;‡ nor from the works of penance, or other good works ; because our church teaches that the " life of a Christian ought to be a perpetual penance,§ and that to *enter into life*, we must *keep God's commandments*,‖ and must *abound in every good work.*"¶ Whether an obligation of all this can be reconciled with the articles of being " justified by faith only,"** and that " works done before grace partake of the nature of sin,"†† I do not here inquire. V. It is inconsistent with our doctrine of *inherent justification*,‡‡ to believe, as the same prelate charges us, that the effect of an indulgence is to transfer " the overplus of the goodness," or justification of the saints, by the ministry of the Pope, to us Catholics on earth. Such an absurdity may be more easily reconciled with the system of Luther and other Protestants concerning *imputed justification ;* which, being like a " clean, neat cloak, thrown over a filthy leper,"§§ may be conceived transferable from one person to another. Lastly, whereas the council of Trent calls

---

* Strictures on Female Education, vol. ii. p. 239.
† Eaton's Honeycomb of Salvation. See also Sir Richard Hill's Letters.
‡ Concil. Trid. Sess. vi. c. 4, c. 13, &c.
§ Sess. xiv. De Extr. Unc.　　　　　　　‖ Sess. vi. can. 19.
¶ Ibid. cap. 16.—N. B. There are eight Indulgences granted to Catholics at the chief festivals, &c. in every year ; the conditions of which are, confession *with sincere repentance*, the H. Communion, alms to the poor, (without distinction of their religion) prayers for the church and strayed souls, the peace of christendom, and the blessing of God on this nation ; finally, a disposition to hear the word of God, and to assist the sick. See Laity's Directory, Keating and Brown.
** Art. XI. of 39 Art.　　　　　　†† Art. XIII.
‡‡ Trid. Sess. vi. can. xi.　　　　§§ Becanus de Justif

indulgences *heavenly treasures,** we hold that it would be a sacrilegious crime in any person whomsoever to be concerned in buying or selling them. I am far, however, Rev. sir, from denying that indulgences have ever been sold†—alas! what is so sacred that the avarice of men has not put up to sale! Christ himself was sold, and that by an apostle, for thirty pieces of silver. I do not retort upon you the advertisements I frequently see in the newspapers about buying and selling benefices, with the cure of souls annexed to them, in your church; but this I contend for, that the Catholic church, so far from sanctioning this detestable simony, has used her utmost pains, particularly in the general councils of Lateran, Lyons, Vienne, and Trent, to prevent it.

To explain, now, in a clear and regular manner, what an indulgence is; I suppose, first, that no one will deny that a sovereign prince, in showing mercy to a capital convict, may either grant him a remission of all punishment, or may leave him subject to some lighter punishment: of course he will allow that the Almighty may act in either of these ways with respect to sinners. II. I equally suppose that no person, who is versed in the Bible, will deny that many instances occur there of God's remitting the essential guilt of sin and the eternal punishment due to it, and yet leaving a temporary punishment to be endured by the penitent sinner. Thus, for example, the sentence of spiritual death and everlasting torments was remitted to our first father, upon his repentance, but not that of corporal death. Thus, also when God reversed his severe sentence against the idolatrous Israelites, he added, *Nevertheless, in the day when I visit, I will visit their sin upon them.* Exod. xxxii. 34. Thus, again, when the inspired Nathan said to the model of penitents, David, *The Lord hath put away thy sin*, he added, *nevertheless, the child that is born unto thee shall die.* 2 Kings, alias Sam. xii. 14. Finally, when David's *heart smote him, after he had numbered the people*, the Lord, in pardoning him, offered him by his prophet, Gad, the choice of three temporal punishments war, famine, and pestilence. *Ibid.* xxiv. III. The Catholic church teaches that the same is still the common course of God's mercy and wisdom, in the forgiveness of sins committed after baptism; since she has formally condemned the proposi-

---

* Sess. xxi. c. 5.

† The bishop tells us that he is in possession of an indulgence, lately granted at Rome, for a small sum of money; but he does not say who granted it. In like manner he may buy forged Bank notes and counterfeit coin in London very cheap, if he pleases.

tion, that " every penitent sinner, who, after the grace of Justi‑
fication, obtains the remission of his guilt and eternal punish‑
ment, obtains also the remission of all temporal punishment."*
The essential guilt and eternal punishment of sin, she declares,
can only be expiated by the precious merits of our Redeemer,
Jesus Christ; but a certain‑temporal punishment God reserves
for the penitent himself to endure, " lest the easiness of his par‑
don should make him careless about falling back into sin."†
Hence *satisfaction* for this temporal punishment has been insti‑
tuted by Christ as a part of the sacrament of penance; and
hence " a Christian life," as the council has said above,
" ought to be a penitential life." This council at the same
time, declares, that this very satisfaction for temporal punish‑
ment *is only efficacious through Jesus Christ.*‡ Nevertheless, as
the promise of Christ to the apostles, and St. Peter in particu‑
lar, and to their successors, is unlimited: WHATSOEVER
you shall loose upon earth, shall be loosed also in heaven, Mat.
xviii. 18—xvi. 19; hence the church believes and teaches that
her jurisdiction extends to this very satisfaction, so as to be able
to remit it wholly or partially, in certain circumstances, by
what is called an INDULGENCE.§ St. Paul exercised this
power in behalf of the incestuous Corinthian, at his conversion
and the prayers of the faithful, 2 *Cor.* ii. 10; and the church
has claimed and exercised the same power ever since the time
of the apostles down to the present.‖ V. Still this power, like
that of absolution, is not arbitrary; there must be a just cause
for the exercise of it, namely, the greater good of the penitent,
or of the faithful, or of Christendom in general; and there must
be a certain proportion between the punishment remitted and
the good work performed.¶ Hence no one can ever be sure
that he has gained the entire benefit of an indulgence, though
he has performed all the conditions appointed for this end :**
and hence, of course, the pastors of the church will have to an‑
swer for it, if they take upon themselves to grant indulgences
for unworthy or insufficient purposes. VI. Lastly, it is the re‑
ceived doctrine of the church that an indulgence, when truly
gained, is not barely a relaxation of the canonical penance en‑
joined by the church, but also an actual remission by God of the

* Conc. Trid. Sess. vi. can. 30.
† Sess vi. cap. 7, cap. 14.　Sess. xiv. cap. 8
‡ Sess. xiv. 8.
§ Trid. Sess. xxv. De Indulg.
‖ Tertul. in Lib. ad Martyr. c. i.　St. Cypr. l. 3.　Epist. Concil. l.　Nic. Ancyr.
&c.　　　　¶ Bellarm. Lib. i. De Indulg. c. 12.　　** Ibid

whole or part of the temporal punishment due to it in his sight.
The contrary opinion, though held by some theologians, has
been condemned by Leo X,* and Pius VI :† and indeed, without the effect here mentioned, indulgences would not be *heavenly treasures*, and the use of them would not be *beneficial*, but rather *pernicious* to Christians, contrary to two declarations of the
last general council, as Bellarmin well argues.‡

The above explanation of an indulgence, conformably to the
doctrine of Theologians, the decrees of Popes, and the definitions of Councils, ought to silence the objections and suppress
the sarcasms of Protestants on this head: but if it be not sufficient for such purpose, I would gladly argue a few points with
them concerning their own indulgences. Methinks, Rev. sir, I
see you start at the mention of this, and hear you ask, what Protestants hold the doctrine of indulgences?—I answer you; all
the leading sects of them, with which I am acquainted. To begin with the church of England: one of the first articles I meet
with in its canons, regards *indulgences* and the use that is to be
made of the *money paid for them.*§ In the synod of 1640, a
canon was made which authorized the employment of commu-
tation-money, namely, of such sums as were paid for indulgences from ecclesiastical penances, not only in charitable, but also
in *public* uses.‖ At this period the established clergy were de-
voting all the money they could any way procure to the war
which Charles I. was preparing in defence of the church and
state against the Presbyterians of Scotland and England: so
that, in fact, the money then raised by indulgences was employed in a real crusade. It has been before stated that the second
offspring of Protestantism, the Anabaptists, claimed an indul-

* Art. 19, inter Art. Damn. Lutheri.
† Const. *Auctor. Fid.*   ‡ L. i. c. 7, prop. 4.
§ " Ne quæ fiat posthac solemnis penitentiæ commutatio nisi rationibus, gravio-
ribus quæ de causis, &c. Deinde quod mulcta illa pecuniaria vel in relevam pau-
perum, vel in alios pios usus erogetur." Articuli pro Clero, A. D. 1584, Sparrow,
p. 194. The next article is, " De moderandis quibusdam indulgentiis pro cele-
bratione matrimonii," &c. p. 195. These indulgences were renewed, under the
same titles, in the Synod held in London in 1597. Sparrow, pp. 248. 252.

‖ " That no Chancellor, Commissary or Official, shall have power to commute
any penance, in whole or in part; but either, together with the bishop, &c. that he
shall give a full and just account of such commutations, to the bishop, who shall
see that all such moneys shall be disposed of for charitable and public uses, according to law—saving always to ecclesiastical officers their *due and accustomable fees.*"
Canon 14, Sparrow, p. 368—In the remonstrance of grievances presented by a
committee of the Irish parliament to Charles I, one of them was, that " Several bishops received great sums of money *for commutation of penance* (that is for indulgences) which they converted to their own use." Commons Journ. quoted by Curry,
Vol. i. p. 169.

gence from God himself, in quality of his chosen ones, to despoil the impious, namely, all the rest of mankind, of their property; while the genuine Calvinists, of all times, have ever maintained that Christ has set them free from the observance of every law of God as well as of man. Agreeebly to this tenet, sir Richard Hill says, "It is a most pernicious error of the schoolmen to distinguish sins according to *the fact*, and not according to the person."* With respect to patriarch Luther, it is notorious that he was in the habit of granting indulgences, of various kinds, to himself and his disciples. Thus, for example, he dispensed with himself and Catharine Boren from their vows of a religious life, and particularly that of celibacy: and even preached up adultery in his public sermons.† In like manner he published Bulls, authorizing the robbery of bishops and bishoprics, and the murder of Popes and cardinals. But the most celebrated of his indulgences is that which, in conjunction with Bucer and Melancthon, he granted to Philip, Landgrave of Hesse, in consideration of the latter's protection of Protestantism, for so it is stated, to marry a second wife, his former being living.‡ But if any credit is due to this same Bucer, who, for his learning, was invited by Cranmer and the duke of Somerset into England, and made the divinity professor of Cambridge, the whole business of the pretended Reformation was an indulgence for libertinism. His words are these: " The greater part of the people seem only to have embraced the Gospel, in order to shake off the yoke of discipline and the obligation of fasting, penance, &c. which lay upon them in Popery, and to live at their pleasure, enjoying their lusts and lawless appetites, without controul. Hence they lent a willing ear to the doctrine that we are saved by faith alone, and not by good works, having no relish for them."§

I am, &c.
J. M.

---

* Fletcher's Checks, vol. iii.
† " Si nolit Domina, veniat ancilla, &c." Serm. De Matrim. t. v.
‡ This infamous indulgence, with the deeds belonging to it, was published from the original by permission of a descendant of the Landgrave, and republished by Bossuet. Variat. book vi.   § Bucer. De Regn. Chris. l. i. c. 4.

LETTER XLIII.

To the Rev. ROBERT CLAYTON, M. A.

ON PURGATORY AND PRAYERS FOR THE DEAD.

Rev. Sir,

In the natural order of our controversies, this is the proper place to treat of purgatory and prayers for the dead. On this subject, bishop Porteus begins with saying, "There is no Scripture proof of the existence of purgatory: heaven and hell we read of perpetually in the Bible; but purgatory we never meet with; though surely, if there be such a place, Christ and his apostles would not have concealed it from us."* I might expose the inconclusiveness of this argument by the following parallel one; the Scripture nowhere commands us to keep the *first day of the week* holy: we perpetually read of sanctifying the *Sabbath*, or Saturday; but never meet with the Sunday, as a day of *obligation;* though, if there be such an obligation, Christ and his apostles would not have concealed it from us! I might likewise answer, with the bishop of Lincoln, that the inspired Epistles (and I may add the Gospels also) "are not to be considered as regular treatises upon the Christian religion."† But I meet the objection in front, by saying, first, that the apostles did teach their converts the doctrine of purgatory, among their other doctrines, as St. Chrysostom testifies, and the tradition of the church proves; secondly, that the same is demonstratively evinced from both the Old and the New Testament.

To begin with the Old Testament; I claim a right of considering the two first Books of Machabees as an integral part of them; because the Catholic church so considers them,‡ from whose tradition, and not from that of the Jews, as St. Austin signifies,§ our sacred canon is to be formed. Now in the second of these books, it is related that the pious general, Judas Machabeus, sent twelve thousand drachmas to Jerusalem for sacrifices, to be offered for his soldiers, slain in battle, after

* Confut. p. 48. † Elem. of Theol. vol. i. p. 277
‡ Concil. Cartag. iii. St. Cyp. St. Aug. Innoc. I. Gelas, &c.
§ Lib. 18. De Civ. Dei.

which narration, the inspired writer concludes thus: *It is there-fore a holy and a wholesome thought to pray for the dead, that they may be loosed from their sins.* 2 Mac. xii. 46. I need not point out the inseparable connexion there is between the prac-tice of praying for the dead and the belief of an intermediate state of souls, since it is evidently needless to pray for the saints in heaven, and useless to pray for the reprobate in hell. But, even Protestants, who do not receive the Books of Machabees, as canonical Scripture, venerate them as authentic and holy records: as such, then, they bear conclusive testimony of the belief of God's people, on this head, one hundred and fifty years before Christ. That the Jews were in the habit of prac-tising some religious rites for the relief of the departed, at the beginning of Christianity, is clear from St. Paul's first Epistle to the Corinthians, who mentions them, without any censure of them;* and that this people continue to pray for their de-ceased brethren, at the present time, may be learned from any living Jew.

To come now to the New Testament: what place, I ask, must that be, which our Saviour calls *Abraham's bosom*, where the soul of Lazarus reposed, *Luke* xvi. 22, among the other just souls, till he by his sacred passion paid their ransom? Not heaven, otherwise Dives would have addressed himself to God instead of Abraham; but evidently a middle state, as St. Austin teaches.† Again, of what place is it that St. Peter speaks, where he says, *Christ died for our sins; being put to death in the flesh, but enlivened in the spirit; in which also coming, he preached to those spirits that were in prison.* 1 Pet. iii. 19. It is evidently the same which is mentioned in the apostles' creed: *He descended into hell:* not the hell of the damned, to suffer their torments, as the blasphemer, Calvin, asserts,‡ but the *prison* above-mentioned, or *Abraham's bosom*, in short, a middle state. It is of this prison, according to the holy fathers,§ our blessed Master speaks, where he says, *I tell thee, thou shalt not depart thence, till thou hast paid the very last mite.* Luke xii. 59. Lastly, what other sense can that passage of St. Paul's Epistle to the Corinthians bear, than that which the holy fa-thers affix to it,‖, where the apostle says, *The day of the Lord*

<hr>

* *Else what shall they do who are baptized for the dead, if the dead rise not at all? Why are they then baptized for them?*   1 Cor. xv. 29.
† De Civit. Dei, L. xv. c. 20.   ‡ Instit. L. li. c. 16.
§ Tertul. St. Cypr. Origen, St. Ambrose, St. Jerom, &c.
‖ Origen, Hom 14 in Levit. &c.   St. Ambrose in Ps. 118.   St. Jerom, L. 2. con-tra Jovin.   St. Aug. in Ps. 37, where he prays thus: " Purify me, O Lord, in this

shall be revealed by fire, and the fire shall try every man's work of what sort it is. If any man's work abide, he shall receive a reward. If any man's work be burnt, he shall suffer loss; but he himself shall be saved, yet so as by fire.* 1 Cor. iii. 13, 15 The prelate's diversified attempts to explain away these Scriptural proofs of purgatory, are really too feeble and inconsistent to merit being even mentioned. I might here add, as a further proof, the denunciation of Christ, concerning *blasphemy against the Holy Ghost:* namely, that this sin *shall not be forgiven either in this world or in the world to come,* Mat. xii. 32: which words clearly imply, that *some sins* are forgiven in the world to come, as the ancient fathers show :* but I hasten to the proofs of this doctrine from tradition, on which head the prelate is so ill-advised as to challenge Catholics.

II. Bp. Porteus, then, advances, that " Purgatory, in the present Popish sense, was not heard of for four hundred years after Christ; nor universally received for one thousand years, nor almost in any other church than that of Rome to this day."† Here are no less than three egregious falsities, which I proceed to show, after stating what his lordship seems not to know, namely, that all which is necessary to be believed, on this subject, is contained in the following brief declaration of the council of Trent: " There is a purgatory, and the souls, detained there, are helped by the prayers of the faithful, and particularly by the acceptable sacrifice of the altar."‡ St. Chrysostom, the light of the eastern church, flourished within three hundred years of the age of the apostles, and must be admitted as an unexceptionable witness of their doctrine and practice. Now he writes as follows: " It was not without good reason OR-DAINED BY THE APOSTLES, that mention should be made of the dead in the tremendous mysteries, because they knew well that these would receive great benefit from it."§ Tertullian, who lived in the age next to that of the apostles, speaking of a pious widow, says, " She prays for the soul of her husband, and begs refreshment‖ for him." Similar testimonies of St. Cyprian, in the following age are numerous: I shall satisfy myself with quoting one of them, where, describing the difference between some souls, which are immediately admitted into heaven, and others, which are detained in purga-

life, that I may not need the chastising fire of those *who will be saved, yet so as by fire.*"

* St. Aug. De Civit. Dei. L 21, c. 24. St. Greg. l. 4. Dialog. Bed in cap. 3, Marc.
† P. 50.   ‡ Sess. xxv. De Purg.
§ In cap. i. Philip. Hom. 3.   ‖ L. De Monogam. c. 10.

tory, he says, " It is one thing to be waiting for pardon; another to attain to glory: one thing to be sent to prison, not to go from thence till the last farthing is paid; another to receive immediately the reward of faith and virtue: one thing to suffer lengthened torments for sin, and to be chastised and purified for a long time in that fire; another to have cleansed away all sin by suffering,"* namely, by martyrdom. It would take up too much time to quote authorities on this subject from St. Cyril of Ierusalem, Eusebius, St. Epiphanius, St. Ambrose, St. Jerom, St. Augustin, and several other ancient fathers and writers, who demonstrate, that the doctrine of the church was the same that it is now, not only within a thousand, but also within four hundred years from the time of Christ, with respect both to prayers for the dead, and an intermediate state, which we call purgatory. How express is the authority of the last named father, in particular, where he says and repeats, " Through the prayers and sacrifices of the church and alms-deeds, God deals more mercifully with the departed than their sins deserve!"† How affecting is this saint's account of the death of his mother, St. Monica, when she entreated him to remember her soul at the altar, and when, after her decease, he performed this duty, in order, as he declares, " to obtain the pardon of her sins!"‡ As to the doctrine of the oriental churches, which the bishop signifies is conformable to that of his own, I affirm, as a fact, which has been demonstrated,§ that there is not one of them which agrees with it, nor one of them which does not agree with the Catholic church, in the only two points defined by her, namely, as to there being a middle state, which we call purgatory, and as to the souls, detained in it, being helped by the prayers of the living faithful. True it is, they do not generally believe, that these souls are punished by a *material fire;* but neither does our church require a belief of this opinion; and accordingly, she made a union with the Greeks in the council of Florence, on their barely confessing and subscribing the aforesaid two articles.

III. I should do an injury, Rev. sir, to my cause, were I to pass over the concessions of eminent Protestant prelates and other writers on the matter in debate. On some occasions Luther admits of purgatory, as an article founded on Scripture.‖ Melancthon confesses that the ancients prayed for the dead, and

---

* S. Cypr. l. 4. ep. 2.　　　　　† Serm. 172. Enchirid. cap. 109, 110.
‡ Confess. l. ix. c. 13.
§ See the Confessions of the different Oriental churches in the Perpetuité, &c
‖ Assertiones, Art. 37.＿ Disput. Leipsic.

says that the Lutherans do not find fault with it.* Calvin intimates, that the souls of all the just are detained in Abraham's
bosom till the day of judgment.† In the first liturgy of the
church of England, which was drawn up by Cranmer and Ridley, and declared by act of parliament to have been *framed by
inspiration of the Holy Ghost*, there is an express prayer for the
departed, that " God would grant them mercy and everlasting
peace."‡ It can be shown that the following bishops of your
church believed that the dead ought to be prayed for, Andrews,
Usher, Montague, Taylor, Forbes, Sheldon, Barrow of St.
Asaph's and Blandford.§ To these I may add the religious Dr.
Johnson, whose published Meditations prove, that he constantly
prayed for his deceased wife. But what need is there of more
words on the subject, when it is clear that modern Protestants,
in shutting up the Catholic purgatory for imperfect just souls,
have opened another general one for them, and all the wicked
of every sort whatsoever! It is well known that the disciples
of Calvin, at Geneva, and, perhaps, every where else, instead
of adhering to his doctrine, in condemning mortals to eternal
torments, without any fault on their part, now hold that the
most confirmed in guilt and the finally impenitent shall, in the
end, be saved:‖ thus establishing, as Fletcher of Madeley observes, " a general purgatory."¶ A late celebrated theological, as well as philosophical writer of our own country, Dr.
Priestly, being on his deathbed, called for Simpson's work *On
the Duration of Future Punishment*, which he recommended in
these terms: " It contains my sentiments: we shall all meet
finally: we only require different degrees of discipline, suited
to our different tempers, to prepare us for final happiness."**
Here again is a general Protestant purgatory: and why should
Satan and his crew be denied the benefit of it? But to confine
myself to eminent divines of the established church. One of
its celebrated preachers, who, of course, " never mentions hell
to ears polite," expresses his wish, " to banish the subject of
everlasting punishment from all pulpits, as containing a doctrine, at once improper and uncertain,"†† which sentiment is
applauded by another eminent divine, who reviews that sermon

* Apolog. Conf. Aug.   † Instit. l. iii. c. 5.
‡ See the form in Collier's Ecc. Hist. vol. ii. p. 257.
§ Collier's Hist.—N. B. The present bishop of Exeter, in a sermon just publish-
ed, prays for the soul of our poor princess Charlotte, " as far as this is lawful and
profitable."
‖ Encyclo. Art. Geneva.   ¶ Checks to Antinom. vol. 4.
** See Edinb. Review. Oct. 1808.
†† Sermons by Rev. W. Gilpin, Preb. of Sarum.

in the British Critic.* Another modern divine censures " the
threat of eternal perdition as a cause of infidelity."† The renowned Dr. Paley, (but here we are getting into quite novel
systems of theology, which will force a smile from its old students, notwithstanding the awfulness of the subject) Dr. Paley,
I say, so far softens the punishment of the infernal regions, as
to suppose that, " There may be very little to choose between
the condition of some who are in hell, and others who are in
heaven !"‡ In the same liberal spirit the Cambridge professor
of divinity teaches, that " God's wrath and damnation are more
terrible in the sound than the sense !§ and that *being damned*
does not imply any fixed degree of evil."‖ In another part of
his Lectures, he expresses his hope, and quotes Dr. Hartley, as
expressing the same, that " all men will be ultimately happy,
when punishment has done its work in reforming principles and
conduct."¶ If this sentiment be not sufficiently explicit in favour of purgatory, take the following, from a passage in which
he is directly lecturing on the subject. " With regard to the doctrine of purgatory, though it may not be founded either in reason or in Scripture, it is not unnatural. Who can bear the
thought of dwelling in everlasting torments? Yet who can say
that a God everlastingly just, will not inflict them? The mind
of man seeks for some resource : it finds one only ; in conceiving that some temporary punishment, after death, may purify
the soul from its moral pollutions, and make it, at last, acceptable, even to a deity, infinitely pure."**

IV. Bishop Porteus intimates that the doctrine of a middle
state of souls was borrowed from Pagan fable and philosophy.
—In answer to this, I say, that, if Plato,†† Virgil, and other
heathens, ancient and modern, as likewise Mahomet and his
disciples, together with the Protestant writers quoted above,
have embraced this doctrine, it only shows how conformable it
is to the dictates of natural religion. I have proved, by various arguments, that a temporary punishment generally remains due, to sin, after the guilt and eternal punishment due to
it, have been remitted. Again, we know from Scripture, that
even the just man falls seven times, Prov. xxiv. 17, and that men

---

* British Critic, Jan. 1802.
† Rev. Mr. Polwhele's Let. to Dr. Hawker.
‡ Moral and Polit. Philos.   § Lect. vol. iii. p. 154.   ‖ Ibid.
¶ Vol. ii. p. 390. It is to be observed that the doctrine of the final salvation of
the wicked is expressly condemned in the 42d Article of the church of England, A.
D. 1552.   ** Vol. iv. p. 112.
†† Plato in Gorgia, Virgil's Æneid, l. 2, the Koran.

must give an account of every idle word that they speak, Mat. xii. 36. On the other hand, we are conscious that there is not an instant of our life, in which this may not suddenly terminate, without the possibility of our calling upon God for mercy. What then, I ask, will become of souls which are surprised in either of those predicaments? We are sure from Scripture and reason that nothing defiled shall enter heaven, *Rev.* xxi. 27: will then our just and merciful Judge make no distinction in guiltiness, as bishop Fowler and other rigid Protestants maintain?* Will he condemn to the same eternal punishment the poor child who has died under the guilt of a lie of excuse, and the abandoned wretch who has died in the act of murdering his father? To say that he will, is so monstrous a doctrine in itself, and so contrary to Scripture, which declares that *God will render to every man according to his deeds*, Rom. ii. 6, that it seems to be universally exploded.† The evident consequence of this is, that there are some *venial* or pardonable sins, for the expiation of which, as well as of the temporary punishment due to other sins, a place of temporary punishment is provided in the next life, where, however, the souls detained may be relieved, by the prayers, alms, and sacrifices of the faithful here on earth. O! how consoling is the belief and practice of Catholics in this matter, compared with those of Protestants! The latter show their regard for their departed friends in costly pomp and feathered pageantry; while their burial service is a cold, disconsolate ceremony; and as to any further communication with the deceased, when the grave closes on their remains, they do not so much as imagine any. On the other hand, we Catholics know, that death itself cannot dissolve the *communion of saints*, which subsists in our church, nor prevent an intercourse of kind and often beneficial offices between us and our departed friends. Oftentimes we can help them more effectually, in the other world, by our prayers, our sacrifices, and our alms-deeds, than we could in this by any temporary benefits we could bestow upon them. Hence we are instructed to celebrate the obsequies of the dead by all such good works; and, accordingly, our funeral service consists of psalms and prayers, offered up for their repose and eternal felicity. These acts of devotion, pious Catholics perform for the deceased, who were near and dear to them, and indeed for the dead in general, every day, but particularly on the respective anniversaries of the deceased.

---

* Calvin, l. iii. c. 12. Fowler in Watson's Tracts, vol. vi. p. 362.
† See Dr. Hey, vol. iii. pp. 384, 451, 453.

26*

Such benefits, we are assured, will be paid with rich interest, by those souls to whose bliss we have contributed, when they attain to it; and if they should not be in a condition to help us, the God of mercy at least will abundantly reward our charity. On the other hand, what a comfort and support must it be to our minds, when our turn comes to descend into the grave, to reflect that we shall continue to live in the constant thoughts and daily devotions of our Catholic relatives and friends!

I am, &c.

J. M

LETTER XLIV.

To the Rev. ROBERT CLAYTON, M. A.

EXTREME UNCTION.

Rev. Sir,

The Council of Trent terms the sacrament of extreme unction, the *Consummation of Penance*, and therefore, as bishop Porteus makes this the subject of a charge against our church, here is the proper place for me to answer it. His lordship writes *a long chapter* upon it, because his business is to gloss over the clear testimony which the apostle St. James bears to the reality of this sacrament: in return, I shall write *a short letter* in refutation of his chapter, because I have little more to do than to cite that testimony, as it stands in the New Testament: it is this: *Is any man sick among you, let him bring in the priests of the church, and let them pray over him, anointing him with oil, in the name of the Lord. And the prayer of faith shall save the sick man; and the Lord shall raise him up, and if he be in sins, they shall be forgiven him,* James v. 14, 15. Here we see all that is requisite, according to the English Protestant Catechism, to constitute a sacrament,* for there " is an outward visible sign," namely, the *anointing with oil:* there " is an inward spiritual grace, given unto us," namely, *the saving of the sick and the forgiveness of his sins.* Lastly, there is the Ordina-

---

* In the Book of Common Prayer.

tion of Christ, as the *means* by which the same *is received;"* unless the bishop chooses to allege, that the holy apostle fabricated a Sacrament, or means of grace, without any authority for this purpose from his heavenly Master. What then does his lordship say, in opposition to this divine warrant for our Sacrament? He says, that the anointing of the sick by elders or old men, was the appointed method of *miraculously curing them* in primitive times, which would imply, that no Christian died in those times, except when either oil or old men were not to be met with! He adds, that *the forgiveness of the sick man's sins* means *the cures of his corporal diseases!*[*] And after all this, he boasts of building his religion on mere Scripture, in its plain, unglossed meaning!† In reading all this, I own I cannot help revolving in my mind the above quoted profane parody of Luther, on the first words of Scripture, in which he ridicules the distortion of it by many Protestants of his time.‡ With the same confidence his lordship adds: " Our laying aside a ceremony (the anointing) which *has long been useless,* &c. can be no loss, while every thing that is truly valuable in St. James's direction is preserved in our office for visiting the sick."§ Exactly in this manner our friends, the Quakers, undertake to prove, that, in laying aside the ceremony of washing catechumens with water, they " have preserved every thing that is truly valuable" in the sacrament of Baptism!‖ But where shall we find an end of the inconsistencies and impieties of deluded Christians, who refuse to hear that church which Christ has appointed to explain to them the truths of religion?

There is not more truth in the prelate's assertion, that there is no mention of anointing with oil, among the primitive Christians, except in miraculous cures, during the first 600 years: for the celebrated Origen, who was born in the age next to that of the apostles, after speaking of an humble confession of sins, as a mean of obtaining their pardon, adds to it, *the anointing with oil, prescribed by St. James.*¶ St. Chrysostom, who lived in the fourth century, speaking of the power of priests in remitting sin, says, they exert it when they are called in to perform the rite mentioned by St. James, &c.** The testimony of Pope Innocent I. in the same age, is so express as to the warrant for this sacrament, the matter, the minister, and the subjects of

---

* P. 59.   † P. 69.
‡ " In principio Deus creavit cœlum et terram: *In the beginning the cuckoo devoured the sparrow and its feathers.*
§ P. 61.   ‖ Barclay's Apology, Prop. 12.
¶ Hom. ii. in Levit.   ** De Sacerd. L. iii.

it;[*] that though the bishop alluded to the testimony, he does not choose to grapple with it, or even to quote it.[†] I pass over the irrefragable authorities of St. Cyril of Alexandria, Victor of Antioch, St. Gregory the Great, and our Venerable Bede, in order once more to recur to that short but convincing proof, that the Catholic church has not invented those sacraments and doctrines in latter ages, which Protestants assert were unknown in the primitive ages. The Nestorians then broke off from the communion of the church in 431, and the Eutychians in 451 : these rival sects exist, in numerous congregations, throughout the east, at the present day, and they both, as well as the Greeks, Armenians, &c. maintain, in belief and practice, *Extreme Unction* as *one of the seven sacraments.* Nothing can so satisfactorily vindicate our church from the charge of imposition or innovation, in the particulars mentioned, as these facts do. How much more consistently has the impious Friar, Martin Luther, acted in denying at once the authority of St. James's Epistle, and condemning it as " a chaffy composition, and unworthy an apostle,"[‡] than Bp. Porteus, with his confederates do, who attempt to explain away the clear proofs of extreme unction, contained in it? In the mean time, in spite of them all, pious Catholics will continue to reap inestimable consolation and grace, in the time of man's greatest need, for the sake of which this and the other helps of their church, were provided by our Saviour Jesus Christ.

I am, &c.
J. M.

Epist. ad Decent. Eugub.   † P. 61.
" Stramminoram."   Prefat. in Ep. Jac. Jenæ de Captiv. Babyl.

LETTER XLV.

To the Rev. ROBERT CLAYTON, M. A

WHETHER THE POPE BE ANTICHRIST.

REV. SIR,

THERE remains but one more question of doctrine to be dis-
·cussed between me and your favourite controvertist, bishop
Porteus, which is concerning the character and power of the
Pope ; and this he compresses into a narrow compass, among a
variety of miscellaneous matters, in the latter part of his book.
However, as it is a doctrine of first-rate importance, against
which I make no doubt but several of your Salopian Society
have been early and bitterly prejudiced, I propose to treat it, at
some length, and in a regular way.   To do this, I must begin
with the inquiry, whether the Pope be really and truly, *the man
of sin*, and *the son of perdition*, described by St. Paul, 2 *Thess.*
ii. 1, 10 ; in short, *the Antichrist* spoken of by St. John, 1 *John*
ii. 18, and called by him, *A beast with seven heads and ten
horns*, Revel. xiii. 1, whose See or church is *the great harlot,
the mother of the fornications and abominations of the earth*, Ibid.
xvii. 5.   I shudder to repeat these blasphemies, and I blush to
hear them uttered by my fellow Christians and countrymen,
who derive their liturgy, their ministry, their Christianity, and
civilization, from the Pope and the church of Rome ; but they
have been too generally taught by the learned, and believed by
the ignorant, for me to pass them by in silence on this occasion.
One of bishop Porteus's colleagues, bishop Hallifax, speaks of
this doctrine concerning the Pope and Rome, as long being
" the common symbol of Protestantism."*   Certain it is, that
the author of it, the outrageous Martin Luther, may be said to
have established Protestantism upon this principle : he had at
first submitted his religious controversies to the decision of the
Pope, protesting to him thus : " Whether you give life or
death, approve or reprove, as you may judge best, I will
hearken to your voice, as to that of Christ himself :"† but no
sooner did Pope Leo condemn his doctrine, than he published

---

* Sermons by bishop Hallifax, preached at the Lecture founded by the late bishop Warburton, to prove the apostasy of Papal Rome, p. 27.
† Epist. ad Leon X. A. D. 1518.

his book " Against the execrable Bull of Antichrist,"* as he qualified it. In like manner, Melancthon, Bullinger, and many others of Luther's followers, publicly maintained, that the Pope is Antichrist, as did afterwards Calvin, Beza, and the writers of that party in general. This party considered this doctrine so essential, as to vote it *an article of faith,* in their synod of Gap, held in 1603.† The writers in defence of this impious tenet in our island, are as numerous as those of the whole continent put together, John Fox, Whitaker, Fulke, Willet, sir Isaac Newton, Mede, Lowman, Towson, Bicheno, Kett, &c. with the bishops, Fowler, Warburton, Newton, Hallifax, Hurd, Watson, and others, too numerous to be here mentioned. One of these writers, whose work has but just appeared, has collected a new and quite whimsical system from the Scriptures concerning Antichrist. Hitherto, Protestant expositors have been content to apply the character and attributes of Antichrist to a succession of Roman pontiffs; but the Rev. H. Kett professes to have discovered, that the said Antichrist is, at the same time, every Pope who has filled the See of Rome, since the year 756, to the number of one hundred and sixty, together with the whole of what he calls " the Mahometan power," from a period more remote by a century and a half, and the whole of infidelity, which he traces to a still more ancient origin than even Mahometanism.‡

That the first Pope, St. Peter, on whom Christ declared, that he built his church, *Mat.* xvi. 18, was not Antichrist, I trust I need not prove, nor, indeed, his third successor in the Popedom, St. Clement, since St. Paul testifies of him, that *his name is written in the book of life,* Phil. iv. 3. In like manner, there is no need of my demonstrating, that the See of Rome was not the harlot of Revelations, when St. Paul certified of its members, that their *faith was spoken of throughout the whole world,* Rom. i. 8. At what particular period, then, I now ask, as I asked Mr. Brown, in one of my former letters, did the grand apostasy take place, by which the head pastor of the church of Christ, became his declared enemy, in short, the Antichrist, and by which the church, whose faith had been divinely authenticated, became *the great harlot, full of the names of blasphemy*? This revolution, had it really taken place, would have been the

* Tom. ii.   † Bossuet's Variat. P. ii. B. 13.
‡ History of the Interpreter of Prophecy, by H. Kett, B. D. This writer's attempt to transform the great supporters of the Pope, St. Jerom, Pope Gregory I. St. Bernard, &c. into witnesses that the Pope is Antichrist, because they condemn certain acts as Antichristian, is truly ridiculous.

greatest and the most remarkable that ever happened since the deluge: hence, we might expect, that the witnesses, who profess to bear testimony to its reality, would agree, as to the time of its taking place. Let us now observe how far this is the fact. The Lutheran Braunbom, who writes the most copiously, and the most confidently of this event, tells us, that the Popish Antichrist was born in the year of Christ 86, that he grew to his full size in 376, that he was at his greatest strength in 636, that he began to decline in 1086, that he would die in 1640, and that the world would end in 1711.* Sebastian Francus affirms, that Antichrist appeared immediately after the apostles, and caused the external church, with its faith and sacraments, to disappear.† The Protestant church of Transylvania published that Antichrist first appeared A. D. 200.‡ Napper declared that his coming was about 313, and that Pope Silvester was the man.§ Melancthon says, that Pope Zozimus, in 420, was the first Antichrist,‖ while Beza transfers this character to the great and good St. Leo, A. D. 440.¶ Fleming fixes on the year 606 as the year of this great event, Bp. Newton on the year 727; but all agree, says the Rev. Henry Kett, " that the Antichristian power was fully established in 757, or 758."** Notwithstanding this confident assertion, Cranmer's brother-in-law, Bullinger, had, long before, assigned the year 763 as the era of this grand revolution,†† and Junius had put it off to 1073. Musculus could not discover Antichrist in the church till about 1200, Fox not till 1300,‡‡ and Martin Luther, as we have seen, not till his doctrine was condemned by Pope Leo in 1520. Such are the inconsistencies and contradictions of those learned Protestants, who profess to see so clearly the verification of the prophecies concerning Antichrist in the Roman pontiffs. I say *contradictions.* because those among them who pronounce Pope Gregory, or Leo the Great, or Pope Silvester, to have been Antichrist, must contradict those others, who admit them to have been respectively Christian pastors and saints. Now what credit do men of sense give to an account of any sort, the vouchers for which contradict each other? Certainly none at all.

Nor are the predictions of these egregious interpreters, concerning the death of Antichrist, and the destruction of Popery, more consistent with one another, than their accounts of the

---

* Bayle's Dict. Braunbom.
‡ De Abolend. Christ. per Antichris.
‖ In locis postremo edit.
** Vol. ii. p. 58.　　†† In Apoc.

† De Alvegand. Stat. Eccles.
§ Upon the Revel.
¶ In Confess General.
‡‡ In Eandem

birth and progress of them both. We have seen above, that Braunbom prognosticated that the death of the papal Antichrist would take place in the year 1640. John Fox foretold it would happen in 1666. The incomparable Joseph Mede, as bishop Hallifax calls him,* by a particular calculation of his own invention, undertook to demonstrate that the Papacy would be finally destroyed in 1653.† The Calvinist minister Jurieau, who had adopted this system, fearing that the event would not verify it, found a pretext to lengthen the term, first to 1690, and afterwards to 1710. But he lived to witness a disappointment at each of these periods.‡ Alix, another Huguenot preacher, predicted that the fatal catastrophe would certainly take place in 1716.§ Whiston, who pretended to find out the longitude, pretended also to discover that the Popedom would terminate in 1714: finding himself mistaken, he guessed a second time, and fixed on the year 1735.‖ At length, Mr. Kett, from the success of his *Antichrist of Infidelity* against his *Antichrist of Popery*, about twenty years ago, (for he feels no difficulty in *dividing Satan against himself*, Mat. xii. 6,) foretold that the long wished-for event was at the eve of being accomplished,¶ and Mr. Daubeny having, with several other preachers, witnessed Pope Pius VI. in chains, and Rome possessed by French Atheists, sounds the trumpet of victory, and exclaims, all is accomplished.** Empty triumph of the enemies of the church! They ought to have learned, from her lengthened history, that she never proves the truth of Christ's promises so evidently as when she seems sinking under the waves of persecution; and that the chair of Peter never shines so gloriously, as when it is filled by a dying martyr, like Pius VI, or a captive confessor, like Pius VII; however triumphant for a time, their persecutors may appear!

But these dealers in prophecy undertake to demonstrate from the characters of Antichrist, as pointed out by St. Paul and St. John. that this succession of Popes is the very man in question: accordingly the bishop of Landaff says; " I have known the infidelity of more than one young man happily removed, by showing him the characters of Popery delineated by St. Paul, in his prophecy concerning *The Man of Sin*, 2 Thess. ii. and

* P 286. † Bayle's Dict. ‡ Ibid. § Ibid
‖ Essay on Revel. ¶ Vol. ii. chap. 1.
** The fall of Papal Rome. In like manner G. S. Faber, in his two Sermons before the University of Oxford, in 1799, boasts that " the immense Gothic structure of Popery, built on superstition and buttressed with tortures, has crumbled to dust."

in that concerning the apostasy of the latter times, 1 *Tim.* iv.
1."* In proof of this point, he republishes the Dissenter, Benson's Dissertation on *The man of Sin;*† I purpose, therefore,
making a few remarks on the leading points of this adoptive
child of his lordship, as also upon some of the Rev. Mr. Kett's
illustrations of them. First, then, we all know that *the Revelation of the Man of Sin* will be accompanied with a *revolt* or
falling off, in other words, with a great apostasy; but it is a
question to be discussed between me and bishop Watson, whether this character of *apostasy* is more applicable to the Catholic church, or to that class of Religionists who adopt his
opinions? To decide this point, let me ask, what are the first
and principal articles of the three creeds professed by his church
as well as by ours, that of the apostles, that of Nice, and that
of St. Athanasius, as likewise of his articles, his liturgy, and
his canons? Incontestably those which profess a belief in the
blessed Trinity, and the incarnation of the consubstantial Son
of the eternal Father. Now it is notorious, that every Catholic
throughout the world, holds these the fundamental articles of
Christianity as firmly now as St. Athanasius himself did fifteen
hundred years ago: but what says his lordship, with numberless other Protestant Christians of this country, on these heads?
Let the preface to his Collection be consulted,‡ in which, if he
does not *openly deny* the Trinity, he excuses the Unitarians,
who deny it, on the ground that they are *afraid of becoming
idolaters by worshipping Jesus Christ.*§ Let his charges be examined: in one of which he says to his clergy, that " he does
not think it *safe* to tell them what the Christian doctrines are;"‖
no, not so much as the unity and trinity of God. In another
charge, however, the bishop assumes more courage, and informs his clergy, that " Protestantism consists in believing
what each one pleases, and in professing what he believes."
How much should I rejoice to have this question of *apostasy*,
between the bishop of Landaff and me, decided by Luther,
Calvin, Beza, Cranmer, Ridley, and James I, only for the
proofs which history affords me, that, not content with excluding him from the class of Christians, they would assuredly
burn him at the stake as an apostate. The second character of
Antichrist, set down by St. Paul, is, that he *opposeth and is
lifted up above all that is called God, or that is worshipped, so*

---

* Bp. Watson's Collect. p. 7.　　　† Ibid. p. 262.
‡ Vol. i. Pref. p. 15, &c.　　　§ P. 17.
‖ Bishop Watson's Charge, 1795.
27

that he sitteth in the Temple of God, showing himself as if he were God, 2 Thess. ii. 4. This character Mr. Benson and bishop Watson think applicable to the Pope, who, they say, claims the attributes and homage due to the Deity. I leave you, Rev. sir, and your friends, to judge of the truth of this character, when I inform you, that the Pope has his confessor, like other Catholics, to whom he confesses his sins in private; and that every day, in saying mass, he bows before the altar, and in the presence of the people confesses, that he has " sinned in thought, word, and deed," begging them to pray to God for him, and that afterwards, in the more solemn part of it, he professes " his hopes of forgiveness, not through his own merits, but through the bounty and grace of Jesus Christ our Lord."[*] The third mark of Antichrist is, that his *coming is according to the working of Satan, in all power, and signs, and lying wonders,* 2 Thess. ii. 9. From this passage of Holy Writ, it appears that Antichrist, whenever he does come, will work false, illusive prodigies, as the magicians of Pharaoh did; but, from the divine promises, it is evident that the disciples of Christ would continue to work true miracles, such as he himself wrought; and from the testimony of the holy fathers and all ecclesiastical writers, it is incontestible, that certain servants of God have been enabled to work them, from time to time, ever since this his promise. This I have elsewhere demonstrated, as likewise, that the fact is denied by Protestants, not for want of evidence, as to its truth, but because this is necessary for the defence of their system.[†] Still it is false that the Catholic church ever claimed *a power of working miracles in the order of nature,* as her opponents pretend : all that we say is, that God is pleased, from time to time, to illustrate the true church with real miracles, and thereby to show, that she belongs to him. The latest dealer in prophecies, who boasts that his books have been revised by the bishop of Lincoln,[‡] by way of showing the conformity between Antichristian Popery and the *beast, that did great signs, so that he made fire to come down from heaven unto the earth, in the sight of men,* Rev. xiii. 13, says of the former, " even fire is pretended to come down from heaven, as in the case of *St. Anthony's fire.*"[§] I am almost ashamed to refute so illiterate a cavil. True it is, that the hospital monks of St. Anthony were heretofore famous for curing the Erysipelas with a peculiar ointment, on which account that disease acquired the

<hr>

[*] Canon of the Mass.   [†] Part ii. Letter. xxiii.
[‡] Interpret. of Prophecy, by H. Kett, LL. B. Pref.
[§] Kett. vol. ii. 22.

name of *St. Anthony's fire ;** but neither these monks, nor any other Catholics, were used to invoke that inflammation, or any other burning whatsoever, from heaven or elsewhere. I beg that you and your friends will suspend your opinion of the fourth alleged resemblance between Antichrist and the Pope, that of persecuting the saints, till I have leisure to treat that subject in greater detail than I can at present. I shall take no notice at all of this writer's chronological calculations, nor of the anagrams and chronograms by which many Protestant expounders have endeavoured to extract the mysterious number six hundred and sixty-six from the name or title of certain Popes, farther than to observe, that ingenious Catholics have extracted the same number from the name *Martinus Lutherus*, and even from that of David Chrytheus, who was the most celebrated inventor of those riddles.

Such are the grounds on which certain refractory children, in modern ages, have ventured to call their true mother *a prostitute*, and the common father of Christians, the author of their own conversion from Paganism, *The Man of Sin*, and the very *Antichrist*. But they do not really believe what they declare; their object being only to inflame the ignorant multitude. I have sufficient reason to think this, when I hear a Luther threatening to unsay all that he had said against the Pope, a Melancthon lamenting, that Protestants had renounced him, a Beza negotiating to return to him, and a late Warburton-lecturer lamenting, on his deathbed, that he could not do the same.

I am, &c.

J. M.

* Pasquotius, In Molanum De Sacr. Imag.

N 2

LETTER XLVI.

To the Rev. ROBERT CLAYTON, M. A.

ON THE POPE'S SUPREMACY.

Rev. Sir,

THIS acknowledges the honour of three different letters from you, which I have not, till now, been able to notice. The objections, contained in the two former, are either answered, or will, with the help of God, be answered by me. The chief purport of your last, is to assure me, that the absurd and impious tenet, of the Pope being Antichrist, never was a part of your faith, nor even your opinion; but that having read over Dr. Barrow's *Treatise of the Pope's Supremacy*, as well as what bishop Porteus has published upon it, you cannot but be of archbishop Tillotson's mind, who published the above named treatise, namely, that " The Pope's Supremacy is not only an indefensible, but also an impudent cause; that there is not one tolerable argument for it, and that there are a thousand invincible reasons against it."* Your liberality, Rev. sir, on the former point, justifies the idea I had formed of you: with respect to the second, whether the Pope's claim of Supremacy, or Tillotson's assertion concerning it, is *impudent*, I shall leave you to determine, when you shall have perused the present letter. But, as this, like other subjects of our controversy, has been enveloped in a cloud of misrepresentation, I must begin with dissipating this cloud, and with clearly stating what the faith of the Catholic church is concerning the matter in question.

It is not, then, the faith of this church, that the Pope has any civil or temporal supremacy, by virtue of which he can depose princes, or give or take away the property of other persons, out of his own domain: for even the incarnate Son of God, from whom he derives the supremacy, which he possesses, did not claim, here upon earth, any right of the above-mentioned kind: on the contrary, he positively declared, that his *kingdom is not of this world'!* Hence, the Catholics of both our Islands, have, without impeachment even from Rome, denied, upon oath, that " the Pope has any civil jurisdiction, power, superi-

* Tillotson's Preface to Barrow's Treatise.

brity, or pre-eminence, directly or indirectly, within this realm."* But, as it is undeniable, that different Popes, in former ages, have pronounced sentence of deposition against certain contemporary princes, and, as great numbers of theologians have held (though not as a matter of faith) that they had a right to do so, it seems proper, by way of mitigating the odium which Dr. Porteus and other Protestants raise against them, on this head, to state the grounds, on which the pontiffs acted and the divines reasoned in this business.. Heretofore, the kingdoms, principalities, and states, composing the Latin church, when they were all of the same religion, formed, as it were, one Christian republic, of which the Pope was the accredited head. Now, as mankind have been sensible at all times, that the duty of civil allegiance and submission cannot extend beyond a certain point, and that they ought not to surrender their property, lives and morality, to be sported with by a Nero or a Heliogabalus; instead of deciding the nice point for themselves, when resistance becomes lawful, they thought it right to be guided by their chief pastor. The kings and princes themselves acknowledged this right in the Pope, and frequently applied to him to make use of his indirect, temporal power, as appears in numberless instances.† In latter ages, however, since Christendom has been disturbed by a variety of religions, this power of the pontiff has been generally withdrawn: princes make war upon each other, at their pleasure, and subjects rebel against their princes, as their passions dictate,‡ to the great detriment of both parties, as may be gather-

* 31. Geo. III. c. 32.

† See in Mat. Paris, A. D. 1195, the appeal of our king Richard I, to Pope Celestin III, against the duke of Austria for having detained him prisoner at Trivallis, and the Pope's sentence of excommunication against that duke for refusing to do him justice.

‡ In every country, in which Protestantism was preached, sedition and rebellion, with the total or partial deposition of the lawful sovereign, ensued, not without the active concurrence of the preachers themselves. Luther formed a league of princes and states in Germany against the emperor, which desolated the empire for more than a century. His disciples, Muncer and Stork, taking advantage of the pretended *evangelical liberty*, which he taught, at the head of 40,000 Anabaptists, claimed the empire and possession of the world, in quality of *the meek ones*, and enforced their demand with fire and sword, dispossessing princes and lawful owners, &c. Zuinglius lighted up a similar flame throughout Switzerland, at Geneva, &c. and died fighting, sword in hand, for the Reformation, which he preached. The United States embraced Protestantism and renounced their sovereign, Philip, at the same time. The Calvinists of France, in conformity with the doctrine of their master, namely, that " princes deprive themselves of their power, when they resist God, and that it is better to spit in their faces than obey them," *Dan.* vi. 28, as soon as they found themselves strong enough, rose in arms against their sovereigns, and dispossessed them of half their dominions. Knox, Goodman, Buchanan, and the other preachers of Presbyterianism in Scotland, having taught the peo-

ed from what sir Edward Sandys, an early and zealous Protestant writes. "The Pope was the common Father, adviser, and conductor of Christians, to reconcile their enmities, and decide their differences."* I have to observe, secondly, that the question here is not about the personal qualities, or conduct of any particular Pope, or of the Popes in general; at the same time, it is proper to state, that in a list of two hundred and fifty-three Popes, who have successively filled the chair of St. Peter, only a small comparative number of them, have disgraced it, while a great proportion of them have done honour to it, by their virtues and conduct. On this head, I must again quote Addison, who says; "the Pope is generally a man of learning and virtue, mature in years and experience, who has seldom any vanity or pleasure to gratify at his people's expense, and is neither encumbered with wife and children, or mistresses."†

In the third place, I must remind you and my other friends, that I have nothing here to do with the doctrine of the Pope's individual infallibility, (when pronouncing *Ex Cathedra*, as the term is, he addresses the whole church, and delivers the faith of it upon some contested article,)‡ nor would you, in case you were to become a Catholic, be required to believe in any doctrines, except such as are held by the whole Catholic church, with the Pope at its head. But, without entering into this or

---

ple, that "princes may be deposed by their subjects, if they be tyrants against God and his truth:" and that "It is blasphemy to say that kings are to be obeyed, good or bad," disposed them for the perpetration of those riots and violences, including the murder of Cardinal Beaton, and the deposition and captivity of their lawful sovereign, by which Protestantism was established in that country. With respect to England, no sooner was the son of Henry dead, than a Protestant usurper, lady Jane, was set up, in prejudice of his daughters, Mary and Elizabeth, and supported by Cranmer, Ridley, Latimer, Sandys, Poynet, and every Reformer of any note, because she was a Protestant. Finally, it was upon the principles of the Reformation, especially that of each man's explaining the Scripture for himself, and a hatred of Popery, that the Grand Rebellion was begun and carried on, till the king was beheaded and the constitution destroyed. Has then the cause of humanity, or that of peace and order, been benefitted by the change in question?

　* Survey of Europe, p. 202.
　† Remarks on Italy, p. 112.
　‡ The following is a specimen of Barrow's and Tillotson's chicanery in their *Treatise of the Supremacy*. Bellarmin, in working up an argument on the Pope's infallibility, says, *hypothetically* by way of proving the falsehood of his opponent's doctrine, that "this doctrine would oblige the church to believe *vices to be good, and virtues to be bad,* in case the Pope were to err in teaching this." Bell. De Rom. Pont. l. iv. c. 5. Hence these writers take occasion to affirm, that Bellarmin *positively teaches,* that "if the Pope should err, by enjoining vices, or forbidding virtues, the church should be bound to believe vices to be good and virtues evil!" p 203. This shameful misrepresentation has been taken up by most subsequent Protestant controvertists.

any other scholastic question, I shall content myself with observing, that it is impossible for any man of candour and learning, not to concur with a celebrated Protestant author, namely, Causabon, who writes thus: " No one, who is the least versed in ecclesiastical history, can doubt, that God made use of the holy See, during many ages, to preserve the doctrines of faith !"*

At length we arrive at the question itself, which is, whether the bishop of Rome, who, by pre-eminence, is called *Papa (Pope,* or *father of the faithful)* is or is not entitled to a superior rank and jurisdiction, above other bishops of the Christian church, so as to be its *spiritual head* here upon earth, and so that his See is *the centre of Catholic unity?* All Catholics necessarily hold the affirmative of this question, while the abovementioned tergiversating primate denies, that there is a tolerable argument in its favour.† Let us begin with consulting the New Testament, in order to see, whether or no the first Pope or bishop of Rome, St. Peter, was any way superior to the other apostles. St. Matthew, in numbering up the apostles, expressly says of him, *THE FIRST, Simon, who is called Peter,* Mat. x. 2. In like manner, the other Evangelists, while they class the other apostles differently, still give the first place to Peter.‡ In fact, as Bossuet observes,§ " St. Peter was the first to confess his faith in Christ ;‖ the first to whom Christ appeared, after his resurrection ;¶ the first to preach the belief of this to the people ;** the first to convert the Jews ;†† and the first to receive the Gentiles."‡‡ Again I would ask, is there no distinction implied, in St. Peter's being called upon by Christ to declare three several times, that he *loved* him, and even that he *loved him more than* his fellow apostles, and in his being each time charged to *feed Christ's lambs,* and, at length, *to feed his sheep also,* whom the lambs are used to follow ?§§ What else is here signified, but that this apostle was to act the part of a shepherd, not only with respect to the flock in general, but also

* Exercit. xv. ad Annal. Baron.

† Tillotson's father was an Anabaptist, and he himself was professedly a Puritan preacher, till the Restoration, so that there is reason to doubt whether he ever received either Episcopal Ordination or Baptism. His successor, Secker, was also a Dissenter, and his baptism has been called in question. The former, with bishop Burnet, was called upon to attend lord Russel at his execution, when they absolutely insisted, as a point necessary for salvation, on his disclaiming the lawfulness of resistance in any case whatever. Presently after, the revolution happening, they themselves declared for lord Russel's principles.

‡ Mark iii. 16. Luke vi. 14. Acts i. 13. § Orat. ad Cler.
‖ Mat. xvi. 16. ¶ Luke xxiv. 34. ** Acts ii. 14.
†† Ver. 37. ‡‡ Ibid. x. 47. §§ John xxi. 15.

with respect to the pastors themselves? The same is plainly signified by our Lord's prayer for the faith of this apostle, in particular, and the charge that he subsequently gave him: *Simon, Simon, behold Satan has desired to have you, that he may sift you, as wheat: but I have prayed for thee, that thy faith fail not; and thou, being once converted, confirm thy brethren.* Luke xxii. 32. Is there no mysterious meaning in the circumstance, marked by the Evangelist, of Christ's *entering into Simon's ship*, in preference to that of James and John, in order to *teach the people out of it*, and in the subsequent miraculous *draught of fishes*, together with our Lord's prophetic declaration to Simon: *Fear not, from henceforth thou shalt catch men.* Luke v. 3. 10. But the strongest proof of St. Peter's superior dignity and jurisdiction consists in that explicit and energetical declaration, of our Saviour to him, in the quarters of Cesarea Philippi, upon his making that glorious confession of our Lord's divinity: *Thou art Christ, the Son of the living God.* Our Lord had mysteriously changed his name, at his first interview with him, when Jesus looking upon him, said, *Thou art Simon, the Son of Jona; thou shalt be called Cephas, which is interpreted Peter,* John i. 42: and, on the present occasion, he explains the mystery, where he says, *Blessed art thou Simon, Bar-Jona: because flesh and blood hath not revealed it to thee, but my Father, who is in heaven: And I say to thee: that thou art Peter* (a rock,) *and UPON THIS ROCK I WILL BUILD MY CHURCH, and the gates of hell shall not prevail against it: and I will give to thee the keys of the kingdom of Heaven: and whatsoever thou shalt bind on earth, shall be bound in heaven; and whatsoever thou shalt loose on earth, shall be loosed also in heaven.* Mat. xvi. 17, 18, 19. Where now, I ask, is the sincere Christian, and especially the Christian who professes to make Scripture the sole rule of his faith, who, with these passages of the inspired text before his eyes, will venture, at the risk of his soul, to deny that any special dignity or charge was conferred upon St. Peter, in preference to the other apostles? I trust no such Christian is to be found in your society. Now, as it is a point agreed upon, at least in your church and mine, that bishops, in general, succeed to the rank and functions of the apostles, so, by the same rule, the successor of St. Peter, in the See of Rome, succeeds to his primacy and jurisdiction. This cannot be questioned by any serious Christian, who reflects, that, when our Saviour gave his orders about *feeding his flock,* and made his declaration about building his church, he was not establishing an order of things to last during the few

years that St. Peter had to live, but one that was to last as long
as he should have a flock and a church on earth, that is to
the end of time; conformably with his promise to the apostles,
and their successors, in the concluding words of St. Matthew :
Behold I am with you always, even to the end of the world. Mat.
xxviii. 20.

That St. Peter (after governing for a time, the patriarchate
of Antioch, the capital of the East, and thence sending his
disciple, Mark, to establish that of Africa at Alexandria) finally fixed his own See at Rome, the capital of the world, that his
successors there have each of them exercised the power of supreme pastor, and have been acknowledged as such by all
Christians, except by notorious heretics and schismatics, from
the apostolic age down to the present, the writings of the fathers, doctors, and historians of the church unanimously testify.
St. Paul, having been converted, and raised to the apostleship
in a miraculous manner, thought it necessary to *go up to Jerusalem to see Peter*, where he *abode with him fifteen days.* Galat.
i. 18.   St. Ignatius, who was a disciple of the apostles, and
next successor, after Evodius, of St. Peter in the See of Antioch, addresses his most celebrated epistle to the church, which
he says, " PRESIDES in the country of the Romans."*
About the same time, dissensions taking place in the church of
Corinth, the case was referred to the church of Rome, to which
the Holy Pope Clement, *whose name is written in the book of
life*, Philip. iv. 3, returned an apostolical answer of exhortatio
and instruction.†

In the second century, St. Irenæus who had been instructed by
St. Polycarp, the disciple of St. John the Evangelist, referring to
the tradition of the apostles, preserved in the church of Rome, calls
it " the greatest, most ancient, and most universally known, as
having been founded by St. Peter and St. Paul; to which (he says)
every church is bound to conform, by reason of its superior
authority."‡   Tertullian, a priest of the Roman church, who
flourished near the same time, calls St. Peter, " the rock of the
church," and says, that " the church was built upon him."§
Speaking of the bishop of Rome, he terms him in different
places, " the blessed Pope, the high priest, the apostolic prelate, &c."   I must add, that, at this early period, Pope Victor
exerted his superior authority, by threatening the bishops of
Asia with excommunication for their irregularity in celebrating

* Πρoκαθηνται, Epist. Ignat. Cotelero.   † Coteler.
‡ " Ad hanc ecclesiam convenire necesse est omnem ecclesiam." Contra
Hæres. l. iii. c. 3.   § Prescrip. l. i. c. 22. De Monogam.

Easter, and the other moveable feasts, from which rigorous measure he was deterred, chiefly by St. Irenæus.* In the third century, we hear Origen† and St. Cyprian repeatedly affirming, that the church was " founded on Peter," that he " fixed his chair at Rome," that this is " the mother church," and " the root of Catholicity."‡ The latter expresses great indignation that certain African schismatics should dare to approach " the See of Peter, the head church and source of ecclesiastical unity."§ It is true, this father afterwards had a dispute with Pope Stephen, about rebaptizing converts from heresy; but this proves nothing more than that he did not think the Pope's authority superior to general tradition, which, through mistake, he supposed to be on his side. To what degree, however, he did admit this authority, appears by his advising this same Pope, to depose Marcian, a schismatical bishop of Gaul, and to appoint another bishop in his place.‖ At the beginning of the fourth century we have the learned Greek historian, Eusebius, explaining in clear terms, the ground of the Roman pontiff's claim to superior authority, which he derives from St. Peter;¶ we have also the great champion of orthodoxy and the patriarch of the second See in the world, St. Athanasius, appealing to the bishop of Rome, which See he terms " the mother and the head of all other churches."** In fact, the Pope reversed the sentence of deposition, pronounced by the saint's enemies, and restored him to his patriarchal chair.†† Soon after this, the council of Sardica confirmed the bishop of Rome, in his right of receiving appeals from all the churches in the world.‡‡ Even the Pagan historian, Ammianus, about the same time, bears testimony to the superior authority of the Roman Pontiff.§§ In the same century, St. Basil, St. Hilary, St. Epiphanius, St. Ambrose, and other fathers and doctors, teach the same thing. Let it suffice to say, that the first named of these scruples not to advise, that the Pope should send visiters to the eastern churches, to correct the disorders, which the Arians had caused in them,‖‖ and that the last mentioned represents communion with the bishop of Rome, as communion with the Catholic church.¶¶ I must add, that the great St. Chrysostom, having been, soon after, unjustly deposed from his seat in the Eastern Metropolis, was restored to it by the au-

---

* Euseb. Hist. Eccles. l. v. c. 24.   † Hom. 5 in Exod. Hom. 17 in Luc.
‡ Ep. ad Cornel. Ep. ad Anton. De Unit. &c.   § Ep. ad Cornel. 55.
‖ Ep. 29.   ¶ Euseb. Chron. An. 44.   ** Epist. ad Marc.
†† Socrat. Hist. l. ii. c. 2. Zozom.   ‡‡ Can. 3.
§§ Rerum Gest. l. xv.   ‖‖ Epist. 52.   ¶¶ Orat. in Obit. Satyr.

thority of Pope Innocent; that Pope Leo termed his church " the head of the world, because its spiritual power, as he alleged, extended farther than the temporal power of Rome had ever extended."* Finally, the learned St. Jerom, being distracted with the disputes among three parties, which divided the church of Antioch, to which church he was then subject, wrote for directions, on this head, to Pope Damasus, as follows: " I, who am but a sheep, apply to my shepherd for succour. I am united with your holiness, that is to say, with the chair of Peter, in communion. I know that the church is built upon that *rock*. He who eats the Paschal Lamb out of that house, is profane. Whoever is not in Noah's Ark will perish by the deluge. I know nothing of Vitalis, I reject Melitius, I am ignorant of Paulinus: he who does not gather with thee, scatters," &c.† It were useless, after this, to cite the numerous testimonies to the Pope's supremacy, which St. Augustin, and all the fathers, doctors, and church historians, and all the general councils bear, down to the present time. However, as the authority of our apostle, Pope Gregory the Great, is claimed by most Protestant divines on their side, and is alluded to by Bp. Porteus,‡ merely for having censured the pride of John, patriarch of C. P. in assuming to himself the title of *Œchumenical* or *universal bishop;* it is proper to show, that this Pope, like all the others who went before him, and came after him, did claim and exercise the power of supreme pastor, throughout the church. Speaking of this very attempt of John, he says, " The care of the whole church was committed to Peter, and yet he is not called the universal apostle."§ With respect to the See of C. P. he says, " Who doubts but it is subject to the apostolic See;" and again, " When bishops commit a fault, I know not what bishop is not subject to it," *(the See of Rome.)*‖ As no Pope was ever more vigilant, in discharging the duties of his exalted station, than St. Gregory, so none of them, perhaps, exercised more numerous or widely extended acts of the supremacy, than he did. It is sufficient to cite here his directions to St. Austin of Canterbury, whom he had sent into this island, for the conversion of our Saxon ancestors, and who had consulted him, by letter, how he was to act with respect to the French bishops, and the bishops of this

* Serm. de Nat. Apos. This sentiment, another father of the church, in the following century, St. Prosper, expressed in these lines: " Sedes Roma Petri, quae pastoralis honoris; Facta caput mundo, quidquid non possidet armis; Religione tenet." † Ep ad Damas.
‡ P. 78. § Ep. Greg. l. v. 20. ‖ L. ix. 59.

island, namely, the British prelates in Wales, and the Pictish and Scotch in the northern parts.　To this question Pope Gregory returns an answer in the following words: " We give you no jurisdiction over the bishops of Gaul, because, from ancient times, my predecessors have conferred the *Pallium* (the ensign of legatine authority) on the bishop of Arles, whom we ought not to deprive of the authority he has received.　But we commit all the bishops of Britain to your care, that the ignorant among them may be instructed, the weak strengthened, and the perverse corrected by your authority."*　After this is it possible to believe that Bp. Porteus and his fellow writers ever read Venerable Bede's History of the English nation ?　But if they could even succeed in proving that Christ had not built his church upon St. Peter and his successors, and had not given them the keys of the kingdom of heaven ; it would still remain for them to prove, that he had founded any part of it on Henry VIII, Edward VI, and their successors, or that he had given the mystical keys to Elizabeth and her successors.　I have shown, in a former letter, that these sovereigns exercised a more despotic power over all the ecclesiastical and spiritual affairs of this realm, than any Pope ever did, even in the city of Rome, and that the changes in religion, which took place in their reigns, were effected by them and their agents, not by the bishops or any clergy whatever; and yet no one will pretend to show from Scripture, tradition, or reason, that these princes had received any greater power from Christ over the doctrine and discipline of his church, than he conferred upon Tiberius, Pilate, or Herod, or than he has given at the present day, to the great Turk or the Lama of Thibet, in their respective dominions.

Before I close this letter I think it right to state the sentiments of a few eminent Protestants respecting the Pope's supremacy. I have already mentioned, that Luther acknowledged it, and submissively bowed to it, during the three first years of his dogmatizing about justification ; and till his doctrine was condemned at Rome.　In like manner, our Henry VIII. asserted it, and wrote a book in defence of it, in reward of which the Pope conferred upon him and his successors the new title of *Defender of the Faith.*　Such was his doctrine ; till, becoming amorous of his queen's maid of honour, Ann Bullen, and finding the Pope conscientiously inflexible in refusing to grant him a divorce from the former, and to sanction an adulterous connexion with the latter, he set himself up, as *supreme head of the*

* Hist. Bed. l. l. c. 27. Resp. 9. Spelm. Concil. p. 98.

church of England, and maintained his claim by the arguments
of halters, knives, and axes.   James I, in his first speech in parliament, termed Rome " the mother church," and in his writings allowed the Pope to be " The patriarch of the West."
The late archbishop Wake, after all his bitter writings against
the Pope and the Catholic church, coming to discuss the terms
of a proposed union between this church and that of England,
expressed himself willing to allow a certain superiority to the
Roman pontiff.*   Bishop Bramhall had expressed the same
sentiment,† sensible as he was, that no peace or order could
subsist in the Christian church, any more than in a political
state, without a supreme authority.   Of the truth of this maxim,
two others, among the greatest men whom Protestantism has to
boast of, the Lutheran Melancthon, and the Calvinist Hugo
Grotius, were deeply persuaded.   The former had written to
prove the Pope to be Antichrist; but seeing the animosities,
the divisions, the errors, and the impieties of the pretended reformers, with whom he was connected, and the utter impossibility of putting a stop to these evils, without returning to the
ancient system, he wrote thus to Francis I, of France : " We
acknowledge, in the first place, that ecclesiastical government
is a thing holy and salutary : namely, that there should be certain bishops to govern the pastors of several churches, and that
THE ROMAN PONTIFF should be above all the bishops.
For the church stands in need of governors, to examine and
ordain those who are called to the ministry, and to watch over
their doctrine; so that, if there were no bishops, they ought to
be created."‡   The latter great man, Grotius, was learned,
wise, and always consistent.   In proof of this he wrote as follows, to the minister, Rivet : " All who are acquainted with
Grotius, know how earnestly he has wished to see Christians
united together in one body. This he once thought might have
been accomplished by a union among Protestants, but afterwards, he saw that this is impossible. Because, not to mention
the aversion of Calvinists to every sort of union, Protestants
are not bound by any ecclesiastical government, so that they
can neither be united at present, nor prevented from splitting
into fresh divisions. Therefore Grotius now is fully convinced,

* " Suo Gaudeat qualicunque Primatu." See Maclain's Third Appendix to
Mosheim's Eccl. Hist. vol. v.
† Answer to Militiere.
‡ D'Argentre, Collect. Jud. t. i, p. 2.—Bercastel and Feller relate, that Melanc
thon's mother, who was a Catholic, having consulted him about her religion, h
persuaded her to continue in it.

ıs many others are also, that Protestants never can be united among themselves, unless they join those who adhere to the Roman See; without which there never can be any general church government. Hence he wishes that the revolt and the causes of it may be removed, among which causes, the primacy of the bishop of Rome was not one, as Melancthon confessed, who also thought that primacy necessary to restore union."[*]

I am, &c.
J. M.

LETTER XLVII.

To JAMES BROWN, Jun. Esq.

ON THE LANGUAGE OF THE LITURGY AND ON READING THE HOLY SCRIPTURES.

DEAR SIR,

I AGREE with your worthy father, that the departure of the Rev. Mr. Clayton, to a foreign country, is a loss to your Salopian Society in more respects than one; and as it is his wish that I should address the few remaining letters I have to write, in answer to bishop Porteus's book, to you, sir, who, it seems, agree with him in the main, but not altogether, on religious subjects, I shall do so, for your own satisfaction and that of your friends, who are still pleased to hear me upon them. Indeed the remaining controversies between that prelate and myself are of light moment, compared with those I have been treating of, as they consist chiefly of disciplinary matters, subject to the control of the church, or of particular facts misrepresented by his lordship.

The first of these points of changeable discipline, which the bishop mentions, or rather declaims upon throughout a whole chapter, is the use of the Latin tongue in the public liturgy of the Latin church. It is natural enough that the church of England, which is of modern date, and confined to its own domain, should adopt its own language, in its public worship;

---

* Apol. ad Rivet.

and, for a similar reason, it is proper that the great Western or Latin church, which was established by the apostles, when the Latin tongue was the vulgar tongue of Europe, and which still is the common language of educated persons in every part of it, should retain this language in her public service. When the bishop complains of " our worship being performed in *an unknown tongue*,"* and of our " wicked and cruel cunning in *keeping people in darkness*,"† by this means, under pretext that 'they reverence what they do not understand,"‡ he must be conscious of the irreligious calumnies he is uttering : knowing, as he does, that Latin is, perhaps, still the most general language of Christianity,§ and that, where it is not commonly understood, it is *not the church which has introduced a foreign language* among the people, but it is the *people* who have *forgotten their ancient language.* So far removed is the Catholic church from " the wicked and cruel cunning of keeping people in ignorance," by retaining her original apostolical languages, the Latin and the Greek ; that she strictly commands her pastors every where, " to inculcate the word of God, and the lessons of salvation, to the people, in their vulgar tongue, every Sunday and festival throughout the year,"|| and " to explain to them the nature and meaning of her divine worship as frequently as possible."¶ In like manner, we are so far from imagining that the less our people understand of our liturgy, the more they reverence it, that we are quite sure of precisely the contrary; particularly with respect to our principal liturgy, the adorable sacrifice of the mass. True it is, that a part of this is performed by the priest in silence, because, being a sacred action, as well as a form of words, some of the prayers which the priest says, would not be proper or rational in the mouths of the people. Thus, the high priest of old went *alone* into the tabernacle, to make the atonement;** and thus Zachary offered incense in the temple by *himself*; while the multitude prayed without.†† But this is no detriment to the faithful, as they have translations of the liturgy, and other books in their hands, by means of which, or of their own devotion, they can join with the priest in every part of the solemn worship ; as

* P. 76. † P. 63. ‡ P. 65.
§ The Latin language is vernacular in Hungary and the neighbouring countries: it is taught in all the Catholic settlements of the universe, and it approaches so near to the Italian, Spanish, and French, as to be understood, in a general kind of way, by those who use these languages.
‖ Concil. Trid. Sess. xxiv. c 7. ¶ Idem. Sess. xxi. c. 8.
** Levit. xvi. 17. †† Luke i. 10.

the Jewish people united with their priests, in the sacrifices above-mentioned.

But we are referred by his lordship to 1 *Cor.* xiv. in order " to see what St. Paul would have judged of the Romanists practice" in retaining the Latin liturgy, (which, after all, he himself and St. Peter established where it now prevails;) I answer, that there is not a word in that chapter which mentions or alludes to the public liturgy, which at Corinth was, as it is still performed in the old Greek; the whole of it regarding an imprudent and ostentatious use of the gift of tongues, in speaking all kinds of languages, which gift many of the faithful possessed, at that time, in common with the apostles. The very reason, alleged by St. Paul, for prohibiting extemporary prayers and exhortations, which no one understood, namely, that *all things should be done decently and according to order*, is the principal motive of the Catholic church, for retaining, in her worship, the original languages employed by the apostles. She is, as I before remarked, a *universal church*, spread over the face of the globe, and composed *of all nations, and tribes, and tongues*, Rev. vii. 9, and these tongues constantly changing; so that instead of the uniformity of worship, as well as of faith, which is so necessary for that *decency and order*, there would be nothing but confusion, disputes, and changes in every part of her liturgy, if it were performed in so many different languages, and dialects; with the constant danger of some alteration or other in the essential forms, which would vitiate the very sacrament and sacrifice. The advantage of an ancient language, for religious worship, over a modern one, in this and other respects, is acknowledged by the Cambridge professor of divinity, Dr. Hey. He says, that such a one " is fixed and venerable, free from vulgarity, and even more perspicuous."* But to return to bishop Porteus's appeal to the judgment of St. Paul, concerning " the Romanists practice" in retaining the language with the substance of their primitive liturgy, I leave you, dear sir, and your friends, to pronounce upon it, after I shall have stated the following facts: 1st, that St. Paul himself wrote an Epistle, which forms part of the liturgy of all Christian churches, to these very *Romanists*, in the *Greek language*, though they themselves made use of the Latin :† 2dly, that the Jews, after they had exchanged their original Hebrew for the Chaldaic tongue, during the Babylonish captivity, continued to perform their liturgy in the former language, though the vul-

---

* Lectures, vol. iv. p. 191.   † St. Jerom, Epist. 123.

gar did not understand it,* and that our Saviour Christ, as
well as his apostles, and other devout friends, attended this service in the temple, and the synagogue, without ever censuring
it : 3dly, that the Greek churches, in general, no less than the
Latin church, retain their original pure Greek tongue in their
liturgy, though the common people have forgotten it, and
adopted different barbarous dialects instead of it :† 4thly that
patriarch Luther maintained, against Carlostad, that the language of public worship, was a matter of indifference : hence,
his disciples professed, in their Ausburg Confession, to retain the
Latin language in certain parts of their service : lastly, that
when the establishment endeavoured, under Elizabeth, and
afterwards, under Charles I. to force their liturgy upon the
Irish Catholics, it was not thought necessary to translate it into
Irish, but it was constantly read in English, of which the natives did not understand a word : thus " furnishing the Papist
with an excellent argument against themselves," as Dr. Heylin
observes.‡

The bishop has next a long letter on what he calls, *the prohibition of the Scriptures*, by the Romanists, in which he con-
fuses and disguises the subjects he treats of, to beguile and inflame ignorant readers. I have treated this matter, at some
length, in a former letter, and therefore shall be brief in what I
write upon it in this : but what I do write shall be explicit and
clear. It is a wicked calumny, then, that the Catholic church
undervalues the Holy Scriptures, or prohibits the use of them:
on the contrary, it is she that has religiously preserved them,
as the inspired word of God, and his invaluable gift to man,
during these eighteen centuries : it is she alone, that can and
does vouch for their *authenticity*, their *purity*, and their *inspiration*. But, then, she knows that there is an *unwritten word
of God*, called tradition, as well as *a written word*, the Scriptures ; that the former is the *evidence* for *the authority* of the
latter, and that, when nations had been *converted*, and churches
formed by the *unwritten word*, the authority of this was nowise
abrogated by the inspired Epistles and Gospels, which the
apostles and evangelists occasionally sent to such nations or
churches. In short, both these words together form the Catholic rule of faith. On the other hand, the church, consisting,
according to its more general division, of two distinct classes,

* Walton's Polyglot Proleg. Hey, &c.
† Mosheim, by Maclaine, vol. ii. p. 575.
‡ Ward has successfully ridiculed this attempt in his *England's Reformation*,
Canto II.

the *pastors* and their *flocks*, the *preachers* and their *hearers*, each has its particular duties in the point under consideration, as well as in other respects. The pastors are bound to study the rule of faith in both its parts, with unwearied application, to be enabled to acquit themselves of the *first of all their duties*, that of *preaching the Gospel* to their people.* Hence St. Ambrose calls the sacred Scripture *the Sacerdotal Book*, and the council of Cologne orders that it should " never be out of the hands of ecclesiastics." In fact, the Catholic clergy must, and do employ no small portion of their time, every day, in reading different portions of Holy Writ. But no such obligation is generally incumbent on the flock, that is, on the laity; it is sufficient for them to hear the word of God from those whom God has appointed to announce and to explain it to them, whether by sermons, or catechisms, or other good books, or in the tribunal of penance. Thus, it is not the bounden duty of all good subjects to read and study the laws of their country: it is sufficient for them to hear and to submit to the decisions of the judges, and other legal officers, pronouncing upon them; and, by the same rule, the latter would be inexcusable if they did not make the law and constitution their constant study, in order to decide right. Still, however, the Catholic church never did prohibit the reading of the Scriptures to the laity; she only required, by way of preparation, for this most difficult and important study, that they should have received so much education, as would enable them to read the sacred books in their original languages, or in that ancient and venerable Latin version, the fidelity of which she guarantees to them; or, in case they were desirous of reading it in a modern tongue, that they should be furnished with some attestation of their piety and docility, in order to prevent their turning this salutary food of souls into a deadly poison, as, it is universally confessed, so many thousands constantly have done. At present, however, the chief pastors have every where relaxed these disciplinary rules, and vulgar translations of the whole Scripture are upon sale, and open to every one, in Italy itself, with the express approbation of the Roman pontiff. In these islands, we have an English version of the Bible, in folio, in quarto, and in octavo forms, against which our opponents have no other objection to make, except that it is too literal,† that is, too faithful. But Dr. Porteus professes not to admit of any restriction whatever " on

* Trid. Sess. v. cap. 2.   Sess. xxv. cap. 4.
† See the bishop of Lincoln's Elements of Theol. vol. ii. p. 16.

the reading of what heaven hath revealed, with respect to any part of mankind." No doubt, *the revealed truths themselves* are to be made known as much as possible, to all mankind ; but it does not follow from hence, that all mankind are to read the Scriptures : there are passages in them, which, I am confident, his lordship would not wish his daughters to peruse ; and which, in fact, were prohibited to the Jews, till they had attained the age of thirty.*   Again, as lord Clarendon, Mr. Grey, Dr. Hey, &c. agree, that the misapplication of Scripture was the cause of the destruction of church and state, and of the murder of the king in the grand rebellion, and as he must be sensible, from his own observation, that the same cause exposed the nation to the same calamities in the Protestant riots of 1780, I am confident the bishop, as a Christian, no less than as a British subject would have taken the Bible out of the hands of Hugh Peters, Oliver Cromwell, lord George Gordon, and their respective crews, if this had been in his power : I will affirm the same, with respect to count Emanuel Swedenborg, the founder of the modern sect of Jerusalemites, who taught, that no one had understood the Scriptures, till the sense of them was revealed to him ; as also with respect to Joanna Southcote, foundress of a still more modern sect, and who, I believe, tormented the bishop himself with her rhapsodies, in order to persuade him, that she was the woman of Genesis, destined *to crush the serpent's head,* and the woman of the Revelations, *clothed with the sun, and crowned with twelve stars.*   Nay, I greatly deceive myself if the prelate would not be glad to take away every hot-brained Dissenter's Bible, who employs it in persuading the people, that the church of England is a rag of Popery, and a spawn of the whore of Babylon.   In short, whatever Dr. Porteus may choose to say of an unrestricted perusal and interpretation of the Scriptures, with respect to all sorts of persons, it is certain, that many of the wisest and most learned divines of his church have lamented this, as one of her greatest misfortunes.   I will quote the words of one of them : " Aristarchus, of old, could hardly find seven wise men in all Greece : but, amongst us, it is difficult to find the same number of ignorant persons.   They are all doctors and divinely inspired.   There is not a fanatic or a mountebank, from the lowest class of the people, who does not vent his dreams for the word of God.   The bottomless pit seems to be opened, and there come out of it locusts with stings ; a swarm of sectaries and heretics, who have renewed

---

* St. Jerom in Proem Ezech. St. Greg. Naz. de Moderand Disp.

2 P

all the heresies of former ages, and added to them numerous
and monstrous errors of their own.*

Since the above was written, the *Bibliomania*, or rage for
the letter of the Bible, has been carried, in this country, to the
utmost possible length, by persons of almost every description,
Christians and Infidels; Trinitarians, who worship God in
three persons, and Unitarians, who hold such worship to be
idolatrous; Pædobaptists who believe they became Christians
by baptism; Anabaptists, who plunge such Christians into the
water, as mere Pagans; and Quakers, who ridicule all baptism, except that of their own imagination; Arminian Methodists, who believe themselves to have been justified without repentance, and Antinomian Methodists, who maintain, that they
shall Be saved without keeping the laws either of God or man;
Churchmen, who glory in having preserved the whole orders
and part of the missal and ritual of the Catholics; and the
countless sects of Dissenters, who join in condemning these
things as Antichristian Popery: all these have forgotten, for a
time, their characteristical tenets, and united in enforcing the
reading of the Bible, as the only thing necessary! The Bible
Societies are content, that all these contending religionists
should affix whatever meaning they please to the Bible, provided only they read the text of the Bible! Nay, they are
satisfied if they can but get the Hindoo worshippers of Juggernaut, the Thibet adorers of the Grand Lama, and the Taboo
cannibals of the Pacific Ocean to do the same thing, vainly
fancying, that this lecture will reform the vicious, reclaim the
erroneous, and convert the Pagans. In the mean time, the experience of fourteen years proves, that theft, forgery, robbery,
murder, suicide, and other crimes go on increasing with the
most alarming rapidity; that every sect clings to its original
errors, that not one Pagan is converted to Christianity, nor one
Irish Catholic persuaded to exchange his faith for a Bible
Book. When will these Bible enthusiasts comprehend, what
learned and wise Christians of every age have known and
taught, that *the word of God consists not in the letter of Scripture, but in the meaning of it!* Hence it follows, that a Catholic child, who is grounded in his short but comprehensive
First Catechism, so called, knows more of the revealed word of
God, than a Methodist preacher does, who has read the whole
Bible ten times over. The sentiment expressed above is not only
that of St. Jerom† and other Catholic writers, but also of the

---

* Walton's Polyglot Prolegom.　　† Cap. 1 ad Galat.

learned Protestant bishop, whom I have already quoted. He
says, " The word of God does not consist in mere letters, but
in the sense of it, which no one can better interpret than the
true church, to which Christ committed this sacred deposite."*

I am, &c.

J. M

LETTER XLVIII.

To JAMES BROWN, Jun. Esq.

ON VARIOUS MISREPRESENTATIONS.

DEAR SIR,

THE learned prelate, who is celebrated for having concen-
trated the five sermons of his patron, archbishop Secker, and
the more diffusive declamation of primate Tillotson against
Popery; having gone through his regular charges on this topic, tries, in the end, to overwhelm the Catholic cause, with an
accumulation of petty, or, at least, secondary objections, in a
chapter which he entitles: *various corruptions and superstitions
of the church of Rome.* The first of these is, that Catholics
" equal the apocryphal with the canonical books" of Scripture :† to which I answer, that the same authority, namely, the
authority of the Catholic church, in the fifth century, which
decided on the canonical character of the Epistle to the Hebrews, the Revelations, and five other books of the New Testament, on the character of which till that time, the Fathers and
ecclesiastical writers were not agreed, decided also on the can-
nonicity of the Books of Toby, Judith, and five other books of
the Old Testament, being those which the prelate alludes to as
apocryphal. If the church of the fifth century deserves to be
heard in one part of her testimony, she evidently deserves to
be heard in the other part.—His second objection is, that " The
Romish church," as he calls *the Catholic church,* has made " a
modern addition of five new sacraments, to the two appointed
by Christ; making also the priest's intention necessary to the

---

* Walton's Proleg.   † P. 70

benefit of them." I have, in the course of these letters, vindicated the divine institution of these five sacraments, and have shown, that they are acknowledged to be sacraments no less than the other two, by the Nestorian and Eutychian heretics, &c. who separated from the church almost 1400 years ago, and in short, by all the Christian congregations of the world, except a comparatively few modern ones, called Protestants, in the north of Europe. Is it from ignorance, or wilful misrepresentation, that the bishop of London charges " the *Romish church* with the *modern* addition of five new sacraments?" With respect to the *intention of the minister* of a sacrament, I presume there is no sensible person who does not see the essential difference there is between an action that is *seriously performed,* and the *mimicking* or *mockery* of it by a comedian or buffoon. Luther, indeed, wrote, that " the Devil himself would perform a true sacrament, if he used the right matter and form :" but I trust, that you, sir, and my other friends, will not subscribe to such an extravagance. I have also discussed the subjects of relics and miracles, which the prelate next brings forward; so that it is not necessary for me to say any thing more about them, than that the church, instead of " venerating fictitious relics, and inventing lying miracles," as he most calumniously accuses her of doing, is strict to an excess, in examining the proofs of them both, as he would learn, if he took pains to inquire. In short, there are but about two or three articles in his lordship's accumulated charges against his *mother church*, which seem to require a particular answer from me at present. One of these is the following: " Of the same bad tendency is their (the Catholics) engaging such multitudes of people in vows of celibacy and useless retirement from the world, their obliging them to silly austerities and abstinences, of no real value, as matters of great merit."* In the first place, the church never *engages* any person whomsoever in a vow of celibacy; on the contrary, she exerts her utmost power and severest censures, to prevent this obligation from being contracted *rashly,* or under any *undue influence.*† True it is, she teaches, that continency is a state of greater perfection than matrimony; but so does St. Paul ‡ and Christ himself,§ in words too explicit and forcible to admit of controversy on the part of any sincere Christian. True it is, also, that having the choice of her sacred ministers, she selects those for the service of her altar, and for

---

* P. 70.   † Concil. Trid. Sess. xxv. De Reg. cap. 15, 16, 17, 18.
‡ See the whole chapter vii. of 1 Cor.   § Mat. xix 12.

assisting the faithful in their spiritual wants, who voluntarily embrace this more perfect state :* but so has the Establishment expressed her wish to do also, in that very act which allows her clergy to marry.† In like manner, I need go no further than the homily on fasting, or the " table of Vigils, fasts, and days of abstinence, to be observed in the year," prefixed to *The Common Prayer Book*, to justify our doctrine and practice, which the bishop finds fault with, in the eyes of every consistent Church-Protestant. I believe the most severe austerities of our saints never surpassed those of Christ's precursor, whom he so much commended,‡ clothed as he was with hair-cloth, and fed with the locusts of the desert.

In a former letter to your society, I have replied to what the bishop here says concerning the deposing of kings by the Roman pontiff, and have established facts by which it appears, that more princes were actually dispossessed of the whole, or a large part, of their dominions, by the pretended gospel-liberty of the Reformation, within the first fifty years of this being proclaimed, than the Popes had attempted to depose during the preceding fifteen hundred years of their supremacy. To this accusation another of a more alarming nature is tacked, that of our " annulling the most sacred promises and engagements, when made to the prejudice of the church."§ These are other words for the vile hackneyed calumny of our *not keeping faith with heretics.*‖ In refutation of this, I might appeal to the doctrine of our Theologians,¶ and to the oaths of the British Catholics ; but I choose rather to appeal to historical facts, and to the practical lessons of the leading men by whom these have been conducted. I have mentioned, that when the Catholic queen Mary came to the throne, a Protestant usurper, lady Jane, was set up against her, and that the bishops Cranmer,

* The second Council of Carthage, can. 3, and St. Epiphanius Hær. 48, 59, trace the discipline of sacerdotal continence up to the Apostles.

† " Although it were not only better for the estimation of priests and other ministers, to live chaste, sole, and separated from women, and the bond of marriage, but also they might thereby the better attend to the administration of the Gospel; and it were to be wished that they would willingly endeavour themselves to a life of chastity, &c." 2 Edw. vi. c. 21. See the injunction of queen Elizabeth against the admission of women into colleges, cathedrals, &c. in Strype's Life of Parker. See likewise a remarkable instance of her rudeness to that archbishop's wife. Ibid. and in Nichol's Progresses, A. D. 1561. ‡ Mat. xi. 9. § P. 71.

‖ In the Protestant Charter-school Catechism, which is taught by authority, the following question and answer occur p. 9. " Q. How do Papists treat those whom they call heretics?—A. They hold that faith is not to be kept with heretics, and that the Pope can absolve subjects from their oath of allegiance to their Sovereigns."

¶ See in particular the Jesuit Becanus *De Fide Hæreticis prestanda.*

Ridley, Latimer, Hooper, Rogers, Poynet, Sandys, and every
other Protestant of any note, broke their allegiance and engagements to her, for no other reason than because she was a
Catholic, and the usurper a Protestant. On the other hand,
when Mary was succeeded by her Protestant sister, Elizabeth,
though the Catholics were then far more numerous and powerful than the Protestants, not a hand was raised, nor a seditious
sermon preached against her. In the mean time, on the other
side of the Tweed, where the new Gospellers had deposed their
sovereign, and usurped her power, their apostle Knox publicly
preached, that " neither promise nor oath can oblige any man
to obey or give assistance to tyrants against God ;"* to which
lesson his colleague, Goodman, added: " If governors fall from
God, to the gallows with them."† A third fellow-labourer in
the same Gospel cause, Buchanan, maintained, that " princes
may be deposed by their people, if they be tyrants against God
and his truth, and that their subjects are free from their oaths
and obedience."‡ The same, in substance, were the maxims
of Calvin, Beza, and the Huguenots of France, in general: the
temporal interest of their religion was the ruling principle of
their morality. But, to return to our own country: the enemies of church and state having hunted down the earl of Straf-
ford, and procured him to be attainted of high treason, the
king, Charles I, declared that he *could not, in conscience, concur
to his death*, when the case being referred to the archbishops,
Usher and Williams, and three other Anglican bishops, they
decided (in spite of his majesty's conscience, and his oath to
administer justice in mercy) that he might, *in conscience*, send
this *innocent peer to the block*, which he did accordingly.§ I
should like to ask bishop Porteus, whether this decision of his
predecessors was not *the dispensation of an oath*, and the *annulling of the most sacred of all obligations?* In like manner,
most of the leading men of the nation, with most of the clergy,
having sworn to the *Solemn League and Covenant*, " for the

* In his book addressed to the nobles and people of Scotland.

† De Obedient.

‡ History of Scotland.—The same was the express doctrine of the Geneva Bible, translated by Coverdale, Goodman, &c. in that city, and in common use
among the English Protestants, till king James's reign: for in a note on verse 12
of 2d Mat. these translators expressly say, " A promise ought not to be kept,
where God's honour and *preaching of his truth* is injured." Hist. Account of Eng.
Translations, by A. Johnson, in Watson's Collect. vol. iii. p. 93.

§ Collier's Church History, vol. ii. p. 801.—On the other hand, when several of
the Parliament's soldiers, who had been taken prisoners at Brentford, had sworn
never again to bear arms against the king, they were " absolved from that oath,"
says Clarendon. " by their divines." Exam. of Neal's Hist. by Grey, vol. iii. p. 10

more effectual extirpation of Popery," they were *dispensed with* from the keeping of it, by an express clause in the act of uniformity.* But whereas, by a clause of the oath in the same act, all subjects of the realm, down to constables and schoolmasters, were obliged to swear, that " It is not lawful, upon *any pretence whatsoever,* to take up arms against the king;" this oath, in its turn, was universally dispensed with, in the churches and in parliament, at the Revolution. I have mentioned these few facts and maxims concerning Protestant dispensations of oaths and engagements, in case any of your society may object, that some Popes have been too free in pronouncing such dispensations. Should this have been the case, they alone, personally, and not the Catholic church, were accountable for it, both to God and man.

I have often wondered, in a particular manner, at the confidence with which bishop Porteus asserts and denies facts of ancient Church History, in opposition to the known truth. An instance of this occurs in the conclusion of the chapter before me, where he says : " The primitive church did not attempt, for several hundreds of years, to make any doctrine necessary, which we do not : as the learned well know from their writings."† The falsehood of this position must strike you, on looking back to the authorities adduced by me from the ancient fathers and historians, in proof of the several points of controversy which I have maintained : but, to render it still more glaring, I will recur to the histories of AERIUS and VIGILANTIUS, two different heretics of the fourth century. Both St. Epiphanius,‡ and St. Austin,§ rank Aerius among the heresiarchs, or founders of heresy, and both give exactly the same account of his three characteristical errors; the first of which is avowed by all Protestants, namely, that " prayers and sacrifices are not to be offered up for the dead," and the two others by most of them, namely, that " there is no obligation of observing the appointed days of fasting, and that priests ought not to be distinguished, in any respect, from bishops."‖ So far were the primitive Christians from tolerating these heresies, that its supporters were denied the use of a place of worship, and were forced to perform it in forests and caverns.¶ Vigilantius likewise condemned prayers for the dead, but he equally reprobated prayers to the saints, the honouring

* Statute 13 and 14 Car. II, cap. 4. † P. 73. ‡ Hæresis 75.
§ De Hæres. tom. vi. Ed. Frob.
‖ Ibid. St. John Damascen and St. Isidore equally condemn these tenets as heretical ¶ Fleury's Hist. ad An. 392.

of their relics, and the celibacy of the clergy, together with vows
of continence in general. Against these errors, which I need
not tell you Dr. Porteus now patronises, as Vigilantius formerly did, St. Jerom directs all the thunder of his eloquence, declaring them to be *sacrilegious*, and the author of them to be a
*detestable heretic.** The learned Fleury observes, that the impious novelties of this heretic made no proselytes, and therefore,
that there was no need of a council to condemn them.† Finally, to convince yourself, dear sir, how far the ancient fathers
were from tolerating different communions or religious tenets
in the Catholic church, conformably to the prelate's monstrous
system, of a Catholic church, composed of all the discordant
and disunited sects in Christendom, be pleased to consult again
the passages which I have collected from the works of the
former, in my fourteenth letter to your society; or, what is still
more demonstrative, on this point, observe, in ecclesiastical
history, how the Quartodecimans, the Novatians,‡ the Donatists, and the Luciferians, though their respective errors are
mere molehills, compared with the mountains, which separate
the Protestant communions from ours, were held forth as heretics by the fathers, and treated as such by the church, in her
councils.

I am, &c.

J. M.

---

* Epist. 1 and 2, adversus Vigilan.   † Ad An. 405.

‡ St. Cyprian being consulted about the nature of Novatian's errors, answers:
" there is no need of a strict inquiry *what errors* he teaches while he *teaches out of
the church.*" He elsewhere writes: " The church being one, cannot he, at the
same time, within and without. If she be with Novatian, she is not with (Pope)
Cornelius; if she be with Cornelius, Novatian is not in her." Epist. 76 ad Mag.

LETTER XLIX.

To *JAMES BROWN*, Jun. *Esq.*

ON RELIGIOUS PERSECUTION.

DEAR SIR,

I PROMISED to treat the subject of religious persecution apart, a subject of the utmost importance in itself, and which is spoken of by the bishop of London in the following terms: " They, the Romish church, zealously maintain their claim of punishing whom they please to call heretics, with penalties, imprisonment, tortures, death."* Another writer, whom I have quoted above, says, that this church " breathes the very spirit of cruelty and murder;"† indeed most Protestant controvertists seem to vie with each other in the vehemence and bitterness of the terms by which they endeavour to affix this most odious charge, of cruelty and murder, on the Catholic church. This is the favourite topic of preachers, to excite the hatred of their hearers against their fellow Christians: this is the last resource of baffled oratorical hypocrites: *if you admit the Papists*, they cry, *to equal rights, these wretches must and will certainly murder you, as soon as they can: the fourth Lateran council has established the principle, and the bloody queen Mary has acted upon it.*

I. To proceed regularly in this matter: I begin with expressly denying the bishop of London's charge; namely, that the Catholic church " *maintains a claim* of punishing heretics with penalties, imprisonment, tortures, and death;" and I assert, on the contrary, that she *disclaims the power* of so doing. Pope Leo the Great, who flourished in the fourth century, writing about the Manichean heretics, who, as he asserted, " laid all modesty aside, prohibiting the matrimonial connexion, and subverting all law, human and divine," says, that " the ecclesiastical lenity was content, even in this case, with the sacerdotal judgment, and avoided all sanguinary punishments,"‡ however the secular emperors might inflict them for reasons of state. In the same century, two Spanish bishops, Ithacius and Idacius, having

---

* P. 71.   † De Coetlogon's Seasonable Caution, p. 15.
‡ Epist. ad Turib.

interfered in the capital punishment of certain Priscillian heretics, both St. Ambrose and St. Martin refused to hold communion with them, even to gratify an emperor, whose clemency
they were soliciting in behalf of certain clients.　Long before
their time, Tertullian had taught, that " It does not belong to
religion to force religion;"* and a considerable time after it,
when St. Austin and his companions, the envoys of Pope Gregory the Great, had converted our king Ethelbert, to the Christian faith, they particularly inculcated to him, not to use forcible means to induce any of his subjects to follow his example,†
But what need of more authorities on this head, since our canon
law, as it stood in ancient times, and as it still stands, renders
all those who have actively concurred to the death or mutilation of any human being, whether Catholic or heretic, Jew or
Pagan, even in a just war, or by exercising the art of surgery,
or by judicial proceedings, *irregular*, that is to say, such persons cannot be promoted to holy orders, or exercise those
orders, if they have actually received them.　Nay, when an
ecclesiastical judge or tribunal has, after due examination, pronounced that any person, accused of obstinate heresy, is actually
guilty of it, he is required by the church, expressly, to declare
in her name, that her power extends no further than such decision; and, in case the obstinate heretic is liable, by the laws
of the state, to suffer death or mutilation, he is required to pray
for his pardon.　Even the council of Constance, in condemning John Huss of heresy, declared that its power extended no
further.‡

II. But, whereas many heresies are subversive of the established governments, the public peace, and natural morality, it
does not belong to the church to prevent princes and states
from exercising their just authority in repressing and punishing
them, when this is judged to be the case; nor would any clergyman incur irregularity by exhorting princes and magistrates
to provide for those important objects, and the safety of the
church itself, by repressing its disturbers, provided he did not
concur to the death or mutilation of any particular disturber.
Thus it appears, that though there have been persecuting laws
in many Catholic states, the church itself, so far from *claiming*,
actually *disclaims the power of persecuting*.

III. But Dr. Porteus signifies,§ that the church itself has
claimed this power in the third canon of the fourth Lateran

---

council, A. D. 1215, by the tenour of which, temporal lords and magistrates were required to exterminate all heretics from their respective territories, under pain of these being confiscated to their sovereign prince, if they were laymen, and to their several churches, in case they were clergymen. From this canon, it has been, a hundred times over, argued against Catholics, of late years, not only that their church claims a right to exterminate heretics, but also requires those of her communion to aid and assist in this work of destruction, at all times, and in all places. But it must first be observed, *who were present* at this council, and by *whose authority* these decrees, of a temporal nature, were passed. There were then present, besides the Pope and the bishops, either in person or by their ambassadors, the Greek and the Latin emperors; the kings of England, France, Hungary, the Sicilies, Arragon, Cyprus, and Jerusalem; and the representatives of a vast many other principalities and states; so that, in fact, this council was a congress of Christendom, temporal, as well as spiritual. We must, in the next place, remark the *principal business*, which drew them together. It was the *common cause of Christianity and human nature;* namely, the extirpation of the Manichean heresy, which taught, that there were two first principles, or Deities; one of them the creator of devils, of animal flesh, of wine, of the Old Testament, &c.; the other, the author of good spirits, of the New Testament, &c.; that unnatural lusts were lawful, but not the propagation of the human species; that perjury was permitted to them, &c.* This detestable heresy, which had caused so much wickedness and bloodshed in the preceding centuries, broke out with fresh fury, in the twelfth century, throughout different parts of Europe, more particularly in the neighbourhood of Albi, in Languedoc, were they were supported by the powerful counts of Tholouse, Comminges, Foix, and other feudatory princes; as also by numerous bodies of banditti, called Rotarii, whom they hired for this purpose. Thus strengthened, they set their sovereigns at defiance, carrying fire and sword through their dominions, murdering their subjects, particularly the clergy, burning the churches and monasteries, and, in short, waging open war with them, and, at the same time, with Christianity, morality, and human nature itself; casting the Bibles into the jakes, profaning the altar-plate, and

* See the Protestant historian Mosheim's account of the the shocking violation of decency and other crimes of which the Albigenses, Brethren of the Free Spirit, &c. were guilty in the 13th century. Vol. iii. p. 284.

29*

practising their detestable rites for the extinction of the human species. It was to put an end to these horrors, that the great Lateran council was held, in the year 1215, when the heresy itself was condemned by the proper authority of the church, and the lands of the feudatory lords, who protected it, were declared to be forfeited to the sovereign princes, of whom they were held, by an authority derived from those sovereign princes. The decree of the council regarded only the *prevailing heretics of that time*, who, though " wearing different faces," being indifferently called Albigenses, Cathari, Poplicolæ Paterini, Bulgari, Bacomilii, Beguini, Beguardi, and Brethren of the Free Spirit, &c. were " all tied together by the tails," as their council expresses it, like Sampson's foxes, in the same band of Manicheism.* Nor was this exterminating canon ever put in force against any other heretics except the Albigenses, nor even against them, except in the case of the above named counts; it was never so much as published, or talked of, in these islands : so little have Protestants to fear from their Catholic fellow-subjects, by reason of the third canon of the council of Lateran.†

IV. But they are chiefly the Smithfield fires of queen Mary's reign, which furnish matter for the inexhaustible declamation of Protestant controvertists, and the unconquerable prejudices of the Protestant populace against the Catholic religion, as " breathing the very spirit of cruelty and murder," according to the expression of the above quoted orators. Nevertheless, I have unanswerably demonstrated elsewhere,‡ that, " if queen Mary was a persecutor, it was not in virtue of the tenets of her religion that she persecuted." I observed, that during almost two years of her reign, no Protestant was molested on account of his religion; that in the instructions, which the Pope sent her for her conduct on the throne, there is not a word to recommend persecution; nor is there one word in the synod, which the Pope's legate, Cardinal Pole, held at that time, as Burnet remarks, in favour of persecution. This representative of his holiness even opposed the persecution project, with all

* For a succinct, yet clear account of Manicheism, see Bossuet's Variations, Book xl ; also, for many additional circumstances relating to it, see Letters to a Prebendary, Letter IV.

† For an account of the rebellions and antisocial doctrine and practices of the Wickliffites and Hussites, see the last quoted work, Letter IV; also History of Winchester, vol. i. p. 296.

‡ Letters to a Prebendary, Letter IV, on persecution; also History of Winchester, vol. i. p. 354, &c. See in the former, p. 149, &c. proofs of the infidelity of the famous martyrologist, John Fox, and of the great abatements which are to be made in his account of the Protestant sufferers.

his influence, as did king Philip's chaplain also, who even preached against it, and defied the advocates of it to produce an authority from Scripture in its favour.   In a word, we have the arguments made use of in the queen's council, by those advocates for persecution, Gardiner, Bonner, &c. by whose advice it was adopted ; yet none of them pretended, that the doctrine of the Catholic church required such a measure   On the contrary, all their arguments are grounded on motives of state policy.   Indeed, it cannot be denied, that the first Protestants, in this, as in other countries, were possessed of, and actuated by a spirit of violence and rebellion.   Lady Jane was set up and supported in opposition to the daughters of king Henry, by all the chief men of the party, both churchmen and laymen, as I have observed. Mary had hardly forgiven this rebellion, when a fresh one was raised against her, by the duke of Suffolk, sir Thomas Wynt, and all the leading Protestants.   In the mean time, her life was attempted by some of them, and her death was publicly prayed for by others; while Knox and Goodman, on the other side of the Tweed, were publishing books *Against the Monstrous regiment of Women*, and exciting the people of this country, as well as their own, to *put their Jezabel to death*.   Still, I grant, persecution was not the way to diminish the number or the violence of the enthusiastic insurgents.   With toleration and prudence, on the part of the governors, the paroxysm of the governed would quickly have subsided.

V. Finally; whatever may be said of the intolerance of Mary, I trust that this charge will not be brought against the next Catholic sovereign, James II.   I have elsewhere * shown, that, when duke of York, he used his best endeavours to get the act, *De Heretico Comburendo*, repealed, and to afford an asylum to the Protestant exiles, who flocked to England, from France, on the revocation of the edict of Nantz, and, in short, that, when king, he lost his crown in the cause of toleration: *his Declaration of Liberty of Conscience,* having been the determining cause of his deposition. But what need of words to disprove the odious calumny, that Catholics " breathe the spirit of cruelty and murder," and are obliged, by their religion, to be persecutors, when every one of our gentry, who has made the tour of France, Italy, and Germany, has experienced the contrary ; and has been as cordially received by the Pope himself, in his metropolis of Rome, where he is both prince and

History of Winchester, vol. i. p. 437, Letters to a Prebendary, p. 376.

bishop, in the character of an English Protestant, as if he were known to be the most zealous Catholic!—Still, I fear, there are some individuals in your society, as there are many other Protestants of my acquaintance elsewhere, who cling fast to this charge against Catholics, of persecution, as the last resource for their own intolerance; and, it being true, that Catholics have, in some times and places, unsheathed the sword against the heterodox, these persons insist upon it, that it is an essential part of the Catholic religion to persecute. On the other hand, many Protestants, either from ignorance or policy, nowadays, claim for themselves, exclusively, the credit of toleration. As an instance of this, the bishop of Lincoln writes: " I consider toleration as a mark of the true church, and as a principle, recommended by the most eminent of our reformers and divines."* In these circumstances, I know but of one argument to stop the mouths of such disputants, which is to prove to them, that persecution has not only been more generally practised by Protestants than by Catholics, but also, that it has been more warmly defended and supported by the most eminent " Reformers and divines" of their party, than by their opponents.

I. The learned Bergier defies Protestants to mention so much as a town, in which their predecessors, on becoming masters of it, tolerated a single Catholic in it.† Rousseau, who was educated a Protestant, says, that " the Reformation was intolerant from it cradle, and its authors universally persecutors."‡ Bayle, who was a Calvinist, has published much the same thing. Finally, the Huguenot minister, Jurieu, acknowledges, that " Geneva, Switzerland, the Republics, electors and princes of the empire, England, Scotland, Sweden, and Denmark, had all employed the power of the state to abolish Popery, and establish the Reformation."§ But to proceed to other more positive proofs of what has been said; the first father of Protestantism, finding his new religion, which he had submitted to the Pope, condemned by him, immediately sounded the trumpet of persecution and murder against the pontiff, and all his supporters in the following terms: " If we send thieves to the gallows, and robbers to the block, why do we not fall on those masters of perdition, the Popes, cardinals, and bishops, with all our force, and not give over till we have bathed our hands in their blood?"‖ He elsewhere calls the Pope, " a mad wolf, against

---

* Charge in 1812.   † Trait. Hist. et Dogmat.
‡ Letters de la Mont.
§ Tab. Lett. quoted by Bossuet, Avertiss, p. 625.
‖ Ad Silvest. Pereir.

whom every one ought to take arms, without waiting for an order from the magistrate." He adds, " if you fall before the beast has received its mortal wound, you will have but one thing to be sorry for, that you did not bury your dagger in its breast. All that defend him must be treated like a band of robbers, be they kings or be they Cæsars."* By these and similar incentives, with which the works of Luther abound, he not only excited the Lutherans themselves to propagate their religion by fire and sword against the emperor and other Catholic princes, but also gave occasion to all the sanguinary and frantic scenes, which the Anabaptists played, at the same time, through the lower part of Germany. Coeval with these was the civil war, which another arch-reformer, Zuinglius, lighted up in Switzerland, by way of propagating his peculiar system, and the persecution which he raised equally against the Catholics and the Anabaptists. Even the moderate Melancthon wrote a book in defence of religious persecution,† and the conciliatory Bucer, who became professor of divinity at Cambridge, not satisfied with the burning of the heretic, Servetus, preached that " his bowels ought to have been torn out, and his body chopped to pieces."‡

II. But the great champion of persecution, every one knows, was the founder of the second great branch of Protestantism, John Calvin. Not content with burning Servetus, beheading Gruet, and persecuting other distinguished Protestants, Castallo, Bolsec, and Gentilis, (who being apprehended in the neighbouring Protestant canton of Berne, was put to death there) he set up a consistorial inquisition at Geneva, for forcing every one to conform to his opinions, and required, that the magistrates should punish whomever this consistory condemned. He was succeeded in his spirit, as well as in his office, by Beza, who wrote a folio work in defence of persecution.§ In this he shows, that Luther, Melancthon, Bullinger, Capito, no less than Calvin, had written works, expressly in defence of this principle, which, accordingly, was firmly maintained by Calvin's followers, particularly in France. Bossuet refers to the public records, of Nismes, Montpelier and other places, in proof of the directions, issued by the Calvinist consistories to their generals, for " forcing the Papists to embrace the Reformation by taxes, quartering soldiers upon them, demolishing their houses, &c."

* Theses apud Sleid. A. D. 1545. Opera Luth. tom. i.
† Beza, De Hæret. puniend.
‡ Ger. Brandt. Hist. Abreg. Refor. Pais Bas, vol. l. p. 454.
§ De Hæreticis puniendis a Civili Magistratu, &c. à Theod. Beza.

and he says, " the wells into which the Catholics were flung,
and the instruments of torture which were used at the first mentioned city, to force them to attend the Protestant sermons, are
things of public notoriety."*　In fact, who has not read of the
infamous baron D'Adrets, whose savage sport it was, to torture
and murder Catholics, in a Catholic kingdom, and who forced
his son literally to wash his hands in their blood?　Who has
not heard of the inhuman Jane, queen of Navarre, who massa-
cred priests and religious persons, by hundreds, merely on account of their sacred character?　In short, Catholic France,
throughout its extent, and during a great number of years, was
a scene of desolation and slaughter, from the unrelenting persecution of its Huguenot subjects.　Nor was the spectacle dis-
similar in the Low Countries, when Calvinism got a footing in
them.　Their first synod, held in 1574, equally proscribed the
Catholics and the Anabaptists, calling upon the magistrates to
support their decrees,† which decrees were renewed in several
subsequent synods.　I have elsewhere quoted a late Protestant
writer, who, on the authority of existing public records, describes the horrible torments with which Vandermerk and Sonoi,
two generals of the prince of Orange, put to death incredible
numbers of Dutch Catholics.‡　Other writers furnish more
ample materials of the same kind.§　But while the Calvinist
ministers continued to stimulate their magistrates to redoubled
severities against the Catholics, for which purpose, among
other means, they translated into Dutch and published the
above-mentioned work of Beza, a new object of their persecution arose in the bosom of their own society; Arminius, Vos-
sius, Episcopius, and some other divines, supported by the illustrious statesmen, Barnevelt and Grotius, declared against the
more rigorous of Calvin's maxims.　They would not admit,
that God decrees men to be wicked, and then punishes them
everlastingly for what they cannot help; nor that many persons
are in his actual grace and favour, while they are immersed in
the most enormous crimes.　For denying this, Barnevelt was
beheaded,‖ Grotius was condemned to perpetual imprisonment,
and all the remonstrant clergy, as they were called, were banished, at the requisition of the synod of Dort, from their families and their country, with circumstances of the greatest cruelty.

---

* Variat. L. x. m. 52.　　　　　　　† Brandt, vol. i. p. 227.
‡ P. 283.　Letters to a Prebend. p. 103.
§ See the learned Estius's History of the Martyrs of Gorcum; De Brandt, &c.
‖ Diodati, quoted by Brandt, says that the canons of Dort carried off the head of
Barnevelt.

In speaking of Lutheranism, I have passed by many persecuting decrees and practices of its adherents against Calvinists and Zuinglians, and many more of Calvinists against Lutherans; while both parties agreed in showing no mercy to the Anabaptists. Before I quit the continent, I must mention the Lutheran kingdoms of Denmark and Sweden, in both which, as Jurieau has signified above, the Catholic religion was extirpated, and Protestantism established by means of rigorous, persecuting laws, which denounced the punishment of death against the former. Professor Messenius, who wrote about the year 1600, mentions four Catholics who had recently been put to death, n Sweden, on account of their religion, and eight others who aad been imprisoned and tortured on that account, of whom he aimself was one.*

III. To pass over now, to the northern part of our own island: the first reformers of Scotland, having deliberately murdered Cardinal Beaton, archbishop of St. Andrew's,† and riotously destroyed the churches, monasteries, and every thing else, which they termed monuments of Popery, assembled in a tumultuous and illegal manner, and before even their own religion was established by law, they condemned the Catholics to capital punishment for the exercise of theirs: " such strangers," says Robertson, " were men, at that time, to the spirit of toleration and the laws of humanity !"‡ Their chief apostle was John Knox, an apostate friar, who, in all his publications and sermons, maintained, that " it is not birth, but God's election, which confers a right to the throne and to magistracy ;" that " no promise or oath, made to an enemy of the truth, that is to a Catholic, is binding ;" and that " every such enemy, in a high station, is to be deposed."§ Not content with threatening to depose her, he told his queen, to her face, that the Protestants had a right to take the sword of justice into their hands, and to punish her, as Samuel slew Agag, and as Elias slew Jezabel's prophets.|| Conformably with this doctrine, he wrote into England, that " the nobility and people were bound in conscience, not only to withstand the proceedings of that Jezabel, Mary, whom they call queen, but also to put her to death, and all her priests with her."¶ His fellow apostles, Goodman, Willox, Buchanan, Rough, Black, &c. constantly inculcated to

* Scandia Illustrat. quoted by Le Brun. Mess. Explic. t. iv. p. 40.
† Gilb. Stuart's Hist. of Ref. in Scot. vol. i. p. 47, &c.
‡ Hist of Scotland, An. 1560.   § See Collier's Ecc. Hist. vol. ii. p 442.
|| Stuart's Hist. vol. i. p. 59.
¶ Cited by Dr. Paterson, in his Jerus. and Babel.

the people the same seditious and persecuting doctrine; and the
Presbyterian ministers, in general, earnestly pressed for the
execution of their innocent queen, who was accused of a murder, perpetrated by their own Protestant leaders.*   The same
unrelenting intolerance was seen among " the most moderate"
of their clergy, " when they were assembled by order of king
James and his council, to inquire whether the Catholic earls of
Huntly, Errol, and their followers, on making a proper concession, might not be admitted into the church, and be exempt
from further punishment?"   These ministers then answered,
that " Though the gates of mercy are always open for those
who repent, yet, as these noblemen had been guilty of idolatry,
(the Catholic religion) a crime deserving death by the laws
both of God and man, the civil magistrate could not legally
pardon them, and that, though the church should absolve them,
it was his duty to inflict punishment upon them."†   But we
need not be surprised at any severity of the Presbyterians
against Catholics, when, among other penances, ordained
by public authority, against their own members who should
break the fast of Lent, *whipping in the church* was one.‡

IV. The father of the Church of England, under the authority of the protector Seymour, duke of Somerset, was confessedly
Thomas Cranmer, whom Henry VIII. raised to the archbishopric of Canterbury; of whom it is difficult to say, whether his
obsequiousness to the passions of his successive masters, Henry,
Seymour, and Dudley, or his barbarity to the sectaries who
were in his power, was the more odious.   There is this circumstance, which distinguishes him from almost every other persecutor, that he actively promoted the capital punishment, not
only of those who differed from him in religion, but also of
those who agreed with him in it.   It is admitted by his advocates,§ that he was instrumental, during the reign of Henry, in
bringing to the stake the Protestants, Lambert, Askew, Frith,
and Allen, besides condemning a great many others to it, for
denying the corporal presence of Christ in the sacrament, which
he disbelieved himself;‖ and it is equally certain, that during
the reign of the child Edward, he continued to convict Arians
and Anabaptists capitally, and to press for their execution.
Two of these, Joan Knell and George Van Par, he got actually

---

* Stuart's Hist. vol. i. p. 255   † Robertson's Hist. An. 1596.
‡ Stuart, vol. ii. p. 94.
§ Fox, Acts and Monum.   Fuller's Church Hist. b. v.
‖ See Letters to a Preb. p. 206.

Burnt: preventing the young king, Edward, from pardoning them, by telling him, that " princes being God's deputies, ought to punish impieties against him."* The two next most eminent fathers of the English church were, unquestionably, bishop Ridley, and bishop Latimer, both of them noted persecutors, and persecutors of Protestants to the extremity of death, no less than of Anabaptists and other sectaries!†

Upon the second establishment of the Protestant religion in England, when Elizabeth ascended the throne, it was again buttressed up here, as in every other country, where it prevailed, by the most severe, persecuting laws. I have elsewhere shown, from authentic sources, that above two hundred Catholics were hanged, drawn and quartered during her reign, for the mere profession or exercise of the religion of their ancestors for almost one thousand years. Of this number fifteen were condemned for denying the queen's spiritual supremacy, one hundred and twenty-six for the exercise of their priestly functions, and the rest for being reconciled to the Catholic church, for hearing mass, or aiding and abetting Catholic priests.‡ When to these sanguinary scenes are added those of many hundreds of other Catholics, who perished in dungeons, who were driven into exile, or who were stripped of their property, it will appear, that the persecution of Elizabeth's reign, was far more grievous than that of her sister Mary; especially when the proper deductions are made from the sufferers under the latter.§ Nor was persecution confined to the Catholics; for, when great numbers of foreign Anabaptists, and other sectaries, had fled into England, from the fires and gibbets of their Protestant brethren in Holland, they found their situation much worse here, as they complained, than it had been in their own country. To silence these complaints, the bishop of London, Edwin Sandys, published a book in vindication of religious persecution.‖ In short, the Protestant church and state concurred to their extirpation. An assembly of them, to the number of twenty-seven, having being seized upon in 1575, some of them

---

* Burnet's Ch. Hist. p. ii. b. i.
† See the proofs of these facts collected from Fox, Burnet, Heylin, and Collier, in Letters to a Preb. Let. V.
‡ Certain opponents of mine have publicly objected to me, that these Catholics suffered for *high treason :* true ; the laws of persecution declared so: but their only treason consisted in *their religion.* Thus the Apostles, and other Christian martyrs, were traitors in the eye of the Pagan law ; and the chief priests declared, with respect to Christ himself ; *we have a law, and according to that he ought to die.*
§ See letters to a Prebendary, pp. 149, 150.
‖ Ger. Brandt, Hist. Reform. Abreg. vol. i. p. 234.

were so intimidated as to recant their opinions, some were
scourged, two of them, Peterson and Terwort, were burnt to
death in Smithfield, and the rest banished.* Besides these
foreigners, the English Dissenters were also grievously persecuted. Several of them, such as Thacker, Copping, Green-
wood, Barrow, Penry, &c. were put to death, which rigours
they ascribed principally to the bishops, particularly to Parker,
Aylmer, Sandys, and Whitgift.† The last named, they accused
of being the chief author of the famous inquisitorial court,
called the Star Chamber, which court, in addition to all its
other vexations and severities, employed the rack and torture,
to extort confession.‡ The doctrines and practice of persecution, in England, did not end with the race of Tudor. James
I, though he was reproached with being favourable to the Catholics, nevertheless signed warrants for twenty-five of them
to be hanged and quartered, and sent one hundred and twenty-
eight of them into banishment, barely on account of their religion, besides exacting the fine of 20*l.* per month from those
who did not attend the church service. Still he was repeatedly
called upon by parliament to put the penal laws in force with
greater rigour; in order, say they, " to advance the glory of
Almighty God, and the everlasting honour of your majesty;"§
and he was warned by archbishop Abbot, against tolerating
Catholics, in the following terms: " Your majesty hath propounded a toleration of religion. By your act you labour to
set up that most damnable and heretical doctrine of the church
of Rome, the whore of Babylon; and thereby draw down upon
the kingdom and yourself, God's heavy wrath and indignation."‖ In the mean time the Puritans complained loudly of
the persecution, which they endured from the court of High
Commission, and particularly from archbishop Bancroft, and
the bishops Neale, of Litchfield, and King, of London. They
charged the former of these, with not only condemning Edward
Wightman for his opinions, but also, with getting the king's
warrant for his execution, who was accordingly burnt at Lich-
field; and the latter, with treating, in the same way, Bartholomew Legat, who was consumed in Smithfield.¶ The same
unrelenting spirit of persecution prevailed in the addresses of
parliament, and of many bishops to Charles I, which had dis-

---

* Brandt, vol. i. p. 234. Hist. of Churches of Eng. and Scotl. vol. ii. p. 199.
† Ibid.   ‡ Mosheim, vol. iv. p. 40.
§ Rushworth's Collect. vol. i. p. 141.   ‖ Rushworth's Collect
¶ Chandler's Introduct. to Limborche's Hist. of Inquis. p. 80. Neal's Hist. of
Purit. vol. ii. p. 96.

graced those presented to his father: one of these, signed by the renowned archbishop Usher, and eleven other Irish bishops of the establishment, declares, that " to give toleration to Papists, is to become accessary to superstition, idolatry, and the perdition of souls; and that, therefore, it is *a grievous sin.*"*
At length the Presbyterians, and Independents, getting the upper hand, had an opportunity of giving full scope to their characteristic intolerance. Their divines, being assembled at Sion college, condemned, as an error, the doctrine of toleration, " under the abused term," as they expressed it, " of liberty of conscience"† Conformably with this doctrine, they procured from their parliament a number of persecuting acts, from those of fining, up to those of capital punishment. The objects of them were not only Catholics, but also church of England men,‡ Quakers, Seekers, and Arians. In the mean time, they frequently appointed national fasts to *atone for their pretended guilt, in being too tolerant.*§ Warrants for the execution of four English Catholics, were extorted from the king, while he was in power, and near twenty others were publicly executed under the parliament and the protector. This hypocritical tyrant afterwards invading Ireland, and being bent on exterminating the Catholic population there, persuaded his soldiers, that they had a divine commission for this purpose, as the Israelites had to exterminate the Canaanites.‖ To make an end of the clergy, he put the same price upon a priest's as upon a wolf's head.¶ Those Puritans who, previously to the civil war, had sailed to North America, to avoid persecution, set up a far more cruel one there, particularly against the Quakers, whipping them, cropping their ears, boring their tongues with a hot iron, and hanging them. We have the names of four of these sufferers, one of them a woman, who were executed at Boston.**

IV. The Catholics had behaved with unparalleled loyalty to the king and constitution, during the whole war which the Puritans waged against these. It has even been demonstrated,†† that three-fifths of the noblemen and gentlemen who lost their lives on the side of royalty, were Catholics, and that more than half of the landed property, confiscated by the rebels, be-

* Leland's Hist. of Ireland, vol. ii. p. 482. Neal's Hist. vol. ii. p. 469.
† Hist. of Churches of Eng. and Scotl. vol. iii. ‡ Ibid.
§ Ibid. Neal's Hist.
‖ Anderson's Royal Geneal. quoted by Curry, vol. ii. p. 11.
¶ Ibid. p. 63. ** Neal's Hist. of Churches.
†† Lord Castlemain's Catholic Apology.

longed to the Catholics; add to this, that they were chiefly instrumental in saving Charles II, after his defeat at Worcester, hence there was reason to expect, that the restoration of the king and constitution, would have brought an alleviation, if not an end of their sufferings: but the contrary proved to be the case: for then all parties seem to have combined to make them the common object of their persecuting spirit and fury. In proof of this, I need allege nothing more than that two different parliaments *voted the reality of Oates's Plot!* and that eighteen innocent and loyal Catholics, one of them a peer, suffered the death of traitors, on account of it: to say nothing of seven other priests, who, about that time, were hanged and quartered for the mere exercise of their priestly functions. Among the absurdities of that sanguinary plot, such as those of shooting the king with silver bullets, and invading the island with an army of pilgrims from Compostella, &c.* it was not the least to pretend, that the Catholics wished to kill the king at all; that king whom they had heretofore saved in Staffordshire, and whom they well knew to be secretly devoted to their religion; but any pretext was good which would serve the purposes of a persecuting faction. These purposes were to exclude Catholics not only from the throne, but also from the smallest degree of political power, down to that of a constable, and to shut the doors of both houses of parliament against them. The faction succeeded in its first design by *the Test Act*, and in its second, by the act requiring *the Declaration against Popery;* both obtained at a period of national delirium and fury. What the spirit of the clergy was, at that time, with respect to the oppressed Catholics, appeared at their solemn procession at sir Edmundbury Godfrey's funeral,† and still appears in the three folio volumes of invective and misrepresentation then published, under the title of *A Preservative against Popery.* On the other hand, such was the unchristian hatred of the Dissenters against the Catholics, that they promoted the Test Act with all their power‡ though no less injurious to themselves than to the Catholics, and on every occasion, they refused a toleration which might extend to the latter.§ There is no need of bringing down the history of persecution in this country to a later period than the revolution, at which time, as I observed before, a Catholic king was deposed, because he would not be a persecutor.

---

* Echard's Hist.   † North's Exam. Echard.
‡ Neal's Hist. of Puritans, vol. iv.   Hist. of Churches, vol. iii.
§ Ibid.

Suffice it to say, that the number of penal laws against the professors of the ancient religion, and founders of the constitution of this country, continued to increase in every reign, till that of his present majesty. In the course of this reign most of the old persecuting laws have been repealed, but the two last mentioned, enacted in a moment of delirium, which Hume represents as our greatest national disgrace, I mean the impracticable *Test Act*, and the unintelligible *Declaration against Popery*, are rigidly adhered to under two groundless pretexts. The first of these is, that they are *necessary for the support of the established church:* and yet it is undeniable, that this church had maintained its ground, and had flourished much more during the period which preceded these laws, than it has ever done since that event. The second pretext is, that the withholding of honours and emoluments *is not persecution.* On this point, let a Protestant dignitary of first rate talents be heard: " We agree, that persecution, merely for conscience sake, is against the genius of the gospel: and so is any law for depriving men of their natural and civil rights, which they claim as men. We are also ready to allow, that the smallest negative discouragements, for uniformity's sake, are so many persecutions. An incapacity by law for any man to be made a judge or a colonel, merely on point of conscience, is a negative discouragement, and, consequently, a real persecution," &c.* In the present case, however, the persecution which Catholics suffer from the disabilities in question, does not consist so much in their being deprived of those common privileges and advantages, as in their being *held out by the legislature, as unworthy of them,* and thus being reduced to the condition of *an inferior cast,* in their own country, the country of freedom; this they deeply feel, and cannot help feeling.

V. But to return to my subject: I presume, that if the facts and reflections, which I have stated in this letter, had occurred to the R. Rev. prelates, mentioned at the beginning of it, they would have lowered, if not quite altered, their tone on the present subject: the bishop of London would not have charged Catholics with claiming a right to punish those whom they call heretics, " with penalties, imprisonment, tortures, and death :" nor would the bishop of Lincoln have laid down " toleration as a mark of the true church, and as a principle, recommended by the most eminent reformers and (Protestant) divines." At all events, I promise myself, that a due consideration of the

   * Dean Swift's works, vol. viii. p. 56

points here suggested, will efface the remaining prejudices of certain persons of your society against the Catholic church, on the score of her alleged "spirit of persecution, and of her supposed claim to punish the errors of the mind with fire and sword." They must have seen, that she does not claim, but that, in her very general councils, she has disclaimed all power of this nature; and that, in pronouncing those to be obstinate heretics, whom she finds to be such, she always pleads for mercy, in their behalf, when they are liable to severe punishment from the secular power: a conduct which many eminent Protestant Churchmen, were far from imitating, in similar circumstances. They must have seen, moreover, that, if persecuting laws have been made and acted upon by the princes and magistrates in many Catholic countries, the same conduct has been uniformly practised in every country, from the Alps to the Arctic Circle, in which Protestants, of any description, have acquired the power of so doing. But, if, after all, the friends alluded to, should not admit of any material difference, on one side or the other, in this matter, I will here point out to them two discriminating circumstances of such weight, as must, at once, decide the question about persecution in disfavour of Protestants.

In the first place, when Catholic states and princes have persecuted Protestants, it was done in favour of *an ancient religion*, which had been established in their country, perhaps, a thousand or fifteen hundred years, and which had long preserved the peace, order, and morality of their respective subjects; and when, at the same time, they clearly saw, that any attempt to alter this religion would, unavoidably, produce incalculable disorders, and sanguinary contests among them. On the other hand, Protestants, every where, persecuted in behalf of *new systems*, in opposition to the established laws of the church, and of the respective states. Not content with vindicating their own freedom of worship, they endeavoured, in each country, by persecution, to force the professors of the old religion to abandon it and adopt theirs; and they acted in the same way by their fellow Protestants, who had adopted opinions different from their own. In many countries, where Calvinism got a head, as in Scotland, in Holland, at Geneva, and in France, they were riotous mobs, which, under the direction of their pastors, rose in rebellion against their lawful princes, and having secured their independence, proceeded to sanguinary extremities against the Catholics.

In the second place, If Catholic states and princes have enforced submission to their church by persecution, they were fully persuaded, that there is *a divine authority in this church to decide in all controversies of religion*, and that those Christians who refuse to hear her voice, when she pronounces upon them, are obstinate heretics. But on what ground can Protestants persecute Christians of any description whatsoever? Their grand rule and fundamental charter is, that the *Scriptures were given by God for every man to interpret them, as he judges best.* If, therefore, when I hear Christ declaring, *Take ye and eat, this is my body,* I believe what he says; with what consistency can any Protestants require me, by pains or penalties, to swear that I do not believe it, and that to act conformably with this persuasion is idolatry? But religious persecution, which is every where odious, will not much longer find refuge in the most generous of nations: much less will the many victorious arguments which demonstrate the true church of Christ, our common mother, who reclaimed us all from the barbarous rites of Paganism, be defeated by the calumnious outcry, that she herself is a bloody Moloch, that requires human victims.

I am &c.
J. M.

LETTER L.

To the *FRIENDLY SOCIETY of NEW COTTAGE.*

CONCLUSION.

MY FRIENDS AND BRETHREN IN CHRIST,

HAVING, at length, finished the task you imposed upon me eight months ago, in my several letters to your worthy president, Mr. Brown, and others of your society, I address this, my concluding letter, to you, in common, as a slight review of them. I observed to you, that, to succeed in any inquiry, it is necessary to know and to follow the right method of making it: hence, I entered upon the present important search after the truths of the Christian Revelation, with a discussion of the rules or methods, followed, for this purpose, by different classes of Christians. Having, then, taken for granted the following

maxims,—that *Christ has appointed some rule* or method of
learning his revelation : that this rule must be *an unerring one;*
and that it must be *adapted to the capacities and situations of
mankind*, in general ; I proceeded to show, that a supposed *private spirit*, or particular inspiration, is not that rule ; because
this persuasion has led numberless fanatics, in every age, since
that of Christ, into the depths of error, folly, and wickedness of
every kind. I proved, in the second place, that the written
Word or Scripture, according to each one's conception of its
meaning, is not that rule ; because it is not adapted to the capacity and situation of the bulk of mankind ; a great proportion of them not being able to read the Scripture, and much
less to form a connected sense of a single chapter of it ; and,
because innumerable Christians, at all times, by following this
presumptuous method, have given into heresies, impieties, contradictions, and crimes, almost as numerous and flagrant as
those of the above mentioned fanatics.   Finally, I demonstrated, that there is a two-fold word of God, the unwritten, and
the written ; that the former was appointed by Christ, and
made use of by the apostles, for converting nations ; and that
it was not made void by the inspired Epistles and Gospels,
which some of the apostles, and the evangelists, addressed, for
the most part, to particular churches or individuals ; that the
Catholic church is the divinely commissioned guardian and interpreter of the word of God, in both its parts ; and that,
therefore, the method, appointed by Christ for learning what
he has taught, on the various articles of his religion, is to
HEAR THE CHURCH propounding them to us from the
whole of his rule.   This method, I have shown, continued to
be pointed out by the fathers and doctors of the church, in constant succession, and that it is the only one which is adapted
to the circumstances of mankind, in general ; the only one,
which leads to the peace and unity of the Christian church ;
and the only one, which affords tranquillity and security to individual Christians during life, and at the trying hour of their
dissolution.

At this point, my labours might have ended ; as the Catholic
church alone follows the right rule, and the right rule infallibly
leads to the Catholic church : but since bishop Porteus, and
other Protestant controvertists, raise cavils, as to which is the
true church ; and whereas this is a question, that admits of a
still more easy and more triumphant answer, than that concerning the right rule of faith, I have made this the subject of a
second series of letters, with which, I flatter myself, the greater

part of you are unacquainted. In fact, no inquiry is so easy, to an attentive and upright Christian, as to discover which is the true church of Christ; because, on one hand, all Christians agree, in their common creeds, concerning the characters or marks, which she bears; and because, on the other hand, these marks are of an exterior and splendid kind, such as require no extensive learning or abilities, and little more than the use of our senses and common reason, to discern them. In short, to ascertain which, among the numerous and jarring societies of Christians, all pretending to have found out the truths of Revelation, is the true church of Christ, that necessarily possesses them, we have only to observe which among them is distinctively, ONE, HOLY, CATHOLIC, and APOSTOLICAL, and the discovery is made. In treating of these characters, or marks, I said it was obvious to every beholder, that there is no bond of union whatever among the different societies of Protestants; and that no articles, canons, oaths, or laws, had the force of confining the members of any one of them, as experience shows, to a uniformity of belief, or even profession, in a single kingdom or island; while the great Catholic church, spread as it is over the face of the globe, and consisting, as it does, *of all nations, and tribes, and peoples, and tongues*, is strictly united together, in the same faith, the same sacraments, and the same church-government; in short, that it demonstratively exhibits the first mark of the true church, *unity*.—With respect to the second mark, *sanctity*, I showed, that she, alone, teaches and enforces the *whole doctrine* of the gospel; that she is the mother of all the saints, acknowledged as such by Protestants themselves; that she possesses many *means* of attaining sanctity, which the latter disclaim; and that God himself attests the truth of this church, by the miracles with which, from time to time, he illustrates her exclusively : and, whereas many eminent Protestant writers have charged the Catholics with deception and forgery on this head, I have unanswerably retorted the charge upon themselves. No words were wanting to show, that the *Catholic church* bears the glorious name of CATHOLIC, and very few to demonstrate, that she is *Catholic* or universal, with respect both to place and time, and that she is also *apostolical*. The latter point, however, I exhibited in a more evident and sensible manner, by means of the sketch of an *apostolical tree*, or genealogical table of the church, which I sent you; showing the succession of her pontifis, her most eminent bishops, doctors and saints, as also, of the most notorious heretics and schismatics, who have been lopped off from this

tree, in every age from that of the apostles down to the present
age.   " No church, but the Catholic, can exhibit any thing of
this kind," as Tertullian reproached the seceders of his time.
Under this head, you must have observed, in particular, the
want of an apostolical succession of ministry, which, I showed,
all Protestant societies labour under, and their want of success
in attempting the work of the apostles, the conversion of Pagan
nations.

The third series of my letters has been employed in tearing
off the hideous mask, with which calumny and misrepresentation
had disfigured the fair face of Christ's true spouse, the Catho
lic church.   In this endeavour, I trust, I have been successful,
and that there is not one of your society who will any more reproach Catholics with being Idolaters, on account of their respect for the memorials of Christ and his saints, or of their de
siring the prayers of the latter ; or on account of the adoration
they pay to the divine Jesus, hidden behind the Sacramental
veils: nor will they, hereafter, accuse us of purchasing, or
otherwise procuring leave to commit sin, or the previous pardon
of sins, to be committed ; or, in short, of perfidy, sedition,
cruelty, or systematic wickedness of any kind.   So far from
this, I have reason to hope, that the view of the church herself
which I have exhibited to your society, instead of the caricature of her, which Dr. Porteus, and other bigoted controvertists
have held up to the public, has produced a desire in several of
them to return to the communion of this original church ; bearing, as she clearly does, all the marks of the true church ;
gifted, as she manifestly is, with so many helps for salvation ;
and possessing the only safe and practicable rule for ascertain-
ing the truths of Revelation.   The consideration which, I understand, has struck some of them, in the most forcible manner,
is that which I suggested from my own knowledge and experience, as well as from the observation of the eminent writers
whom I named ; namely, that *no Catholic, at the near approach
of death, is ever found desirous of dying in any other religion,
while numbers of Protestants, in that situation, seek to be recon
ciled to the Catholic religion.*

Some of your number have said, that, though they are of
opinion that the Catholic religion is the true one, yet they have
not that evidence of the fact, which they think sufficient to justify a change in so important a point as that of religion.—God
forbid that I should advise any person to embrace the Catholic
religion, without having sufficient evidence of its truth: but I
must remind the persons in question, that they have not a meta-

physical evidence, or a mathematical certainty of the truth of
Christianity, in general; they have only a moral evidence, and
certainty of it: with all the miracles and other arguments,.by
which Christ and his apostles proved this divine system, it was
still *a stumbling block to the Jews, and folly to the Gentiles,* 1
Cor. i. 23: in short, there is light enough in it to. guide the
sincere faithful, and obscurity enough to mislead the perverse
unbelievers, according to the observation of St. Austin; because, after all, faith is not merely, a divine illustration of the
understanding, but also, a divine, and yet voluntary motion of
the will.   Hence, if, in travelling through this darksome vale
a Locke, I think, observes with respect to Revelation in general, God is pleased to give us the light of the moon or of the
stars, we are not to stand still on our journey, because he does
not afford us the light of the sun.   The same is to be said, with
espect to the evidence in favour of the Catholic religion: it is
moral evidence of the first quality; far superior to that on which
we manage our temporal affairs and guard our lives; and not,
in the least, below that which exists for the truth of Christianity
at large.—At all events, it is wise to choose the safer part: and
it would be madness to act otherwise, when eternity is at stake.
The great advocates of Christianity, SS. Austin, Pascal, Abbadie, and others, argue thus, in recommending it to us, in preference to infidelity: now, the same argument evidently holds
good, for preferring the Catholic religion to every Protestant
system.   The most eminent Protestant divines, such as Luther
Melancthon, Hooker, Chillingworth, with the bishops, Laud,
Taylor, Sheldon, Blanford, and the modern prelates, Marsh
and Porteus himself, all acknowledge, that *salvation may be
found in the communion of the original Catholic church:* but no
divine of this church, consistently with her characteristical unity, and the constant doctrine of the holy fathers and of the
Scripture itself, as I have elsewhere demonstrated, can allow,
that salvation is to be found out of that communion; except in
the case of invincible ignorance.

It remains, my dear friends and brethren, for each of you to
take his and her part: but remember, that the part you several-
ly take, is taken for eternity!   On this occasion, therefore, if
ever you ought to do so, reflect and decide seriously and conscientiously, dismissing all worldly respects, of whatever kind,
from your minds; for *what* exchange shall a man receive for
his soul!* and what will the prejudiced opinion of your fellow

* Mat. xvi. 20.

'mortals avail you at the tribunal, where we are all so soon to appear! and in the vast abyss of eternity in which we shall quickly be all ingulfed! Will any of them plead your cause at that bar? And will your punishment be more tolerable from their sharing in it? Finally, beseech your future judge, who is now your merciful Saviour, with all the fervour and sincerity of your souls, to bestow upon you the light to see your way, and the strength to follow it, which he merited for you, when he hung, for three hours, your agonizing victim, on the cross.

Adieu, my dear friends and brethren, we shall soon meet together at the tribunal I have mentioned; and be assured, that I look forward to that meeting with a perfect confidence, that you and I, and the Great Judge himself, will then approve, in common, of the advice I now give you.

I am, &c

J. M

W——. May 29, 1802.

A

POSTSCRIPT

TO THE SECOND EDITION OF THE

ADDRESS

TO THE

RIGHT REV. LORD BISHOP OF ST. DAVID'S,

OCCASIONED BY HIS LORDSHIP'S

'ONE WORD TO THE REV. DR. MILNER.'

————

My Lord,

Should a grave and dignified author be found unsettled in his opinions, and contradictory in his assertions, he would unavoidably puzzle his readers to make out his meaning, and distress his literary opponents to preserve a due respect towards him; but much more so, should such a venerable character descend to the regions of burlesque and of ridiculous absurdity.

In the course of last summer, the Right Reverend Bishop of St. David's published, what he called, THE PROTESTANT'S CATECHISM, a work professedly intended, not only to defeat the claims of them Catholics to more extensive religious and civil freedom, but also to deprive them of that portion of it which they actually enjoy. Among the other articles, announced in *The Table of Contents*, at the head of this work, is the following: ' Section the 24th: Means of co-operating with the laws for preventing the danger and increase of Popery'.—From this and other passages in his Lordship's work, we had too much reason to fear, that he was disposed to vote for and promote, to the utmost of his power, the re-enactment of Elizabeth's sanguinary Statutes against us: which fear was augmented by his twice quoting the following awful words from Milton's prose works: ' Popery, as being idolatrous, *is not to be tolerated,* either in public or in *private;* it must now be

31

thought how to *remove it,* and hinder the growth thereof. If they say that, by removing their idols, we violate their consciences, *we have no warrant to regard conscience, which is not grounded on Scripture.'* The adoption of these intolerant sentiments by a Lord of Parliament naturally alarmed us, not barely for our own lives, that is to say, for those of five millions of his Majesty's European subjects, who, though they are not idolaters, yet pass for such in his Lordship's eyes, but also for the lives of fifty more millions of his Majesty's subjects in Asia, Africa and America, who are, in the strict sense of the word, idolaters. Accordingly, when I had read the Contents of the Catechism, I hastily turned over the leaves of it to page 54, where these Contents had informed me I should find the means in question, that is to say, the precise nature and extent of the religious persecution with which the Bishop of St. David's threatens us. But instead of finding these, I met the following note : ' The means of co-operating with the laws for preventing the danger and increase of Popery, intended for the Conclusion, as noticed in *The Table of Contents,* being intimately *connected with the credit* and usefulness of our Ecclesiastical establishment, as I conceive, but admitting a difference of opinion, are omitted for further consideration.' Now, my Lord, I appeal to your Lordship's knowledge of literature, whether another author can be named, who in the same work exhibits such an opposition of sentiment and language, as this Prelate does in his Catechism? In a word, can either his readers or his critics pay any serious attention to what he writes, when it is evident that he has not made up his mind, and contradicts himself concerning it ?

Soon after the appearance of this Catechism, its Right Rev. Author advertised, at the head of the *Gentleman's Magazine,* a new work, as being then actually in the press, under the title of THE GRAND SCHISM. Being then engaged in answering the Catechism, I own, I hailed this promise of fresh paradoxes, to support those which I was refuting; for I was perfectly aware that the farther his Lordship advanced in the thorny and miry lane, in which he was resolved to walk, the more he would get entangled in contradictions, and the deeper he would sink into absurdity. Accordingly, month after month, I inquired of all his publishers for *The Bishop of St. David's GRAND SCHISM :* but none of them had heard a word about it. In the end, it appeared that his Lordship had changed his mind about this publication also : but, whether ' for the credit and usefulness of the Establishment,' or his own, he best knows.

Hitherto the Prelate had not, to my knowledge, taken any public notice of my *End to Controversy*, or of my *Address* to him, at the beginning of it; but, meeting soon after with *The Protestant Advocate's Retrospect for October*, I found them both mentioned by his lordship, or by some one else, who professed to know his mind, and who was evidently imbued with his bigotted notions, in the following manner. Speaking of this *chef d'œuvre*, as the Prelate or his intimate friend sarcastically calls the present work, he says: 'The address is made to the Bishop of St. David's in a style of peculiar acrimony and *insolence*, assuredly intended to prevent that most estimable and learned Prelate from descending to notice such an *arrogant* writer. Then he will cry *Victory*, and his partizans will re-echo the exclamation, and will attribute to their arguments what is due only to their insolence.' Now, my Lord, as I know that this is not the general character of my publication, and, otherwise, as I feel that no language can be too strong in arguing with any man who himself has the *insolence* to tell me that I am a *traitor* and an *idolater*, when I know and have demonstrated the contrary, I consider the passage I have quoted, as an apology for the prelate's declining to meet me in the field of argument; and such I believe to have been his intention, till very lately, when he again changed his mind, and put forth his THREE WORDS ON GENERAL THORNTON'S SPEECH, AND ONE WORD ON DOCTOR MILNER'S END OF CONTROVERSY: which work itself betrays the greatest unsteadiness and inconsistency in its author. In fact, THE THREE WORDS take up nine octavo pages, and the ONE WORD fourteen! It is true, the Prelate excuses himself for 'expanding,' as he calls it, his ONE WORD: but could he not, while the manuscript was in his possession, have made his title accord with his work; as, in a former instance, he might have made his Table of Contents agree with the Sections of his Catechism!

But, after all, such instances of fickleness, are not calculated to raise more than a *smile* at any grave and venerable character, who might exhibit them; but, should such a character, with a mitre on his head, and a Catechism in his hand, begin an Episcopal lecture with the travesty or burlesque of an immoral sentiment, borrowed from a loose poet,* and should we

---

* The motto of the Bishop's last theological lecture is the following:
  'Let him write now who never wrote before:
  'Let those, who always wrote, now write the more.—*Trav. Anon.*'
These lines are burlesqued from the following, which are inscribed on the Temple

hear him venting, with oracular sententiousness and solemnity,
a great number of whimsical falsehoods and glaring contradictions; what educated man or woman could refrain from *laugh-
ing* in his face? Indeed who could suppose that such a personage meant any thing else but to be laughed at? Now, my
Lord, has not the Public lately witnessed the verification of
this supposition? In fact, what other lectures does this bur-
lesquing Prelate, alluded to, deliver, as a system of religious
instructions to the ignorant Welsh Jumpers, English Methodists,
Baptists, Independents, &c. but these: *I bring you here, good
people, a new Catechism, and* Three Words *and* One Word
*more, in defence of it, which I have just composed for your com-
mon use. This Catechism will not perplex you with any articles
of belief, concerning God, or Christ, or Redemption, or Grace;
nor will it incommode you with any ordinances of the Commandments, the Sacraments, the love of God and man, and the like: it
requires nothing of you but to adhere to your common Protestancy; which essentially consists in two points; first, in ' the abjuration of Popery and the exclusion of Papists from all power,
ecclesiastical or civil:'** and secondly, in ' holding that the worship of the Church of Rome is idolatrous: for they, who do not
hold this latter doctrine, are not Protestants, whatever they may
profess to be.'†* You have hitherto believed that the Catholics
(*as all the world calls them, but whom I call* Papists) *existed before the* Protestants, *and, unfortunately, all writers of all countries, ancient and modern, have combined to propagate this false
opinion; but I, the present Bishop of St. David's, assure you,
upon my own authority, that ' the Catholics are not our elder
but our younger brothers :'‡ that ' their Religion, consisting, as
it does, in acknowledging the Pope's supremacy§ is a novelty of
the seventh century.'‖* Hence you clearly see that the Protestants*

---

of Venus, in certain celebrated gardens, and are borrowed from the *Pervigilium
Veneris,* ascribed to Catullus:

   ' Cras amet, qui nunquam amavit:
   ' Quique amavit, cras amet.'

See the translation of this distich in Parnel's Poems.

* Prot. Catech. p. 12.
† Ibid. p. 46.
‡ THREE WORDS, p. 17.
§ Catech. p. 11.
‖ Ibid. p. 14.—N. B. This learned Prelate, contradicting himself, says in another
page of his Catechism, p. 22, that ' the Papal domination did not exist before the
time of Hildebrand, whom he calls Clement VII. in the eleventh century.' Now,
we have hitherto been taught that Clement VII. was not chosen Pope till the
year 1523, and that he was the Pope who refused to divorce Henry VIII. from his
lawful wife, and thus gave occasion to the English schism! What a system of
new lights is this *Protestant's Catechism!*

*abjured Popery and excluded the Papists from all power, six
hundred years before Popery was invented: you see, moreover,
that all their Popes, to the number of sixty-six, who lived during
those ages, and, among the rest, Gregory the Great, ' the most
learned and virtuous of the Roman Popes,'* whose missionaries
converted our ancestors from Paganism, were all Protestants.
But, though Gregory himself was a Protestant, and ' reprobated
the supremacy,'† yet, his missionary, Augustin, and his other
Papal envoys, laboured to bring over our British and Irish Bishops to submit to his supremacy, that is, to embrace Popery!‡
You are further to learn that, although Popery is essentially
Idolatry, it did not become a* schism *till the sixteenth century!
' Happy would it be if their (the Catholics) eyes could be opened to the false foundations of a foreign jurisdiction, which led to
that most unnational* schism of the sixteenth century, *and could
be induced to repair the evils of their past* defection, *by returning to the bosom of their* Mother Church *in England and Ireland!'§——But, alas! these ' Catholics* separated from their
Mother Church, *and this separation was* THE GRAND
SCHISM *of the sixteenth century.'‖——Such, my Lord, are
the humorous self-confuting lectures which this good-natured
Bishop puts on his Mitre to deliver to us in his *Protestant's
Catechism;* and which, besides the amusement they afford us,
inform us of what I so much wanted to learn, namely, at what
period the Prelate dates the defection of Catholics from the
Protestant Church, and the commencement of his *Grand
Schism.* It is probable, however, that some difficulties which
he met with in bringing the reigns of Queen Mary and Oliver
Cromwell in England, as well as that of Francis I. in France,
and of Philip II. in Holland, into his system, caused him to
give up his promised work on the *Grand Schism,* in despair.

In proof, however, that his Lordship was serious when he
published his *Catechism,* he offers different pleas in his *Three
Words, and One Word.* He says, in the first place: ' If I
taught nothing about God, or Christ, or the commandments, in
my *Catechism,* Dr. M. may see these subjects treated in some
of my other works.'¶ To this I answer, very possibly this
may be the case; still, *a Bishop's Catechism,* which contains
not a word of Christian doctrine or practice, and which teaches

* Catech. p. 16.
† Ibid. ‡ Catech. P. 24.
§ Three Words, Advertisem. p. iv.
‖ Ibid. p. 16.
¶ Three Words, Advertisem. p. 12.

nothing but intolerance and persecution, is an unexampled phe-
nomenon in Christianity.—Besides this, I may say, that I have
applied at the shops of all the Bishop's publishers to purchase some of his best publications, and at the shop in
the Strand, No. 107, barely to get a sight of them, without
success. The Prelate adds, 'There is, at least, one great moral
and practical lesson inculcated in the Protestant's Catechism,
which Dr. M. has overlooked, though taught by St. Peter himself, namely, submission to the king's entire sovereignty.'*—
And does the Right Rev. Author of the Catechism allege
this, in proof of his seriousness in composing and publishing it,
which, if it means any thing, evidently means that we are always to submit the business of Religion to the supreme power
of the state, whether Christian, Jewish, or Pagan! In fact,
did St. Peter so submit, when he answered *the Magistrates*,
who had forbidden him and his fellow Apostles to preach the
name of Christ : *We ought to obey God rather than men*, Acts
v. 29.? And if the first Protestants had adopted this doctrine,
may we not presume, that the Bishop of St. David's would be
found, at the present day, delivering lectures of an opposite
tenour to those contained in his Protestant's Catechism?

But the Prelate advances in his career, so far as to say
'The six and thirty pages addressed to the author of the Protestant's Catechism, afford no answer to that Catechism, and
invalidate none of his positions.'†—*Heu prisca fides! Heu can-
dida veritas!* whither are you fled, when a Christian Bishop,
professing ' to follow truth, whithersoever she leads, in the utmost sincerity and ardour of his soul,'‡ with the Protestant
Catechism in one hand, and the *Address to the Bishop of St.
David's* in the other, can deliberately affirm, that the latter
work is no answer to the former, and that it does not so much
as invalidate its positions! Is it then no answer to his loose
conjectures concerning St. Paul's having visited Britain, and
his still more groundless assertion of St. Paul having converted
its inhabitants, to refer to the positive testimony of all the original writers of our history, British, Saxon, Roman, and Gallic,
in proof that the Britons were generally converted by Fugatius and Duvianus, legates of Pope Eleutherius, in the second
century?—Does it not invalidate his positions to trace a succession of communications with, and of submission to, the See
of Rome, on the part of the British Bishops, by their frequenting her synods and receiving her legates, and to demonstrate,

* P. 20.   † P. 15.   ‡ P. 20.

that even the Prelate's own predecessor in the See of St. David's, and his favourite author Giraldus Cambrensis, claimed before the Pope himself, in the twelfth century, to have legatine jurisdiction throughout Wales, by the grant of St. Germanus, one of these Papal envoys!—Are not his positions invalidated by the evidence I have brought from authentic documents, and acknowledged by Usher himself, that the Irish and Anglo-Saxon Christians were equally indebted, for their conversion, to the Popes; the former to Pope Celestine, the latter to Pope Gregory the Great; and that they ever continued united with the See of Rome in the belief of Purgatory, the Invocation of Saints, the sacrifice of the Mass, Transubstantiation, and the Pope's Supremacy? Have I not shaken his system, when I evinced, in particular, that every one of our Primates, from St. Augustin, in the sixth century, down to Cranmer, in the sixteenth, received his *confirmation* or *institution* [from which alone he derives his Archiepiscopal jurisdiction,] by a *Special grant of the Pope?*—Should the Right Rev. Prelate, after this, signify, in my hearing, that I have not sufficiently answered him, he will not find me backward in so doing.

But, it seems, the work itself was, in the opinion of the Prelate to whom the Address is made, answered a century before it was written. In fact, he says: ' In this elaborate correspondence, though not without its interest of learning and research, there is nothing material advanced in defence of Popery, to which the reader will not find an answer in Bishop Bull's *Letters to Bossuet,* and Smith's *Errors of the Church of Rome detected.*'* Bull, who was Bishop of St. David's at the beginning of the last century, was certainly an able and learned divine, and drove his Arian adversaries before him; but, after this, levelling his horns at the rock of St. Peter, they were broken short by a Catholic Divine of equal talents and superior learning, Dr. Edward Hawarden, S. T. P.† Smith, of Dover, was one of those wretched Priests, who, wanting the grace necessary for living up to the strictness of their obligations, have attempted to excuse their breach of them, by abusing the Church which imposes them upon them. His puny embryo was stifled in the birth, and he himself, soon after his fall, met with that awful end, which has been the general fate, within our own memory, of this class of *converts,*‡ as the Prelate calls them.§ But,

---

* P. 14. † See Preface to his *True Church of Christ,* vol. ii.

‡ Dean Swift used to say of such ' converts from Popery;' *I wish, when the Pope weeds his garden, he would not throw his nettles over our wall.*

§ Smith dropped down dead in Canterbury Cathedral, about the year 1780.

my Lord, as that adamantine chain of demonstration, which encircles the three parts of the work in question, was not broken before it was knit together, so it never will be broken, till *the Gates of Hell prevail against the Church of Christ.*

The Right Rev. Author evidently flatters himself that, at all events, he has solved three of the enigmas, or paradoxes, which I had pointed out in his Catechism : nevertheless, they still are as fast closed as ever. For is it not evident, that *Religion,* of no description whatever, excludes any man from Parliament, except the Catholic? Did not Lord George Gordon, a M. P. profess himself a Jew, wear a beard about a foot long, and die in the embraces of a Jewish harlot? Did not Edward Wortley Montague, another M. P. believing himself to be the son of the Great Turk, declare himself a Mahometan? And those our civil and military officers, who, in the island of Ceylon, a few years ago, joined in the public worship of Budho, the brother idol of the blood-stained Jaggernaut, are they excluded from Parliament on this account?—As to ' the *inviolable* covenants of the two unions,' which the Prelate maintains, must ever exclude Catholics from all power : it is still matter of demonstration that one of them, which, according to him, *has been violated* more than once, does not so much as allude to them ; and that the other alludes to them for the express purpose of acknowledging, that they *may* be admitted into Parliament!—As to his third paradox, it suffices to say, that its Right Rev. Author still maintains that his Majesty cannot lawfully accept of *The Veto*, and yet that we violate our alle-

About the same time an unprincipled priest of Staffordshire, of the name of Tayler, met with the same awful fate in stepping into a stage coach. Another still more unprincipled priest, who chose to incur excommunication, and who even denied the inspiration of Scripture, Dr. Geddes, used to send for the helps of the Church when he was sick, and to laugh at them when he recovered. At last a priest actually coming to reconcile him to God and the Church, found that he had unexpectedly expired. Lewis of Leominster, having sent his concubine to bring up his breakfast to his bed, was found a corpse by her. Holmes of Essex, and Rogers, alias Rozier, of Birmingham, who the evening before ailed nothing, were found in the morning breathless. James Quesnel and James Nolan, having both been warned by their friends, to my certain knowledge, of the fate they might expect, but continuing to waver about returning to their duty, dropped down dead in the streets, the former at Worcester, the latter in London. My townsman, Billinge, finding himself summoned away, sunk into despair, starting continually, and exclaiming: ' *I am a lost man! I am a lost man!* I dream of nothing but of hellfire!' How unlike the end of his confrere, Austin Jennison, who having been struck dumb by his conscience, in the pulpit, which so ill became him, hurried the same day from his living, near Edinburgh, his pretended wife and property, first to London and thence into France, about the year 1788, where he died in penance and peace. Doran blew out his brains, near Newbury. A detailed history of the converts to, and apostates from, the Catholic Church, in this kingdom, since the defection of Henry VIII. would form a most interesting and useful work.

giance, by not conferring it upon him! Thus, according to the Prelate, we are *traitors* for not committing an unlawful act!

Thus much I have said, in answer to the Prelate's ONE WORD to me, which word, however, is seen to embrace so great a variety of subjects! With respect to his Lordship's THREE WORDS to General Thornton, they are confined to *The Declaration,* by which every Member of Parliament is required to swear—not his belief in the Articles of the Church of England;—nor in the truth of Christianity;—nor in the existence of God—but that ' the invocation of any Saint, and the *Sacrament,* (as it is ignorantly termed of the Mass) as they are now used in *the Church of Rome,* are superstitious and idolatrous.' Thus we see that a M. P. *may invoke the Devil* to take away his own soul or that of his neighbour, and may proclaim that the Mass, as *used by the Russians, Greeks,* and many other sects, believing in Transubstantiation, is *holy and salutary,* and still keep his seat; provided he swear that these *self-same things,* as used by *Catholics,* are *idolatrous!* Gracious heaven! was ever such a qualification for legislating devised or thought of by any human beings, except by the last Parliament of Charles II.! If history had been quite silent on the subject, would not the Act itself prove that the Parliament and the nation were in a crisis of frenzy when it was passed? In fact, history does inform us, that they both were then worked up, by an unprincipled hypocrite, who was brought up a rebel and died a regicide assassin,* [assisted by the perjury of an unnatural monster,]† to believe that the Catholics, who had saved the King's life in their Priests' hiding-holes, when he was a Protestant, at the risk of their own lives, and when they might have gained £100,000 by betraying him, had plotted, now that he was a Catholic, to murder him, by stabbing him, by poisoning him, and by shooting him with silver bullets, and afterwards to bring over 30,000 pilgrims, armed with black bill-hooks, from St. Jago in Spain, to overturn the government! History tells us, moreover, that, on the credit of this plot, near 20 Catholics were actually hanged and quartered, and all their nobility confined in prison! ——I have spoken of our ancestors, I now speak of our posterity, concerning whom I will confidently affirm, that if any thing will equal their astonishment, that so unjust, false, malicious, and absurd an Act, as that containing the *Declaration,* should have passed through the Houses in the 17th century,

---

* Lord Shaftsbury   † Dr. Titus Oates.

and this under the hypocritical pretext of ' An Act for the better preservation of his Majesty's person and Government,' it will be that the same Act, and under the same hypocritical title, should have remained unrepealed till the present period in the nineteenth century. And yet it does stand unrepealed at the present hour,—a signal monument of the *religious and moral integrity* of the Catholics, in still refusing to purchase honours and emoluments at the expense of a false oath, [which persons of other religions have taken, with the consciousness either of swearing a falsehood, or of swearing what they do not understand, when they swear that the Catholic worship is *idolatrous*] as likewise in their bearing the *infamy* or perjury rather than the *guilt* of it. In fact, the whole latter part of the Declaration is swelled out with implied charges against Catholics, of evading the obligation of oaths by ' equivocations, mental reservations, and Papal dispensations,' which vile expedients, if they actually possessed them, it is self-evident, would render the whole Declaration nugatory.

General Thornton, in his late Parliamentary Speech, against the *Declaration*, which pronounces the Catholics guilty of *Idolatry*, takes up the subject on the grounds just stated, that is to say, upon Protestant grounds. Accordingly, he feelingly appeals to the Members of Parliament themselves, whether it be not ' abhorrent from their religious and moral feelings,' to charge their fellow Christians upon oath, with the guilt of idolatry, while they not only clear themselves of that crime, but also were acquitted of it by the most learned Protestant Bishops and Divines this country could boast of, when the Declaration was devised.* The general then argues as follows : ' How is it to be accounted for, on any just principle, that those, who, preparatory to their going into holy orders, are called upon to subscribe to the 39 Articles of Religion, after it ras been their duty to make this subject their particular study, should only be required to consider the practice as having *given occasion to many superstitions*, when the Members of both Houses of Parliament, on taking their seats, are obliged to declare, that they solemnly and sincerely, in the presence of God, do believe the practice not only to be superstitious, but likewise *idolatrous?* —Let me beseech the House to consider well the consequences

---

* Such as the Bishops Jeremy Taylor, Blandford, Montague, Forbes, Gunning, Archbishop Sheldon, Prebendary Thorndike, Chillingworth, &c. When the Declaration was under consideration in the House of Peers, Bishop Gunning, of Ely, protested that he could not in conscience swear it. *Burnet's Hist. of his own Times.*

of it.'——Here the Rt. Rev. Prelate chooses to make a vigor-
ous assault upon the General, by way of proving that the law
requires no stronger declarations against the Catholics, from
Members of Parliament, than it does from the Clergy of the
Establishment; and that the latter, in subscribing the 39 Articles, do, in fact, charge the Catholics with *idolatry.* Let
us now attend to his proofs. He says: ' The Articles, besides saying that the doctrine of Transubstantiation has *given
occasion to many superstitions*, say moreover, that it is *repugnant to the plain sense of scripture, and overthroweth the nature
of a Sacrament :* and that the Sacrament *was not, by Christ's
ordinance, reserved, carried about, lifted up, and worshipped.'*
Atqui :—Ergo.——Now, my Lord, I appeal to your Lordship's theological learning, first, whether a thousand tenets and
practices may not be *repugnant to scripture*, and may not *overthrow the nature of a Sacrament*, without constituting *idolatry?*
Secondly, whether a Member of Parliament, for example, or
his *worship* the Mayor, or a *worshipful* Alderman, or any man's
own wife, whom he has married according to the form in The
Common Prayer Book, may not be *reserved*, and *carried about*,
and *lifted up*, and *worshipped*, without making such a person
an object of *idolatry?* In case your Lordship answers these
two questions, as every other man of sense will do, it is evident
at once, that the Act of 30 Car. II. by the Declaration in
question, does impose an infinitely heavier burden on the consciences of Parliament-men, than the 39 Articles do on those
of Churchmen. Thus it is demonstrated, that the Right Rev.
Bishop has made a false attack on the gallant General; and
that he has been completely beaten on his own ground.——As
to the Prelate's disingenuous statements of the arguments in
my foregoing Letters on the Real Presence and Transubstantiation, and his feeble nibbling at them, in his Appendix, I shall
leave them to make whatever effect they are capable of making
on the minds of intelligent readers, satisfying myself with barely requesting them, after they have perused the Prelate's statements and objections, to look back again upon the arguments
themselves.

In conclusion, my Lord, I am so little apprehensive that the
Catechism and the defence of it, put together, will induce a
single member of the Great Universal Church to quit what the
Prelate, whimsically and by *Antonomasia*, calls *The Grand
Schism* of the sixteenth century, that I might safely promise
without danger of being called upon to make my promise good,
that, upon satisfactory proof of this having happened in one

instance, I would furnish a second instance in myself. Nor
am I, in the least, fearful that a single Peer or Gentleman, who
is not otherwise induced to vote in Parliament against the Catholic Claims, will be influenced to do so by these episcopal
lectures. All I dread is, that, as the Catechism is now reduced
in size and expense, for the evident purpose of being widely
circulated among the furious jumpers of Wales, and the no less
ignorant and infuriate mobility of the metropolis, who have already deeply imbibed his Lordship's grand principle of Protestantism, the swearing against Popery, they may be worked
up by it to equal demonstrations of zeal with those which we
witnessed in the former champion of Protestantism, Lord
George Gordon, and his associators. These, we remember,
argued the Catholic Question against Members of the Legislature with their fists and clubs, confuted the Catholics by burning down their chapels and houses, and demonstrated the purity
of their Religion, by demolishing the prisons and storming the
Bank.

I have the honour to remain, my Lord,
Your Lordship's obedient Servant,
J. M. D. D.

Wolverhampton, March 7, 1819.